Intermediate Logic

Intermediate Logic

Logic

DAVID BOSTOCK

CLARENDON PRESS · OXFORD

This book has been printed digitally and produced in a standard specification
in order to ensure its continuing availability

OXFORD
UNIVERSITY PRESS

Great Clarendon Street, Oxford OX2 6DP

Oxford University Press is a department of the University of Oxford.
It furthers the University's objective of excellence in research, scholarship,
and education by publishing worldwide in

Oxford New York

Auckland Bangkok Buenos Aires Cape Town Chennai
Dar es Salaam Delhi Hong Kong Istanbul Karachi Kolkata
Kuala Lumpur Madrid Melbourne Mexico City Mumbai Nairobi
São Paulo Shanghai Singapore Taipei Tokyo Toronto
with an associated company in Berlin

Oxford is a registered trade mark of Oxford University Press
in the UK and in certain other countries

Published in the United States
by Oxford University Press Inc., New York

© David Bostock 1997

The moral rights of the author have been asserted
Database right Oxford University Press (maker)

Reprinted 2002

ISBN 0-19-875141-9
ISBN 0-19-875142-7 (pbk)

Preface

This book is intended for those who have studied a first book in logic, and wish to know more. It is concerned to develop logical theory, but not to apply that theory to the analysis and criticism of ordinary reasoning. For one who has no concern with such applications, it would be possible to read this book as a first book in the subject, since I do in fact introduce each logical concept that I use, even those that I expect to be already familiar (e.g. the truth-functors and the quantifiers). But it would be tough going. For in such cases my explanations proceed on a fairly abstract level, with virtually no discussion of how the logical vocabulary relates to its counterpart in everyday language. This will be difficult to grasp, if the concept is not in fact familiar.

The book is confined to elementary logic, i.e. to what is called first-order predicate logic, but it aims to treat this subject in very much more detail than a standard introductory text. In particular, whereas an introductory text will pursue just one style of semantics, just one method of proof, and so on, this book aims to create a wider and a deeper understanding by showing how several alternative approaches are possible, and by introducing comparisons between them. For the most part, it is orthodox classical logic that is studied, together with its various subsystems. (This, of course, includes the subsystem known as intuitionist logic, but I make no special study of it.) The orthodox logic, however, presumes that neither names nor domains can be empty, and in my final chapter I argue that this is a mistake, and go on to develop a 'free' logic that allows for empty names and empty domains. It is only in this part of the book that what I have to say is in any way unorthodox. Elsewhere almost all of the material that I present has been familiar to logicians for some time, but it has not been brought together in a suitably accessible way.

The title of the book shows where I think it belongs in the teaching of the subject. Institutions which allow a reasonable time for their first course in logic could certainly use some parts of this book in the later stages of that course. Institutions which do not already try to get too much into their advanced courses could equally use some parts of it in the earlier stages of those courses. But it belongs in the middle. It should provide a very suitable background for those who wish to go on to advanced treatments of model theory, proof theory, and other such topics; but it should also prove to be an entirely satisfying resting-place for those who are aware that a first course in logic leaves many things unexplored, but who have no ambition to master the mathematical techniques of the advanced courses. Moreover, I do not believe that the book needs to be accompanied by a simultaneous course of instruction; it should be both comprehensible and enjoyable entirely on its own.

While I have been interested in logic ever since I can remember, I do not think that I would ever have contemplated writing a book on the topic, if it had not been for my involvement fifteen years ago in the booklet *Notes on the Formalization of Logic*. This was compiled under the guidance of Professor Dana Scott, for use as a study-aid in Oxford University. Several themes in the present work descend from that booklet, and I should like to acknowledge my indebtedness not only to Dana Scott himself, but also to the others who helped with the compilation of that work, namely Dan Isaacson, Graeme Forbes, and Gören Sundholm. But, of course, there are also many other works, more widely known, which I have used with profit, but with only occasional acknowledgement in what follows.

David Bostock

Merton College, Oxford

Contents

Part III. FURTHER TOPICS 321

8. Existence and Identity 323

Part I

SEMANTICS

1

Introduction

1.1. **Truth**

The most fundamental notion in classical logic is that of truth. Philosophers, of course, have long debated the question 'what is truth?', but that is a debate which, for the purposes of the present book, we must leave to one side. Let us assume that we know what truth is.

We are concerned with truth because we are concerned with the things that are true, and I shall call these things 'propositions'. Philosophers, again, hold differing views on what is to count as a proposition. A simple view is that a proposition is just a (declarative) sentence, but when one thinks about it for a moment, there are obvious difficulties for this suggestion. For the same sentence may be used, by different speakers or in different contexts, to say different things, some of them true and others false. So one may prefer to hold that it is not the sentences themselves that are true or false, but particular utterings of them, i.e. utterings by particular people, at particular times and places, in this or that particular situation. A more traditional view, however, is that it is neither the sentences nor the utterings of them that are true, but a more abstract kind of entity, which one can characterize as *what is said* by one who utters a sentence. Yet a further view, with a longer history, is that what one expresses by uttering a sentence is not an abstract entity but a mental entity, i.e. a judgement, or more generally a thought. Again, we must leave this debate on one side. Whatever it is that should properly be said to be true, or to be false, that is what we shall call a proposition. At least, that is the official position. But in practice I shall quite often speak loosely of sentences as being true or false. For whatever propositions are, they must be closely associated with sentences, since it is by means of sentences that we express both truths and falsehoods.

We assume, then, that there are these things called propositions, and that every one of them is either true or not. And if it is not true, we say that it is false. So there are just two truth-values, truth and falsehood, and each proposition has exactly one of them. In fact we assume more strongly that a given proposition has, *in every possible situation*, just one of these two truth-values, so that when we have considered the case in which it is true, and the case in which it is false, no *possibility* has been omitted. Since the vast majority of the propositions that we actually express in daily life suffer from vagueness in one way or another, one must admit that this assumption is something of an idealization. For with a vague proposition there are some situations in which it seems natural to say that it is neither true nor false, but classical logic makes no allowance for this. For the most part this idealization seems to do no harm, but there are occasions when it leads to trouble, i.e. when we apparently get the wrong result by applying the precise rules of classical logic to the vague propositions of everyday life.[1] But, once more, for the purposes of the present book we can only note the problem and pass by on the other side, with the excuse that our present subject is not the application of logical theory but the development of the theory itself. And that theory does depend upon the stated assumption about propositions and truth. Indeed, that assumption is what distinguishes classical logic from most of its rivals.

In developing our theory of logic we shall wish to speak generally of all propositions, and we introduce the schematic letters 'P','Q','R',... to facilitate this. They are called sentence-letters (or, in some books, propositional letters) because they are to be understood as standing in for, or taking the place of, sentences which are or express propositions. We can therefore generalize by letting such a letter represent any proposition, arbitrarily chosen. But we shall also speak of 'interpreting' a sentence-letter, or assigning an 'interpretation' to it, and it is natural to say that here we are thinking of the letter as representing some particular and specified proposition. That is just how one does proceed when applying logical theory, for example to test actual arguments containing actual propositions. However, for our purposes in

[1] The best-known example is the so-called 'Sorites paradox'. See e.g. C. Wright, 'Language-Mastery and the Sorites Paradox', in G. Evans and J. McDowell (eds.), *Truth and Meaning* (Oxford University Press: Oxford, 1976).

this book, the *only* feature of the assigned proposition that will ever be relevant is its truth-value. So in fact we shall 'interpret' a sentence-letter just by assigning to it a truth-value, either T (for truth) or F (for falsehood). We shall not pause to specify any particular proposition which that letter represents and which has the truth-value in question.

1.2. Validity

The word 'valid' is used in a variety of ways, even within the orthodox terminology of logic. But its primary application is to arguments, so we may begin with this.

In an argument some propositions are put forward as premisses, and another proposition is claimed to follow from them as conclusion. Of course, an actual case will often involve rather more than this, for the arguer will not just *claim* that his conclusion follows from his premisses; he will also try to *show* (i.e. to prove) that it does, and this may involve the construction of long and complicated chains of reasoning. It is only in rather simple cases that a mere claim is deemed to be enough. Nevertheless, the classical definition of validity ignores this complication, and it counts an argument as valid if and only if the conclusion does in fact follow from the premisses, whether or not the argument also contains any demonstration of this fact. To say that the conclusion does follow from the premisses is the same as to say that the premisses do entail the conclusion, and on the classical account that is to be defined as meaning: it is impossible that all the premisses should be true and the conclusion false. Once more, we must simply leave on one side the philosophers' debate over the adequacy of this definition, either as a definition of validity or as a definition of entailment.

Now logic is often characterized as the study of validity in argument, though in fact its scope is very much narrower than this suggests. In what is called elementary logic we study just two ways in which an argument may be valid, namely (1) when its validity is wholly due to the truth-functional structure of the propositions involved, and (2) when it is due to both truth-functional and quantificational structure working together.[2] In other areas of logic, not usually called elementary, one studies the contribution to validity of various other features of propositions, for example their tense or modality. But there is no end to the list of propositional features that *can*

---

[2] If the words 'truth-functional' and 'quantificational' are not familiar, then please be patient. Detailed explanations will come in the next two chapters.

contribute to validity, since *any* necessary connection between premises and conclusion will satisfy the definition, and it would be foolish to suppose that some one subject called 'logic' should study them all. In response to this point it used to be said that logic is concerned with 'form' rather than with 'content', and accordingly that its topic can be circumscribed as 'validity in virtue of form'. My impression is that that suggestion is not looked upon with much favour these days, because of the difficulty of making any suitable sense of the notion of 'form' being invoked. In any case, I mention the point only to set it aside, along with the many other interesting problems that affect the very foundations of our subject. So far as this book is concerned, we will confine attention just to the way that truth-functional and quantificational complexity can affect validity. (But later we shall add a brief consideration of identity.)

Because our subject is so confined, we can usefully proceed by introducing what are called 'formal languages', in which the particular kind of complexity that we are studying is the *only* complexity that is allowed to occur at all. For example, to study the effects of truth-functional complexity we shall introduce a 'language' in which there are symbols for certain specified truth-functions—and these, of course, are assigned a definite meaning—but all the other symbols are merely schematic. Indeed, in this case the other symbols will be just the schematic sentence-letters already mentioned. They will occupy positions where one might write a genuine sentence, expressing a genuine proposition, but they do not themselves express any propositions. Accordingly, this so-called 'formal language' is not really a *language* at all, for the whole point of a language is that you can use it to say things, whereas in this 'formal language' nothing whatever can be said. So it is better regarded, not as a language, but as a *schema* for a language—something that would become a language if one were to replace its schematic letters by genuine expressions of the appropriate type (in this case, sentences). Let us say, then, that we shall introduce language-schemas, in which the particular kinds of complexity that we are interested in will be represented, but everything else will be left schematic.

The 'sentences' of such a language-schema are similarly not really sentences, but sentence-schemas, picking out particular patterns of sentence-construction. We shall call them 'formulae'. By taking several such formulae as our premiss-formulae, and another as a conclusion-formula, we can represent an argument-schema, which again is a pattern of argument which many particular arguments will exemplify. Then, in a new use of the word 'valid', we may say that an argument-schema is to be counted as a *valid schema* if and only if every actual argument that exemplifies it is a *valid argument*, in the sense defined earlier (i.e. it is impossible that all its pre-misses should be true and its conclusion false). It is the validity of these argument-schemas that we shall actually be concerned with. At least, that is the basic idea, though in practice we shall set up our definitions a little differently.

When any formal language is introduced, we shall specify what is to count as an 'interpretation' of it. At the moment, we have introduced just one such language, namely the language which has as its vocabulary just the sentence-letters '*P*','*Q*','*R*',..., and nothing else. In this *very* simple lan-guage, each sentence-letter is a formula, and there are no other formulae. Moreover, we have explained what is to count as interpreting a sentence-letter, namely assigning to it either T or F as its value. So this tells us how to interpret every formula of the language. We therefore know what it would be to consider all interpretations of some specified set of formulae. Suppose, then, that we take an argument-schema in this language. It will consist of some set of sentence-letters, each of which is to be counted as a premiss-formula, together with a single sentence-letter to be counted as the conclusion-formula. Then we shall say that such an argument-schema counts as a valid schema if and only if *there is no interpretation* in which each of the premiss-formulae comes out true and the conclusion-formula comes out false. (With the present very simple language, it is clear that this will be the case if and only if the conclusion-formula is itself one of the premiss-formulae.)

When the argument-schema is valid in this sense, then it will *also* be valid in the sense first suggested, i.e. every actual argument that exemplifies the schema will be a valid argument. Why so? Because when we consider 'every interpretation' of the schema, we are thereby considering 'every possibility' for the arguments that exemplify the schema, and this in turn is because—as I stressed in Section 1.1—we are assuming that a proposition must always be either true or false, and there is no third possibility for it.

The formal languages that we shall actually be concerned with in the remainder of this book are, of course, rather more complicated than the very simple example just given, but the same general principles will continue to apply. When the language is introduced, we shall specify what is to count as an interpretation of it, and the aim will be to ensure that the permitted inter-pretations cover all the possibilities. Provided that this is achieved, the res-ults that we obtain for our formal or schematic languages by looking at all interpretations of them will carry with them results about what is and is not possible in the genuine languages that exemplify them. For example, if we have a formula that is not true under any interpretation, then all the propositions exemplifying that formula will be propositions that cannot possibly be true. This is the relationship required if the study of formal languages is to be a significant contribution to the study of validity in arguments, as classically conceived. But, for *most* of what follows, this relationship will simply be assumed; it will be the formal languages themselves that directly engage our attention.

1.3. **The Turnstile**

Just as an argument is valid (according to the classical definition) if and only if its premises entail its conclusion, so we may also say that an argument-schema is a valid schema if and only if its premiss-formulae entail its conclusion-formula. This uses the word 'entails' in a new way, to signify a relation between formulae, and that is how the word will be used from now on. In fact it proves more convenient to work with this notion of entailment, rather than the notion of an argument-schema being valid, so I now introduce the sign '⊨' to abbreviate 'entails' in this sense. The sign is pronounced 'turnstile'. But before I proceed to a formal definition it will be helpful to introduce some further vocabulary, of the kind called 'metalogical'.

At the moment, our only formulae are the sentence-letters. Let us now specify these a little more precisely as the letters in the infinite series

$$P,Q,R,P_1,Q_1,R_1,P_2,...$$

These are schematic letters, taking the place of sentences which are or express propositions, and used to speak generally about all propositions. More kinds of formulae will be introduced shortly. But whatever kind of formulae is under consideration at any stage, we shall wish to speak generally about all formulae of that kind, and for this purpose it will be useful to have some further schematic letters which take the place of formulae. I therefore introduce the small Greek letters

$$\varphi,\psi,\chi,\varphi_1,\psi_1,\chi_1,\varphi_2,...$$

in this role.[3] Their function is like that of the sentence-letters, but at one level up. For they take the place of formulae, while formulae take the place of genuine sentences expressing propositions. I also introduce the capital Greek letters

---

[3] 'φ','ψ','χ' are spelled 'phi', 'psi', 'chi' respectively, and pronounced with a long 'i' in each case. The 'c' in 'chi' is hard (as in Scottish 'loch').

$\Gamma, \Delta, \Theta, \Gamma_1, ...,$

whose role is to generalize, in an analogous way, not over single formulae but over *sets* of formulae.[4] Using this vocabulary we can say that the basic notion to be defined is

$\Gamma \vDash \varphi,$

where φ is any formula and Γ is any set of formulae. And the definition is

There is no interpretation in which every formula in Γ is true and the formula φ is false.

Any sentence that exemplifies the schema '$\Gamma \vDash \varphi$', with actual formulae in place of the metalogical schematic letters 'Γ' and 'φ', will be called a *sequent*. A sequent, then, makes a definite claim, that certain formulae are related in a particular way, and it is either true or false.

My introduction of the capital Greek letters 'Γ','Δ',... was a little curt, and indeed some further explanation is needed of how all our metalogical letters are actually used in practice. As I have said, the turnstile '$\vDash$' is to be understood as an abbreviation for 'entails'. Grammar therefore requires that what occurs to the right of this sign is an expression that refers to a formula, and what occurs to the left of it is an expression—or a sequence of expressions—referring to several formulae, or to a set of formulae, or a sequence of formulae, or something similar. But in standard practice the letter 'φ' is used to take the grammatical place, not of an expression which *refers to* a formula, but of an expression which *is* a formula. Similarly the letter 'Γ' is used to take the grammatical place, not of an expression that *refers to* one or more formulae, but of one or more expressions that *are* formulae. To illustrate this, suppose that we wish to say that if you take any set of formulae Γ, and if you form from it a (possibly) new set by adding the particular formula 'P' to its members, then the result is a set of formulae that entails the formula 'P'. Apparently the correct way of writing this would be

$\Gamma \cup \{'P'\} \vDash 'P',$

(where '$\cup$' indicates the union of two sets, and the curly brackets round 'P' mean 'the set whose only member is "P"'). But in practice we never do use the notation in this way. Instead, we write just

$\Gamma, P \vDash P.$

---

[4] 'Γ','Δ','Θ' are spelled 'gamma', 'delta', 'theta' respectively, and the 'e' in 'theta' is long. (The corresponding lower-case Greek letters are 'γ','δ','θ'.)

Similarly, if we wish to generalize and say that the same holds for any other formula in place of 'P', then we write

$\Gamma, \varphi \vDash \varphi$.

Supposing, then, that '$\vDash$' really does abbreviate the verb 'entails', the notation that we actually use must be regarded as the result of the following further conventions:

(1) where an expression to the left of '$\vDash$' specifies a set by using the sign '$\cup$' of set union, this sign is always to be replaced by a comma;
(2) where an expression to the left of '$\vDash$' specifies a set by listing its members, and enclosing the list in curly brackets, the curly brackets are always to be omitted;
(3) quotation marks, needed in English to form from a formula an expression which refers to that formula, are always to be omitted.

So it comes about that in actual practice we avoid both the use of quotation marks, and the explicitly set-theoretical notation, that the explanation of '$\vDash$' as 'entails' appears to demand.

It may seem more natural, then, to adopt a different explanation of '$\vDash$', not as abbreviating the verb 'entails', but simply as representing the word 'therefore'. What grammar requires of an ordinary use of the word 'therefore' is that it be preceded by one or more whole sentences, stating the premisses of the argument, and followed by another whole sentence, stating its conclusion. Of course it would be quite wrong to enclose each of these sentences in its own quotation marks. So when we abstract from this an argument-schema, which many different arguments may exemplify, we shall naturally do this just by writing formulae in place of the original sentences, again without adding any quotation marks. And similarly when we wish to generalize about our argument-schemas, we shall do this by using 'φ' to take the place of any formula, and 'Γ' to take the place of any sequence of formulae. So the grammar that is actually used with the turnstile, not only in this book but (so far as I am aware) in every other, is very much more natural if we take it to mean 'therefore' rather than 'entails'.

There is of course a difference between the two interpretations. On the first approach, whereby '$\vDash$' means 'entails', the schema '$\Gamma \vDash \varphi$' is a schema whose instances are sentences which make a definite claim, true or false. On the second, whereby '$\vDash$' means 'therefore', the schema '$\Gamma \vDash \varphi$' is a schema whose instances are argument-schemas, such as 'P; not both P and Q; therefore not Q'. An argument-schema does not itself make any claim at all;

rather, we may make claims about that schema, e.g. the claim that it is valid. So, on this second approach, if one wishes to claim that the formulae Γ entail the formula φ one writes not

$$\Gamma \vDash \varphi$$

but

'$\Gamma \vDash \varphi$' is valid.

In practice, it makes very little difference which interpretation is adopted. Some books use the one, others use the other, and in several cases the sign appears to be being used in both ways at once. But no serious confusion results.

In this book I shall adopt the first interpretation, and what is written to the left of '$\vDash$' will be taken as indicating a set of formulae, even though that may not be what the notation naturally suggests.

One reason for this—not a very important one—is that the order in which the premiss-formulae are listed, and the number of times that any formula occurs in the list, evidently make no difference to the correctness of an entailment claim. This is automatically catered for if we say that what is in question is the *set* of all the premiss-formulae, since it will still be the same set whichever way we choose to list its members, so long as it is the same members that are listed. (But of course we could obtain this result in other ways too, as we shall do in Chapter 7.) The more significant reason is that the notion of a *set* of premiss-formulae very naturally includes two cases which we shall want to include, but which would be unnatural as cases of arguments or argument-schemas. These are the case when we have infinitely many premisses, and the case when we have none at all. The idea of an argument with no premisses—an 'argument' which begins with the word 'therefore' (i.e. 'for that reason') referring back to no statement previously given as a reason—is certainly strange; so too is the idea of an argument with so many premisses that one could *never* finish stating them, and so could never reach the stage of drawing the conclusion. But if we are speaking simply of what is entailed by this or that set of propositions (or formulae), then these two cases are less strange. In any case I stipulate that they are to be included: the set of formulae Γ may be infinite, and it may be empty. Both cases are automatically covered by the definition already given.

It may be noted that, in accordance with our convention for omitting curly brackets to the left of the turnstile, we shall write simply

$$\vDash \varphi$$

to say that the formula φ is entailed by the empty set of formulae, and its definition can of course be simplified to

There is no interpretation in which φ is false.

At a later stage in the book (Chapter 7) I shall generalize the definition of the turnstile so that what is to the right of it may also be a set of formulae, and not just a single formula. I do not introduce that generalization now, since in the earlier chapters there would be no use for it. But it is convenient to introduce now what is, in effect, one special case of the generalization to come later: we shall allow that what is to the right of the turnstile may be either a single formula or no formula, and consequently a new definition is needed now for the case where there is no formula to the right. It is easy to see what this definition should be, namely

$$\Gamma \vDash$$

is to mean

There is no interpretation in which every formula in Γ is true.

Any instance of the schema '$\Gamma \vDash$', with actual formulae in place of 'Γ', will also be called a sequent.

It is worth noting at once that our definition includes the special case in which Γ is empty, so that in the notation we actually use there are no formulae either to the right or to the left of the turnstile, and we are faced with just this claim:

$$\vDash.$$

This is a false claim. It says that there is no interpretation in which every formula in the empty set is true. But there is such an interpretation, indeed *any* interpretation whatever will suffice, including the interpretation in which every sentence-letter is assigned F. For since there are no formulae in the empty set anyway, it follows that there are none which are not true, in this interpretation and in any other. (As always in logic, we understand 'Every A is B' to mean the same as 'There is no A which is not B', and so it is true if there is no A at all.) Here we have reached our first result about '$\vDash$', namely that when it stands by itself to make a claim about the empty set of formulae, it is false. It is convenient to write '$\nvDash$' in place of '$\vDash$' to express the negation of what '$\vDash$' expresses. Using this convention, we can set down our result in this way:

$$\nvDash.$$

But perhaps it is less confusing to express the point more long-windedly in English: the empty sequent is false.

Further results about '$\models$' are best postponed until we have introduced the formulae to which it will relate. Meanwhile, let us summarize what has been said so far. In logic we study sequents, which have the turnstile '$\models$' as their main verb. In the standard case, a sequent

$$\Gamma \models \varphi$$

will have several formulae to the left of the turnstile, and one formula to the right, and in this case the turnstile abbreviates 'entails'. But we also allow for a sequent of the form

$$\Gamma \models$$

with no formula on the right. In this case the turnstile can be read as 'is inconsistent'. And we allow too for a sequent of the form

$$\models \varphi$$

with no formula on the left. In this case we shall say that the sequent claims that the formula φ is valid. Note that this is yet a third use of the word 'valid', in which it is applied not to an argument, nor to an argument-schema, but to a single formula. This is the only way in which the word will be used henceforth. Despite these different ways of reading the turnstile in English, depending on whether one or other side of the sequent is empty, nevertheless it is recognizably the same notion in each case. For every sequent claims:

> There is no interpretation in which everything on the left is true and everything on the right is false.

2

Truth-Functors

The most elementary part of logic is often called 'propositional logic' (or 'sentential logic'), but a better title for it is 'the logic of truth-functors'. Roughly speaking, a truth-functor is a sign that expresses a truth-function, so it is the idea of a truth-function that first needs attention.

2.1. Truth-Functions

A truth-function is a special kind of function, namely a function from truth-values to truth-values.

Functions in general may be regarded as rules correlating one item with another. A function will be 'defined on' items of some definite kind (e.g. numbers), and these items are the possible inputs to the function. To each such item as input, the function assigns another item (or possibly the same item) as its output for that input. The outputs may be items of the same kind as the inputs, or they may be items of a different kind. For example, the expression 'the square of . . .' expresses a function defined on numbers; given any number x as input to the function, the function yields another number, namely x^2, as its output for that input. Similarly, the expression 'the father of . . .' expresses a function defined on people; given any person x as input, the function yields another person, namely the father of x, as its output for that input. So the first is a function from numbers to numbers, and the second a function from people to people. In each of these cases the outputs are items of the same kind as the inputs, but a function does not have to be like this. For example, 'the number of . . .'s children' expresses a function from people to numbers. The important thing about a function is just that it does always have one and only one output for each input of the specified kind. We call the input to the function an 'argument' to the function, and its output for that input is called its 'value' for that argument. Thus the function expressed by 'the square of . . .' has the value 4 for the argument 2, the value 9 for the argument 3, the value 16 for the argument 4, and so on.

A truth-function is a function which takes truth-values as arguments and which yields truth-values as values; that is to say, it is a function from truth-values to truth-values. A nice simple truth-function is the one which yields F as value for T as argument and T as value for F as argument. It is briefly specified by this truth-table:

Argument	Value
T	F
F	T

This is an example of a *one-place* truth-function (also called a *unary*, or *monadic*, truth-function). There are not many one-place truth-functions. (In fact there are only three others. Write down their truth-tables.) But there are also *two-place* truth-functions (also called binary, or dyadic), and *three-place* truth-functions (also called ternary, or triadic), and so on indefinitely. It is natural to think of a two-place function as taking two arguments simultaneously, and this is perfectly all right, so long as one distinguishes them as the *first* argument and the *second*. Alternatively, one can think of a two-place function as taking just one argument, where that one argument is an ordered *pair* of items. In that case, the truth-functions should be described as functions which take as arguments either single truth-values, or ordered pairs of truth-values, or ordered trios of truth-values, and so on. (To express

15

the point generally, it is usual to speak of ordered n-tuples.) But if we speak in the first way, which is perhaps more natural, then the truth-functions are functions which take as arguments one or more truth-values, in a specified order. The values of a truth-function are always single truth-values.

For example, among the two-place truth-functions there is one specified by the following truth-table:

First argument	Second argument	Value
T	T	T
T	F	F
F	T	T
F	F	T

Among the three-place truth-functions there is one specified by the following truth-table:

First argument	Second argument	Third argument	Value
T	T	T	T
T	T	F	F
T	F	T	F
T	F	F	F
F	T	T	F
F	T	F	F
F	F	T	F
F	F	F	T

It is clear that with the two-place function just specified the order of the arguments does make a difference, for the function takes the value F only when the *first* argument takes the value T, and the *second* takes the value F. But, as it happens, the order of the arguments is irrelevant to the three-place function just specified: it takes the value T when and only when all its three arguments take the *same* value, and this does not depend upon which order they are taken in.

In general, the number of n-place truth-functions is 2^{2^n}. Thus, as already mentioned, there are 4 one-place functions. We can add that there are 16 two-place functions, 256 three-place functions, and so on. In the other direction there are 2 *zero-place* functions. Admittedly it is stretching the notion of a function somewhat to suppose that there could be such a thing as a zero-place function. Such a 'function' is not in any natural sense a 'correlation', but it can be regarded as something that has an 'output' for a 'zero input'. For example, among functions from numbers to numbers one might regard a particular numeral, say '2', as expressing a zero-place function; it requires no number as input, and it yields the number 2 as output. Similarly among functions from truth-values to truth-values one may regard as a sign for a zero-place function any symbol that always takes the value T as its value, without requiring any argument to enable it to do so, and similarly any symbol that always takes the value F as its value. I shall shortly introduce signs that work just like this.

EXERCISES

2.1.1. Write out the truth-tables of the following truth-functions:
- (a) The three-place function which takes the value T if and only if just one of its arguments takes the value T.
- (b) The three-place function which takes the value T if and only if at least two of its arguments take the value T.
- (c) The three-place function that takes the value T if and only if its first argument takes the value F.

2.1.2. Describe the relation between the three-place function in 2.1.1(c) and the two-place function that takes the value T if and only if its first argument takes the value F. Can a two-place function be the *same* function as a three-place function?

2.1.3. Write out the truth-tables of all the two-place truth-functions. Estimate how long it would take you to do the same for all the three-place truth-functions.

2.2. Truth-Functors

Given any proposition '*P*' one can form from it another proposition which is its negation. In English this is usually done by inserting the word 'not' in some appropriate place in the sentence expressing it, though ambiguity is better avoided by tediously writing out 'It is not the case that' at the front of the sentence. In this book we shall use '¬' as our negation sign, written in front of what it negates, as in '¬*P*'. (Some other books use '–' or '~' instead.) Similarly, given any propositions '*P*' and '*Q*' one can form from them another proposition which is their conjunction. In English this is usually done by writing the word 'and' between the two sentences in question, though again one can prevent some possible misunderstanding by using instead the long-winded construction 'It is the case both that . . . and that . . .'. In this book we shall use '∧' as our conjunction sign, written between what it conjoins, as in 'P ∧ Q'. (Some other books use '&' or '·' instead.)

A word such as 'not' or 'and', when used in this way, may be regarded as expressing a function from sentences to sentences; for you supply it with a sentence, or a pair of sentences, as input, and it forms from them a new sentence as its output for that input. So we may call it a sentence-functor. Clearly there is no end to the different ways of forming new sentences from given sentences, but we shall at once confine our attention to those, such as inserting 'not' or 'and', that are truth-functional. This means simply that the sentence-functor which gives a sentence as output for one or more sentences as input corresponds to a truth-function, namely the truth-function which yields the truth-value of the output sentence as its output when it is given the truth-value(s) of the input sentence(s) as its input. A sentence-functor which corresponds in this way to a truth-function will be called, simply, a truth-functor.

Just as a truth-function is given by a truth-table, so too a corresponding truth-functor is also characterized by the same truth-table. For example, the negation sign '¬' has this truth-table:

P	$\neg P$
T	F
F	T

And the conjunction sign '∧' has this truth-table.

P	Q	$P \wedge Q$
T	T	T
T	F	F
F	T	F
F	F	F

This tells us that the negation '¬P' is false when 'P' is true and true when 'P' is false; and that the conjunction 'P ∧ Q' is true if both of its conjuncts are true, and false otherwise. To put this kind of information succinctly, let us write '|P|' as an abbreviation for 'the truth-value of "P"', and similarly for any other letter in place of 'P'. Let us also abbreviate 'if and only if' simply to 'iff'. Then the information contained in these tables can also be put briefly like this:

$$|\neg P| = T \quad \text{iff} \quad |P| = F$$
$$|P \wedge Q| = T \quad \text{iff} \quad |P| = T \text{ and } |Q| = T.$$

Notice that it is enough if we just spell out the conditions under which a proposition is true, for it then follows that in all other conditions it will be false, in view of our assumption that a proposition always is either true or false.

In addition to the truth-functors '¬' and '∧' we shall also use '∨', '→', and '↔' as truth-functors which correspond, in a rough and ready way, to the English words 'or', 'if ... then ...', and 'if and only if'. Their truth-tables are

P	Q	$P \vee Q$	$P \to Q$	$P \leftrightarrow Q$
T	T	T	T	T
T	F	T	F	F
F	T	T	T	F
F	F	F	T	T

In view of the correspondence with English just noted, the same information can also be given in this way:

$$|P \vee Q| = T \quad \text{iff} \quad |P| = T \text{ or } |Q| = T$$
$$|P \to Q| = T \quad \text{iff} \quad \text{if } |P| = T \text{ then } |Q| = T$$
$$|P \leftrightarrow Q| = T \quad \text{iff} \quad |P| = T \text{ iff } |Q| = T.$$

(In some other books one finds '⊃' in place of '→', and '≡' in place of '↔'.) When two sentences are joined by '∨' we call the whole a disjunction and the two sentences are its disjuncts; when they are joined by '→' we call the whole a conditional, the first sentence being its antecedent and the second its consequent; when they are joined by '↔' we call the whole a biconditional (and there is no special name for its parts).

We shall also use 'T' and '⊥' as 'zero-place truth-functors', i.e. as sentences which take a constant truth-value, the first being true in every possible situation and the second false. So their 'truth-tables' amount just to this:

$$|T| = T \qquad |\bot| = F$$

If you wish, you may think of 'T' and '⊥' as abbreviating some entirely familiar propositions, the first necessarily true and the second necessarily false, for example '0 = 0' and '0 = 1'. That is an approach which will give entirely the right results for the purposes of this book. But from a more philosophical perspective one might well wish to quarrel with it. For it is very often held that our other truth-functors are *defined* by their truth-tables, and so have no other meaning than the truth-table gives to them. If that is so, then presumably 'T' and '⊥' should equally be regarded as defined by their truth-tables, so that '⊥' is a sentence with no other meaning than that what it says is, in all possible situations, false. In that case, '⊥' is a wholly unfamiliar sentence. (And so is 'T'.)

Setting aside the rather odd case of 'T' and '⊥', the other truth-functors just listed are chosen partly because it proves convenient to have a short way of expressing the truth-functions in question, and partly because they have a rough correspondence (as noted) with familiar English expressions. No doubt these two reasons are connected with one another, though one may well debate just how this connection should be understood. (Does one of the reasons given explain the other? If so, which way round does the explanation go?) One may also debate upon how close the correspondence is between these truth-functors and their English counterparts, and why it is not perfect. But, as usual, we shall forgo the pleasures of such a debate, since our concern is with the logical theory itself and not with its application to English. From this perspective, there is certainly some arbitrariness in choosing to introduce simple signs for just these truth-functions but not others. In Sections 2.7 and 2.9 we shall explore some consequences that would flow from selecting one set of truth-functors rather than another, but although these introduce some constraints, they still leave a great deal of freedom. So I do not in fact specify any definite list of truth-functors as *the* ones to be employed. Instead, the treatment will be general enough to allow for any choice of truth-functors, though the ones just listed will be the ones most commonly employed in illustrations.

EXERCISES

2.2.1. Determine whether the following sentence-functors are truth-functors. (Method: see whether it is possible to construct a complete truth-table for them.)

(a) *P* because *Q*.
(b) Even if *P*, still *Q*.
(c) John believes that *P*.
(d) Either John believes that *P* or he does not.

2.2.2. Discuss the following proposals:

(a) that '¬' and 'not' mean the same.
(b) that '∨' and 'or' mean the same.
(c) that '→' and 'only if' mean the same.

2.3. **Languages for Truth-Functors**

We shall now introduce suitable formal languages for studying the effects that truth-functors have on entailment. As already noted (p. 6), these are not really languages, in the ordinary sense of the word, but rather language-schemas. For they will be built from a vocabulary which includes some truth-functors—it does not matter which—and otherwise only schematic sentence-letters, together with brackets to show punctuation. The full list of sentence-letters is the infinite list

$$P,Q,R,P_1,Q_1,R_1,P_2,...$$

A formal language for truth-functors may contain all of these letters in its vocabulary, or it may contain only some. If we take as an example the language which contains them all, and which contains all the truth-functors of the previous section, and nothing else, then this language is specified by the following *formation rules*:

(1) Each sentence-letter is a formula.
(2) 'T' and '⊥' are formulae.
(3) If φ is a formula, so is $\neg\varphi$.
(4) If φ and ψ are formulae, so are $(\varphi\wedge\psi)$, $(\varphi\vee\psi)$, $(\varphi\rightarrow\psi)$, $(\varphi\leftrightarrow\psi)$.
(5) Nothing else is a formula.

It is easy to see how the rules are to be varied to accommodate different choices of the initial vocabulary. For example, our rule (1) might just say: 'The letters "P", "Q", and "R" are formulae', and then in view of clause (5) no other letters would be included in the language. Any or all of rules (2)–(4) might be omitted, and some other truth-functor might be added. For example, one might wish to consider a language with just the one truth-functor '↑' (to be introduced later, p. 58), so that in place of all of rules (2)–(4) we should just have

If φ and ψ are formulae, so is $(\varphi\uparrow\psi)$.

But so long as at least one expression is given outright as a formula by rule (1) (or rule (2)), and so long as at least one truth-functor is introduced by a rule with the form of rules (3) or (4), saying that that truth-functor may be applied to any formulae to yield new formulae, then we shall have a language with infinitely many formulae in it. For there is no upper bound on the length of a formula, and indeed the rules will not allow of there being any such bound.

The only limit on the length of a formula is that every formula must be of

finite length, and rule (5) is intended to be so understood that it has this consequence. One should think of this rule as saying that there are no formulae
other than the ones that there *have* to be in order to satisfy the other rules. It
comes to the same thing to say that the set of formulae is the *smallest* set that
satisfies the other rules, because it is a subset of every set that satisfies them.
So, since we do not need formulae of infinite length in order to satisfy those
rules, there are none. On the contrary, every formula is built up by starting
with some *atomic formulae*, given by rules (1) and (2), and then applying
rules (3) and (4) to bind these together into successively longer and longer
formulae, until, after some finite number of applications, the last truth-
functor is added and the whole formula is completed.

The formulae that are formed along the way are called the *subformulae* of
the whole formula (and the whole formula is trivially counted as a subformula of itself). The subformulae of a given formula are just those parts of it
that are themselves formulae, except that for this purpose we do not count a
sentence-letter as having any parts smaller than itself. (For example, 'P' is
not a subformula of 'P_2', and 'P_2' is not a subformula of 'P_{22}'.) We may add
that for each occurrence of a truth-functor in our whole formula there will
be a definite stage in the process of building up the whole at which it was first
incorporated, and that will be the stage when the shortest subformula containing that occurrence was formed. This shortest subformula is called the
scope of the given occurrence, and the truth-functor concerned is said to be
the *main* functor of that subformula. It is easily seen that the punctuation
supplied by the brackets that figure in rule (4) ensures that each formula
does have a unique decomposition into subformulae, so that there is never
any ambiguity over the scope of an occurrence of a truth-functor.

Nevertheless, all these brackets are rather tedious in practice, and it is
convenient to have some conventions for omitting them. Without any ambiguity we may always omit the outer pair of brackets in any formula that
begins and ends with a bracket. Where we have a continued conjunction,
as in

$$((\varphi \wedge \psi) \wedge \chi) \quad \text{or} \quad (\varphi \wedge (\psi \wedge \chi))$$

we may also omit the inner pair of brackets and write simply

$$(\varphi \wedge \psi \wedge \chi).$$

This increases readability, and should not be misleading, since it will make
no difference which way the inner brackets are restored. The same convention applies to a continued disjunction

$$((\varphi \vee \psi) \vee \chi) \quad \text{or} \quad (\varphi \vee (\psi \vee \chi)).$$

Finally we may regard the functors $\rightarrow$ and $\leftrightarrow$ as 'outranking' $\wedge$ and $\vee$ in the sense that, where brackets are not shown, they should be restored in a way that gives a larger scope to $\rightarrow$ or $\leftrightarrow$, and a smaller scope to $\wedge$ and $\vee$, rather than vice versa. Thus

$$\varphi \vee \psi \rightarrow \chi$$

is to be understood as an abbreviation for

$$(\varphi \vee \psi) \rightarrow \chi$$

and not for

$$\varphi \vee (\psi \rightarrow \chi).$$

Similarly,

$$\varphi \vee (\psi \wedge \chi) \quad \leftrightarrow \quad (\varphi \vee \psi) \wedge (\varphi \vee \chi)$$

is short for

$$(\varphi \vee (\psi \wedge \chi)) \quad \leftrightarrow \quad ((\varphi \vee \psi) \wedge (\varphi \vee \chi))$$

and not for any of the many other ways in which brackets might be restored.

It would be possible to avoid brackets altogether by a change in the notation for two-place truth-functors, i.e. by writing the functor *before* its two arguments, rather than *between* them. That is, one writes '$\vee \varphi \psi$' rather than '$\varphi \vee \psi$', and similarly for any other two-place functor. In this notation (which is known as Polish notation), the potential ambiguity in

$$\varphi \vee \psi \rightarrow \chi$$

cannot be reproduced. For on one way of construing it (i.e. the correct way), it is written as

$$\rightarrow \vee \varphi \psi \chi$$

and on the other way it is written as

$$\vee \varphi \rightarrow \psi \chi.$$

But most people find this notation difficult to read, and in any case it will not be used in this book.

EXERCISES

2.3.1.(*a*) Write formation rules for a language which contains all the sentence-letters, but just one truth-functor, namely the three-place truth-functor $\leftrightarrow(\varphi,\psi,\chi)$, which takes the value T when and only when φ, ψ, and χ each have the same value.

(*b*) Outline an argument to show that in this language no formula has an even number of sentence-letters. (A fully detailed argument for this conclusion would require the method of Section 2.8. But you should be able to give the *idea* of an argument without reading that section.)

2.3.2. How many different ways are there of restoring brackets to the formula

$$P \wedge Q \wedge Q \wedge P?$$

Why is it reasonable to say that it will not make any difference which way you choose to do it?

2.4. Semantics for these Languages

An *interpretation* I of a formal language $\mathcal{L}$ for truth-functors consists of:

(1) an assignment of a truth-value, either T or F, to each sentence-letter in $\mathcal{L}$. This assignment is arbitrary, i.e. *any* such assignment is allowed.

(2) an assignment of truth-values to all the remaining formulae in $\mathcal{L}$, which is not arbitrary, but is calculated from the values assigned to the sentence-letters in accordance with the truth-tables of the truth-functors involved. For example, if the truth-functors of $\mathcal{L}$ are just $\neg, \wedge, \vee$, then the interpretation of the remaining formulae is determined by the rules

$$|\neg\phi| = T \quad \text{iff} \quad |\phi| = F$$
$$|\phi\wedge\psi| = T \quad \text{iff} \quad |\phi| = T \text{ and } |\psi| = T$$
$$|\phi\vee\psi| = T \quad \text{iff} \quad |\phi| = T \text{ or } |\psi| = T.$$

Occasionally it will be useful to consider a non-standard interpretation, which does not obey the stipulations (1) and (2) above. In such a case we shall distinguish the interpretations obeying (1) and (2) as the *standard* interpretations. But 'interpretation' will mean 'standard interpretation' unless there is some indication to the contrary.

The definitions of entailment, inconsistency, and validity for languages for truth-functors are as given in the previous chapter (Section 1.3). For example, a set of formulae Γ is inconsistent iff there is no (standard) interpretation of any language for truth-functors in which all of those formulae are interpreted as true. But it is perhaps easier to think of it in a slightly different way. We will say that the *language* of a set Γ of formulae is the language which has as its vocabulary just the sentence-letters and truth-functors that occur in Γ. Then the set Γ is inconsistent iff in every interpretation of the language of Γ some formula in Γ is interpreted as false. Similarly Γ entails ϕ

24

iff, in every interpretation of the language of $\Gamma \cup \{\phi\}$, either some formula in Γ is false or the formula ϕ is true. Similarly again, ϕ is valid iff, in every interpretation of the language of $\{\phi\}$, ϕ is true. The point that we are here relying on is this: provided that we restrict attention to interpretations which do interpret every sentence-letter, and every truth-functor, in the formulae we are concerned with, then we may take it for granted that what is not true in that interpretation is false, and that what is not false is true. Moreover, we shall never need to consider interpretations which include more letters, or more truth-functors, than occur in the formulae under consideration. For the interpretation of the extra vocabulary cannot in any way affect the truth-values of formulae which lack that vocabulary.

The most straightforward test for validity or entailment or inconsistency is a truth-table test. So long as we may confine our attention to finite sets of formulae, this test can always be applied and will always yield a definite result. One begins by listing all the letters in the formula or formulae to be tested, and then all the different ways of assigning truth-values to those letters. For each assignation we shall construct a separate line of the truth-table, so when we have 2 letters to consider there will be 4 lines in the table, when we have 3 letters there will be 8 lines, and in general when we have n letters there will be 2^n lines. Each line thus represents one of the possible interpretations for the language of the formula or formulae to be tested, and we simply calculate the resulting truth-value for each whole formula in that interpretation, using the tables already stipulated for the various functors involved. The method of calculation is to work up from the shorter subformulae to the longer ones.

Here is a simple example to show that $P \rightarrow (\neg P \rightarrow Q)$ is a valid formula. The table is

P	Q	P	$\rightarrow$	$(\neg P$	$\rightarrow$	$Q)$
T	T	T	T	F	T	T
T	F	T	T	F	T	F
F	T	F	T	T	T	T
F	F	F	T	T	F	F

We have just two letters to consider, P and Q, so we begin by writing these on the left, and underneath them the four possible interpretations. Then on the right we write the formula we are interested in, and we begin by considering its shortest subformulae, which are the letters P and Q again. Under the first occurrence of P, and under the occurrence of Q, we have simply repeated the value they receive in each assignment. Under the second occurrence of P we have written nothing, because in this case we have at once put in the values of the next longer subformula ¬P. These values are written under the main truth-functor of ¬P, namely ¬. Using the truth-table for → we can now calculate the values, in each line, of the next longer subformula ¬P→Q, and again we write these values under its main truth-functor, namely →. Finally, we are now in a position to calculate the values of the whole formula, which we write under its main truth-functor, namely the first occurrence of → in the formula. For ease of reading, this column is sidelined, since it is the goal of the calculation. It turns out that only the value T occurs in this column, which is to say that in every interpretation of the language of the formula that formula is true, i.e. that the formula is valid.

Here is another example, to verify the entailment

$$P{\to}R, Q{\to}R \ \models \ (P{\lor}Q) \to R.$$

The relevant table is

P	Q	R	P→R	Q→R	(P∨Q)→R
T	T	T	T	T	T
T	T	F	F	F	F
T	F	T	T	T	T
T	F	F	F	T	F
F	T	T	T	T	T
F	T	F	T	F	F
F	F	T	T	T	T
F	F	F	T	T	T

In this table we have saved ink by not bothering to repeat the value of a single letter under that letter, but otherwise the procedure is just the same: the value of each formula is calculated from the values of its shorter subformulae. The table shows that whenever the two premiss-formulae are both true—i.e. in lines 1, 3, 5, 7, 8—the conclusion formula is true too; or equivalently (and easier to check) that whenever the conclusion formula is false—i.e. in lines 2, 4, 6—then at least one of the premiss-formulae is also false. This shows that the proposed entailment is indeed correct.

When setting out truth-tables, it is standard practice always to consider the various interpretations in the order illustrated in my last two examples. So, for instance, in a truth-table of 16 lines the column under the first letter would consist of 8 occurrences of T followed by 8 occurrences of F; the column under the second letter would have 4 occurrences of T alternating with 4 occurrences of F; the column under the third letter would have pairs of T alternating with pairs of F; and the column under the last letter would have T alternating with F. Each column begins with T and ends with F, so that the first interpretation considered is that in which all the letters are interpreted as true, and the last considered is that in which they are all interpreted as false. A sequent which can be shown to be correct by the truth-table test is called a *tautologous* sequent, and a single formula which can be shown to be valid by this test is called a *tautology*.

It is obvious that the task of writing out a full truth-table can become very laborious, especially when there are many letters to be considered. So it is natural to seek for some short cuts. One method which is often handy is this: seek to construct just *one* line of the truth-table, which will falsify the suggested entailment. If the construction succeeds, then obviously the entailment is not correct; if the construction fails, then this will be because it runs up against some obstacle which shows that *no* such construction could succeed. In that case, there is no falsifying line, and therefore the entailment is correct. To apply this method, one works in the opposite direction to that of the truth-tables, i.e. one calculates the values of subformulae from the values of the longer formulae that contain them.

Here is an example, testing an entailment which involves four letters, and which therefore would have 16 lines in its full truth-table. The finished diagram which records the reasoning is this:

$$P \to R, \quad Q \to S \quad \vDash \quad (P \lor Q) \to (R \lor S)$$

$$\text{F T F} \quad \text{F T F} \qquad \text{T} \quad \text{F} \quad \text{F F F}$$

$$\underline{\underline{5}}\ 1\ 4 \quad \underline{\underline{5}}\ 1\ 4 \qquad \underline{\underline{2}} \quad 1 \quad 3\ 2\ 3$$

(The numbers on the bottom line are put in only to help in the explanation of the reasoning.) We begin by writing down the entailment to be tested, which has two premiss-formulae and one conclusion-formula. Then our first step is to suppose that this suggested entailment is not correct, i.e. we suppose that there is an interpretation which makes both the premiss-formulae true, and the conclusion-formula false. We therefore put T under the main functor of each premiss-formula, and F under the main functor of the conclusion-formula. These three entries are labelled '1' on the diagram. Now there is nothing more that we can do with the premiss-formulae for the time being, so for our second step we just consider the conclusion. We observe that if the whole conditional $(P \lor Q) \to (R \lor S)$ is to be false, then its antecedent $P \lor Q$ must be true and its consequent $R \lor S$ must be false, so we write in T under the main functor of the first, and F under the main functor of the second. These two entries are labelled '2' on the diagram. The third step then notes that if the disjunction $R \lor S$ is to be false, then both R and S must be false, so F is entered twice more at the entries labelled '3'. We have

now discovered that if there is an interpretation which falsifies our entailment, it must be one in which both R and S are interpreted as false. So our
fourth step just writes in this information for the two premiss-formulae,
and allows us to complete the argument. For if the premiss $P \rightarrow R$ is to be
true, and the consequent R is now given as false, then the antecedent P must
be false as well. So as a fifth step we can write F under P, and by the same reasoning we can also write F under Q. But now we have reached an impossibility, for if P is false, and Q is false, then the disjunction $P \vee Q$ must also be
false, and yet we had said at step 2 that it would have to be true. We therefore
underline the conflicting truth-values, and draw our conclusion: the proposed entailment must be correct. For the attempt to find a falsifying interpretation has run into a contradiction.

Reasoning by this method does not always work out quite so straightforwardly. Here is another example, which in this case does work out, but
which begins to show how problems may arise. Let us see whether the entailment we have just tested also holds the other way round. In this case, our
diagram works out like this:

$$
\begin{array}{ccccccccccc}
(P \vee Q) & \rightarrow & (R \vee S) & \vDash & (P \rightarrow R) & \wedge & (Q \rightarrow S) \\
\text{T T} & \text{T} & \text{F T T} & & \text{T F F} & \text{F} & \text{T T} \\
& & & & \text{A} & & \\
4 \ 5 & 1 & 4 \ 6 \ 7 & & 3 \ 2 \ 3 & 1 & 9 \ 8 \\
\end{array}
$$

Step 1 enters T for the left formula, and F for the right formula, as before. But
these values in fact do not determine any further values at all, so in order to
get any further we must now make an *assumption*. There are several assumptions that one could make. We shall explore later a method which makes
assumptions about the values of the individual sentence-letters. (This is
Quine's method of truth-value analysis, introduced in Section 2.11.) But it
is more in keeping with the present method to make an assumption about
the value of a longer formula, in fact of a longest subformula that is not yet
assigned a value. So we choose to consider the conclusion-formula $(P \rightarrow R)$
$\wedge (Q \rightarrow S)$. Our initial supposition is that this conjunction is false. So it follows that one or other of the two conjuncts, $P \rightarrow R$ and $Q \rightarrow S$, is false, but we
do not know which. We shall assume, then, that it is $P \rightarrow R$ that is false, marking this in on the diagram as step 2, but also labelling it 'A' for 'Assumption'.
Now suppose that in following out the consequences of this assumption we
meet an impossibility, as we did with the last example. Then what we have
to do is to run the test again, this time making the alternative assumption
that $Q \rightarrow S$ is false. If *both* assumptions lead to an impossible distribution of
truth-values, then we know that there cannot be any falsifying interpreta-

tion. But that is not what happens with the present example, as we soon see. The assumption at step 2, that $P{\to}R$ is false, allows us to mark P as true and R as false at step 3. Step 4 then carries this information across to the left formula, and step 5 then notes that, since P is true, $P{\vee}Q$ must be true too. Combining this with the initial supposition that the left formula as a whole is true, we deduce in step 6 that $R{\vee}S$ must be true, and hence in step 7 that S must be true. Step 8 then carries this information across to the other occurrence of S, and step 9 infers that the clause $Q{\to}S$ must therefore be true. At this point we may stop. Admittedly, the value of Q has not yet been determined, and for completeness we should make some assumption about it. But it is easily seen that we could make either assumption, and the rest of the diagram will not be affected. So we have not run up against any impossibility. On the contrary, we have succeeded in constructing a line of the truth-table in which the premiss-formula is true and the conclusion-formula is false, thus showing that the proposed entailment is *not* correct.

As will be evident from these two examples, using this method requires more thought than constructing a full truth-table, but it can save a great deal of time. The method can also become rather complicated, if we are forced to make several different assumptions, one after the other, in testing the same entailment. But I shall not say any more about it at this stage, for in fact the basic idea that we are using here will be developed into an elegant and fool-proof procedure in Chapter 4, with a simple technique for handling a number of assumptions.

EXERCISES

2.4.1. Use truth-tables to determine whether the following sequents are correct. (We use '$\phi =\!\!\models \psi$' as short for '$\phi \models \psi$' and '$\psi \models \phi$'.)

(a) $\neg(P{\to}P) \models (P{\to}\neg P)$

(b) $\models (P{\to}Q) \vee (P{\to}\neg Q)$

(c) $\models (P{\to}Q) \vee (R{\to}P)$

(d) $(P{\to}Q) \wedge (P{\to}\neg Q) \models$

(e) $(P{\leftrightarrow}Q) \wedge (P{\leftrightarrow}\neg Q) \models$

(f) $P \to (Q{\vee}R)$ $=\!\!\models$ $(P{\to}Q) \vee (P{\to}R)$

(g) $(Q{\vee}R) \to P$ $=\!\!\models$ $(Q{\to}P) \vee (R{\to}P)$

(h) $P \leftrightarrow (Q{\vee}R)$ $=\!\!\models$ $(P{\wedge}Q) \vee (P{\wedge}R) \vee (\neg P{\wedge}\neg Q{\wedge}\neg R)$

(i) $P \leftrightarrow (Q{\vee}R)$ $=\!\!\models$ $(P{\wedge}Q{\wedge}R) \vee (\neg P{\wedge}\neg Q) \vee (\neg P{\wedge}\neg R)$.

2.4.2. Without writing out a full truth-table, determine whether the following sequents are correct. (Indicate your reasoning.)

(a) $P{\rightarrow}Q, Q{\rightarrow}R, R{\rightarrow}S \vDash P{\rightarrow}S$
(b) $P{\vee}Q, \neg(P{\wedge}R), \neg(Q{\wedge}S) \vDash \neg(R{\wedge}S)$
(c) $P \rightarrow (Q{\vee}R), R \rightarrow (P{\rightarrow}S), \neg(S{\wedge}P) \vDash Q{\rightarrow}P$
(d) $P \rightarrow (Q{\vee}R), R \rightarrow (P{\rightarrow}S), \neg(S{\wedge}P) \vDash P{\rightarrow}Q$.

2.5. Some Principles of Entailment

It is useful to be familiar with a number of general principles concerning entailment (or inconsistency). We may first note three that are often called 'structural' principles, since they apply to formulae of any kind whatever, and not just to formulae of the languages for truth-functors that we are presently concerned with. They are called the principles of *Assumptions*, of *Thinning*, and of *Cutting*.

2.5.A. Assumptions   This is the principle that any formula entails itself, i.e.

$$\phi \vDash \phi.$$

(The reason why it is called the principle of assumptions will emerge in Chapters 6 and 7.) When we bear in mind the definition of entailment in terms of truth and falsehood in an interpretation, we see that this principle depends just upon the fact that no interpretation assigns *both* T *and* F to the same formula. It should be obvious enough that this is a fact, at least for (standard) interpretations of a language of truth-functors. You might like to reflect upon how it could be proved. (I give a proof in Section 2.8 below.)

2.5.B. Thinning   This is the principle that if a set of premisses entails a conclusion, and we *add* further premisses to that set, then the enlarged set still entails the conclusion. We have two versions of this principle to record, first for the ordinary case where our sequent has a conclusion, and second for the special case where there is no conclusion

(a) If $\Gamma \vDash \phi$ then $\Gamma, \psi \vDash \phi$.
(b) If $\Gamma \vDash$ then $\Gamma, \psi \vDash$.

(The principle is called 'Thinning' simply because thinning is a way of weakening, and '$\Gamma, \psi \vDash \phi$' makes a weaker claim than does '$\Gamma \vDash \phi$'.) In both these versions the principle allows us, if we wish, to add an extra formula to the *left* of the turnstile, so we may distinguish this as *Thinning on the left*.

Later, when we come to consider sequents with more than one formula on the right (in Chapter 7), a precisely analogous principle will allow us to add an extra formula to the right of the turnstile, and this is *Thinning on the right*. One special case of this can be stated now, namely where the number of formulae on the right is increased from zero to one:

(c) If $\Gamma \models$ then $\Gamma \models \psi$.

One has only to consider the definition of the turnstile, in these various contexts, and it is at once obvious that each of (*a*), (*b*), and (*c*) is a correct principle.

2.5.C. Cutting

This principle is a generalization of the point that entailment is transitive, i.e. that if one formula entails a second, and the second entails a third, then the first formula entails the third. The generalization extends this to cover also entailments which have more than one premiss. Again, we have two versions to record, one where our 'third formula' is indeed a formula, and one where it is instead the absence of any formula:

(a) If $\Gamma \models \phi$ and $\phi,\Delta \models \psi$ then $\Gamma,\Delta \models \psi$
(b) If $\Gamma \models \phi$ and $\phi,\Delta \models$ then $\Gamma,\Delta \models$.

(It is called the principle of Cutting because the intermediate conclusion ϕ is 'cut out'.) This principle is not quite so obvious as the preceding two, so I here give a proof of version (*a*). (The modification to yield version (*b*) is obvious.)

Assume, for *reductio ad absurdum*, that the principle is not correct, i.e. that (for some Γ,Δ,ϕ,ψ) we have[1]

(1) $\Gamma \models \phi$ (2) $\phi,\Delta \models \psi$ (3) $\Gamma,\Delta \not\models \psi$.

Then by assumption (3) there is an interpretation *I* which assigns T to each formula in Γ, and to each in Δ, but assigns F to ψ. We ask: what value does *I* assign to ϕ? It may be that *I* assigns no value to ϕ, but if so that can only be because ϕ contains vocabulary which does not occur in Γ or Δ or ψ, and is not interpreted by *I*. In that case, we can evidently expand the interpretation *I*, by adding to it interpretations of the extra vocabulary of ϕ, to form a new interpretation I^+. Since I^+ agrees with *I* on the interpretation of all the vocabulary in Γ and Δ and ψ, it will still be the case that I^+ assigns T to all formulae in Γ, and T to all formulae in Δ, and F to ψ. But I^+ now does assign

---

[1] Recall that '$\not\models$' negates '$\models$'. So (3) means: not ($\Gamma,\Delta \models \psi$).

some value, either T or F, to ϕ. However, by assumption (1) $\Gamma \vDash \phi$, so I^+ cannot assign F to ϕ (since it assigns T to all in Γ); and by assumption (2) $\phi, \Delta \vDash \psi$, so I^+ cannot assign T to ϕ (since it assigns T to all in Δ but F to ψ). This is a contradiction. It follows, then, that assumptions (1), (2), and (3) cannot all be true, so that if (1) and (2) are true, then (3) must be false, as desired.

I now proceed to another principle which is not usually called 'structural', though again it is a principle that continues to apply, whatever kinds of formula are under consideration.

2.5.D. Uniform substitution for schematic letters

In the logic of truth-functors the only schematic letters that we have are sentence-letters, so the principle concerns the substitution of arbitrary formulae in place of sentence-letters. It says that if we have any correct sequent, and if we substitute any formula for a sentence-letter in it—substituting the *same* formula for *every* occurrence of the sentence-letter, all through the sequent—then the result is again a correct sequent. It is useful to introduce a succinct notation for substitution. If ϕ and ψ are formulae, and P_i is a sentence-letter, we shall write $\phi(\psi/P_i)$ for the result of substituting an occurrence of the formula ψ for each occurrence of the letter P_i in ϕ. (If there is no occurrence of P_i in ϕ, then $\phi(\psi/P_i)$ is just ϕ.) Similarly, if Γ is a set of formulae, then we shall write $\Gamma(\psi/P_i)$ for the result of substituting an occurrence of ψ for each occurrence of P_i throughout all the formulae in Γ. Then we may state our principle in two versions, corresponding to the two kinds of sequent we are recognizing:

(*a*) If $\Gamma \vDash \phi$ then $\Gamma(\psi/P_i) \vDash \phi(\psi/P_i)$.

(*b*) If $\Gamma \vDash$ then $\Gamma(\psi/P_i) \vDash$.

The justification for the principle is obvious at once. If we have a correct sequent containing a letter P_i, then that sequent satisfies the truth-table test whichever value is assigned to P_i. But when we replace P_i by a different formula, still that formula as a whole can only take one of the values that P_i could take, and therefore the truth-table test must still be satisfied. That means that the sequent is still correct.

Here are some simple illustrations. It is easily checked that the following is a correct entailment:

$$P \rightarrow \neg P \ \vDash \ \neg P.$$

We may therefore substitute any other formula for all the occurrences of P in this entailment, and the result will again be an entailment; for example:

$$\bot \to \neg\bot \vDash \neg\bot$$
$$Q \to \neg Q \vDash \neg Q$$
$$\neg P \to \neg\neg P \vDash \neg\neg P.$$

These result by substituting for P first $\bot$, then Q, then $\neg P$, which are very simple substitutions. But we may also substitute more complex formulae, say $P \wedge Q \wedge \neg R$, or $(P \to \neg P) \to \neg P$, to obtain

$$(P \wedge Q \wedge \neg R) \to \neg(P \wedge Q \wedge \neg R) \vDash \neg(P \wedge Q \wedge \neg R)$$
$$((P \to \neg P) \to \neg P) \to \neg((P \to \neg P) \to \neg P) \vDash \neg((P \to \neg P) \to \neg P)$$

To check the correctness of these last two sequents, it is a good deal easier to note that they are substitution-instances of a simple sequent already known to be correct, than it is to apply the truth-table test directly to them.

I now turn to consider principles of entailment that are specific to particular truth-functors. There is some embarrassment of riches here, for many correct principles present themselves. But for definiteness I choose one principle for each of the common truth-functors, which I will call the *basic* principle for that functor.

2.5.E. Negation

$$\Gamma, \neg\phi \vDash \quad \text{iff} \quad \Gamma \vDash \phi.$$

2.5.F. Conjunction

$$\Gamma \vDash \phi \wedge \psi \quad \text{iff} \quad \Gamma \vDash \phi \text{ and } \Gamma \vDash \psi.$$

2.5.G. Disjunction

$$\Gamma, \phi \vee \psi \vDash \quad \text{iff} \quad \Gamma, \phi \vDash \text{ and } \Gamma, \psi \vDash.$$

2.5.H. The Conditional

$$\Gamma \vDash \phi \to \psi \quad \text{iff} \quad \Gamma, \phi \vDash \psi.$$

Each of these is easily verified by considering the definition of the turnstile, and of the truth-functor in question. For illustration I give just the argument for the basic negation principle.

First we observe that any interpretation that does not interpret the negation sign can of course be expanded to one that does, just by adding to it the relevant clause for negation, and leaving everything else unchanged. And an interpretation that does interpret the negation sign will assign T to $\neg\phi$ iff it assigns F to ϕ. It follows that there is an interpretation which assigns T to all the formulae in Γ, and assigns T to $\neg\phi$, iff there is an interpretation which assigns T to all the formulae in Γ, and assigns F to ϕ. In other words,

$$\Gamma, \neg\phi \not\vDash \quad \text{iff} \quad \Gamma \not\vDash \phi.$$

But that is the same as to say,

$$\Gamma, \neg\phi \vDash \quad \text{iff} \quad \Gamma \not\vDash \phi.$$

This basic principle for negation is only one of many useful principles concerning negation, but in fact all the others can be deduced from it. I give just a few examples. First, it implies, as we should expect, that a formula and its negation are together inconsistent, i.e.

(a) $\phi, \neg\phi \vDash.$

(To see this, put ϕ for Γ in the basic principle, and observe that the right-hand side is then given by the principle of assumptions.) From this, by thinning on the right, we also have the principle called *ex falso quodlibet*:[2]

(b) $\phi, \neg\phi \vDash \psi.$

From the same starting-point, i.e. from (a), we can also obtain the useful principle of double negation. As a special case of (a) we have $\neg\phi, \neg\neg\phi \vDash$, and so by applying the basic principle to this (with $\neg\neg\phi$ for Γ) we obtain

(c) $\neg\neg\phi \vDash \phi.$

As a special case of (c) we have $\neg\neg\neg\phi \vDash \neg\phi$, and if we put this together with (a), namely $\phi, \neg\phi \vDash$, we can apply the principle of Cutting to 'cut out' the formula $\neg\phi$. The result is $\neg\neg\neg\phi, \phi \vDash$. So we now apply the basic principle to this to obtain

(d) $\phi \vDash \neg\neg\phi.$

(c) and (d) together tell us that any formula is logically equivalent to its double negation. Finally, I observe that the basic principle also implies a form of the law of excluded middle, telling us that if a conclusion ψ follows both from ϕ and from $\neg\phi$ then it must be true. Moreover, we can add extra premisses Γ without disturbing this point, thus

(e) If $\Gamma, \phi \vDash \psi$ and $\Gamma, \neg\phi \vDash \psi$ then $\Gamma \vDash \psi$.

---

[2] *Ex falso quodlibet* means 'from what is false there follows anything you like'. The principle is therefore misnamed, for the truth is that a *contradictory* premiss will imply anything you like, but a mere falsehood will not.

(Applying the basic principle once to the first antecedent, and twice to the second, these become $\Gamma,\phi,\neg\psi \vDash$ and $\Gamma,\neg\psi \vDash \phi$. From these two we may 'cut out' the formula ϕ, and the result then follows by one or more applications of the basic principle.) There are many more useful principles concerning negation. The position will be analysed in more detail in Sections 5.4 and 6.2.

Some deductions from the principles cited as 'basic' principles for conjunction, disjunction, and the conditional are left as exercises. But I observe here that the principle cited for disjunction may be regarded as having two versions, one where there is a formula to the right of the turnstile, and one where there is not:

(a) $\Gamma,\phi\vee\psi \vDash \chi$ iff $\Gamma,\phi \vDash \chi$ and $\Gamma,\psi \vDash \chi$.
(b) $\Gamma,\phi\vee\psi \vDash$ iff $\Gamma,\phi \vDash$ and $\Gamma,\psi \vDash$.

Given suitable principles for negation, either of these versions can be obtained from the other. For example if, as I have proposed, we start with version (b), then we may take the case in which Γ includes a negated formula $\neg\chi$ to deduce

$\Gamma,\neg\chi,\phi\vee\psi \vDash$ iff $\Gamma,\neg\chi,\phi \vDash$ and $\Gamma,\neg\chi,\psi \vDash$.

Applying to this our basic principle for negation, we at once have version (a). The converse deduction is left as an exercise. If, then, we can assume that suitable principles for negation are already present, it does not matter whether we take version (a) or version (b) of this principle for disjunction, and I prefer version (b) because it is nicely related to our basic principle for conjunction (as Section 2.10 will show). But if we are not already given any other principles which allow us to show that the two versions are equivalent, then I think that all we could say is that each is equally basic. (For example, it is version (b) that appears basic from the viewpoint of Chapter 4, but version (a) that appears basic from the viewpoint of Chapter 6. Both versions are special cases of the more general approach pursued in Chapter 7.)

The question of what to count as 'basic' principles for the truth-functors will be taken up in more detail in Chapters 6 and 7. For the present, I set it aside, in order to come to an important principle which is naturally associated with the biconditional, though it is not at all the same in character as the principles proposed for the other truth-functors. In fact there are versions of it which do not rely on the biconditional at all, as we shall see.

2.5.l. Interchange of equivalent formulae   The gist of this principle is that if two formulae are equivalent then either may be substituted for the

other. In the strongest version of the principle, which I take first, formulae are taken to be equivalent if (in a given interpretation) they have the same truth-value. To state this more exactly, let ϕ and ψ be any two formulae; let $\delta(\phi)$ be any formula which contains within itself one or more occurrences of the formula ϕ as a subformula; let $\delta(\psi)$ be the result of substituting the formula ψ in place of the formula ϕ, at one or more occurrences in $\delta(\phi)$. Then the principle in question is

$$\phi \leftrightarrow \psi \quad \vDash \quad \delta(\phi) \leftrightarrow \delta(\psi).$$

The proof is straightforward. The principle claims that any interpretation which verifies $\phi \leftrightarrow \psi$, and which also interprets $\delta(\phi)$, will verify $\delta(\phi) \leftrightarrow \delta(\psi)$. An interpretation which verifies $\phi \leftrightarrow \psi$ is one that assigns the same truth-value to both formulae. But then it must follow that that interpretation also assigns the same truth-value to $\delta(\phi)$ and $\delta(\psi)$. For $\delta(\phi)$ and $\delta(\psi)$ are exactly alike, except that the one has ϕ in some places where the other has ψ. But if ϕ and ψ have the same value, then this difference will not affect the calculation of the values of $\delta(\phi)$ and $\delta(\psi)$.

This is the basic form of the principle of interchange of equivalent formulae. In practice, the principle is often used in a weaker form, which confines attention to formulae which are *logically* equivalent, i.e. which have the same truth-value in *all* interpretations. In this form the principle is

$$\text{If } \vDash \phi \leftrightarrow \psi \text{ then } \vDash \delta(\phi) \leftrightarrow \delta(\psi).$$

It is clear that this follows (by the principle of Cutting) from the first version. We may rephrase this derived form in a way which eliminates the truth-functor $\leftrightarrow$. For as a special case of our basic principle for the conditional we have

$$\vDash \phi \rightarrow \psi \quad \text{iff} \quad \phi \vDash \psi$$

and hence also

$$\vDash \phi \leftrightarrow \psi \quad \text{iff} \quad \phi \vDash \psi \text{ and } \psi \vDash \phi.$$

Abbreviating the right-hand side of this to '$\phi \dashv\vDash \psi$', we may therefore write the derived form of the principle in this way:

$$\text{If } \phi \dashv\vDash \psi \text{ then } \delta(\phi) \dashv\vDash \delta(\psi).$$

There will be several applications of this form of the principle in what follows.

EXERCISES

2.5.1. Show that the basic principle for negation can in fact be deduced from

(a) $\phi, \neg\phi \vDash$
(b) If $\Gamma, \phi \vDash \psi$ and $\Gamma, \neg\phi \vDash \psi$ then $\Gamma \vDash \psi$.

2.5.2. Fill a gap in the text by showing that version (a) of the disjunction principle (p. 35) implies version (b), given a suitable principle for negation.

2.5.3.(a) Show that the basic principle for conjunction implies

(1) $\phi, \psi \vDash \phi \wedge \psi$.
(2) $\phi \wedge \psi \vDash \phi$ and $\phi \wedge \psi \vDash \psi$.

((1) is known as the *introduction* rule for conjunction, (2) as the *elimination* rule.)
(b) Show that this deduction may be reversed, i.e. that (1) and (2) together imply the basic principle for conjunction.

2.5.4.(a) Show that the basic principle for the conditional, *together with* a suitable principle for negation (e.g. *ex falso quodlibet*), implies

(1) $\psi \vDash \phi \rightarrow \psi$ and $\neg\phi \vDash \phi \rightarrow \psi$
(2) $\phi, \phi \rightarrow \psi \vDash \psi$.

((2) is known as *Modus Ponens*, and is the usual elimination rule for the conditional; (1) is not usually regarded as a suitable introduction rule, since it involves $\neg$ as well as $\rightarrow$.)
(b) Show that this deduction may be reversed.

2.5.5. Show that version (a) of the basic principle for disjunction implies the introduction rule

$\phi \vDash \phi \vee \psi$ and $\psi \vDash \phi \vee \psi$.

Speculate upon what would be a suitable elimination rule, bearing in mind the desideratum that an elimination rule for a given truth-functor should not also involve any other truth-functor. (For the answer, see Sections 6.2 and 7.4.)

2.6. Normal Forms (DNF, CNF)

It is often convenient to be able to confine one's attention to languages which contain only a limited number of truth-functors. In this section we shall suppose that our language contains only $\top, \bot, \neg, \wedge, \vee$, and no other truth-functors. We shall show that in this case we can without loss confine our attention yet further, to formulae that are written in a specially tidy form.

First, we can confine attention to formulae in which the negation sign is always immediately followed by a sentence-letter, so that no other truth-functor ever occurs in the scope of a negation sign. This is because every formula in our language is logically equivalent to a formula obeying this condition. To establish this point, we need only consider the laws

$$
\begin{array}{rcl}
\neg\top & =\!\models & \bot \\
\neg\bot & =\!\models & \top \\
\neg\neg\varphi & =\!\models & \varphi \\
\neg(\varphi\wedge\psi) & =\!\models & \neg\varphi\vee\neg\psi \\
\neg(\varphi\vee\psi) & =\!\models & \neg\varphi\wedge\neg\psi.
\end{array}
$$

(The first two have no special name; the third is of course the law of double negation; the last two are called De Morgan's laws, after the logician Augustus de Morgan. You should check with a truth-table test that these laws are indeed correct.) Now consider any occurrence of the negation sign that does have some truth-functor in its scope. This means that it must be followed either by $\top$ or by $\bot$ or by another negation sign or by a bracket, introducing a formula with either $\wedge$ or $\vee$ as its main functor. In the first three cases that occurrence of the negation sign can simply be deleted, at the same time interchanging $\top$ and $\bot$ in the first two cases, and deleting the other negation sign in the third case. In the remaining two cases we apply De Morgan's laws, exchanging the one negation sign outside the bracket for two that are inside it, at the same time changing the $\wedge$ to $\vee$, or the $\vee$ to $\wedge$, whichever is appropriate. Then we look again at the two negation signs that result. Either they are now followed immediately by sentence-letters, as desired, or if they are not, then we apply the whole procedure once more. And we continue to do this as often as is needed to bring *every* negation sign into the required position.

It is clear that we must eventually reach the result desired. For in the first three cases the negation sign disappears altogether, and in the other two the negation sign is exchanged for two others, each of which has *fewer* truth-functors in its scope (for there must be fewer truth-functors in φ than there are in $\varphi\wedge\psi$, and similarly with ψ). Finally, note that the formula we end with, after making all these transformations, must still be logically equivalent to the formula we began with. This, of course, is because each transformation exchanges one subformula for another that is logically equivalent to it, and we noted at the end of the last section that such an interchange of logically equivalent subformulae must preserve the equivalence of the whole.

Having got the negation signs into the right position, we can now carry out some further transformations. In particular we can rearrange the occurrences of ∧ and ∨ so that no conjunction sign has any disjunction in its scope, or alternatively so that no disjunction sign has any conjunction in its scope. The first is called disjunctive normal form (DNF), and the second is conjunctive normal form (CNF). These transformations rely on the laws of *distribution*, which are

$$\varphi \wedge (\psi \vee \chi) \quad =\!\!\models \quad (\varphi \wedge \psi) \vee (\varphi \wedge \chi).$$
$$(\varphi \vee \psi) \wedge \chi \quad =\!\!\models \quad (\varphi \wedge \chi) \vee (\psi \wedge \chi).$$
$$\varphi \vee (\psi \wedge \chi) \quad =\!\!\models \quad (\varphi \vee \psi) \wedge (\varphi \vee \chi).$$
$$(\varphi \wedge \psi) \vee \chi \quad =\!\!\models \quad (\varphi \vee \chi) \wedge (\psi \vee \chi).$$

One uses the first pair to obtain DNF, and the second pair to obtain CNF. Let us concentrate just on the first, where our object is to ensure that no conjunction sign has any disjunction in its scope. If any does, then there must be somewhere a conjunction sign that *immediately* governs a disjunction, i.e. that conjoins two formulae at least one of which *is* a disjunction, as in the formulae on the left-hand side of the first pair of distribution laws. So we replace this by the right-hand side. The result is that the conjunction sign is split into two, but each of these has *fewer* disjunction signs in its scope than the one we began with. So if we continue the procedure we must eventually reach the desired position, where there are *no* disjunction signs in the scope of any conjunction signs. And, as before, these transformations simply interchange logically equivalent subformulae, so the formula that we end with must be logically equivalent to the one that we began from. (The argument in the case of CNF is exactly similar.)

At this point we may delete the superfluous brackets from a continued conjunction, and from a continued disjunction (p. 22), and our whole formula in DNF looks like this. It is as a whole a disjunction of one or more disjuncts, where each of the disjuncts is a conjunction of one or more conjuncts, and where each of the conjuncts is either an atomic formula—i.e. a sentence-letter or ⊤ or ⊥—or the negation of an atomic formula. Let us write $\pm P_i$ to indicate that there may or may not be a negation sign in front of the atomic formula P_i. Then the whole formula takes this form

$$(\pm P_i \wedge \pm P_j \wedge ...) \vee (\pm P_k \wedge \pm P_l \wedge ...) \vee ...$$

A formula in CNF has the corresponding structure with ∧ and ∨ everywhere interchanged, i.e.

$$(\pm P_i \vee \pm P_j \vee ...) \wedge (\pm P_k \vee \pm P_l \vee ...) \wedge ...$$

But it should be noted that in this description of the structure of formulae in DNF and CNF we have made use of the degenerate case of a 'disjunction' which has only one 'disjunct', and similarly of a 'conjunction' which has only one 'conjunct'.

It follows that some formulae have both structures simultaneously, i.e. they are both in DNF and in CNF. The simplest example is a formula which is a single sentence-letter

$P.$

This formula is a disjunction of only one disjunct, where the disjunct is itself a conjunction of only one conjunct, namely P. So it is in DNF. Of course, we can say the same thing the other way round too. This formula is a conjunction of only one conjunct, where the conjunct is itself a disjunction of only one disjunct, namely P. So it is equally in CNF. Or one can make this point in the terminology with which I began: in this formula, no occurrence of $\neg$ has any truth-functor in its scope; no occurrence of $\land$ has any $\lor$ in its scope; and no occurrence of $\lor$ has any $\land$ in its scope. You should verify in a similar way that both of the following formulae are also both in DNF and in CNF:

$P \land \neg Q \land R$
$P \lor \neg Q \lor R.$

By contrast, of the following formulae the first is in DNF but not CNF, and the second is in CNF but not DNF:

$P \lor (Q \land \neg R)$
$(P \lor Q) \land (P \lor \neg R).$

Finally, the following formulae are neither in DNF nor in CNF:

$\neg(P \land Q)$
$(P \land (Q \lor \neg R)) \lor \neg Q.$

The normal forms DNF and CNF, as characterized so far, can still be very untidy. To introduce a greater tidiness we may start by rearranging each conjunction, in a case of DNF, or each disjunction, in a case of CNF, so that in each one the sentence-letters occur in alphabetical order. In view of the laws of *commutativity* and *associativity*, namely

$$\varphi \land \psi \quad \mathbin{=\!\mid\!\mid\!=} \quad \psi \land \varphi \qquad\qquad \varphi \lor \psi \quad \mathbin{=\!\mid\!\mid\!=} \quad \psi \lor \varphi$$
$$\varphi \land (\psi \land \chi) \quad \mathbin{=\!\mid\!\mid\!=} \quad (\varphi \land \psi) \land \chi \qquad \varphi \lor (\psi \lor \chi) \quad \mathbin{=\!\mid\!\mid\!=} \quad (\varphi \lor \psi) \lor \chi,$$

the order in which the conjuncts or disjuncts are written makes no difference. This will bring to light any repetitions, where the same sentence-letter occurs twice, and these may then be deleted in view of the laws of *idempotence*, namely

$$\varphi\wedge\varphi \quad =\!\!\models\quad \varphi \qquad \varphi\vee\varphi \quad =\!\!\models\quad \varphi.$$

It will also bring to light any case in which we have both a sentence-letter and its own negation. These can then be simplified by the following laws of *contradiction* and *excluded middle*:

$$\varphi\wedge\neg\varphi \quad =\!\!\models\quad \bot \qquad \varphi\vee\neg\varphi \quad =\!\!\models\quad \top.$$

The occurrences of $\top$ and $\bot$ thus introduced, and any other occurrences of $\top$ and $\bot$ that there may be in our formula can then be eliminated (except in one special case) by applying the laws

$$\bot\wedge\varphi \quad =\!\!\models\quad \bot \qquad \top\vee\varphi \quad =\!\!\models\quad \top$$
$$\bot\vee\varphi \quad =\!\!\models\quad \varphi \qquad \top\wedge\varphi \quad =\!\!\models\quad \varphi.$$

For example, suppose that we have a formula in DNF, and one of the disjuncts contains the conjunction $P_i \wedge \neg P_i$. We begin by replacing this by $\bot$, using the law of contradiction. Then, if this is part of a longer conjunction, we replace the whole conjunction by $\bot$, using the law next cited in the left column. Thus $\bot$ becomes one of the disjuncts in our overall disjunction. If there are any other disjuncts, then this disjunct can simply be eliminated, using the final law cited in the left column. If there are no other disjuncts, our whole formula has already been reduced just to $\bot$, and we make no further simplifications. Generalizing upon this, it is easy to see that any occurrence of $\bot$ in a formula in DNF either can be eliminated or can replace the whole formula. Using the laws cited in the right column, the same holds for any occurrence of $\top$. And, using both columns together, the same result holds for formulae in CNF just as well as for formulae in DNF. We can always assume, then, that our formulae do not contain either $\top$ or $\bot$, except in the special case when $\top$ or $\bot$ is the whole formula.

The final 'tidying up' operation is to transform the formula so that each disjunct, in a case of DNF, or each conjunct, in a case of CNF, contains exactly the same sentence-letters. This is done by applying the laws of *elaboration*:

$$\varphi \quad =\!\!\models\quad (\varphi\wedge\psi)\vee(\varphi\wedge\neg\psi) \qquad \varphi \quad =\!\!\models\quad (\varphi\vee\psi)\wedge(\varphi\vee\neg\psi)$$

For example, suppose we have a formula in DNF. We begin by listing all the sentence-letters that occur anywhere in that formula, and we check to see whether each disjunct contains one occurrence of each of them. If we find a disjunct φ which lacks some letter, say P_i, then we use the law of elaboration in the left column to replace φ by $(\varphi\wedge P_i)\vee(\varphi\wedge\neg P_i)$. (Each of the new disjuncts $\varphi\wedge P_i$ and $\varphi\wedge\neg P_i$ is then rearranged alphabetically.) By repeating this step as often as necessary, we can evidently expand each conjunction to the desired length. Then we make one final step of simplification: if it now turns out that any disjunct is repeated, we delete the repetition as superfluous (by the law of idempotence), and we have now reached our goal. Our formula is now in *perfect DNF*, which is to say: it is in DNF; no disjunct is superfluous; each disjunct contains the same sentence-letters; no disjunct contains the same letter twice; the truth-functors $\top$ and $\bot$ do not occur, except in the special case where one of them is the whole formula. (*Perfect CNF* is defined similarly, with 'conjunct' for 'disjunct' throughout.)

The method just explained is a method for transforming any formula, step by step, into a logically equivalent formula in perfect DNF, or in perfect CNF, whichever is desired. The method relies throughout on the principle that logically equivalent subformulae may be substituted for one another and the results will also be logically equivalent. It has some quite interesting applications, as will be shown later (Exercises 6.2.2 and 6.5.1). But in practice it can be very tedious indeed, so it is relevant that there is an alternative method that is often quicker. This involves (*a*) constructing the full truth-table for the formula in question, and then (*b*) simply reading the desired normal form off the truth-table. I give first an example to show how this is done, and afterwards a general description of the technique.

Suppose we have a formula $\varphi(P,Q,R)$, containing just the sentence-letters P,Q,R, and we wish to find for it a logically equivalent formula in perfect DNF. We first calculate its truth-table, which is, say, this

P	Q	R	$\varphi(P,Q,R)$
T	T	T	T
T	T	F	F
T	F	T	F
T	F	F	T
F	T	T	T
F	T	F	F
F	F	T	F
F	F	F	T

We look down the truth-table to see in which rows the formula is true, i.e. in this case rows 1, 4, 5, 8, and we ignore the others. For each such row we then form a conjunction of the sentence-letters or their negations which corresponds to the truth-values assigned to the letters in that row in this way: if the letter P_i is assigned T in that row, we write P_i, and if it is assigned F, then we write $\neg P_i$. So in the present case we write down four such conjunctions, namely

$P{\wedge}Q{\wedge}R$
$P{\wedge}\neg Q{\wedge}\neg R$
$\neg P{\wedge}Q{\wedge}R$
$\neg P{\wedge}\neg Q{\wedge}\neg R.$

The point of this is that each formula we have written down is true if and only if the letters are assigned the values in the corresponding rows of the truth-table. Now our whole formula $\varphi(P,Q,R)$ is true if and only if the letters are assigned values as in one or other of the four rows being considered, so it is true if and only if one or other of the four conjunctions that we have written down is true, i.e. if and only if the disjunction of those four conjunctions is true. So finally we write down the disjunction of those four conjunctions, namely

$$(P{\wedge}Q{\wedge}R) \vee (P{\wedge}\neg Q{\wedge}\neg R) \vee (\neg P{\wedge}Q{\wedge}R) \vee (\neg P{\wedge}\neg Q{\wedge}\neg R).$$

This is the formula desired. As we have argued, it is logically equivalent to the formula we began with, since it must have the same truth-table, and it is in perfect DNF.

Here is a general statement of the method. Consider any formula φ with sentence-letters $P_1,...,P_n$. List the interpretations of the sentence-letters under which the whole formula is true. If there are none, then simply write $\bot$, for this is a formula in perfect DNF that is logically equivalent to φ. If there are some, then form for each the corresponding conjunction $\pm P_1 \wedge \pm P_2 \wedge ...$ $\wedge \pm P_n$, where $\pm P_i$ is P_i if P_i is true in that interpretation, and $\neg P_i$ otherwise. The disjunction of all these conjunctions is then the formula required.

The method is easily adapted to the case of CNF. Here what we need to do is to consider the interpretations in which our formula is false. If there are none, then we simply write $\top$, and the task is done. If there are some, then again we form the corresponding conjunctions for each. For example, in the case of the formula $\varphi(P,Q,R)$ considered earlier there are four such conjunctions, namely

$P{\wedge}Q{\wedge}\neg R$
$P{\wedge}\neg Q{\wedge}R$
$\neg P{\wedge}Q{\wedge}\neg R$
$\neg P{\wedge}\neg Q{\wedge}R.$

Now our formula $\varphi(P,Q,R)$ is false iff one of these conjunctions is true, and hence it is true iff all of these conjunctions are false. We therefore form a formula which says that they are false, namely by conjoining the negations of them:

$$\neg(P\wedge Q\wedge\neg R) \wedge \neg(P\wedge\neg Q\wedge R) \wedge \neg(\neg P\wedge Q\wedge\neg R) \wedge \neg(\neg P\wedge\neg Q\wedge R).$$

This is logically equivalent to our original formula. Moreover, it is easily transformed into a formula in perfect CNF, simply by applying De Morgan's laws (and double negation) to obtain

$$(\neg P\vee\neg Q\vee R) \wedge (\neg P\vee Q\vee\neg R) \wedge (P\vee\neg Q\vee R) \wedge (P\vee Q\vee\neg R).$$

Thus for every formula there is a logically equivalent formula in perfect DNF, and there is also a logically equivalent formula in perfect CNF, and we have now proved this result in two ways, first by showing how to transform any formula that is not already in the required form into one that is, by systematically exchanging its subformulae for others that are logically equivalent; and second by showing how to read the required normal form off the truth-table. The first method yielded only a limited result, for we began by restricting attention to a language that contained only the truth-functors $\top,\bot,\neg,\wedge,\vee$. To remove the limitation, we should have to show that any truth-functor whatever is equivalent to one that can be expressed in this language. But that is just what the second method does. For any truth-functor will have a truth-table, and the second method shows us how to find an expression in our preferred language that has that same truth-table. It is the second method, therefore, that yields the more significant result. The next section will develop this further.

EXERCISES

2.6.1. Find perfect disjunctive normal forms for the following formulae, first by the method of successive transformations, and then by constructing a truth-table and reading the result off that

(a) $\neg((P\wedge(\neg P\vee\bot)) \vee P$
(b) $(P\vee\neg Q) \wedge (Q\vee\neg P)$
(c) $(P\vee Q) \wedge (P\vee\neg Q) \wedge (\neg P\vee Q) \wedge (\neg P\vee\neg Q)$.

Note that to deal with the last example you will need to restore the missing brackets; restore them in whatever way seems likely to abbreviate labour. (You may wish to experiment with this.) Note also that when applying the method of successive transformations there is no need to follow the order used in the previous section. We know that if that order is followed then the desired result must be reached in the end, but a different order may well get there more quickly. (You may wish to experiment on this point with example (a).)

2.6.2. Show that, in a language with $\neg$ and $\leftrightarrow$ as its only truth-functors, every formula is logically equivalent to one in which no occurrence of $\neg$ has any truth-functor in its scope.

2.7. **Expressive Adequacy I**

A set of truth-functors is said to be *expressively adequate* (or, sometimes, *functionally complete*) iff, for every truth-function whatever, there is a formula containing only those truth-functors which expresses that truth-function, i.e. which has as its truth-table the truth-table specifying that function. The method introduced in the last section, of reading off from a truth-table a formula in perfect DNF, or in perfect CNF, establishes this basic result on expressive adequacy:

The set of truth-functors $\{\top, \bot, \neg, \wedge, \vee,\}$ is expressively adequate.

There is just one slight modification that needs to be made to the argument already given.

Consider, for example, the two-place truth-function which always yields the value F, whatever its arguments. The method given for writing a formula in perfect DNF to fit this truth-table was that one should simply write $\bot$. But $\bot$ itself is a zero-place truth-functor, expressing a zero-place truth-function and not a two-place truth-function. (It is *logically equivalent* to any formula expressing our two-place function.) What is wanted, then, is a formula containing two sentence-letters, say P and Q, which always takes the value F, and the fact is that there is no such formula in perfect DNF. The closest that we can come is

$(P \wedge \neg P) \vee (Q \wedge \neg Q).$

This is a formula in DNF, and it does have the right truth-table, but it is not counted as being in perfect DNF, since it does not obey the condition that no disjunct is to contain the same letter twice. However, the point is of no importance if we are just concerned with expressive adequacy, for our formula expresses the required truth-function perfectly well, even though it is not in perfect DNF. An alternative way of dealing with this case is to note that it is automatically covered by our method of finding a formula in perfect CNF to fit this truth-function. Generalizing this point, it is easy to see that we can always find formulae whose only truth-functors are $\neg, \wedge, \vee$, to express any truth-function *except* for the two zero-place functions. It is only in these two special cases that $\top$ or $\bot$ need to be used. Moreover, we noted earlier that the whole notion of a zero-place function is somewhat artificial, and so it is usual to ignore these two cases when discussing expressive adequacy. If we do ignore them, then clearly the basic result on expressive adequacy can be stated more simply:

The set of truth-functors $\{\neg, \wedge, \vee\}$ is expressively adequate.

Having obtained this basic result on expressive adequacy, it is easy to obtain further positive results by showing how other sets of truth-functors can be used to express the functions expressed by $\neg, \wedge, \vee$. For example, the set $\{\neg, \wedge\}$ is expressively adequate, since it can also express disjunction, and the set $\{\neg, \vee\}$ is expressively adequate, since it can also express conjunction. To see this, we need only note these two logical equivalences:

$$\varphi \vee \psi \quad =\!\Vdash \quad \neg(\neg\varphi \wedge \neg\psi)$$
$$\varphi \wedge \psi \quad =\!\Vdash \quad \neg(\neg\varphi \vee \neg\psi).$$

(These are simple variations on De Morgan's laws.) It is usual to say that the first shows how to *define* $\vee$ in terms of $\neg$ and $\wedge$, and the second shows how to *define* $\wedge$ in terms of $\neg$ and $\vee$, and this is a convenient way of talking. But it is a somewhat loose use of the word 'define', for we do not really mean to claim that the formula on the left *has the same meaning as* the formula on the right. (On the contrary, the usual view about the meaning of the truth-functors, as stated earlier, is that each is defined by its own truth-table, independently of any other truth-functor.) All that we mean to claim is that the two formulae are logically equivalent, and so for most logical purposes they behave as if they had the same meaning; in particular, by the principle allowing interchange of equivalent formulae, either may be substituted for the other whenever we wish.

The set of truth-functors $\{\neg, \rightarrow\}$ is also expressively adequate, for we can define $\wedge$ and $\vee$ in terms of it, e.g. thus:

$$\varphi \wedge \psi \quad =\!\Vdash \quad \neg(\varphi \rightarrow \neg\psi)$$
$$\varphi \vee \psi \quad =\!\Vdash \quad \neg\varphi \rightarrow \psi.$$

One may note, incidentally, that these definitions can be reversed to yield definitions of $\rightarrow$ in terms of $\neg$ and $\wedge$, and in terms of $\neg$ and $\vee$

$$\varphi \rightarrow \psi \quad =\!\Vdash \quad \neg(\varphi \wedge \neg\psi)$$
$$\varphi \rightarrow \psi \quad =\!\Vdash \quad \neg\varphi \vee \psi.$$

Another curiosity is that $\vee$ can be defined in terms of $\rightarrow$ alone, and without using $\neg$, by

$$\varphi\lor\psi \quad =\!\!\!\Vdash \quad (\varphi\to\psi)\to\psi.$$

But by contrast there is no way of defining $\land$ in terms of $\to$ alone (see Exercise 2.9.2).

I observe finally that the set of functors $\{\to,\bot\}$ is expressively adequate, since $\neg$ can be defined in terms of $\to$ and $\bot$ by

$$\neg\varphi \quad =\!\!\!\Vdash \quad \varphi\to\bot.$$

Thus whatever truth-functions can be expressed by $\neg$ and $\to$ can also be expressed by $\to$ and $\bot$, and, as we have already observed, the set $\{\neg,\to\}$ is adequate. Of all the two-membered sets mentioned so far, this set $\{\to,\bot\}$ has a claim to be counted as the 'most' adequate, since it can express the two zero-place truth-functions, which the others cannot. For one of them is expressed by $\bot$ on its own, and the other by $\neg\bot$, i.e. by $\bot\to\bot$, as the definition of $\neg$ tells us.

Now the sets $\{\land,\bot\}$ and $\{\lor,\bot\}$ are not adequate; nor is the set $\{\neg,\leftrightarrow\}$. There are many ways of defining $\leftrightarrow$ in terms of our other truth-functors, for example:

$$\varphi\leftrightarrow\psi \quad =\!\!\!\Vdash \quad (\varphi\to\psi)\land(\psi\to\varphi)$$
$$\varphi\leftrightarrow\psi \quad =\!\!\!\Vdash \quad (\varphi\land\psi)\lor(\neg\varphi\land\neg\psi)$$
$$\varphi\leftrightarrow\psi \quad =\!\!\!\Vdash \quad (\varphi\lor\psi)\to(\varphi\land\psi).$$

However, there is no way of defining either $\land$ or $\lor$ or $\to$ just in terms of $\leftrightarrow$ and $\neg$. But how are such negative claims to be established? Given one positive result on expressive adequacy, the method of obtaining further positive results is simply to specify the needed definitions. But we do not yet have a method of obtaining any negative results. Consequently, I break off the discussion of expressive adequacy at this point in order to introduce the method required.

EXERCISES

The truth-functor $\not\leftrightarrow$ is defined by this truth-table

φ	ψ	$\varphi \not\leftrightarrow \psi$
T	T	F
T	F	F
F	T	T
F	F	F

2.7.1. Define ∧ in terms of ↔ and ¬, and deduce that the set {¬,↔} is expressively adequate.

2.7.2. Define ⊥ in terms of ↔ alone, and deduce that the set {→,↔} is expressively adequate.

2.7.3. Define ∧ in terms of ↔ alone. (If you cannot solve this problem now, try again when you have read Section 2.10.)

2.8. Argument by Induction

A well-known principle of argument in elementary arithmetic is the principle of mathematical induction, which is this:

> Suppose that the first number, 0, has a certain property; and suppose also that if any number has that property, then so does the next; then it follows that all numbers have the property.

When we speak of 'all numbers' here, we mean, of course, all those numbers that can be reached by starting with 0 and going on from each number to the next some finite number of times. For example, negative numbers, fractional numbers, or infinite numbers are not to count, but only those numbers that are called the 'natural' numbers. I take it that it is sufficiently obvious that the principle of induction is a correct principle for reasoning about such numbers.

The principle as I have just stated it is the *ordinary* principle of (mathematical) induction, but there is also another version of the principle, which is called the principle of complete induction. This is a bit more difficult to grasp. It may be stated thus:

> Suppose that, for every number, if all the numbers less than it have a certain property, then so does it; then it follows that every number has the property.

It may help to see how this principle works if I begin by deducing it from the ordinary principle of induction.

Assume as a premiss, then, that for some property *P*,

(1) For any number *x*, if every number less than *x* has *P*, then so does *x*.

We wish to show that it then follows that every number has the property *P*. We shall show first that it follows that, for every number *x*, every number less than x has P. And we shall show this using the ordinary principle of induction. So we observe first:

(a) Every number less than 0 has P.

This is trivially true for every property, since there are no numbers less than 0. (Recall that negative numbers are not to count.) Here is something, then, that holds for 0. Next we let n be any arbitrary number and assume that the same thing holds for n, i.e. that

(b) Every number less than n has P.

Taking x as n in our premiss (1), it then follows that n also has P. But further, the numbers less than $n+1$ are just the numbers less than n together with n itself, so this shows

(c) Every number less than $n + 1$ has P.

This establishes the premisses for an ordinary inductive argument. For in (a) we have established our result for 0, and then in (b) we assumed the result for n and deduced in (c) that it must then hold for $n + 1$ as well. So by ordinary induction it holds for all numbers, i.e.

(2) For every number x, every number less than x has P.

Finally, from (1) and (2) together we at once have the desired conclusion

(3) For every number x, x has P.

Thus we have shown that (1) implies (3), and that is the principle of complete induction.

    In logic we shall apply this principle in connection with some special uses of numbers, and the first of these is the use of numbers to measure what we call the *length* of a formula.[3] (Other books sometimes speak instead of the *degree* of a formula.) By this we mean simply the *number of occurrences of truth-functors* in that formula. For example, the formula $\neg\neg\neg P$ has length 3, since it contains three occurrences of truth-functors (each an occurrence of the same functor); the formula $P \vee (Q{\rightarrow}R)$ has length 2, since it contains only two occurrences of truth-functors (each an occurrence of a different functor). (So the formula $\neg\neg\neg P$ counts as *longer than* the formula $P \vee (Q{\rightarrow}R)$, despite the fact that it occupies less space on paper.) Now suppose that we wish to show that all formulae have a certain property. Since every formula is of some definite length, it will evidently be enough to prove:

---

[3] Later we shall also argue by induction on the length of a proof.

For all numbers x, all formulae of length x have the property.

In order to prove this by the principle of complete induction what we need to do is to set up the *inductive hypothesis*, for an arbitrary number n,

(1) For all numbers y less than n, all formulae of length y have the property.

From this hypothesis we then seek to deduce that

(2) All formulae of length n have the property.

If the deduction succeeds, then—since n was arbitrary—we have established the premiss for the induction, and our result is therefore proved.

As a matter of fact we shall not set out our inductive arguments in quite this form, but in a simpler form which makes no explicit reference to numbers. For in order to deduce our consequence (2), what we need to do is to take an arbitrary formula ϕ of length n, and to show that it has the property. But the inductive hypothesis, from which we hope to deduce this, evidently tells us that all formulae of length less than ϕ have the property, or in other words that all formulae shorter than ϕ have the property. So this is the form in which the inductive hypothesis will actually be stated, namely

(1′) All formulae ψ shorter than ϕ have the property.

And from this hypothesis we then aim to deduce:

(2′) The formula ϕ has the property.

In the deduction, ϕ is to be any arbitrary formula. If the deduction succeeds, then it shows directly that (1′) implies (2′), and hence indirectly that (1) implies (2). Since (1) implies (2) it follows, as we have seen, that all formulae of any length have the property, or simply,

All formulae have the property.

So we shall not actually mention particular numbers in the course of the argument, though it helps to think in terms of numbers when reflecting on why this form of argument is justified.

In these arguments by (complete) induction on the length of a formula, it will nearly always be necessary to distinguish, and to consider separately, a number of different cases. The different cases will be the different possibilities for the structure of the formula ϕ, and which these are will depend upon which formulae our argument is intended to cover, i.e. on which *language* is in question. Supposing that the language is that specified by the formation rules set out on p. 21, there will be four basic kinds of formulae to consider:

    (1) where φ is a sentence-letter;
    (2) where φ is either ⊤ or ⊥;
    (3) where φ is the negation of some formula, i.e. where φ is ¬ψ for some formula ψ;
    (4) where φ is the conjunction or disjunction of two other formulae, or some other two-place truth-function of them; i.e. where φ is (ψ∗χ) for some formulae ψ and χ, and some two-place truth-functor ∗.

The formation rules specify that every formula must be of one or other of these four kinds, because every formula is constructed by some finite number of applications of the formation rules, and the last rule applied must be one of the four just listed.

    In practice, we usually do not need to distinguish between cases (1) and (2), but can roll them together under the case where φ is an *atomic* formula, i.e. has no subformulae except itself. In this case, the inductive hypothesis is generally useless. For where φ is a sentence-letter there are no formulae shorter than φ, and where φ is ⊤ or ⊥ it has no *components* shorter than itself, which has much the same effect. The inductive hypothesis is useful in cases (3) and (4). For if φ is ¬ψ, then since ψ is shorter than φ we can assume that the hypothesis holds of ψ; and, similarly, if φ is (ψ∗χ), then we can assume that it holds both of ψ and of χ. It is quite often the case that we need to consider separately the cases of (ψ∧χ), (ψ∨χ), (ψ→χ), and so on. It sometimes happens that we need to consider subcases within these, or (more usually) subcases within the case in which φ is ¬ψ. I proceed now to illustrate these remarks by several examples of inductive arguments. All the examples in this section will be arguments for results that should be obvious anyway. So the interest is in seeing the technique at work, and is not (yet) in the new results that one can prove by it.

I begin with a couple of theses that follow simply from the formation rules given in Section 2.3.

    2.8.A. In any formula, the brackets pair uniquely.

By this I mean that there is one and only one function which pairs each left-hand bracket with just one right-hand bracket, and each right-hand bracket with just one left-hand bracket, and which satisfies the following further conditions: (1) the pair of the pair of any bracket is itself; (2) any left-hand bracket is always to the left of its paired right-hand bracket; (3) for any paired brackets x and y, a bracket that lies between x and y is paired with another bracket that also lies between x and y, and (hence) a bracket that lies outside x and y is paired with another bracket that also lies outside x and y.

The proof is by induction on the length of an arbitrary formula ϕ. The inductive hypothesis is

In any formula shorter than ϕ, the brackets pair uniquely.

We distinguish cases thus:

Case (1): ϕ is atomic. Then ϕ contains no brackets, and there is nothing to prove.

Case (2): ϕ is ¬ψ. Then ψ is a formula shorter than ϕ, so by the inductive hypothesis the brackets in ψ pair uniquely. But the brackets in ϕ just are the brackets in ψ. So it follows that the brackets in ϕ pair uniquely.

Case (3): ϕ is (ψ*χ) for some two-place truth-functor *. Then ψ is a formula shorter than ϕ, so by the inductive hypothesis the brackets in ψ pair uniquely with one another. The same holds for the brackets in χ. The brackets in ϕ are just the brackets in ψ, and the brackets in χ, and the two outer brackets shown. So if we retain the pairing already given for ψ and for χ, and pair the two outer brackets with one another, then clearly we have a pairing that satisfies the conditions. But no other pairing would satisfy them. For by condition (3) the two outer brackets can only be paired with one another, and by condition (2) no bracket in ψ can be paired with any bracket in χ. For by this condition every right-hand bracket in ψ must still be paired with a bracket in ψ, and by the inductive hypothesis there is only one way of doing this, and it does not leave any spare left-hand bracket in ψ to be paired with something in χ.

This completes the induction, and so establishes the desired result for all formulae.

2.8.B. In any formula, the initial symbol is not a symbol of any of its proper subformulae.

A 'proper' subformula is a subformula other than, and so shorter than, the whole formula. By 'the initial symbol' I mean, more precisely, the first *occurrence* of a symbol. (For example ¬P is a proper subformula of ¬¬P, and both begin with a negation sign. But the first occurrence of the negation sign in ¬¬P does not fall within any of its proper subformulae. By contrast, the final occurrence of a symbol in ¬¬P, namely the occurrence of P, is an occurrence that falls within both of its proper subformulae.)

The proof is by induction on the length of an arbitrary formula ϕ. The inductive hypothesis is

> In any formula shorter than ϕ, the initial symbol is not a symbol of any proper subformula.

We distinguish cases as before:

> *Case (1)*: ϕ is atomic. Then ϕ has no proper subformula, so there is nothing to prove.

> *Case (2)*: ϕ is $\neg\psi$. Suppose that there were a proper subformula $\neg\chi$ of $\neg\psi$, beginning with the same occurrence of $\neg$. Then equally χ would be a proper subformula of ψ, beginning with the same occurrence of its initial symbol. But ψ is shorter than ϕ, and so by the inductive hypothesis this cannot happen.

> *Case (3)*: ϕ is $(\psi*\chi)$ for some two-place truth-functor $*$. By our first result, the outer brackets in ϕ pair with one another, and cannot be paired in any other way. Hence any subformula of ϕ that includes its first left-hand bracket, i.e. its first occurrence of a symbol, must also include its last right-hand bracket. But that is to say that it cannot be a *proper* subformula of ϕ, but must be the whole of ϕ.

This completes the induction, and so establishes the result.

I postpone to the exercises a further result about the syntax of our formulae, resting upon the results 2.8.A–B already reached. Here I turn to another example of an inductive argument, this time based upon the semantics introduced in Section 2.4.

2.8.C. In any interpretation I, every formula of the language interpreted is assigned one and only one truth-value.

Take any interpretation I of a language for truth-functors, and assume for simplicity that the language is specified by some subset of the formation rules on p. 21. Let ϕ be any formula in that language. We prove the result by induction on the length of ϕ. The inductive hypothesis is

> To any formula shorter than ϕ, I assigns a unique truth-value.

We distinguish four cases according to the four kinds of formation rule on p. 21.

> *Case (1)*: ϕ is a sentence-letter. Then, by definition of an interpretation, I assigns to ϕ either T or F, but not both.

Case (2): φ is T or ⊥. Then it is stipulated that I assigns T (and only T) to T, and assigns F (and only F) to ⊥.

Case (3): φ is ¬ψ. By the inductive hypothesis I assigns either T or F, but not both, to ψ. Then it is stipulated that I assigns to φ either F or T (respectively), but not both.

Case (4): φ is (ψ∗χ), for some two-place truth-functor ∗. By the inductive hypothesis I assigns unique truth-values to ψ and to χ. Hence, by whatever is the truth-table for ∗, it is stipulated that I also assigns a unique truth-value to φ.

This completes the induction.

Finally I take up an example from Section 2.6, namely the first step of the procedure for reducing any formula to an equivalent formula in DNF or in CNF. This argument should be compared with the informal argument given earlier.

2.8.D. If the language of φ contains no truth-functors other than T,⊥,¬,∧,∨, then there is a formula logically equivalent to φ in which no occurrence of ¬ has any other occurrence of a truth-functor in its scope.

We assume throughout that our language contains only the five truth-functors listed. To introduce a convenient abbreviation, let us call a formula 'satisfactory' if no occurrence of ¬ in it has any other occurrence of a truth-functor in its scope. Then we have to show that any formula φ is logically equivalent to some satisfactory formula. The proof is by induction on the length of φ. The inductive hypothesis is

> For any formula ψ shorter than φ there is a logically equivalent formula ψ′ which is satisfactory.

We distinguish cases as expected, but within case (2) for negation we must further distinguish a variety of subcases. It is in these subcases that the work of the argument is done.

Case (1): φ is atomic. Then φ contains no occurrence of ¬, and therefore is already satisfactory.

Case (2): φ is ¬ψ. We distinguish five subcases, being the five possibilities for the formula ψ.

Subcase (*a*): ψ is a sentence-letter. Then φ, i.e. ¬ψ, is already satisfactory.

Subcase (*b*): ψ is T or ⊥. Then φ, i.e. ¬ψ, is equivalent either to ⊥ or to T (respectively), and these are each satisfactory.

Subcase (c): ψ is $\neg\chi$. Then ϕ is logically equivalent to χ, and χ is shorter than ϕ. Hence by inductive hypothesis χ is logically equivalent to some satisfactory formula χ'. So ϕ is also equivalent to χ'.

Subcase (d): ψ is $\chi_1 \wedge \chi_2$. Then by De Morgan's law ϕ is logically equivalent to $\neg\chi_1 \vee \neg\chi_2$. Moreover, $\neg\chi_1$ and $\neg\chi_2$ are each shorter than ϕ. So by inductive hypothesis there are logically equivalent satisfactory formulae $(\neg\chi_1)'$ and $(\neg\chi_2)'$. Hence ϕ is logically equivalent to $(\neg\chi_1)' \vee (\neg\chi_2)'$, and this also is satisfactory.

Subcase (e): ψ is $\chi_1 \vee \neg\chi_2$. The argument is as in subcase (d), with $\wedge$ and $\vee$ interchanged.

Case (3): ϕ is $\psi * \chi$, for $*$ either $\wedge$ or $\vee$. By inductive hypothesis there are logically equivalent formulae ψ' and χ' which are satisfactory. Hence ϕ is equivalent to $\psi' * \chi'$, which also is satisfactory.

In view of the restricted language that we are here considering, this completes the review of all possible cases, and so establishes our result.

The following exercises offer a few further examples where the reader may practise the technique of arguing by induction. But we are now in a position to turn to something more interesting, and in particular to take up once more the topic of expressive adequacy.

EXERCISES

2.8.1. Return to Exercise 2.3.1, and give an inductive argument for the result there stated.

2.8.2. Show that in every non-atomic formula there is one and only one occurrence of a truth-functor which does not fall within any proper subformula of that formula. (This is the *main* truth-functor of the formula.) [You will need to use the results 2.8.A and 2.8.B established in the text.]

2.8.3.(a) Show that the principle of distribution can be strengthened, first to

$$\phi \wedge (\psi_1 \vee \psi_2 \vee ... \vee \psi_n) \quad =\!\!|\!\!= \quad (\phi \wedge \psi_1) \vee (\phi \wedge \psi_2) \vee ... \vee (\phi \wedge \psi_n)$$

and then further to

$$(\phi_1 \vee \phi_2 \vee ... \vee \phi_m) \wedge (\psi_1 \vee \psi_2 \vee ... \vee \psi_n)$$
$$=\!\!|\!\!= \quad (\phi_1 \wedge \psi_1) \vee (\phi_1 \wedge \psi_2) \vee ... \vee (\phi_1 \wedge \psi_n)$$
$$\vee (\phi_2 \wedge \psi_1) \vee (\phi_2 \wedge \psi_2) \vee ... \vee (\phi_2 \wedge \psi_n)$$
$$\vee ... \qquad\qquad\qquad ...$$
$$\vee (\phi_m \wedge \psi_1) \vee (\phi_m \wedge \psi_2) \vee ... \vee (\phi_m \wedge \psi_n).$$

[Method: in this case use the *ordinary* principle of mathematical induction, applying it to n in the first case and to m in the second. (That is: show that the first principle holds when n is 1, and show that if it holds when n is any number, then it also
holds when n is the next greater number. Deduce that it holds whatever number n
may be. Similarly for the second principle.)]

(*b*) Using this strengthened principle of distribution, give an inductive argument
to establish the second stage of the procedure in Section 2.6 for reducing a formula
to an equivalent in DNF. That is, show that an equivalent formula can always be
found in which no occurrence of $\wedge$ has any occurrence of $\vee$ in its scope. [You may
assume that the language is restricted as in Section 2.6; you will need to use 2.8.D,
verifying the first stage of the procedure.]

2.9. Expressive Adequacy II

In Section 2.7 we saw how to show that various sets of truth-functors *are*
expressively adequate, but we had no method of showing that any are *not*.
We now have such a method. Let us start with an extremely simple example.
It is fairly obvious that the set which consists just of the one functor $\wedge$, and
nothing else, will not be adequate. But how is this to be proved?

In this case the basic idea is very simple. The truth-table for $\wedge$ has a T in its
first row, since the conjunction of two true formulae is itself true. It follows
that in *any* formula whose only truth-functor is $\wedge$, however long and complex it may be, the top row of the truth-table must be T. But this means that
we can easily specify a truth-function which cannot be expressed by such a
formula, namely any which has F and not T in the top row of its truth-table.
A simple example is evidently the one-place truth-function of negation, so
let us concentrate just on this. A formula which expresses a one-place truth-
function is one that uses only a single sentence-letter, perhaps occurring
many times over. So if negation could be expressed in terms of $\wedge$ alone, then
there would be a formula built up just from occurrences of a single letter, say
P, and occurrences of $\wedge$, which had the same truth-table as $\neg P$. But, as we
have just said, there can be no such formula, since any that is built up in the
way specified must take the value T when P takes the value T.

That last assertion is, in practice, sufficiently obvious to pass without
proof. But if proof is desired, then we can easily supply it, arguing by induction on the length of the formula. We aim to prove:

If ϕ contains only occurrences of P and of $\wedge$, then $|\phi| = $ T if $|P| = $ T.

The inductive hypothesis is

If ψ is shorter than ϕ, and ψ contains only occurrences of P and of $\wedge$, then $|\psi| = $ T if $|P| = $ T.

We have two cases to consider, which exhaust the relevant possibilities:

Case (1): ϕ is a letter. Then if ϕ contains only occurrences of P and of $\wedge$, ϕ must be the letter P. So, of course, $|\phi| = $ T if $|P| = $ T.

Case (2): ϕ is $\psi\wedge\chi$. Then if ϕ contains only occurrences of P and of $\wedge$, the same must be true of ψ and of χ, which are shorter than ϕ. Hence, by the inductive hypothesis, if $|P| = $ T then $|\psi| = $ T and $|\chi| = $ T. Hence, by truth-tables, if $|P| = $ T then $|\psi\wedge\chi| = $ T, i.e. $|\phi| = $ T.

This completes the induction, and so establishes the required conclusion. It also illustrates the general method of establishing a negative result on expressive adequacy, namely: find some property which must be possessed by *every* formula containing only the truth-functors in question, no matter how long, but which is not possessed by all formulae whatever. Once a suitable property is discovered, it will usually be easy to prove, by induction on the length of the formula, that it is suitable.

It is easy to see that a single one-place truth-functor, such as negation, cannot possibly be expressively adequate on its own. For if we only have one-place truth-functors to play with, then we cannot construct any formula which contains more than one sentence-letter. We have just argued that the two-place truth-functor $\wedge$ is not expressively adequate on its own, and exactly the same reasoning applies also to $\vee, \rightarrow, \leftrightarrow$, as you should check. This raises the question: is there any two-place functor that is adequate on its own? The answer turns out to be yes; in fact there are just two such functors.

For the reason just given, we can rule out as inadequate all functors which have T in the first row of their truth-tables. For a precisely similar reason, we can also rule out all functors which have F in the last row of their truth-tables. This leaves us just four candidates to consider, which for the moment we shall label $f_1, f_2, f_3,$ and f_4, and which have these truth-tables:

ϕ	ψ	$f_1(\phi,\psi)$	$f_2(\phi,\psi)$	$f_3(\phi,\psi)$	$f_4(\phi,\psi)$
T	T	F	F	F	F
T	F	T	T	F	F
F	T	T	F	T	F
F	F	T	T	T	T

But a brief consideration of the tables for f_2 and f_3 should show that neither of these could be adequate, for they are in fact equivalent to one-place functors. In fact

$$f_2(\phi,\psi) \quad =\!\!\Vdash \quad \neg\psi, \qquad f_3(\phi,\psi) \quad =\!\!\Vdash \quad \neg\phi.$$

There would be many ways of demonstrating that this must make them inadequate. Perhaps the simplest would be this: any formula that contains only occurrences of P and of f_2, or only occurrences of P and of f_3, must be equivalent either to P or to $\neg P$. That is, it must express a one-place function that is contingent, i.e. that has both a T and an F in its truth-table. (You are invited to work out an inductive argument for this claim.) Hence no such formula can express either the one-place tautologous function expressed by $P\vee\neg P$, or the one-place contradictory function expressed by $P\wedge\neg P$.

   We have shown, then, that only the truth-functors given above as f_1 and f_4 could be, on their own, expressively adequate. They are usually called the *stroke* functors, written as $\uparrow$ and $\downarrow$, so let us reintroduce them in the more familiar notation

ϕ	ψ	$\phi\uparrow\psi$	$\phi\downarrow\psi$
T	T	F	F
T	F	T	F
F	T	T	F
F	T	T	T

$\downarrow$ is the denial of 'or', expressed in English by 'neither . . . nor . . .', and usefully abbreviated just to 'nor'. $\uparrow$ is the denial of 'and', and so sometimes abbreviated, by analogy, to 'nand'. ($\uparrow$ is also written just as $|$, and called in particular the *Sheffer stroke*, after Professor Sheffer, who first drew attention to it.) Of course, it needs to be argued separately that these *are* adequate by themselves, but this only requires us to draw attention to the relevant defining equivalences, namely

$$
\begin{aligned}
\neg\phi &\quad =\!\!\Vdash \quad \phi\uparrow\phi & \neg\phi &\quad =\!\!\Vdash \quad \phi\downarrow\phi \\
\phi\wedge\psi &\quad =\!\!\Vdash \quad (\phi\uparrow\psi)\uparrow(\phi\uparrow\psi) & \phi\wedge\psi &\quad =\!\!\Vdash \quad (\phi\downarrow\phi)\downarrow(\psi\downarrow\psi) \\
\phi\vee\psi &\quad =\!\!\Vdash \quad (\phi\uparrow\phi)\uparrow(\psi\uparrow\psi) & \phi\vee\psi &\quad =\!\!\Vdash \quad (\phi\downarrow\psi)\downarrow(\phi\downarrow\psi).
\end{aligned}
$$

In consequence, it would be possible to choose one of the stroke functors, say $\uparrow$, and to conduct the whole of one's investigation of the logic of truth-functions using just this one truth-functor and no other. But it would not be particularly convenient.

   It turns out, then, that none of the familiar truth-functors $\wedge,\vee,\rightarrow,\leftrightarrow$ is expressively adequate on its own, though there are two other two-place truth-functors that are. We have also seen that the familiar functors $\wedge,\vee,\rightarrow$ do each yield an adequate set when taken together with negation. But we have not yet considered the set $\{\neg,\leftrightarrow\}$. It turns out that in terms of $\neg$ and $\leftrightarrow$

one can express every one-place truth-function, but only half the two-place functions, namely those that have an even number of Ts and Fs in their truth-tables. That is to say, a formula which contains only occurrences of P, of Q, of $\neg$, and of $\leftrightarrow$ must have an even number of Ts and Fs in its truth-table *when* that truth-table is considered as the table for a two-place truth-function. The reason for adding the last condition is this. The formula P, or the formula $Q\leftrightarrow\neg Q$, are formulae satisfying our constraint, but of course they may be considered as expressing *one*-place truth-functions. So considered, the formula P has just one T in its truth-table. But we shall insist upon looking at it differently, as having the following truth-table with two Ts:

P	Q	P
T	T	T
T	F	T
F	T	F
F	F	F

Taking this proviso for granted, let us just say, for brevity, that all formulae of the kind in question 'have an even truth-table'.

As will be expected, the proof is by induction on the length of the formula ϕ. Our inductive hypothesis is

If ψ is shorter than ϕ, and contains only occurrences of $P,Q,\neg,\leftrightarrow$, then ψ has an even truth-table.

We wish to show that the same holds of ϕ. We have three cases to consider:

Case (1): ϕ is a letter. So if ϕ contains only occurrences of $P,Q,\neg,\leftrightarrow$, then ϕ must be either the letter P or the letter Q. We have already explained that in this case ϕ has an even truth-table.

Case (2): ϕ is $\neg\psi$. So if ϕ contains only occurrences of $P,Q,\neg,\leftrightarrow$, then so does ψ, which is shorter than ϕ. Hence by the inductive hypothesis ψ has an even truth-table. But the truth-table for $\neg\psi$ has as many Ts as the table for ψ has Fs, and as many Fs as the table for ψ has Ts. It follows that the table for $\neg\psi$, i.e. for ϕ, must also be even.

Case (3): ϕ is $\psi\leftrightarrow\chi$. So if ϕ contains only occurrences of $P,Q,\neg,\leftrightarrow$, then so do ψ and χ, which are shorter than ϕ. Hence by the inductive hypothesis both ψ and χ have even truth-tables. If in fact ψ has four Ts in its table, then the table for $\psi\leftrightarrow\chi$ is simply that for χ; and if ψ has four Fs then the table for $\psi\leftrightarrow\chi$ is that for $\neg\chi$. So in either of these cases the table for $\psi \leftrightarrow \chi$ is certainly even; similarly, if χ has either four Ts or four Fs in its table. The cases remaining to be considered, then, are those where each of ψ and χ have two Ts and two Fs. We can distinguish these as follows. Either (1) the two Ts in each table are opposite one another; or (2) the two Ts in one table are opposite two Fs in the other; or (3) one T in one table is opposite a T in the other, and the other T in that table is opposite an F in the other. Inspection shows that in case (1) the table for $\psi \leftrightarrow \chi$ has four Ts, in case (2) it has four Fs, and in case (3) it has two Ts and two Fs. In all cases, then, the table for $\psi \leftrightarrow \chi$, i.e. for ϕ, is even.

This completes the induction, and so establishes the result. (It is perhaps the first time in this book so far that we have used induction to prove a point that was not very obvious to unaided intuition.)

The result that we have just established about the set of functors $\{\neg, \leftrightarrow\}$ can be quite significantly improved. The argument can easily be extended to show that in terms of $\neg$ and $\leftrightarrow$ one can express only those three-place functions that have an even truth-table, and similarly for four-place functions, and so on. It happens to be true, but would not be easy to prove by a similar argument, that of three-place functions one can express with $\neg$ and $\leftrightarrow$ only those with a number of Ts that is divisible by 4 (i.e. either 0 or 4 or 8). But still one cannot express *all* such functions, so this does not give a very close description of what *can* be expressed using just $\neg$ and $\leftrightarrow$. For this we need a rather different line of argument.

Let us first consider what can be expressed by $\leftrightarrow$ alone. There are two crucial points here. The first is that $\leftrightarrow$ is both commutative and associative, i.e.

$$\phi \leftrightarrow \psi \quad =\!\!\models \quad \psi \leftrightarrow \phi$$
$$\phi \leftrightarrow (\psi \leftrightarrow \chi) \quad =\!\!\models \quad (\phi \leftrightarrow \psi) \leftrightarrow \chi.$$

We are familiar with the fact that, because $\wedge$ and $\vee$ are both commutative and associative, the order and grouping of a continued conjunction or disjunction makes no difference, and can be varied at will. The same therefore applies to $\leftrightarrow$: order and bracketing are immaterial. (The associativity of $\leftrightarrow$ is not altogether expected. You should check it by a truth-table test.) The second point is that $\leftrightarrow$ is not idempotent, as $\wedge$ and $\vee$ are, but instead obeys these simple laws:

$$\phi \leftrightarrow \phi \quad =\!\!\models \quad \top$$
$$\top \leftrightarrow \phi \quad =\!\!\models \quad \phi.$$

When we put these points together we can infer the following result:

Any formula whose only truth-functor is $\leftrightarrow$ is equivalent to one in which each letter occurs either just once or not at all. (And if the formula is equivalent to one in which no letter occurs at all, then it is equivalent to T.)

The argument is simple. Suppose a formula ϕ, whose only truth-functor is $\leftrightarrow$, contains more than one occurrence of some letter, say P_i. Then by rearranging the order and the bracketing we can form an equivalent formula of the pattern $(P_i \leftrightarrow P_i) \leftrightarrow \psi$, where ψ lacks two occurrences of P_i but otherwise contains just the same letters as ϕ. But this formula is equivalent to $T \leftrightarrow \psi$, which in turn is equivalent to ψ if the formula ψ exists (i.e. if there are letters in ϕ other than the two displayed occurrences of P_i), and otherwise is equivalent just to T. In this way we can always remove from a formula ϕ any pair of occurrences of the same letter, still preserving equivalence. By repeated steps of the same manœuvre we can evidently find a formula equivalent to ϕ in which no letter occurs more than once. (You are invited to state this argument as an induction on the length of ϕ.)

It follows that the one-place truth-functions that can be expressed by formulae containing only the functor $\leftrightarrow$ are just the two expressed by

T, P.

The two-place functions are just the four expressed by

$T, P, Q, P \leftrightarrow Q$.

The three-place functions are just the eight expressed by

$T, P, Q, R, P \leftrightarrow Q, Q \leftrightarrow R, P \leftrightarrow R, (P \leftrightarrow Q) \leftrightarrow R$.

And so on. To put it another way, for each n there is just *one* $n+1$-place function that can be expressed, and is not equivalent to some n-place function.

Let us now turn to consider the effect of adding occurrences of the negation sign. Here again we begin by noting some significant equivalences, namely

$$\phi \leftrightarrow \neg\psi \quad =\!\!\models\quad \neg(\phi \leftrightarrow \psi)$$
$$\neg\phi \leftrightarrow \psi \quad =\!\!\models\quad \neg(\phi \leftrightarrow \psi).$$

These equivalences show that the placing of a negation sign makes no difference. For example, a negation sign that is placed somewhere in the middle of a formula which otherwise contains only $\leftrightarrow$ can always be brought to the front of it by successive applications of these equivalences. So in particular, if we have several negation signs in the formula, then they can each be brought to the front so that the formula begins with a string of negation signs. Then, by double negation, they can be cancelled in pairs, until either one or none is left. So it follows that

> Any formula whose only truth-functors are $\leftrightarrow$ and $\neg$ is equivalent to one in which each letter occurs either once or not at all, and $\neg$ occurs either once or not at all.

(Again, you may like to reflect upon how this result could be more rigorously proved by an inductive argument.) The truth-functions that can be expressed by $\leftrightarrow$ and $\neg$ together are, then, just those that can be expressed by $\leftrightarrow$, together with their negations. This leaves very many truth-functions that cannot be expressed.

EXERCISES

2.9.1. Let $\underline{\vee}$ be the two-place truth-functor of exclusive disjunction, so that $|\phi\underline{\vee}\psi|$ is T iff just one of $|\phi|$ and $|\psi|$ is T. Let $\underline{\vee}_3$ be the analogous three-place truth-functor, so that $|\underline{\vee}_3(\phi,\psi,\chi)|$ is T iff just one of $|\phi|$, $|\psi|$, $|\chi|$ is T. Show that $\underline{\vee}_3$ cannot be defined in terms of $\underline{\vee}$ alone. [Hint: $\underline{\vee}$ can be defined in terms of $\leftrightarrow$ and $\neg$. Use the result in the text.]

2.9.2.(*a*) Show that $\wedge$ cannot be defined in terms of $\rightarrow$ alone. [Method: show by induction that no formula containing only occurrences of P,Q,$\rightarrow$, has a truth-table with more than two Fs.]
(*b*) Show that $\wedge$ can be defined in terms of $\rightarrow$ and $\leftrightarrow$, and hence deduce that $\leftrightarrow$ cannot be defined in terms of $\rightarrow$ alone.
(*c*) Just which two-place truth-functions can be expressed in terms of $\rightarrow$ alone?

2.9.3. Let us call a truth-function 'positive' iff the top row of its truth-table is T.
(*a*) Show that all truth-functions which can be expressed by $\wedge$ and $\rightarrow$ are positive.
(*b*) Show that all positive truth-functions can be expressed by $\wedge$ and $\rightarrow$. [Method: consider how to form a formula in perfect CNF that expresses the truth-function, and show how—if the truth-function is positive—all occurrences of $\neg$ in that formula can be exchanged for occurrences of $\rightarrow$. Thus the function is expressed in terms of $\rightarrow,\wedge,\vee$. Finally observe that $\vee$ can be defined in terms of $\rightarrow$ alone.]

2.10. Duality

At several places in this chapter, but particularly in Section 2.6 on DNF and CNF, you must have noticed that there is a kind of correspondence between

∧ and ∨. Roughly speaking, to any law for ∧ there will be a corresponding law for ∨ and vice versa. This is because ∧ and ∨ are, as we say, *duals* of one another. In this section I give a brief treatment of the duality of ∧ and ∨ in particular; in the exercises there is an invitation to think of duality more generally.

Let us confine attention to formulae with no truth-functors other than ¬,∧,∨. For any such formula ϕ, we shall say that its *dual formula* ϕ^D is the formula obtained just by interchanging ∧ and ∨ throughout ϕ. The first point to prove about duality is this:

> First duality theorem. Let $\bar{\phi}$ be the result of writing a negation sign immediately in front of every sentence-letter in ϕ. Then
>
> $$\phi^D \dashv\vdash \neg\bar{\phi}.$$

The proof is a straightforward induction on the length of the formula ϕ. The hypothesis of induction is

If ψ is shorter than ϕ, then $\psi^D \dashv\vdash \neg\bar{\psi}$.

We have four cases to consider, thus:

Case (1): ϕ is a letter. Then

$$
\begin{array}{lll}
\phi^D & = & \phi & \text{case hypothesis} \\
 & \dashv\vdash & \neg\neg\phi & \text{double negation} \\
 & = & \neg\bar{\phi} & \text{case hypothesis}
\end{array}
$$

Case (2): ϕ is $\neg\psi$. Then

$$
\begin{array}{lll}
\phi^D & = & (\neg\psi)^D & \text{case hypothesis} \\
 & = & \neg(\psi^D) & \text{definition of D} \\
 & \dashv\vdash & \neg(\neg\bar{\psi}) & \text{inductive hypothesis} \\
 & = & \neg(\overline{\neg\psi}) & \text{definition of } \overline{} \\
 & = & \neg\bar{\phi} & \text{case hypothesis}
\end{array}
$$

Case (3): ϕ is $\psi\wedge\chi$. Then

$$
\begin{array}{lll}
\phi^D & = & (\psi\wedge\chi)^D & \text{case hypothesis} \\
 & = & (\psi^D\vee\chi^D) & \text{definition of D} \\
 & \dashv\vdash & (\neg\bar{\psi}\vee\neg\bar{\chi}) & \text{inductive hypothesis} \\
 & \dashv\vdash & \neg(\bar{\psi}\wedge\bar{\chi}) & \text{De Morgan} \\
 & = & \neg(\overline{\psi\wedge\chi}) & \text{definition of } \overline{} \\
 & = & \neg\bar{\phi} & \text{case hypothesis}
\end{array}
$$

Case (4): ϕ is $\psi\vee\chi$. Then

$$
\begin{array}{lll}
\phi^D & = & (\psi\vee\chi)^D & \text{case hypothesis} \\
& = & (\psi^D\wedge\chi^D) & \text{definition of D} \\
& =\!\|\!= & (\neg\bar\psi\wedge\neg\bar\chi) & \text{inductive hypothesis} \\
& =\!\|\!= & \neg(\bar\psi\vee\bar\chi) & \text{De Morgan} \\
& = & \neg\overline{(\psi\vee\chi)} & \text{definition of} \; \overline{} \\
& = & \neg\bar\phi & \text{case hypothesis}
\end{array}
$$

This completes the induction, and so establishes the result.

Without pausing to comment on this, I proceed at once to the next theorem, which follows easily from it.

Second duality theorem. If $\phi \vDash \psi$ then $\psi^D \vDash \phi^D$.

The proof is straightforward:

Assume $\phi \vDash \psi$	
Then $\bar\phi \vDash \bar\psi$	by uniform substitution of $\neg P_i$ for P_i
Hence $\neg\bar\psi \vDash \neg\bar\phi$	by contraposition
So finally $\psi^D \vDash \phi^D$	by the first duality theorem.

We may at once note a corollary

Third duality theorem: if $\phi =\!\|\!= \psi$ then $\phi^D =\!\|\!= \psi^D$.

The 'correspondences' that were striking in Section 2.6 were mainly instances of the third theorem, since the laws there in question were mainly equivalences. But we have already met some instances of the second theorem, for example

$$P\wedge Q \vDash P \qquad P \vDash P\vee Q$$
$$P \vDash P\wedge P \qquad P\vee P \vDash P.$$

I note here one further example. It is obvious that $\phi^{DD} = \phi$, so the second duality theorem can evidently be improved to

$$\phi \vDash \psi \quad \text{iff} \quad \psi^D \vDash \phi^D.$$

Now let us recall a central case of our basic principle for conjunction (p. 33)

$$\chi \vDash \phi\wedge\psi \quad \text{iff} \quad \chi \vDash \phi \text{ and } \chi \vDash \psi$$

Since ϕ,ψ,χ may here be any formulae, it follows that

$$\chi^D \vDash \phi^D\wedge\psi^D \quad \text{iff} \quad \chi^D \vDash \phi^D \text{ and } \chi^D \vDash \psi^D.$$

But $(\phi^D\wedge\chi^D) = (\phi\vee\chi)^D$. Applying this, and applying our second duality theorem, we therefore have

$\phi \lor \psi \vDash \chi$ iff $\phi \vDash \chi$ and $\psi \vDash \chi$.

So it emerges that, in virtue of the second duality theorem, a central case of our basic principle for conjunction implies the corresponding central case of our basic principle for disjunction (and, incidentally, vice versa).

EXERCISES

2.10.1. Recall the truth-functor $\twoheadleftarrow$ defined in the exercises to Section 2.7. It is dual to $\rightarrow$. Thus if ϕ is any formula containing only the functors $\neg, \rightarrow, \twoheadleftarrow$, and if ϕ^D is formed from ϕ by interchanging $\rightarrow$ and $\twoheadleftarrow$, then we again have

If $\phi \vDash \psi$ then $\psi^D \vDash \phi^D$.

Verify this assertion.

2.10.2. Compare the truth-tables of $\land$ and $\lor$, and of $\rightarrow$ and $\twoheadleftarrow$. In the light of this comparison, devise a general definition of duality. What truth-functors are dual to $\leftrightarrow, \top, \neg, \bot$? How are we to understand the dual of a three-place truth-functor?

2.10.3. In the light of your answer to Exercise 2.10.2 state the three theorems on duality in a more general way, without any restriction on the languages to be considered.

2.11. **Truth-value Analysis**

In his *Methods of Logic* (1952) W. V. Quine introduced a way of simplifying formulae which can often assist understanding. He called it 'the method of truth-value analysis', and we may state its basic principle in this way. Let $\phi(\top/P)$ be the result of substituting $\top$ for all occurrences of P in ϕ; similarly, let $\phi(\bot/P)$ be the result of substituting $\bot$ for all occurrences of P in ϕ. Then by the principle allowing interchange of equivalent formulae, we have

$$P \leftrightarrow \top \;\vDash\; \phi \leftrightarrow \phi(\top/P)$$
$$P \leftrightarrow \bot \;\vDash\; \phi \leftrightarrow \phi(\bot/P).$$

And, of course, it is obvious that

$$\vDash \;\; (P \leftrightarrow \top) \lor (P \leftrightarrow \bot).$$

We may therefore analyse a formula into two alternatives, one got by substituting $\top$ for some letter within it, and the other by substituting $\bot$. The point of this is that a formula containing $\top$ or $\bot$ can always be simplified in such a way that either those symbols are eliminated altogether, or they become the whole formula. The laws by which this is done are very obvious, and we have had many of them already. I simply list them

$$
\begin{array}{llll}
\phi \wedge \top & =\!\!\models & \phi & \qquad \phi \wedge \bot & =\!\!\models & \bot \\
\top \wedge \phi & =\!\!\models & \phi & \qquad \bot \wedge \phi & =\!\!\models & \bot \\
\phi \vee \top & =\!\!\models & \top & \qquad \phi \vee \bot & =\!\!\models & \phi \\
\top \vee \phi & =\!\!\models & \top & \qquad \bot \vee \phi & =\!\!\models & \phi \\
\phi \rightarrow \top & =\!\!\models & \top & \qquad \phi \rightarrow \bot & =\!\!\models & \neg\phi \\
\top \rightarrow \phi & =\!\!\models & \phi & \qquad \bot \rightarrow \phi & =\!\!\models & \top \\
\phi \leftrightarrow \top & =\!\!\models & \phi & \qquad \phi \leftrightarrow \bot & =\!\!\models & \neg\phi \\
\top \leftrightarrow \phi & =\!\!\models & \phi & \qquad \bot \leftrightarrow \phi & =\!\!\models & \neg\phi \\
\neg\top & =\!\!\models & \bot & \qquad \neg\bot & =\!\!\models & \top
\end{array}
$$

(You might like to construct an inductive argument, using these laws, to show formally that any formula containing $\top$ or $\bot$ is either equivalent to $\top$ or $\bot$, or equivalent to some shorter formula lacking $\top$ and $\bot$.)

Here is an example of such simplification (taken from Quine 1952: 24–7). Consider the formula

$$((P \wedge Q) \vee (\neg P \wedge \neg R)) \rightarrow (Q \leftrightarrow R).$$

Substituting $\top$ for P, we obtain

$$((\top \wedge Q) \vee (\neg\top \wedge \neg R)) \rightarrow (Q \leftrightarrow R).$$

By the laws noted above, this simplifies to

$$((\top \wedge Q) \vee (\bot \wedge \neg R)) \rightarrow (Q \leftrightarrow R)$$
$$(Q \vee \bot) \rightarrow (Q \leftrightarrow R)$$
$$Q \rightarrow (Q \leftrightarrow R).$$

To finish off this line of investigation let us now suppose[4] in addition (a) that Q is true and (b) that Q is false. This yields

(a) $\top \rightarrow (\top \leftrightarrow R)$ (b) $\bot \rightarrow (\bot \leftrightarrow R)$
   $\top \leftrightarrow R$ $\top$
   R

Thus in case (b) the whole formula will be true, irrespective of the value of R, and in case (a) the formula is equivalent to R, and hence true or false according as R is true or false. Now we go back to the original formula and substitute $\bot$ for P, to obtain

---

[4] Note that we choose to make assumptions about Q, rather than R, because Q occurs more often than R in the formula under consideration. This abbreviates labour.

$$((\bot \wedge Q) \vee (\neg \bot \wedge \neg R)) \rightarrow (Q \leftrightarrow R).$$

This then simplifies to

$$((\bot \wedge Q) \vee (T \wedge \neg R)) \rightarrow (Q \leftrightarrow R)$$
$$(\bot \vee \neg R) \rightarrow (Q \leftrightarrow R)$$
$$\neg R \rightarrow (Q \leftrightarrow R).$$

To finish off this line of investigation, let us now add the assumptions (*a*) that R is true and (*b*) that R is false.[5] This yields

(*a*) $\neg T \rightarrow (Q \leftrightarrow T)$ (*b*) $\neg \bot \rightarrow (Q \leftrightarrow \bot)$
 $\bot \rightarrow (Q \leftrightarrow T)$ $T \rightarrow (Q \leftrightarrow \bot)$
 T $(Q \leftrightarrow \bot)$
                                                  $\neg Q.$

Thus in case (*a*) the whole formula is again true, irrespective of the value of Q, and in case (*b*) the formula is equivalent to $\neg Q$, and hence true or false according as Q is false or true. What this analysis has shown is that the whole truth-table of our formula is as follows:

P	Q	R	$((P \wedge Q) \vee (\neg P \wedge \neg R)) \rightarrow (Q \leftrightarrow R)$
T	T	T	T
T	T	F	F
T	F	T	T
T	F	F	T
F	T	T	T
F	T	F	F
F	F	T	T
F	F	F	T

But it has shown this without the tedium of having to calculate separately the values of each of the subformulae in each of the eight rows. This is a real saving of effort when the formula we are concerned with contains four or more distinct sentence-letters (see Exercise 2.11.2(*a*)).

Another point worth observing is that this truth-value analysis gives us a further way of showing that every formula has an equivalent in DNF. In fact our assumptions about the truth and falsehood of P led us to this equivalent for the whole formula

$$(P \wedge (Q \rightarrow (Q \leftrightarrow R))) \vee (\neg P \wedge (\neg R \rightarrow (Q \leftrightarrow R))).$$

---

5 Note that this time R occurs more often than Q.

Our further assumptions, about Q in the first disjunct and R in the second, then led us to this further equivalent

$$(P \wedge Q \wedge R) \vee (P \wedge \neg Q) \vee (\neg P \wedge R) \vee (\neg P \wedge \neg Q \wedge \neg R).$$

This is, of course, an equivalent in DNF, and could easily be improved to an equivalent in perfect DNF if that was wanted.

A final point to notice is the relevance of this technique to a well-known result about truth-functional logic, namely:

> *The interpolation theorem.* If $\phi \models \psi$, then there exists a formula χ, containing only the sentence-letters common to both ϕ and ψ, such that $\phi \models \chi$ and $\chi \models \psi$. (The formula χ is called an 'interpolant'.)

Suppose, for example, that $\phi \models \psi$, and that some letter, say P, occurs in ϕ but not in ψ. Then if we substitute either T for P, or $\bot$ for P, throughout the sequent $\phi \models \psi$, we shall not alter the formula ψ. Hence, by the principle of uniform substitution for sentence-letters, we may infer

$$\phi(T/P) \models \psi$$
$$\phi(\bot/P) \models \psi.$$

And so, by the basic principle for disjunction

$$\phi(T/P) \vee \phi(\bot/P) \models \psi.$$

But we also have, as an evident corollary of the principle underlying truth-value analysis,

$$\phi \models \phi(T/P) \vee \phi(\bot/P).$$

It follows that $\phi(T/P) \vee \phi(\bot/P)$ is suited for the role of an interpolant, and of course it does not contain the letter P, which was present in ϕ but not in ψ. There may be another letter present in ϕ but not in ψ, and hence present in $\phi(T/P) \vee \phi(\bot/P)$ but not in ψ, but if so we repeat the same procedure to find an interpolant, lacking that letter, between $\phi(T/P) \vee \phi(\bot/P)$ and ψ. By sufficiently many repetitions of this manœuvre we must eventually reach, as desired, an interpolant χ which contains only those letters in ϕ that are also in ψ.

Two points may be noted about this argument. First, the formula $\phi(T/P) \vee \phi(\bot/P)$ will certainly be more complex than the formula ϕ with which we began, but it will also be capable of simplification, as we have seen. Either it will reduce to T or to $\bot$, or all occurrences of T and $\bot$ can be eliminated from it. Second, therefore, in the extreme case in which ϕ and ψ have *no* sentence-letters in common, the interpolant formed by this method must reduce either to T or to $\bot$. So we have

Either $\phi \models \top$, $\top \models \psi$ or $\phi \models \bot$, $\bot \models \psi$.

In the first case, ψ is a tautology; in the second case, ϕ is inconsistent.

EXERCISES

2.11.1. Use truth-value analysis to show that the following formulae are valid:

  (a) $(P{\to}Q) \vee (Q{\to}P)$
  (b) $(P{\leftrightarrow}Q) \vee (P{\leftrightarrow}\neg Q)$
  (c) $(P{\leftrightarrow}Q) \vee (Q{\leftrightarrow}R) \vee (P{\leftrightarrow}R)$.

2.11.2. Use truth-value analysis to determine under what conditions the following formulae are true, and under what conditions they are false:

  (a) $(P{\wedge}Q)\vee(P{\wedge}\neg R)\vee(\neg P{\wedge}R)\vee(\neg P{\wedge}S)\vee(\neg Q{\wedge}R)\vee(\neg R{\wedge}\neg S)$
  (b) $((((P\vee Q)\wedge(P\vee\neg Q))\vee(\neg P\wedge Q)) \leftrightarrow Q) \to ((P{\wedge}R)\vee(P{\wedge}\neg R))$.

Use your analysis for (b) to find a formula in DNF equivalent to it.

2.11.3. Find an interpolant, containing only the letters common to the premiss and conclusion, and not containing $\top$ or $\bot$, for the following entailments:

  (a) $(\neg Q{\to}P) \to \neg Q \models (R{\to}\neg Q) \to \neg Q$
  (b) $\neg((P{\to}R) \vee \neg Q) \models (Q{\leftrightarrow}R) \to S$
  (c) $\neg((P{\to}Q) \to (\neg R{\to}Q)) \models (P\vee\neg R) \wedge (S\vee\neg P)$.

2.11.4. Suppose that $\phi \models \psi$, and that every sentence-letter in ϕ is also in ψ, but not conversely. Then the method given for finding an interpolant cannot be applied. Has something gone wrong? Explain.

3

Quantifiers

3.1. Names and Extensionality

The logic to be studied in this chapter is standardly called 'predicate logic', as the logic of the last chapter is standardly called 'propositional logic'. But a much better name for it is the logic of quantifiers, or, more fully, the logic of 'elementary' or 'first-order' quantifiers. However, there is a more basic notion to be considered before we can come to the quantifiers, and that is the idea of a *name*, or more generally of a *logical subject*. For the elementary, or first-order, quantifiers take the place of names, and sentences containing these quantifiers are most easily understood in terms of the simpler sentences that result from them, when the quantifiers are dropped and names restored in their place. However, there is no agreement amongst philosophers on what is to count as a name, or logical subject, and this is not the place to explore the issues involved. I therefore offer only a bare outline of what are, from the logician's point of view, the crucial assumptions.

The paradigm of a name is an ordinary proper name, written (in English) with an initial capital, whose role is to make a singular reference to a particular object of some kind, e.g. the name of a person, a place, a ship, a hurricane, or whatever. What is important about names, for logical purposes, is this job of singular reference that they perform. So we generalize the idea and say that any other expression too may be counted as a name, for our purposes, if it too performs the same job. I think there would be general agreement that demonstrative expressions, such as 'this book' or 'that chair', may be so counted, though, of course, they are not ordinarily thought of as 'names'. But there is no agreement on other examples. In particular there is a category of expressions called 'definite descriptions' on which philosophers are deadlocked. I shall return to this topic in Chapter 8, but meanwhile I simply leave the question open. The important thing about a name is that it is an expression used to make a singular reference to a particular object; just which expressions do play this role must for the time being remain undetermined.

An expression that is commonly used as a name may nevertheless be functioning in some different way in a particular context. To take a simple example, consider the sentence

'Horace' rhymes with 'Doris' and with 'Maurice'.

The three expressions here quoted are standardly used as names that refer to people, but it is clear that that is not their role here. On the contrary, we say that in this sentence the name 'Horace' is not being *used* at all, but only mentioned, and the different name '"Horace"' is being used to refer to it. In other words, '"Horace"' is functioning here, as it usually does, as a name of 'Horace', whereas 'Horace' is not functioning as a name at all. The important point is that for our purposes we do not count an expression as a name unless it is actually functioning as a name in whatever context is under consideration, i.e. unless it is, in that context, being used to refer to a particular object. By an extension of the same idea, we do not count anything as a repetition of the *same* name unless it is, in the context, being used to refer to the same object. And this implies that an expression is not counted as a name unless it *succeeds* in referring to an object, i.e. unless there really is an object to which it refers.

This is the first assumption that we make about names, i.e. that they always do refer. (In Chapter 8 I shall consider abandoning this assumption, but for the time being it is imposed.) There is also a second assumption, which may naturally be regarded as an extension of the first: for logical purposes, it is only the object referred to that is important, and not the name that is used to refer to it. To put this more precisely: the truth-value of a proposition which contains a name will (usually) depend upon which object that name refers to, but it will never depend upon which name is being used to refer to it; consequently, any other name with the same reference could have been used instead, and the truth-value of the whole would not be affected. That is, if two names each refer to the same object, then in any proposition which contains either of them the other may always be substituted in its place, and the truth-value of the proposition will be unaltered. This assumption is called the *Principle of Extensionality*.

Any natural language will abound with counter-examples to this principle. To adapt what must count as the case best known to philosophers (see Frege 1892/1960), it is true (given a suitable understanding of 'Ancient') that

> The Ancient Egyptians did not know that the Morning Star and the Evening Star are the same heavenly body.

Now in fact the expressions 'the Morning Star' and 'the Evening Star' are names of the same heavenly body, to wit the planet Venus. So, according to the principle of extensionality, it should always be possible to substitute either for the other without affecting truth-value. Accordingly, it should be equally true that

> The Ancient Egyptians did not know that the Morning Star and the Morning Star are the same heavenly body.

But this conclusion is manifestly absurd. Nor can one say that this apparent counter-example arises only because we have taken as names the expressions 'the Morning Star' and 'the Evening Star', whereas these expressions are not really names (but, say, disguised descriptions). For with *any* two names '*a*' and '*b*', which are in fact names of the same object, it will surely be possible to know that $a = a$ without knowing that $a = b$. What is causing the trouble in this example is not the particular names involved, but the kind of claim that is being made by the sentence as a whole.

There are many other examples of this phenomenon in an ordinary language. They are cases where we have a name which is apparently being used to refer to something, but where it makes a difference if we substitute some other name with the same reference. In such a case, the function that the name is performing cannot *just* be to refer to that object; it must be playing some other role as well, which a different name might fail to play, even though it too referred to the same object. So the name is not being used *purely* to refer. We shall say, in such a case, that the name does not occur *extensionally*. Where, however, the substitution of any other name with the same reference must preserve the same truth-value, there the name does occur extensionally. For logical purposes, it is only the extensional occurrences of names that we shall count as being occurrences of names. (I observe in parenthesis that it is common to find names occurring non-extensionally where they occur in a clause which specifies what is going on in someone's mind—e.g. what he knows, believes, fears, doubts, is thinking of, and so on. The same phenomenon also occurs when we are concerned with what is necessary, or possible, or probable; or with the question of how some fact is to be explained, or some conduct justified; and in other cases too.)

EXERCISES

3.1.1. The names in italics in the following sentences do not occur there as names, from a logical point of view. Explain why not.

(*a*) Many people have painted pictures of *Pegasus*.
(*b*) It is not likely that *King Arthur* existed.
(*c*) *The Pope* is usually an Italian.
(*d*) Trieste is no *Vienna*.
(*e*) *Giorgione* was so-called because of his size.

3.1.2. Discuss whether the names in italics in the following sentences do occur there as names, from a logical point of view. (Be prepared to find that some examples are ambiguous, and that we can accept them as using names when taken in one way, but not when taken in another.)

(*a*) *George Eliot* was Mary Ann Evans.
(*b*) At the time, no one knew that *George Eliot* was Mary Ann Evans.
(*c*) There are some who believe that Shakespeare was *Bacon*.
(*d*) Oedipus did not know that *Laius* was his father.
(*e*) No one is afraid of *Dr Jekyll*.
(*f*) It is most improbable that *Dr Jekyll* is a murderer.
(*g*) *The Morning Star* and the Evening Star might have turned out to be different planets.
(*h*) The police took no action because it was *Prince Charles* who was driving.

3.2. **Predicates, Variables, Quantifiers**

A simple way of approaching the modern[1] notion of a predicate is this: given any sentence which contains a name, the result of dropping that name and leaving only a gap in its place is a predicate. Given a suitable context, the sentence as a whole will express some proposition, true or false, about some object. The name refers to the object, and the rest of the sentence, i.e. the predicate, says something about it, something that will be either *true of* the object, or *false of* the object, as the case may be. (And as we commonly say, for short, that sentences themselves are true or false, so we shall similarly speak of predicates themselves being true of certain objects and false of others.) It should be noted that this way of speaking already presupposes that the name we began with occurred extensionally, for we do not allow for the idea that a predicate may be 'true of' an object under one name, but 'false of' it under another. On the contrary, the predicate is either true or false of the object itself, without room for any further qualification. So, if we remove from a sentence a *non-extensional* occurrence of a name, then what is left is *not* to be counted as a predicate, for our purposes.

In fact it will not quite do to say, as I have just done, that a predicate is just a sentence with a gap in it. Some simple *one*-place predicates may be regarded in this way, without creating any problem, but more will need to be said as soon as we move on to consider sentences with several gaps in them. These can arise either because we began with a sentence containing several names, and dropped more than one of them; or because we began with a sentence containing the same name several times over, and dropped that name at more than one of its occurrences; or, of course, from any mixture of these two reasons. To avoid the ambiguity that can result, we shall never in fact write a simple gap, but will always mark that gap by writing in it a letter that is called a *variable*. As variables we introduce the following alphabet

$$u,v,w,x,y,z,u_1,...$$

The point of marking a gap in this way is that two gaps which are each marked with the same variable must each be filled by the same name, if we are to form a sentence containing the predicate in question; whereas gaps which are marked by different variables may be filled by different names.

A sentence which contains some variables in place of names is called an *open sentence,* so in practice we shall use open sentences to represent our

---

[1] Note that the use of the words 'subject' and 'predicate' from Aristotle to Kant was very different from that introduced here.

predicates. An open sentence which contains just one variable, occurring one or more times, represents a one-place (or monadic) predicate, true or false of single objects; one obtains a genuine sentence from it and a single name, upon substituting that name for all occurrences of its variable. An open sentence which contains just two variables replacing names represents a two-place (or dyadic) predicate—also called a dyadic relation—true or false of ordered pairs of objects; one obtains a genuine sentence from it and a pair of names, by substituting the first name of the pair for all occurrences of the first variable, and the second name for all occurrences of the second variable. (Note that, as a special case, the first name of the pair might happen to be the *same* name as the second.) The generalization is obvious: an open sentence containing just n distinct variables replacing names[2] represents an n-place predicate, true or false of ordered n-tuples of objects. Two special notes may be added to this statement. (1) It is convenient to count the generalization as covering *zero-place* predicates; these are represented by 'open' sentences with *no* variables replacing names, i.e. they are just ordinary sentences. (2) There is no need to distinguish between the 'one-tuple' of an object and the object itself, so we shall not bother to do so.

As schematic letters to take the place of names we shall use the alphabet

$a,b,c,d,e,a_1,...$

As schematic letters for predicates we shall use

$F,G,H,P,Q,R,S,T,F_1,...$

A predicate-letter will be followed by one or more name-letters, as in '*Fa*' or '*Gab*', to stand in for a sentence containing those names; or by one or more variables, as in '*Fx*' or '*Gxy*', to stand in for the corresponding open sentences; or by a mixture of the two, as in '*Gxb*'. For official purposes each predicate-letter is regarded as having some definite numeral superscripted, so that F^n represents only the n-place predicates, needing to be followed by n-tuples of name-letters or variables.[3] But in practice we shall always omit these superscripts, for since a predicate-letter is always followed by some definite number of name-letters and variables, this itself allows us to reconstruct its superscript. There is, however, one point arising from the omission to which it is worth drawing attention. Both '*Fa*' and '*Fab*' will be counted as formulae, and therefore so also is '*Fa* ∧ *Fab*'. But, despite appearances, this formula does not contain the *same* predicate-letter twice over. For the first

---

[2] The qualification 'replacing names' is essential. It restricts attention to *free* occurrences of variables. (See further pp. 79–80).

[3] An n-tuple is a series of n items, not necessarily distinct (cf. p. 16 above). E.g. $\langle a,b,a,c,a \rangle$ is a 5-tuple.

occurrence of '*F*' is short for '*F¹*', and the second is short for '*F²*', and these are different predicate-letters.

We have now introduced names, variables, and predicates, which form the auxiliary vocabulary needed to express quantification, so we can proceed to the quantifiers themselves. For the time being[4] we shall recognize only two quantifiers, namely the universal quantifier '∀', which does the work of the English 'all' or 'every' or 'any', and the existential quantifier '∃', which does the work of the English 'some' or 'a'. (The inverted 'A' is intended to suggest 'All'; the reversed 'E' is intended to suggest the Existence expressed by 'there is a' or 'there are some'.) But from a grammatical point of view our quantifiers ∀ and ∃ do not work in the same way as their English counterparts.

If we begin with an open sentence, containing (say) just the one variable *x* and no other, then in English one could form an ordinary sentence from it in two main ways: either one could replace the variable *x* by a name, or one could replace it by a quantifying expression such as 'everything' or 'something' or 'all men' or 'some girls'. But in logic we never write a quantifier in the same position as one could write a name. On the contrary, we do not replace the variable *x* by a quantifier, but we *prefix* a quantifier which, as we say, *binds* that variable. (The point of this departure from natural languages is that it makes clear what the *scope* of the quantifier is.) We show which variable a quantifier is binding by writing that variable itself immediately after the quantifying expression ∀ or ∃. Thus one writes '∀*x*' for the universal quantifier binding the occurrences of '*x*' in what follows, or '∃*y*' for the existential quantifier binding the variable '*y*' in what follows; and so on. The closest analogue to this in English is to prefix a phrase such as 'Everything is such that' or 'Something is such that', and then to replace the subsequent occurrences of the relevant variable by occurrences of the pronoun 'it', all governed by the opening prefix. So it comes about that English sentences such as

> All men are mortal
> Some girls wear blue stockings

are rephrased in our logical notation as

> ∀*x*(if *x* is a man then *x* is mortal)
> ∃*x*(*x* is a girl and *x* wears blue stockings)

and are represented in our schematic language by formulae such as

---

[4] The situation will alter in Section 8.1.

$$\forall x(Fx \to Gx)$$
$$\exists x(Fx \land Gx).$$

As in the case of the truth-functors, there is plenty of room for debate over the relation between the quantifiers of logic and their analogues in ordinary languages, but that is not a topic for the present book.

EXERCISE

3.2.1. Briefly explore the topic that is not for this book. Let us label the four statements thus:

(1) All men are mortal.
(2) Some girls wear blue stockings.
(3) $\forall x(x$ is a man $\to x$ is mortal$)$.
(4) $\exists x(x$ is a girl $\land x$ wears blue stockings$)$.

Consider the following arguments for saying that (1) does not mean the same as (3), and that (2) does not mean the same as (4):

(*a*) (2) implies that more than one girl wears blue stockings; (4) does not.
(*b*) (2) implies that there are also girls who do not wear blue stockings; (4) does not.
(*c*) (1) implies (or presupposes) that there are men; (3) does not.
(*d*) Indeed, (3) is true if there are no men; (1) is not.
(*e*) (1) is about men and nothing else; (3) is apparently about all objects. So the two have different subject-matters.
(*f*) In fact there is no saying what (3) is about, since its domain is just left unspecified. (And the specification 'all objects' is no help, for 'object' is so vague a word that we do not know what is to count as an object for this purpose.) Thus (3) has no clear domain of quantification, whereas (1) does; for (1) quantifies just over men.

How good are these arguments? Would it be possible to meet them by adopting more complex versions of (3) and (4)?

3.3. Languages for Quantifiers

In order to study the effect of quantifiers upon entailment we shall again concentrate on so-called 'formal' languages—i.e. schematic languages—in which definite quantifiers occur, but no definite names or predicates. We shall allow definite truth-functors to occur too, so that the languages in question are really schematic languages for truth-functors *and* quantifiers, and the languages of the previous chapter will be a special case of those to be introduced now. The vocabulary from which the languages are built therefore consists of

name-letters: $a,b,c,d,e,a_1,...$
variables: $u,v,w,x,y,z,u_1,...$
n-place predicate-letters: $F^n, G^n, H^n, P^n, Q^n, R^n, S^n, T^n, F_1{}^n,...$ (for $n \geqslant 0$).

(The zero-place predicate-letters are the sentence-letters of the previous chapter.) It is convenient to add here a further definition:

The *terms* of a language are its name-letters and its variables together.

In addition to this vocabulary the languages may contain any desired truth-functors (which will add brackets to the notation) and either none, or one, or both of the quantifiers $\forall$ and $\exists$.

For definiteness, let us suppose that we wish to include both quantifiers in our language, but of truth-functors only $\neg, \wedge, \vee$. Then the formation rules are:

(1) An n-place predicate-letter, followed by n terms, is a formula.
(2) If ϕ is a formula, so is $\neg\phi$.
(3) If ϕ and ψ are formulae, so are $(\phi\wedge\psi)$ and $(\phi\vee\psi)$.
(4) If ϕ is a formula, and ξ a variable, $\forall\xi\phi$ and $\exists\xi\phi$ are formulae.
(5) There are no other formulae.

Apart from variations in the truth-functors and quantifiers that may be included in the language, we also permit variations in the name-letters, variables, and predicate-letters: the language may contain only some, or perhaps none, of those listed. For example, we may consider a language which has no name-letters (as several authors do), or one which has only the one-place predicate-letters, and so on.

The formation rules just given have some rather unnatural consequences. One might, indeed, look askance even at rule (1), which provides for the *atomic formulae*. For this rule allows as a formula not only schematic expressions such as 'Fa', which take the place of sentences containing names, but also expressions such as 'Fx', which take the place of *open* sentences. An open sentence, however, is not a proper sentence; it cannot express any definite proposition, and it makes no sense to assign it a truth-value. Do we want such a thing to be counted as a formula? But a far more serious difficulty arises with rule (4), which says that if ϕ is *any formula whatever* then we can always form another formula by adding a prefix such as '$\forall x$' or '$\exists y$', whether or not there are any further occurrences of '*x*' or '*y*' in the formula, to be bound by this prefix. So, for example, the following count as formulae: '∀*xP*', '∃*yFxx*', '∀*x*∃*x*∀*xFa*', and so on. But these are expressions which correspond to no English sentences or open sentences; it is natural to say that they make no sense at all.

To consider this point more accurately, we need some further definitions:

(6) The *scope* of an occurrence of a quantifier (or a truth-functor) is the shortest formula in which it occurs.

(7) An occurrence of a quantifier ∀ or ∃, immediately followed by an occurrence of the variable ξ, as in ∀ξ or ∃ξ, is said to be ξ-*binding*.[5]

(8) An occurrence of a variable ξ in a formula φ is *free in* φ iff it is not in the scope of any ξ-binding quantifier in φ; otherwise it is *bound in* φ.

(9) A *closed* formula is one in which no variable occurs free; a formula which is not closed is *open*.

(10) An occurrence of a quantifier ∀ξ or ∃ξ is *vacuous* iff its scope is ∀ξψ or ∃ξψ, and the variable ξ does not occur free in ψ.

A vacuous quantifier, then, is one which is ξ-binding but which fails to bind any occurrence of ξ, except for the occurrence which forms part of the quantifying prefix itself. All the examples of quantifiers in the apparently 'senseless' formulae just noted are vacuous.

In some books the formation rules are so arranged that formulae with free variables, and formulae with vacuous quantifiers, are not counted as formulae at all. It is easy to see how to achieve this. We restrict formation rule (1) to

(1′) An *n*-place predicate-letter, followed by *n name-letters*, is a formula,

and we allow the introduction of variables only with rule (4), at the same time as we provide for the quantifiers that bind them. Further, to ensure that these quantifiers should not be vacuous, we now phrase rule (4) in this way:

(4′) If φ is a formula containing a name α, and if φ(ξ/α) is what results upon substituting the variable ξ for all occurrences of α in φ, then ∀ξφ(ξ/α) and ∃ξφ(ξ/α) are formulae, *provided that* φ(ξ/α) is not *itself* a formula.[6]

---

[5] I use the small Greek letters 'ξ' and 'ζ' ('xi' and 'zeta', with long 'i' and long 'e') as metalogical symbols to stand in for any variables.
[6] I use the small Greek letters 'α', 'β', 'γ' ('alpha', 'beta', 'gamma', with a long 'e' in 'beta') as metalogical symbols to stand in for any name-letters.

Notice that the proviso ensures that at least one occurrence of ξ in φ(ξ/α) is a *free* occurrence, not already bound by any ξ-binding quantifier in φ(ξ/α), so that the newly prefixed quantifier cannot be vacuous.[7] So on these revised rules no formula is allowed to contain a free variable or a vacuous quantifier.

But there is a price to pay. From one point of view it is convenient not to count open formulae as formulae, namely because they cannot be assigned truth-values. But on the other hand we cannot just ignore open formulae, since one frequently needs to say things about them, and they must be given some name or other. Since in fact the name 'open formula' (corresponding to 'open sentence') is now well established, it seems perverse not to use it. But then one might as well go along with what the name implies, and accept that open formulae are indeed formulae. When necessary, one can always explicitly restrict attention to such formulae as are not open, but closed. There is no similar motivation for accepting formulae with vacuous quantifiers. Apart from one or two very recherché purposes,[8] these are for the most part just a nuisance, for one has to keep remembering that sensible-looking rules which apply to all normal quantifiers may not apply to them. But in order to rule them out, while still accepting open formulae as formulae, it turns out that the rules of formation must be given in a much more complicated form, which it is not worth stating here.[9] I therefore return to rules (1)–(5) as first stated, which do permit vacuous quantifiers, but I adopt a ruling about them which renders them harmless. The ruling is that a vacuous quantifier alters nothing, i.e. if ξ does not occur free in φ, then ∀ξφ and ∃ξφ are each logically equivalent to φ.

Having decided what a language for quantifiers is to be, our next task is to say what counts as an interpretation for such a language. This is the task of the next section. Before we come to that I pause here to introduce a notation for substitution that will be convenient in what follows. If φ is any formula, α any name, and ξ any variable, then φ(α/ξ) is to be the formula that results from φ upon substituting occurrences of the name α for every occurrence of the variable ξ in φ that is *free* in φ. If ξ has no free occurrence in φ, then φ(α/ξ) is just φ itself. Similarly, φ(ξ/α) is to be the formula that results from φ upon substituting for each occurrence of α in φ an occurrence of ξ that is *free* in φ. If either there are no occurrences of α in φ, or there is one such that, when an

---

[7] Observe that we cannot explicitly use the notion of a 'free occurrence' when framing rule (4'), for at this stage that notion has not been defined.

[8] For example, vacuous quantifiers in the logic of one-place predicates are a useful model for 'vacuous' modal operators in the modal logic S5.

[9] One must simultaneously define *both* what counts as a formula *and* what counts as a free occurrence in that formula.

occurrence of ξ is substituted for it, that occurrence is bound in ϕ, then in either case $\phi(\xi/\alpha)$ is just ϕ itself. The point is that this notation concerns the substitution of names for *free* variables, and vice versa; if we wish to consider substitution of or for bound variables (as on p. 103), then we must say so explicitly.

EXERCISES

3.3.1. Let us call a formula 'sensible' iff it contains no vacuous quantifiers. Allowing reasonable conventions for omitting brackets, which of the following expressions are (*a*) formulae, (*b*) closed formulae, (*c*) sensible formulae? Give reasons.

(1) *Fax*

(2) $\forall x Fax \rightarrow Fax$

(3) $\forall x(Fax \rightarrow \exists xFax)$

(4) $\forall x(\exists yFyy \rightarrow Fxy)$

(5) $\forall a(\forall yFyy \vDash Faa)$

(6) $\exists x \forall y Fyx \wedge \forall x \exists z Fzy$

(7) $\forall x(Fab \wedge Ga \rightarrow \exists x(Fxb \wedge Gx))$

(8) $\forall x(Fab \wedge Ga \rightarrow \exists xFxb \wedge Gx)$

(9) $\exists x \wedge \exists y Fxy$

(10) $\forall x(P \rightarrow Fx) \vDash P \rightarrow \forall xFx$

3.3.2. Argue in detail that any expression which is counted as a formula on the revised rules (1′) and (4′) of p. 79 is also counted as a formula which is both closed and sensible on the rules originally given on p. 78. [Method: use induction on the length of the expression, noting that length is now to be measured by the number of occurrences of truth-functors *and quantifiers*.]

3.3.3. Compare rule (4′) with this rule:

(4″) If ϕ is a formula containing a name-letter α, and if $\phi(\xi/\alpha)$ is what results upon substituting the variable ξ for all occurrences of α in ϕ, then $\forall \xi \phi(\xi/\alpha)$ and $\exists \xi \phi(\xi/\alpha)$ are formulae, *provided that* ξ does not already occur in ϕ.

(Several books adopt (1′) and (4″), in place of (1′) and (4′).) Show that there are expressions which are permitted as formulae by (4′) but not by (4″), and discuss whether they should be permitted.

3.3.4. The *main* logical symbol in a formula is that symbol in it, either truth-functor or quantifier, which has the whole formula as its scope. Prove that in any formula, apart from atomic formulae, there is always one and only one such symbol. [Method: adapt Exercise 2.8.2.]

3.4. Semantics for these Languages

What is to count as an *interpretation* of a language which contains names, predicates, and quantifiers, as well as truth-functors, is very much more complicated than it was when only the truth-functors needed to be considered. There are also, as we shall see, two rather different methods of providing such interpretations. The method that I give first is I think the simpler: it concentrates just on truth-values, as in the previous chapter, and consequently it ignores open formulae altogether. It is this method that I shall use in subsequent discussions. But since most books these days use a different method, I shall give a brief outline of this too.

We may start with what is common to both methods. An interpretation for a language of the kind that we are now interested in will always begin with the selection of a *domain*, to be what is called 'the domain of the interpretation'. (We abbreviate this to $\mathcal{D}$.) It is also called 'the domain of discourse', since it is thought of as containing all the things that the language in question can speak about. What we choose as the domain is arbitrary; it can be any set of things whatever, finite or infinite, with this one proviso: it cannot be *empty*. I comment briefly on some consequences of this proviso in this section and the next, but I shall not examine its merits until Chapter 8. For the present it is simply a stipulation on what is to count as a (standard) interpretation.

The next step is to provide an interpretation, *on that domain*, of the name-letters and predicate-letters in our language. This means that for each name-letter in the language we must specify some object of the domain for it to be the name of. Since one of our central assumptions about names was that a name must succeed in naming something, we are not permitted to interpret any name-letter as lacking in denotation, but otherwise there are no restrictions. For example, we may, if we wish, interpret all the names as naming the *same* object in the domain, or we may interpret them as all naming different objects, and so on. Similarly, we interpret the predicate-letters on the domain by saying which objects in the domain they count as true of. More accurately, we interpret a zero-place predicate-letter, i.e. a sentence-letter, just by assigning it a truth-value, T or F. We interpret a one-place predicate-letter by assigning it some set of objects from the domain which it is true of. (It is then also specified as false of all other objects in the domain.) Any set of objects from the domain is permitted; in particular we may include *all* the objects in the domain, which interprets the predicate-letter as true of everything; or we may interpret it as true of nothing, or anything in between. We interpret a two-place predicate-letter by assigning to it some set of the ordered pairs that can be formed from members of the domain; and so on.

In order to have a brief notation, for any symbol σ let us write $|\sigma|$ for the 'semantic value' assigned to the symbol σ by whatever interpretation is in question. (If we need to distinguish different interpretations, say I and J, we shall add suitable subscripts as in $|\sigma|_I$ and $|\sigma|_J$.) Also, where $\mathcal{D}$ is the domain of the interpretation, let us write $\mathcal{D}^n$ (for $n>0$) for the set of all n-tuples that can be formed from the objects of that domain. Then we can say: an interpretation I for a language L for quantifiers, will always specify

(1) A non-empty domain $\mathcal{D}$.
(2) For each name-letter α in L some object in $\mathcal{D}$ as its denotation (i.e. what it names). Thus $|\alpha| \in \mathcal{D}$.
(3) For each zero-place predicate-letter Φ^0 in L a truth-value.[10] Thus $|\Phi^0| = T$ or $|\Phi^0| = F$.[11]
(4) For each n-place predicate-letter Φ^n in L ($n>0$), a set of n-tuples formed from the objects in $\mathcal{D}$ as its extension (i.e. what it is true of). Thus $|\Phi^n| \subseteq \mathcal{D}^n$.

These clauses (1)–(4) concern the interpretation of the non-logical vocabulary of L, which will be different from one interpretation to another. We now need to consider the interpretation of the logical vocabulary of L, and this is not chosen arbitrarily, but is designed to conform to the intended meaning of the logical signs. It is therefore the same for all interpretations of the same language.

Let us suppose, again, that we are dealing with a language which contains just $\neg, \wedge, \vee$ as truth-functors, and $\forall$ and $\exists$ as quantifiers. There is also another piece of 'logical vocabulary' that needs explanation, and that is the significance of writing name-letters immediately after a predicate-letter in an atomic formula. So we also need a clause which tells us how atomic formulae are to be evaluated. In the first method that I give, we confine attention throughout to *closed* formulae, so that the atomic formulae that are relevant are just those that contain name-letters but no variables. The obvious clause is this:

(5) $|\Phi^n \alpha \beta \ldots \gamma| = T$ iff $\langle |\alpha|, |\beta|, \ldots, |\gamma| \rangle \in |\Phi^n|$.[12]

---

[10] I use the capital Greek letter 'Φ' ('phi') as a metalogical symbol to stand in for any predicate-letter. (I add that '$\in$' abbreviates 'is a member of' and '$\subseteq$' abbreviates 'is a subset of'.)

[11] We *could* avoid a special clause for zero-place predicates in this way. We may suppose that $\mathcal{D}^0$ is the set of 0-tuples that can be formed from members of $\mathcal{D}$, and that there is just one such 0-tuple, namely 'the empty tuple' (i.e. the empty sequence) which is represented by $\langle\ \rangle$. Then $\mathcal{D}^0 = \{\langle\ \rangle\}$, and if $|\Phi^0| \subseteq \mathcal{D}^0$ then either $|\Phi^0| = \{\langle\ \rangle\}$ or $|\Phi^0| = \{\ \}$ (i.e. the empty set). For a continuation of this approach, see n. 12.

[12] If this clause is intended to include zero-place predicate-letters (cf. n. 11), then in their case it is interpreted as meaning

$|\Phi^0| = T$ iff $\langle\ \rangle \in |\Phi^0|$.

Thus a sentence-letter is true if its value is $\{\langle\ \rangle\}$, and false if its value is $\{\ \}$. (I am indebted to Dana Scott for this ingenious suggestion.)

In words, this says: an atomic formula consisting of an n-place predicate-letter followed by n names counts as true (in the interpretation in question) iff the n-tuple formed by taking the objects which are the denotations of the names (in that interpretation), in the order in which the names occur in the formula, is a member of the set of n-tuples which is the extension of the predicate-letter (in that interpretation). It is long-winded to say it, but the thought is surely very simple. We may add to this the expected clauses for the truth-functors, namely (in the present case)

(6) $|\neg\phi| = T$ iff $|\phi| \neq T$

(7)(a) $|\phi \wedge \psi| = T$ iff $|\phi| = T$ and $|\psi| = T$

(b) $|\phi \vee \psi| = T$ iff $|\phi| = T$ or $|\psi| = T$.

This brings us, then, to the problem of what we are to say about the quantifiers.

Let us suppose that $\forall x \phi(x)$ and $\exists x \phi(x)$ are closed and sensible formulae, so that x, but only x, occurs free in $\phi(x)$. Then the basic idea is evidently this: $\forall x \phi(x)$ is to count as true iff the predicate represented by the open sentence $\phi(x)$ is *true of* all the objects in the domain; and similarly $\exists x \phi(x)$ is to count as true iff that predicate is *true of* some object in the domain. But this way of putting things evidently introduces a difficulty. In clauses (5)–(7) we have been working towards a definition of *true* for our language, but have not said anything about *being true of*. Either, then, we must think of some way of explaining the truth-values of quantified sentences in terms of the *truth* of their simpler instances, or we must go back and revise clauses (5)–(7) so that they are concerned, not—or not only—with truth, but also with being true of. My first method takes the first course, and my second method takes the second.

The first method starts from the thought that if $\forall x \phi(x)$ is true, then so is every simpler formula $\phi(\alpha)$ obtained from it by substituting some name α for the occurrences of x that are free in $\phi(x)$. Provided that the interpretation we are concerned with has assigned a name to each object in the domain, then we can also say conversely that if every formula $\phi(\alpha)$ is true, then so is $\forall x \phi(x)$. But this proviso is not something that we can take for granted. In many cases it is not fulfilled, and in some cases it could not be, since there may be *more* objects in the domain than there are name-letters.[13] The solution to this problem is not to try to ensure an adequate supply of names, but just to think of the many ways of interpreting a single name-letter. The idea

---

[13] There are as many name-letters as there are natural numbers; Cantor proved that there are more real numbers than there are natural numbers.

is, roughly speaking, that $\forall x \phi(x)$ is true iff $\phi(\alpha)$ is true *for every way of interpreting* the name-letter α. Let us try to put this more precisely.

We are trying to settle the truth-values of quantified sentences in an interpretation I. To do this we need also to consider other interpretations which are *variants* of I. In particular, for any name α, let us say that I_α is an α-variant of I iff I_α does interpret the name α, and it differs from I either not at all or just on the interpretation that it assigns to α and in no other way. This may be because I does not assign any interpretation to α whereas I_α does, or because the two assign different interpretations. In all other ways, however, the two interpretations are to be the same. It should be noted here that, for any name α, and any interpretation I, there always is at least one α-variant interpretation I_α. This would not be true if we had permitted the domain of an interpretation to be empty. For if we have a language which contains no name-letters, then it can be interpreted on an empty domain; truth-values may be assigned arbitrarily to its sentence-letters, and all other predicate-letters are assigned the empty set as their extension. But this is an interpretation which has no α-variant interpretation for any name α. For an α-variant interpretation *does* assign a denotation to the name α, which cannot be done if at the same time the domain has to be kept empty. As things are, however, we are debarring the empty domain, so this problem does not arise.

The idea, then, is to specify the truth-value of a quantified formula $\forall \xi \phi$ in terms of the truth-values of its singular instances $\phi(\alpha/\xi)$, not only in the interpretation I that we began with, but also in variant interpretations which treat the substituted name differently.[14] We must, then, specify that the substituted name should be one that does not *already* occur in $\forall \xi \phi$. For we want to hold all the symbols in $\forall \xi \phi$ to their *existing* interpretation while nevertheless considering other interpretations for the name that is introduced in place of the quantified variable. There is no problem about this, for no single formula can already contain all the name-letters that there are. This leads us, then, to adopt the following clauses for the quantifiers:

(8)(a) $|\forall \xi \phi|_I = T$ iff   for every name α not in ϕ, and every α-variant interpretation I_α, $|\phi(\alpha/\xi)|_{I_\alpha} = T$.

  (b) $|\exists \xi \phi|_I = T$ iff   for some name α not in ϕ, and some α-variant interpretation I_α, $|\phi(\alpha/\xi)|_{I_\alpha} = T$.

An alternative formulation, which is quite easily seen to yield the same results, is this:

---

[14] This method is used in Mates (1972: 60 ff.).

(8′) Let β be the alphabetically earliest name that is not in ϕ. Then

    (a) $|\forall\xi\phi|_I = T$ iff   for every β-variant interpretation I_β, $|\phi(\beta/\xi)|_{I_\beta}$
       = T.

    (b) $|\exists\xi\phi|_I = T$ iff   for some β-variant interpretation I_β, $|\phi(\beta/\xi)|_{I_\beta}$
       = T.

For the fact is that for any two names α and β, neither of which occur in ϕ, the α-variant interpretations of $\phi(\alpha/\xi)$ exactly match the β-variant interpretations of $\phi(\beta/\xi)$, and all of the first will be true (or false) iff all of the second are also. (I give a proof of this claim in the next section, as 3.5.C.)

This completes the account of an interpretation, according to the first method. Clauses (1)–(8) have specified what an interpretation is in a way that ensures that the interpretation assigns a definite truth-value, T or F, to every *closed* formula of the language being interpreted. In this method, open formulae are simply ignored. They cannot significantly be assigned truth-values, and no other kinds of values have been considered for them. (Because it concentrates entirely on truth-values, the method is said to give a *recursion on truth*.[15]) I now pass on to the second method, which does assign values of a kind to open formulae.

As I explained the problem initially it was this. A simple quantification creates a closed formula from an open formula. So apparently the truth-value of the quantification should be determined by the 'value' of the open formula that is quantified. But an open formula simply does not have a *truth-value*. What kind of value, then, does it have?

Well, the suggestion that we shall pursue is basically this: an open formula can be regarded as having a truth-value if at the same time we artificially treat its free variables as if they were names. Of course there will be many ways of so treating the variables, i.e. of assigning them denotations. But if we can specify what value the formula has for *each* possible way of assigning denotations to its free variables, then this can be regarded as assigning a non-arbitrary value to the formula itself. In effect, it assigns to the formula an *extension*, for to speak of those ways of assigning objects to the variables that make the formula true is much the same as to speak of those n-tuples of objects that the formula counts as true of. But it is not quite the same. For our technique will specify extensions in a way which *also* allows us to calculate the extensions of complex formulae from the extensions of their simpler components. A simple illustration will make clear how this works.

---

[15] It is called a *recursion* because—very roughly—it determines the truth-values of complex formulae by *going back* to the truth-values of their simpler components (or instances).

Let us take a simple two-place predicate-letter F. The interpretation will specify an extension for this letter; let us suppose it is just the pair of objects $\langle a,b \rangle$ and nothing else. Then it is natural to say that this pair $\langle a,b \rangle$ can equally well be regarded as the extension, in this interpretation, of the open formula 'Fxy'. But it is then equally natural to say that the same pair is the extension of the open formula 'Fyx'. Considered as open formulae, which may be true of, or satisfied by, pairs of objects, there is surely no significant difference between 'Fxy' and 'Fyx'. For it does not matter *which* variables we use to mark the gaps in an open sentence; all that is significant is whether the various gaps are filled by the same variables or different variables. But then, if we are to say that the extensions of 'Fxy' and 'Fyx' are the same, we cannot suppose that the extensions of the two conjuncts of a conjunction determine the extension of the conjunction itself. For clearly the conjunctions '$Fxy \land Fxy$' and '$Fxy \land Fyx$' need not have the same extensions as one another. On the contrary, in the interpretation given, the first has the extension $\langle a,b \rangle$ again, while the second has a null extension (assuming that $a \neq b$). To keep track of this kind of thing, our ways of assigning objects to variables will not lose sight of which variables are involved where. So we shall have one assignment which assigns a to 'x' and b to 'y', and this assignment satisfies 'Fxy' but not 'Fyx'. There will also be another assignment which assigns b to 'x' and a to 'y', and this assignment satisfies 'Fyx' but not 'Fxy'. But there will be no assignment of objects to variables that satisfies both 'Fxy' and 'Fyx', and hence no assignment that satisfies the conjunction '$Fxy \land Fyx$'. Let us now put this idea more precisely.

We suppose given an interpretation I, which specifies a domain, and the interpretation on that domain of the name-letters and predicate-letters in our language L. In fact, let us begin with the simplifying assumption that L contains no name-letters, so that all formulae are built up just from predicate-letters and variables. We now introduce the idea of an assignment s of denotations to the variables of L, i.e. a function which, for each variable ξ of L as input, yields as output some object $s(\xi)$ of the domain $\mathcal{D}$ of the interpretation I. We shall speak of such an assignment s in I as *satisfying* a formula, meaning by this that the formula comes out true (in the interpretation I) when each variable ξ that occurs free in that formula is taken as denoting $s(\xi)$.[16] We give a recursive definition of satisfaction (abbreviating 'satisfies' to 'sats') which starts in the expected way:

---

[16] An alternative method, adopted in Tarski's pioneering work of 1931, and still employed in many books, is this. We take the infinitely many variables of L to be alphabetically ordered, and we consider the infinite sequences (allowing repetitions) of objects from the domain. We then stipulate that the nth variable of the alphabet is *always* to be taken as denoting the nth member of any sequence, and with this

(1) s sats $\Phi^n\xi_1\xi_2...\xi_n$ iff $\langle s(\xi_1), s(\xi_2),...,s(\xi_n)\rangle \in |\Phi^n|$.[17]

(2) s sats $\neg\phi$ iff   not (s sats ϕ).

(3) s sats $\phi\wedge\psi$ iff   (s sats ϕ) and (s sats ψ).

     s sats $\phi\vee\psi$ iff   (s sats ϕ) or (s sats ψ).

To state the clause for the quantifiers we now introduce the idea of one assignment being a *variant* on another. In particular, given an assignment s, and a particular variable ξ, an assignment s_ξ will be a ξ-variant on s iff either it is s or it differs from s just in the denotation it assigns to ξ and in no other way. Then the quantifier clauses are

(4) s sats $\forall\xi\phi$ iff   for every ξ-variant s_ξ on s, s_ξ sats ϕ

     s sats $\exists\xi\phi$ iff   for some ξ-variant s_ξ on s, s_ξ sats ϕ.

These clauses specify what it is for any assignment s to satisfy any formula ϕ of L, whether ϕ is closed or open. In fact they ensure that a closed formula is either satisfied by all assignments or by none, so we can now complete our account of the interpretation I by adding: for any closed formula ϕ

$$|\phi|_I = T \quad \text{iff} \quad \text{for every s in } I, \text{ s sats } \phi.$$

Now let us go back to remove the simplification imposed earlier, that the language should contain no name-letters. If we do have name-letters to take into consideration, it turns out that the simplest way of doing so is to enlarge our assignments of denotations to variables so that they also include assignments of denotations to names. But, of course, there will be this very clear difference: within a given interpretation I, *every* assignment s of denotations will assign the *same* denotation to each name-letter α interpreted by I, namely $|\alpha|$; but they will differ from one another by assigning different denotations $s(\xi)$ to the variables ξ. Each assignment s, then, is to be a function from the *terms* of the language (i.e. its name-letters and its variables) to the objects in the domain of the interpretation. To each term τ it assigns a denotation $s(\tau)$ but in such a way that[18]

for a name-letter α, always $s(\alpha) = |\alpha|$;
for a variable ξ, $s(\xi)$ is an arbitrary member of $\mathcal{D}$.

---

convention we can speak directly of a formula being satisfied by a sequence of objects. (But the sequences in question are infinitely long.) See Tarski (1956, ch. 8), which contains an English translation including corrections.

[17] For the case of zero-place predicate-letters, see nn. 11 and 12 earlier. We have

    s sats Φ^0 iff $\langle\ \rangle \in |\Phi^0|$.

[18] I use the small Greek letter 'τ' ('tau') as a metalogical symbol to stand in for any term.

To accommodate this ruling into the overall scheme, we therefore generalize clause (1) above so that it deals with *all* atomic formulae, both those containing names and those containing variables:

(1′) s sats $\Phi^n \tau_1 ... \tau_n$ iff $\langle s(\tau_1), ..., s(\tau_n) \rangle \in |\Phi^n|$.

The other clauses (and the definition of truth in terms of satisfaction) remain unchanged.

I bring this section to a close with a brief remark on entailment and inconsistency. Now that we have defined what an interpretation is, and what truth in an interpretation is, there is no problem over defining these notions. A set of formulae Γ is inconsistent, i.e. $\Gamma \vDash$, iff (*a*) all the formulae in the set are closed (so that there are interpretations in which they have truth-values), and (*b*) there is no interpretation in which they are all true. A set of formulae Γ entails a formula ϕ, i.e. $\Gamma \vDash \phi$, iff (*a*) ϕ and all the formulae in Γ are closed, and (*b*) there is no interpretation in which all the formulae in Γ are true and the formula ϕ is false. As a special case of this, a formula ϕ is valid, i.e. $\vDash \phi$, iff (*a*) ϕ is closed, and (*b*) there is no interpretation in which ϕ is false. This is equivalent to saying: in every interpretation of the language of ϕ, ϕ is true. For if ϕ is closed, then in every interpretation of its language it must receive one, and only one, of the two truth-values.

On our second method of explaining what an interpretation is, it may seem reasonable to say that it is not *only* closed formulae that can be true. For truth was defined as satisfaction by all assignments, and this is a notion that applies to open formulae too. In fact this suggestion treats an open formula, standing alone, as identical with what is called its *universal closure*, i.e. the result of prefixing to it (in any order[19]) enough universal quantifiers to bind all its free variables. For the one will count as true (in a given interpretation) iff the other does. Now there would be no harm in extending the notion of truth in this way, so long as we take validity as our basic semantic notion, and either we do not talk of entailment and inconsistency at all, or we define them in terms of validity (as on p. 123). That is, it does no harm to count certain open formulae as valid, namely those whose universal closures are valid. But it can lead to a breakdown in expected relationships if we apply this idea to entailment or to inconsistency as these notions are ordinarily understood. For example, if the open formula *Fx* is true when and only

---

[19] Since we speak of *the* universal closure of a formula, we should strictly speaking specify some definite order, say alphabetical. But the order will make no difference to the truth-conditions of the formula.

when its universal closure $\forall x F x$ is true, then according to the usual definition of entailment it must hold that

$$Fx \models \forall x F x.$$

On the other hand it does *not* hold that

$$\models Fx \rightarrow \forall x F x.$$

For the universal closure of this formula is $\forall x(Fx \rightarrow \forall x F x)$, which is certainly not valid. Similarly with inconsistency. It will hold that

$$Fx, \neg \forall x F x \models$$

but not

$$Fx \wedge \neg \forall x F x \models.$$

These seem to me to be very paradoxical results. Some authors avoid them by revising the usual definitions of entailment and inconsistency so that these are now defined in terms of satisfaction rather than truth (e.g. Newton-Smith 1985: 193), but it is surely more straightforward to prevent the problem arising in the first place by insisting that it is only closed formulae that have truth-values. At any rate, that is the course that I shall take, and I shall not count $\models$ as defined in application to open formulae.

EXERCISES

Throughout these exercises suppose that we are given some interpretation I which is specified in the second way, with a recursion on satisfaction, as on pp. 86–9. (This set of exercises is the only part of the book that will work with interpretations specified in this way.) To abbreviate labour, assume that the only logical symbols in the language of I are $\neg, \wedge, \forall$.

3.4.1. Let $\phi(\tau_1)$ and $\phi(\tau_2)$ be any formulae which result from one another upon replacing some free occurrences of τ_1 by free occurrences of τ_2, or vice versa. (If τ_i is a name-letter, every occurrence counts vacuously as 'free'.) Let s be an assignment in I of denotations to terms in which $s(\tau_1) = s(\tau_2)$. Prove

   s sats $\phi(\tau_1)$ iff   s sats $\phi(\tau_2)$.

[Method: use induction on the length of $\phi(\tau_1)$. The inductive hypothesis should be that the result holds for all formulae $\psi(\tau_1)$ shorter than $\phi(\tau_1)$ *and all assignments* s in I. It may help to compare the analogous result for a semantics specified in the first way, by a recursion on truth, which is proved in the next section as 3.5.B, but you will find that the present proof is much simpler than that one.]

3.4.2. Prove that, if ϕ is a closed formula, then ϕ is satisfied either by all assignments in I or by none. [Method: induction on the length of ϕ. In the clause for $\forall$ you will need to introduce a new name in place of the quantified variable, so that the inductive hypothesis can be brought to bear, and to use Exercise 3.4.1.]

3.4.3. Let I^* be an interpretation specified in the first way, with a recursion on truth rather than satisfaction, as on pp. 84–6. Suppose that I and I^* have the same domain, and the same interpretation on that domain of all name-letters and predicate-letters in ϕ. Using the result of Exercise 3.4.2 prove that

If ϕ is closed, then $|\phi|_I = |\phi|_{I^*}$.

3.5. **Some Lemmas on these Semantics**

From now on I shall assume that our semantics is specified in the first way, by a recursion on truth rather than on satisfaction. This seems to me to be the more natural and direct approach. But even so it is quite tricky to work with, so I here insert a short section which illustrates in some detail how this is done. I prove three lemmas which will be put to use in the next section. You will see that the claims to be argued for are very straightforward, but in the second case the argument is quite complex.

The first two arguments will proceed by induction on the length of a formula, and as you will know (unless you have skipped the exercises) the length of a formula is now defined as the number of occurrences of truth-functors *and quantifiers* that it contains. To save labour, I shall therefore assume that we are dealing with a language that contains only $\neg, \wedge, \forall$ as its logical symbols. You will find that further cases can easily be argued in the same way as these. (Or you may rely upon the fact that other truth-functors and quantifiers may be defined in terms of these.)

My first lemma is something which was obvious enough to go without saying in languages for truth-functors, but now deserves a proper treatment:

3.5.A. Lemma on interpretations. If two interpretations I and J have the same domain, and the same interpretations (on that domain) of all the name-letters and predicate-letters in a (closed) formula ϕ, then they also assign the same value to ϕ.

The proof, as I have said, is by induction on the length of the formula ϕ, which we assume to be a closed formula. So assume also that I and J are interpretations with the same domain, which assign the same values to all the letters in ϕ. We must show that they assign the same value to ϕ, i.e. that $|\phi|_I = |\phi|_J$. The hypothesis of induction is

> For all closed formulae ψ shorter than ϕ, and all interpretations $\mathcal{K}_1$ and $\mathcal{K}_2$ with the same domain, which assign the same values to all the letters in ψ, $|\psi|_{\mathcal{K}_1} = |\psi|_{\mathcal{K}_2}$.

We have four cases to consider.

Case (1): ϕ is atomic, i.e. it consists of an n-place predicate-letter followed by n name-letters. Since I and J assign the same values to all these letters, the result follows at once from the clause for evaluating atomic formulae (i.e. clause (5) on p. 83).

Case (2): ϕ is $\neg\psi$. Since I and J assign the same values to all the letters in ϕ, they also assign the same values to all the letters in ψ, which is shorter than ϕ. Hence by the inductive hypothesis we have $|\psi|_I = |\psi|_J$. So the result follows by the clause for evaluating negations (i.e. clause (6) on p. 84).

Case (3): ϕ is $\psi\wedge\chi$. As in case (2), the inductive hypothesis implies $|\psi|_I = |\psi|_J$ and $|\chi|_I = |\chi|_J$, so the result follows by the clause for conjunctions (i.e. clause (7) on p. 84).

Case (4): ϕ is $\forall\xi\psi$. Assume first that $|\forall\xi\psi|_I = F$. By the clause for quantifications (i.e. clause (8) on p. 85), this means that for some name α not in ψ, and some α-variant interpretation I_α of I, we have $|\psi(\alpha/\xi)|_{I_\alpha} = F$. Now let $\mathcal{K}$ be an interpretation which agrees in all respects with J, except that it interprets the name α as I_α does. Since I and J agree on all letters in $\psi(\alpha/\xi)$, except possibly on α, it follows that I_α and $\mathcal{K}$ agree on all letters in $\psi(\alpha/\xi)$, and so by the inductive hypothesis we have $|\psi(\alpha/\xi)|_{\mathcal{K}} = F$. But also, $\mathcal{K}$ is an α-variant on J, and so by the clause for quantifications we also have $|\forall\xi\psi|_J = F$.

Thus if $|\phi|_I = F$ then $|\phi|_J = F$. By an exactly similar argument, if $|\phi|_J = F$ then $|\phi|_I = F$. This establishes the desired result $|\phi|_I = |\phi|_J$.

This completes the induction.

My second lemma shows that our semantics does obey the principle of extensionality discussed earlier, in Section 3.1. That is, if α and β are name-letters which are assigned the same denotation in some interpretation I, then either may be substituted for the other, at one or more places in a formula, without changing the value of that formula in I. To state this more concisely, let $\phi(\alpha)$ be any closed formula containing the name α, and let $\phi(\beta)$

result from it upon replacing some occurrences of α in $\phi(\alpha)$ by occurrences of β.[20] Then the lemma is

3.5.B. Lemma on extensionality. If $|\alpha|_I = |\beta|_I$ then $|\phi(\alpha)|_I = |\phi(\beta)|_I$.

The proof is by induction on the length of the formula $\phi(\alpha)$. The inductive hypothesis is

> For all formulae $\psi(\alpha)$ shorter than $\phi(\alpha)$, for all name-letters α and β, and for all interpretations $\mathcal{I}$: if $|\alpha|_\mathcal{I} = |\beta|_\mathcal{I}$, then $|\psi(\alpha)|_\mathcal{I} = |\psi(\beta)|_\mathcal{I}$.

We have four cases to consider, but the argument for the last case has to be somewhat roundabout. We assume $|\alpha|_I = |\beta|_I$.

Case (1): $\phi(\alpha)$ is atomic; it might be for example $\Phi^3\alpha\beta\gamma$. Then $\phi(\beta)$ is $\Phi^3\beta\beta\gamma$. Since we are given that $|\alpha|_I = |\beta|_I$, it evidently follows that

$$\langle |\alpha|_I, |\beta|_I, |\gamma|_I \rangle = \langle |\beta|_I, |\beta|_I, |\gamma|_I \rangle.$$

Applying the clause for atomic formulae, it at once follows that $|\Phi^3\alpha\beta\gamma|_I = |\Phi^3\beta\beta\gamma|_I$. The same reasoning evidently applies to any atomic formula, so we may conclude that $|\phi(\alpha)|_I = |\phi(\beta)|_I$ as desired.

Case (2): $\phi(\alpha)$ is $\neg\psi(\alpha)$. By inductive hypothesis we have $|\psi(\alpha)|_I = |\psi(\beta)|_I$, and so the result follows by the clause for negations.

Case (3): $\phi(\alpha)$ is $\psi(\alpha) \wedge \chi(\alpha)$, where α may perhaps be present in only one of the conjuncts. Then by inductive hypothesis we have $|\psi(\alpha)|_I = |\psi(\beta)|_I$ and $|\chi(\alpha)|_I = |\chi(\beta)|_I$, where again β may perhaps be present in only one of these formulae. This makes no difference to the argument, for in either case the result follows by the clause for conjunctions.

Case (4): $\phi(\alpha)$ is $\forall\xi\psi(\alpha)$. Assume $|\forall\xi\psi(\alpha)|_I = F$. That is to say: there is some name γ, which is not in $\psi(\alpha)$, and some γ-variant interpretation I_γ of I, such that $|\psi(\alpha)(\gamma/\xi)|_{I_\gamma} = F$. We have two cases to consider, according as the name γ is or is not in $\psi(\beta)$. Suppose first that it is. In that case γ can only be β itself (since it is in $\psi(\beta)$ but not in $\psi(\alpha)$). It follows that β is not in $\psi(\alpha)$, and what we are given is that there is a β-variant interpretation I_β of I such that

(a) $|\psi(\alpha)(\beta/\xi)|_{I_\beta} = F.$

We shall show that in that case there is *also* a suitable γ-variant, using a new name γ other than β, so that this case reduces to the other case first distinguished.

---

[20] Thus $\phi(\alpha)$ is $\phi'(\alpha/\xi)$ and $\phi(\beta)$ is $\phi'(\beta/\xi)$ for some formula ϕ' which contains free occurrences of ξ just where α and β are to be interchanged.

Consider a new name γ, not in $\psi(\alpha)$ or $\psi(\beta)$, and a new interpretation $I_{\beta\gamma}$ which agrees with I_β on the interpretation of all the symbols in the language of I_β, but which also interprets the name γ so that $|\gamma|_{I_{\beta\gamma}} = |\beta|_{I_\beta}$, and hence $|\gamma|_{I_{\beta\gamma}} = |\beta|_{I_{\beta\gamma}}$. Now $I_{\beta\gamma}$ and I_β agree on the interpretation of all the symbols in $\psi(\alpha)(\beta/\xi)$. Hence by lemma 3.5.A on interpretations we have

(b) $\quad |\psi(\alpha)(\beta/\xi)|_{I_\beta} = |\psi(\alpha)(\beta/\xi)|_{I_{\beta\gamma}}$.

And by the inductive hypothesis we have

(c) $\quad |\psi(\alpha)(\beta/\xi)|_{I_{\beta\gamma}} = |\psi(\alpha)(\gamma/\xi)|_{I_{\beta\gamma}}$.

Further, let I_γ be an interpretation which is just like $I_{\beta\gamma}$ except that in I_γ the name β is interpreted as in I and not as in I_β. Now we are given that β does not occur in $\psi(\alpha)$, nor therefore in $\psi(\alpha)(\gamma/\xi)$. Hence I_γ and $I_{\beta\gamma}$ agree on all the symbols in that formula, and so by the lemma on interpretations we have

(d) $\quad |\psi(\alpha)(\gamma/\xi)|_{I_{\beta\gamma}} = |\psi(\alpha)(\gamma/\xi)|_{I_\gamma}$.

Thus I_γ is the required interpretation. For by construction it is a γ-variant on I, and if we put together the four equations (a)–(d), we at once have

(e) $\quad |\psi(\alpha)(\gamma/\xi)|_{I_\gamma} = F.$

It is now easy to complete the proof. In either of the cases first distinguished, equation (e) holds for some name γ not in $\phi(\beta)$. And since I_γ agrees with I on the denotations of α and β we have $|\alpha|_{I_\gamma} = |\beta|_{I_\gamma}$, and so by inductive hypothesis

(f) $\quad |\psi(\alpha)(\gamma/\xi)|_{I_\gamma} = |\psi(\beta)(\gamma/\xi)|_{I_\gamma}$.

Putting (e) and (f) together we have: there is a name γ not occurring in $\phi(\beta)$, and a γ-variant interpretation I_γ of I, such that

(g) $\quad |\psi(\beta)(\gamma/\xi)|_{I_\gamma} = F.$

But in view of the clause for the universal quantifier, that is to say

$$|\forall\xi\psi(\beta)|_I = F.$$

Conditionalizing this whole argument so far, what we have shown is

If $\quad |\phi(\alpha)|_I = F$ then $|\phi(\beta)|_I = F.$

Interchanging α and β throughout the argument, we equally have

If $\quad |\phi(\beta)|_I = F$ then $|\phi(\alpha)|_I = F.$

And therefore finally

$$|\phi(\alpha)|_I = |\phi(\beta)|_I.$$

This completes the induction.

The awkward part of this last argument was to show that if we are given some result with one new name in place of a quantified variable, then we can always obtain the same result with any other new name instead. It is worth recording this point explicitly. Perhaps the most useful way of doing so is by noting that it allows us to give an alternative statement of the truth-conditions for quantified formulae, in terms of their singular instances:[21]

3.5.C. Lemma on alternative semantics for the quantifiers.

$|\forall\xi\phi|_I = T$ iff, for *some* name-letter α not in ϕ, for all α-variants I_α of I, $|\phi(\alpha/\xi)|_{I_\alpha} = T$.

$|\exists\xi\phi|_I = T$ iff, for *every* name-letter α not in ϕ, for some α-variant I_α of I, $|\phi(\alpha/\xi)|_{I_\alpha} = T$.

I shall show that these semantics for $\forall$ are equivalent to those first given (in clause (8) on p. 85), leaving the application to $\exists$ as an exercise. Now it is obvious that if $\forall\xi\phi$ is true according to the original semantics, then it is also true according to these alternative semantics, since it is obvious that what holds for all name-letters not in ϕ must also hold for some. (This depends upon the point that there must be some name-letters that are not in ϕ, whatever formula ϕ may be.) Suppose, then, that $\forall\xi\phi$ is false in some interpretation I according to the original semantics. That is to say: suppose that there is some name-letter, say β, not occurring in ϕ, and some β-variant interpretation I_β of I, such that

(a) $|\phi(\beta/\xi)|_{I_\beta} = F.$

We have to show that $\forall\xi\phi$ is also false according to the alternative semantics, i.e. that for *any* name-letter α not in ϕ there is an α-variant interpretation I_α such that $|\phi(\alpha/\xi)|_{I_\alpha} = F.$

Let α be any name not in ϕ other than β. Let $I_{\beta\alpha}$ be an interpretation exactly the same as I_β, except that it assigns to α the same denotation as I_β assigns to β. Now since α is not in ϕ, it is not in $\phi(\beta/\xi)$ either, so I_β and $I_{\beta\alpha}$ agree on all the symbols in $\phi(\beta/\xi)$. Hence by lemma 3.5.A on interpretations we have

(b) $|\phi(\beta/\xi)|_{I_\beta} = |\phi(\beta/\xi)|_{I_{\beta\alpha}}.$

Further, since α and β are assigned the same denotation in $I_{\beta\alpha}$, by lemma 3.5.B. on extensionality we have

---

[21] Compare the further alternative given on p. 86. (It is clear that the present argument also establishes the correctness of that alternative.)

(c) $|\phi(\beta/\xi)|_{I_{\beta\alpha}} = |\phi(\alpha/\xi)|_{I_{\beta\alpha}}.$

Finally, let I_α be an interpretation exactly the same as $I_{\beta\alpha}$, except that it assigns to β whatever denotation (if any) it was assigned in I. Then since β is not in ϕ, it is not in $\phi(\alpha/\xi)$ either, so I_α and $I_{\beta\alpha}$ agree on all the symbols in $\phi(\alpha/\xi)$. Hence by the lemma on interpretations we have

(d) $|\phi(\alpha/\xi)|_{I_{\beta\alpha}} = |\phi(\alpha/\xi)|_{I_\alpha}.$

Moreover, I_α is by construction an α-variant of I. So putting (a)–(d) together, I_α is an α-variant of I such that

(e) $|\phi(\alpha/\xi)|_{I_\alpha} = F.$

This completes the proof.

We are now ready to move on to some principles of entailment for our languages with quantifiers which extend those given in Section 2.5 for languages with truth-functors.

EXERCISES

3.5.1. Extend the argument for 3.5.A, by adding new clauses to the induction, so that the result is proved also for languages containing $\vee$ and $\exists$.

3.5.2. The argument for clause (4) of the induction proving 3.5.B establishes that

$$|\forall\xi\psi(\alpha)|_I = |\forall\xi\psi(\beta)|_I.$$

Use the equivalence noted below as 3.6.E to show how that argument also establishes the result for $\exists$ in place of $\forall$.

3.5.3. In a similar way, extend the argument given for 3.5.C to cover $\exists$ as well as $\forall$.

3.6. Some Principles of Entailment

It is easy to see that the so-called 'structural' principles of pp. 30–2 apply to our languages for quantifiers just as well as to our languages for truth-functors. These were

    3.6.A. The principle of Assumptions (ASS)
    3.6.B. The principle of Thinning (THIN)
    3.6.C. The principle of Cutting (CUT).

Nothing more needs to be said about the proofs of the first two, which are the same as before in each case, but it is useful to add something here about the third.

If you look back to the proof of CUT given on pp. 31–2, you will see that it relies on this assumption:

> An interpretation I which interprets a set of formulae Γ, but does not interpret a formula ϕ, can always be expanded to an interpretation I^+ which assigns the same values to the formulae in Γ and assigns some value to ϕ as well.

The assumption would not have been correct if we had allowed an interpretation to have an empty domain of discourse. For, as I have noted (p. 85), if the formulae in Γ contain no name-letters, then they can all be interpreted on an empty domain, whereas if ϕ does contain a name-letter, then it cannot be. But changing the domain from an empty one to a non-empty one may well disturb the values assigned to the formulae in Γ. (For example, the two formulae $\exists x Fx$ and $\exists x \neg Fx$ can both be false only if the domain is empty.) As things are, however, we are not permitting a domain to be empty, so every formula can be interpreted on every domain, and this obstacle is avoided. It then follows from our lemma 3.5.A on interpretations that the assumption just cited is satisfied by our semantics for quantifiers, and CUT can therefore be proved in the same way as before.

I now move on to four principles for the quantifiers, though each has two versions, one for $\forall$ and one for $\exists$. Since entailment is defined only for closed formulae, it must of course be assumed that all the formulae here mentioned are closed. The first principle states that vacuous quantification achieves nothing:

3.6.D.(*a*) If ξ is not free in ϕ, $\forall \xi \phi \vDash\!\!\vDash \phi$.
    (*b*) If ξ is not free in ϕ, $\exists \xi \phi \vDash\!\!\vDash \phi$.

The second shows how each quantifier may be defined in terms of the other:

3.6.E.(*a*) $\exists \xi \phi \vDash\!\!\vDash \neg \forall \xi \neg \phi$.
    (*b*) $\forall \xi \phi \vDash\!\!\vDash \neg \exists \xi \neg \phi$.

The third is usually called the elimination rule for $\forall$, paired with the introduction rule for $\exists$, and the final one is the introduction rule for $\forall$, paired with the elimination rule for $\exists$:

3.6.F.(*a*) $\forall \xi \phi \vDash \phi(\alpha/\xi)$.
    (*b*) $\phi(\alpha/\xi) \vDash \exists \xi \phi$.

3.6.G.(*a*) If $\Gamma \vDash \phi$ then $\Gamma \vDash \forall \xi \phi(\xi/\alpha)$, provided α does not occur in Γ.

(*b*) If $\Gamma, \phi \vDash$ then $\Gamma, \exists \xi \phi(\xi/\alpha) \vDash$, provided α does not occur in Γ.[22]

I give proofs just of the first version in each case. Using the fact that $\exists$ can be defined in terms of $\forall$, as 3.6.E states, the second version can always be derived from the first. Or the second version can be argued directly from the semantics for $\exists$, by an entirely parallel argument.

Proof of 3.6.D(a)

It is sufficient to prove here that if ξ is not free in ϕ then $\phi \vDash \forall \xi \phi$, for the converse will follow as a special case of 3.6.F, to be proved later. Assume, then, that I is any interpretation in which ϕ is true. We have to show that $\forall \xi \phi$ is also true in I, i.e. that for every name α not in ϕ, and every α-variant interpretation I_α, $\phi(\alpha/\xi)$ is true in I_α. Since ξ is not free in ϕ, $\phi(\alpha/\xi)$ just is ϕ, so the problem is to prove that ϕ is true in I_α. But this follows at once from our lemma on interpretations, for I and I_α agree on the interpretation of all the letters in ϕ, since they differ only on α, and α is not in ϕ.

Proof of 3.6.E(a)

Consider any interpretation I which does interpret $\forall, \exists, \neg$, and all the letters in ϕ. Then $|\neg \forall \xi \neg \phi|_I = T$ iff $|\forall \xi \neg \phi|_I = F$, i.e. iff for some name α not in ϕ, and some α-variant interpretation I_α, we have $|\neg \phi(\alpha/\xi)|_{I_\alpha} = F$. But since $|\neg \phi(\alpha/\xi)| = F$ iff $|\phi(\alpha/\xi)| = T$, this is just the condition for $|\exists \xi \phi|_I = T$.

Proof of 3.6.F(a)

Assume that I does interpret the name α, and that $|\forall \xi \phi|_I = T$. Let β be any name other than α, and not occurring in ϕ. Then for every β-variant interpretation I_β we have $|\phi(\beta/\xi)|_{I_\beta} = T$. Choose in particular the interpretation I_β which assigns to β the same interpretation as I assigns to α. Then $|\beta|_{I_\beta} = |\alpha|_I = |\alpha|_{I_\beta}$, so by the lemma on extensionality we have

$$|\phi(\beta/\xi)|_{I_\beta} = |\phi(\alpha/\xi)|_{I_\beta}.$$

But also, β does not occur in ϕ, nor therefore in $\phi(\alpha/\xi)$, so I and I_β have the same interpretation for all the symbols in $\phi(\alpha/\xi)$. Hence by the lemma on interpretations we have

---

[22] As with the principle for Disjunction (p. 35), 3.6.G(*b*) is to be regarded as carrying with it the more usual form of $\exists$-elimination:

If $\Gamma, \phi \vDash \psi$ then $\Gamma, \exists \xi \phi(\xi/\alpha) \vDash \psi$, provided that α does not occur in Γ or in ψ.

(The reason why this is called an 'elimination' rule will become clear in Ch. 6.)

$$|\phi(\alpha/\xi)|_{I_\beta} = |\phi(\alpha/\xi)|_I.$$

Putting these two equations together we may evidently infer $|\phi(\alpha/\xi)|_I = T$, as required.

Proof of 3.6.G(a)

Assume that $\Gamma \vDash \phi$, and that α does not occur in Γ, and let I be any interpretation such that all the formulae in Γ are true in I. We have to show that $\forall\xi\phi(\xi/\alpha)$ is also true in I. Using our lemma on alternative semantics for the quantifiers, it will be sufficient to show that there is *some* name β not in $\phi(\xi/\alpha)$ such that $\phi(\xi/\alpha)(\beta/\xi)$ is true in every β-variant I_β of I. And for this it will be sufficient to show that, in particular, $\phi(\xi/\alpha)(\alpha/\xi)$ is true in every α-variant interpretation I_α, for clearly α does not occur in $\phi(\xi/\alpha)$. But since ϕ is a closed formula, the formula $\phi(\xi/\alpha)$ contains a free ξ wherever and only where ϕ contains α, so the formula $\phi(\xi/\alpha)(\alpha/\xi)$ is just the formula ϕ again. Hence what has to be shown is just that ϕ is true in every α-variant interpretation I_α. And this is simple. For it is given that α does not occur in any formula in Γ, so by the lemma on interpretations I and I_α assign the same value to all formulae in Γ, and hence all formulae in Γ are true in every interpretation I_α. But it is also given that Γ entails ϕ, so ϕ too must be true in every such interpretation.

All further entailments involving quantifiers can in fact be deduced from the principles 3.6.A–G, as we shall eventually establish (in Chapter 7). By way of illustration, I give a deduction of just one further entailment at this stage, since it will be needed as a lemma for what is to follow. It is

Lemma. $\forall\xi(\phi\leftrightarrow\psi) \vDash \forall\xi\phi \leftrightarrow \forall\xi\psi.$

The derivation may be given thus. Choosing some name α which does not occur in ϕ or in ψ, by two applications of the principle 3.6.F for $\forall$-elimination we have

$$\forall\xi(\phi\leftrightarrow\psi) \vDash (\phi\leftrightarrow\psi)(\alpha/\xi)$$
$$\forall\xi\phi \vDash \phi(\alpha/\xi).$$

Next we note that $(\phi\leftrightarrow\psi)(\alpha/\xi)$ is the same as $\phi(\alpha/\xi) \leftrightarrow \psi(\alpha/\xi)$, so by a simple truth-functional inference we obtain from this

$$\forall\xi(\phi\leftrightarrow\psi), \forall\xi\phi \vDash \psi(\alpha/\xi).$$

But we began by choosing a name α that does not occur in the premisses to this entailment, so we may now apply the principle 3.6.G for $\forall$-introduction and infer

$$\forall\xi(\phi\leftrightarrow\psi),\forall\xi\phi \vDash \forall\xi\psi.$$

Applying our basic principle for the conditional, this may also be written in the form

$$\forall\xi(\phi\leftrightarrow\psi) \vDash \forall\xi\phi \to \forall\xi\psi.$$

By an entirely similar argument we also have

$$\forall\xi(\phi\leftrightarrow\psi) \vDash \forall\xi\psi \to \forall\xi\phi.$$

And we have only to put these two together to obtain our desired conclusion. I leave it to you as an exercise to find a similar argument to justify this similar entailment:

$$\forall\xi(\phi\leftrightarrow\psi) \vDash \exists\xi\phi \leftrightarrow \exists\xi\psi.$$

We are now in a position to move on to the two remaining principles to be introduced in this section, namely the principle of uniform substitution for schematic letters, and the principle of interchange of equivalent formulae. These principles hold for our languages with quantifiers just as they did for our languages for truth-functors, but they are now very much more complicated to state and to justify. I begin with the interchange of equivalent formulae.

In the languages for truth-functors of the last chapter, there was no distinction to be made between open and closed formulae, for all formulae were closed. Consequently, the principle allowing for interchange of equivalent formulae was there confined to closed formulae, which makes it very simple to state and to prove. But now we have open formulae to consider as well, for they too can be equivalent to one another, and if so then they too can be interchanged while preserving the equivalence of the whole. If ϕ and ψ are open formulae, then they are interpreted as equivalent iff the universal closure of the biconditional formed from them is interpreted as true. Thus if the free variables in ϕ are just x and y, and the same holds for ψ, then to say that ϕ and ψ are equivalent in an interpretation I is just to say that $\forall x\forall y(\phi\leftrightarrow\psi)$ is true in I (and to say that ϕ and ψ are *logically* equivalent is to say $\forall x\forall y(\phi\leftrightarrow\psi)$ is true in all interpretations, i.e. is valid). More generally, where ϕ and ψ are any formulae, with any number of free variables $\xi_1...\xi_n$, I shall write

$$\forall\xi_1...\xi_n(\phi\leftrightarrow\psi)$$

to signify the closure of their biconditional. (If ϕ and ψ are both *closed* formulae, then $n=0$.)

Now, equivalent formulae may be substituted for one another, preserving truth-value. To state this succinctly, let ϕ and ψ be any formulae, whether closed or open, and let $\delta(\phi)$ be any closed formula containing ϕ as a subformula, and $\delta(\psi)$ be the result of interchanging ϕ and ψ at one or more places in $\delta(\phi)$. Then the basic principle that we require can be stated in this way:

3.6.H. $\forall \xi_1...\xi_n(\phi \leftrightarrow \psi) \vDash \delta(\phi) \leftrightarrow \delta(\psi)$.

If we had adopted the semantics on pp. 86–9 based on the notion of satisfaction, then it would at once be obvious that this entailment is correct. For if two formulae are equivalent in a certain interpretation, then it is easy to see that they must be satisfied by all the same assignments in that interpretation. Consequently, they must make the same contribution to the values of any longer formula that contains them. (That is the analogue of the justification given on p. 32, for the simple version of this principle that applies in quantifier-free languages.) But as things are, the semantics that we have adopted assigns no values to open formulae, so our justification must be more roundabout. For the sake of later developments (Exercise 6.2.2) I shall here give an argument by induction, namely an induction on the number of occurrences of truth-functors and quantifiers that are in $\delta(\phi)$ but not in ϕ.

In fact, it turns out to be convenient to prove slightly more than 3.6.H as just formulated. Let ϕ' be any formula resulting from ϕ by substituting name-letters for zero or more of the variables free in ϕ (substituting the same name-letter for each occurrence of the same variable), and let ψ' result from ψ by the same substitutions. Then what we shall prove is

$$\forall \xi_1...\xi_n(\phi \leftrightarrow \psi) \vDash \delta(\phi') \leftrightarrow \delta(\psi').$$

The hypothesis of induction is

If $\theta(\phi')$ is shorter than $\delta(\phi')$ then
$$\forall \xi_1...\xi_n(\phi \leftrightarrow \psi) \vDash \theta(\phi') \leftrightarrow \theta(\psi').$$

We shall again suppose that the language we are concerned with contains only $\neg, \wedge, \forall$ as its logical vocabulary, so that we have four cases to consider.

Case (1): $\delta(\phi')$ is no longer than ϕ', i.e. $\delta(\phi')$ is ϕ'. Then since $\delta(\phi')$ is closed (by hypothesis), ϕ' is closed, and therefore it must result from ϕ by substituting name letters for the variables (if any) that are free in ϕ. So the entailment to be established in this case is

$$\forall \xi_1...\xi_n(\phi \leftrightarrow \psi) \vDash (\phi \leftrightarrow \psi)(\alpha_1/\xi_1, \alpha_2/\xi_2,...,\alpha_n/\xi_n).$$

But this is obviously a correct entailment, as may be shown by repeated use of the principle of $\forall$-elimination.

Case (2): $\delta(\phi')$ is $\neg\theta(\phi')$. Then by inductive hypothesis we have

$$\forall\xi_1...\xi_n(\phi\leftrightarrow\psi) \vDash \theta(\phi') \leftrightarrow \theta(\psi')$$

and by a simple truth-functional inference we have

$$\theta(\phi') \leftrightarrow \theta(\psi') \vDash \neg\theta(\phi') \leftrightarrow \neg\theta(\psi').$$

From these two the result evidently follows, by CUT.

Case (3): $\delta(\phi')$ is $\theta_1(\phi') \wedge \theta_2(\phi')$, where ϕ' may perhaps be missing from one of the conjuncts. (This will not affect the argument.) Then by inductive hypothesis we have

$$\forall\xi_1...\xi_n(\phi\leftrightarrow\psi) \vDash \theta_1(\phi') \leftrightarrow \theta_1(\psi')$$
$$\forall\xi_1...\xi_n(\phi\leftrightarrow\psi) \vDash \theta_2(\phi') \leftrightarrow \theta_2(\psi').$$

From this the result follows by a simple truth-functional inference, as in case (2).

Case (4): $\delta(\phi')$ is $\forall\zeta\theta(\phi')$. Let β be a new name, not occurring in $\theta(\phi')$ or $\theta(\psi')$. (Note that it follows that β does not occur in ϕ or in ψ.) Then by inductive hypothesis we have

$$\forall\xi_1...\xi_n(\phi\leftrightarrow\psi) \vDash (\theta(\phi'))(\beta/\zeta) \leftrightarrow (\theta(\psi'))(\beta/\zeta).$$

That is

$$\forall\xi_1...\xi_n(\phi\leftrightarrow\psi) \vDash (\theta(\phi') \leftrightarrow \theta(\psi'))(\beta/\zeta).$$

Since β does not occur in the premiss, we may apply $\forall$-introduction to this to obtain

$$\forall\xi_1...\xi_n(\phi\leftrightarrow\psi) \vDash \forall\zeta(\theta(\phi') \leftrightarrow \theta(\psi'))(\beta/\zeta)(\zeta/\beta).$$

But since β does not occur in $(\theta(\phi') \leftrightarrow \theta(\psi'))$, this is just

$$\forall\xi_1...\xi_n(\phi\leftrightarrow\psi) \vDash \forall\zeta(\theta(\phi') \leftrightarrow \theta(\psi')).$$

And we have already proved as a lemma (pp. 99–100)

$$\forall\zeta(\theta(\phi') \leftrightarrow \theta(\psi')) \vDash \forall\zeta\theta(\phi') \leftrightarrow \forall\zeta\theta(\psi').$$

So the desired result now follows by CUT.

This completes the induction.

I remark that in the statement of this principle we have required $\delta(\phi')$ and $\delta(\psi')$ to be closed, as this simplifies the argument above. But we could allow them to be open formulae, with free variables $\zeta_1...\zeta_m$, and in this case the correct statement of the principle will be

    3.6.H.(*a*) $\forall\xi_1...\xi_n(\phi\leftrightarrow\psi) \vDash \forall\zeta_1...\zeta_m(\delta(\phi') \leftrightarrow \delta(\psi')).$

It is easy to see how this version can be established from what we have already. For if in $(\delta(\phi') \leftrightarrow \delta(\psi'))$ we write new name-letters in place of the free variables, then we have an entailment that is an instance of 3.6.H, as already established. But then by repeated applications of ∀-introduction these name-letters can be restored to variables, and universally quantified, as the new version requires.

As before, there is a weaker version of this principle, stating that *logically equivalent* formulae may be interchanged, i.e.

3.6.H.(b) If $\vDash \forall\xi_1...\xi_n(\phi\leftrightarrow\psi)$ then $\vDash \forall\zeta_1...\zeta_m(\delta(\phi') \leftrightarrow \delta(\psi'))$.

From this weaker version (which in practice is mo : often useful) we can again eliminate the functor $\leftrightarrow$ if we wish, but I leave hat as an exercise.

It is worth mentioning one simple corollary of his principle of interchange, namely that we may always introduce a *alphabetic change of bound variable*. Consider first any formula that be ins with a quantifier, say $Q\xi\phi(\xi)$, where Q is either ∀ or ∃. Let $\phi(\zeta)$ be th : result of substituting occurrences of the different variable ζ for all free o :currences of ξ in $\phi(\xi)$, assuming that the substituted occurrences are free in $\phi(\zeta)$, and that $\phi(\xi)$ does not already contain any free occurrences of ζ. T us $\phi(\xi)$ contains ξ free wherever and only where $\phi(\zeta)$ contains ζ free. In tl at case it is easy to see that

$$Q\xi\phi(\xi) =\!\vDash Q\zeta\phi(\zeta),$$

for the truth-conditions for each formula are exactl the same. By the principle of interchange, then, we have

$$\delta(Q\xi\phi(\xi)) =\!\vDash \delta(Q\zeta\phi(\zeta))$$

for any added matter δ. And, as we have seen, the re: ilt can also be generalized to cover the case where $Q\xi\phi(\xi)$, and hence $Q\zeta\phi \zeta)$, are open formulae, containing other variables free. So we may say tha , in any context whatever, one bound variable may always be exchanged f r another (by 'relettering'), so long as the same bondage links are prese red. This operation of relettering is quite often useful, as we shall see in the next section.

Our final principle in this section is that which perm: s uniform substitution for schematic letters throughout a sequent. In the lo ic of truth-functors we had only one kind of schematic letter to conside namely the sentence-letters, and so again the principle was simple to stat and to prove. We now have two kinds of schematic letters, i.e. name-letter and predicate-letters, and the principle of substitution holds for both of th :se. So we must take it in two parts. I consider first substitution for name-letters, since this is very straightforward. For the only expression that we have, that is of the same syntactical category as a name-letter, is another name-letter; and thus the principle simply permits us to substitute one name-letter for another. (The position will become a little more interesting in Chapter 8, where complex name-symbols will be introduced.) But substitution for a predicate-letter is a more complex operation, as we shall see.

I write $\Gamma(\beta/\alpha)$ for the result of substituting the name-letter β for all occurrences of the name-letter α throughout all the formulae in Γ, and $\phi(\beta/\alpha)$ for the result of making the same substitution in the formula ϕ. We can now state the principle required in two versions, according to the two kinds of sequent that we are recognizing.

3.6.I.(a) Uniform substitution for name-letters.

(1) If $\Gamma \vDash \phi$ then $\Gamma(\beta/\alpha) \vDash \phi(\beta/\alpha)$.

(2) If $\Gamma \vDash$ then $\Gamma(\beta/\alpha) \vDash$.

I sketch a proof just for the second case.

Assume that $\Gamma(\beta/\alpha) \nvDash$. That is, there exists an interpretation I such that, for all formulae ψ in Γ, $|\psi(\beta/\alpha)|_I = T$. Let I_α be an α-variant of I, agreeing with I in all respects, except that I_α interprets α as having the same denotation as does β in I. Now α does not occur in $\psi(\beta/\alpha)$, and hence by the lemma on interpretations we have $|\psi(\beta/\alpha)|_{I_\alpha} = |\psi(\beta/\alpha)|_I$. Moreover, $|\alpha|_{I_\alpha} = |\beta|_{I_\alpha}$, and the formulae ψ and $\psi(\beta/\alpha)$ result from one another by interchanging α and β at suitable places. Hence by the lemma on extensionality $|\psi(\beta/\alpha)|_{I_\alpha} = |\psi|_{I_\alpha}$. Putting these equations together, $|\psi|_{I_\alpha} = T$. That is to say: there is an interpretation, namely I_α, such that, for all formulae ψ in Γ, $|\psi|_{I_\alpha} = T$. In other words, $\Gamma \nvDash$.

This argument shows: if $\Gamma(\beta/\alpha) \nvDash$, then $\Gamma \nvDash$. Contraposing, we have our result.

Turning to substitution for predicate-letters, we must first pause to explain what the relevant operation is. An n-place predicate-letter is immediately followed by a series of n terms (either name-letters or variables), but it may be followed by different terms at different occurrences in the same formula. When we substitute for the predicate-letter, we are not at the same time substituting for the terms that follow it, so they must be preserved (in the right order) even though the predicate-letter is replaced by something else. Of course, this presents no problem if the predicate-letter is simply replaced by another predicate-letter, but in fact we have more interesting substitutions to consider. We said earlier (pp. 74–5) that an open sentence, with n

free variables, represents an *n*-place predicate. Similarly, an open *formula*, with *n*-free variables, is a complex schematic expression for complex *n*-place predicates of a certain structure. For example, the open formula

$Fxy \wedge \neg Fyx$

represents such complex predicates as can be obtained by substituting genuine open sentences in place of its atomic parts, as in

x loves $y \wedge \neg y$ loves x
x married $y \wedge \neg y$ married x
x weighs more than $y \wedge \neg y$ weighs more than x.
etc.

Clearly, what holds for *all* two-place predicates also holds for all two-place predicates of this particular structure. That is to say that if we have a correct sequent, which holds no matter what two-place predicate a letter G is taken to be, and if we substitute for that letter G the open formula $Fxy \wedge \neg Fyx$, then the result must again be a correct sequent. In a word, the substitutions to be considered are these: for a zero-place predicate-letter (i.e. a sentence-letter), we may substitute any formula with zero free variables (i.e. any closed formula); and for an *n*-place predicate-letter ($n>0$), we may substitute any open formula with n free variables. In the course of substituting an open formula for a predicate-letter, the free variables of that formula will disappear, to be replaced by the terms immediately following the predicate-letter on that occurrence. More precisely, the free variables of the open formula must be ordered in some way, say alphabetically, and we shall let this ordering correspond to the natural ordering of the terms immediately following an occurrence of the predicate-letter, namely from left to right. Then, each occurrence of the predicate-letter is replaced by the open sentence in question, and the alphabetically first free variable of the open sentence is replaced by the first from the left of the terms following the predicate letter at that occurrence, the second by the second, and so on. Here is an example. Suppose we begin with a sequent which claims (correctly) that an asymmetrical relation must be irreflexive:

$\forall x \forall y (Fxy \rightarrow \neg Fyx) \models \forall x \neg Fxx.$

For the schematic letter F in this sequent we then substitute the open sentence

$\exists z(Fxz \wedge Fzy).$

The result is

$$\forall x \forall y (\exists z (Fxz \wedge Fzy) \rightarrow \neg \exists z (Fyz \wedge Fzx)) \vDash \forall x \neg \exists z (Fxz \wedge Fzx).$$

Since the original sequent was in fact a correct sequent, so too is this one obtained from it by substitution.

There is one caveat that needs to be entered. Variables immediately following a predicate-letter are, of course, free in the atomic formula so formed. When an open sentence is substituted for the predicate-letter, and the variables following the predicate-letter are substituted into that open sentence at appropriate positions, *they must remain free* in the open sentence so formed. If the result of a substitution would be that some previously free variables become bound by quantifiers in the open sentence, then the substitution cannot be performed. For example, in the sequent

$$\forall x \forall y (Fxy \rightarrow \neg Fyx) \vDash \forall x \neg Fxx$$

one cannot substitute for the schematic letter the open formula

$$\exists y (Fxy \wedge Fyz).$$

The result could only be

$$\forall x \forall y (\exists y (Fxy \wedge Fyy) \rightarrow \neg \exists y (Fyy \wedge Fyx)) \vDash \forall x \neg \exists y (Fxy \wedge Fyx).$$

But in this first formula the two atomic subformulae *Fyy* each contain an occurrence of *y* that *should* be bound by the initial quantifier $\forall y$, if the overall structure of the formula is to be preserved, whereas it has instead got captured by the nearer occurrence of the quantifier $\exists y$. This is illegitimate, and there is no way of substituting just that open formula for the schematic letter in that particular context. (Instead, one must first 'reletter' the bound variables of the open formula.)

To have a succinct notation, let us write Φ^n for an n-place predicate-letter, ϕ^n for a formula with n variables free, and $\psi(\phi^n/\Phi^n)$ for the result of substituting the formula for the letter, according to the method just given, throughout the formula ψ. We assume that the substitution is a legitimate one. Similarly, we may write $\Gamma(\phi^n/\Phi^n)$ for the result of making such a substitution in every formula in Γ. Then our principle may again be stated in two versions:

3.6.I.(b) Uniform substitution for predicate-letters.

   (1) If $\Gamma \vDash \psi$ then $\Gamma(\phi^n/\Phi^n) \vDash \psi(\phi^n/\Phi^n)$.

   (2) If $\Gamma \vDash$ then $\Gamma(\phi^n/\Phi^n) \vDash$.

I give a proof just for the second version.

The proof will make the simplifying assumption that the letter Φ^n does not occur in the formula ϕ^n that is substituted for it. This restricted form of the principle in fact implies its unrestricted form, as we may see in this way. Let Ψ^n be a new n-place predicate-letter, different from Φ^n and not occurring in ϕ^n or in any formula in Γ. Then by the restricted principle we may first substitute Ψ^n for Φ^n throughout all the formulae in Γ, and next substitute ϕ^n for Ψ^n. The result of these two steps of substitution is just the same as the result of substituting ϕ^n for Φ^n directly. Let us come now to the proof.

Assume that $\Gamma(\phi^n/\Phi^n) \not\models$, i.e. that there is an interpretation I such that, for all formulae ψ in Γ, $|\psi(\phi^n/\Phi^n)|_I = \text{T}$. Now the interpretation I must assign some extension to the open formula ϕ^n, i.e. a set of n-tuples from the domain which ϕ^n may be counted as true of. Let us suppose that the free variables of ϕ^n, in alphabetical order, are $x_1,...,x_n$. Then in our second method of defining an interpretation (pp. 86–9) the relevant n-tuples are just the n-tuples $\langle s(x_1),...,s(x_n)\rangle$ for those assignments s that satisfy ϕ^n in I. Alternatively, if we retain our first way of defining interpretations, we must first substitute new names $a_1,...,a_n$, not already occurring in ϕ^n, for its free variables $x_1,...,x_n$, thus forming the closed formula ϕ^*. Then the n-tuples that we require are just those n-tuples $\langle |a_1|,...,|a_n|\rangle$ formed from the denotations of these names in all interpretations which (1) agree with I on all symbols other than the names $a_1,...,a_n$, and (2) make ϕ^* true. We can therefore introduce a new interpretation J, which agrees with I in all respects except that it assigns this set of n-tuples to the predicate-letter Φ^n as its extension. Since we are assuming that Φ^n does not occur in ϕ^n, this leaves unchanged the interpretation of all symbols in $\Gamma(\phi^n/\Phi^n)$, so that we have $|\psi(\phi^n/\Phi^n)|_J = \text{T}$, for all ψ in Γ. But also, we have constructed J so that ϕ^n and Φ^n have the same extension in it, i.e. they are equivalent formulae. That is, we have as true in J

$$\forall x_1...x_n(\phi^n \leftrightarrow \Phi^n).$$

Moreover, ψ differs from $\psi(\phi^n/\Phi^n)$ just by having Φ^n at some places where the other has ϕ^n. So, by our principle for interchanging equivalent formulae, it follows that ψ and $\psi(\phi^n/\Phi^n)$ are equivalent in J. Hence $|\psi|_J = \text{T}$ for all ψ in Γ, and therefore $\Gamma \not\models$, as desired. This completes the proof.

EXERCISES

3.6.1. Establish the principles 3.6.D(b)–G(b) left unproved in the text.

3.6.2. The following diagram shows what entailments hold between formulae constructed from the quantifiers, and otherwise just one occurrence of Fx, one occurrence of Gx, and one occurrence of $\wedge$.

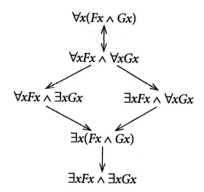

Construct similar diagrams first for ∨, then for →. [Method for ∨: by substitution for predicate-letters we may put ¬F for F, and ¬G for G, in the above entailments. Then the result emerges by noting that each quantifier can be defined in terms of the other, together with ¬, and that ∨ can be defined in terms of ∧ and ¬. The method for → is similar.]

3.6.3.(a) Using the principles for ∀-introduction and ∀-elimination (3.6.F–G) show that the following formulae are valid:

(1) $\forall x \forall y Fxy \to \forall y \forall x Fxy$.
(2) $\exists x \exists y Fxy \to \exists y \exists x Fxy$.
(3) $\exists x \forall y Fxy \to \forall y \exists x Fxy$.

(Observe that (1) and (2) do *not* follow from the principle allowing alphabetic change of bound variable.)

(*b*) Referring to the semantics for the quantifiers, show that the following formula is not valid:

(4) $\forall x \exists y Fxy \to \exists y \forall x Fxy$

(If you are stumped, see p. 133.)

3.6.4. Using 3.6.3.(*a*), show that any string of universal quantifiers, however long, may be rearranged in any desired order, preserving equivalence: (*a*) when that string appears at the beginning of a formula, and (*b*) when it appears at any other place in a formula. [Method: for part (*a*) it will be sufficient to show that any two adjacent quantifiers may be interchanged, i.e. that (for $n \leqslant 0, m \leqslant 0$)

$$\forall \xi_1 ... \xi_n \forall x \forall y \forall \zeta_1 ... \xi_m \phi \quad =\!|\!= \quad \forall \xi_1 ... \xi_n \forall y \forall x \forall \zeta_1 ... \zeta_m \phi.$$

Using ∀-introduction and ∀-elimination this can be shown to follow from

$$\forall x \forall y \forall \zeta_1 ... \zeta_m \phi(\alpha_1/\xi_1,...,\alpha_n/\xi_n) \quad =\!|\!= \quad \forall y \forall x \forall \zeta_1 ... \zeta_m \phi(\alpha_1/\xi_1,...,\alpha_n/\xi_n)$$

(for any names $\alpha_1,...,\alpha_n$ not already in ϕ). Using substitution for predicate-letters, this in turn can be shown to follow from 3.6.3(*a*). For part (*b*), use the principle of interchange of equivalent formulae, i.e. 3.6.H.]

3.7. **Normal Forms (PNF)**

The techniques of the last chapter (Section 2.5) for forming disjunctive or conjunctive normal forms are obstructed by the presence of quantifiers. But we can restore them, at least partially, if we first consider ways of separating quantifiers from truth-functors. The most straightforward result here is this. A formula is said to be in *prenex normal form* (PNF) iff all its quantifiers occur in a block at the beginning, so that no quantifier is in the scope of any truth-functor. We can now show that every formula is equivalent to some formula in PNF.

The idea of the proof is to demonstrate that a quantifier which occurs somewhere in the middle of a formula can always be moved one step to the left, and by sufficiently many such steps we can bring all the quantifiers as far to the left as possible, so that they do all occur in a block at the beginning. So we must begin by establishing, as lemmas, the various equivalences needed to show that a single shift to the left is always possible. For this purpose let us suppose that the truth-functors we are dealing with are just $\neg, \wedge, \vee$. Then the lemmas required are

$$1(a) \quad \neg\forall\xi\phi \;=\!|\!=\; \exists\xi\neg\phi \qquad (b) \quad \neg\exists\xi\phi \;=\!|\!=\; \forall\xi\neg\phi$$

and, *where ξ is not free in ψ,*

$$2(a) \quad \psi \wedge \forall\xi\phi \;=\!|\!=\; \forall\xi(\psi \wedge \phi) \qquad (b) \quad \psi \wedge \exists\xi\phi \;=\!|\!=\; \exists\xi(\psi \wedge \phi)$$
$$3(a) \quad \psi \vee \forall\xi\phi \;=\!|\!=\; \forall\xi(\psi \vee \phi) \qquad (b) \quad \psi \vee \exists\xi\phi \;=\!|\!=\; \exists\xi(\psi \vee \phi).$$

The proofs of $1(a)$ and $1(b)$ have in effect been given in the previous section, since they are obvious consequences of the interdefinability of the two quantifiers. But the point of listing them again here is, I hope, clear: $1(a)$ shows how a universal quantifier governed by a negation sign can be 'shifted to the left' by exchanging it for an existential quantifier governing a negation sign, and $1(b)$ does the same for the existential quantifier. Similarly, $2(a)$ and $3(a)$ show how a universal quantifier governed by a conjunction or a disjunction sign can again be shifted to the left, while $2(b)$ and $3(b)$ do this for the existential quantifier. (We are taking it for granted here that conjunction and disjunction are commutative, so what holds for $\psi \wedge \forall\xi\phi$ will also hold for $\forall\xi\phi \wedge \psi$.)

Here is a simple example. Suppose that we start with the formula

$$\exists x Fx \wedge \exists x Gx \wedge \neg\exists x(Fx \wedge Gx).$$

Using lemma $2(b)$, the leftmost quantifier can then be moved to the front without more ado, to get

109

$$\exists x(Fx \wedge \exists x Gx \wedge \neg \exists x(Fx \wedge Gx)).$$

Now we cannot move the second occurrence of $\exists x$ to the left just as things are, since its variable x *does* occur free in the clause Fx, and so the quantifier would come to capture the x in Fx, which it must not. So as a preliminary we must reletter the next quantifier before we can move it. And while we are at it we shall reletter the third quantifier as well, since this too will need to be done at some time. So we rewrite the formula as

$$\exists x(Fx \wedge \exists y Gy \wedge \neg \exists z(Fz \wedge Gz)).$$

Now the quantifier $\exists y$ can be moved to the left quite straightforwardly, using lemma 2(b) once more, to get

$$\exists x \exists y(Fx \wedge Gy \wedge \neg \exists z(Fz \wedge Gz)).$$

Finally, we may move the quantifier $\exists z$. The first move takes it past the negation sign, using lemma 1(b), to get

$$\exists x \exists y(Fx \wedge Gy \wedge \forall z \neg(Fz \wedge Gz)).$$

The second move then places it where we want it, using lemma 2(a):

$$\exists x \exists y \forall z(Fx \wedge Gy \wedge \neg(Fz \wedge Gz)).$$

This is the desired formula in PNF. It is equivalent to the original, because each step of the transformation has replaced a part of our formula by an equivalent part.

Incidentally, this example also illustrates the general point that a formula in PNF is usually difficult to understand, and comprehensibility is improved by pushing the quantifiers *into* a formula, as far as they will go, not by pulling them all out to the front. The formula that we began with was easy to understand: it said that something is F and something is G but nothing is both. But it takes some practice to see that the formula in PNF that we ended with is also saying the same thing. PNF, then, does not much help with comprehension, but it does have other uses, as we shall see (e.g. in Section 3.9). Let us now come back to our proof.

In order to prove that lemmas 2(a)–3(b) are correct, one could, of course, use the technique extensively employed in the previous section, of going back to the semantics originally given for the quantifiers. But perhaps it is more instructive to show how the results can be deduced from principles of entailment that we have already introduced and justified. This involves in each case giving first a proof from left to right (L→R) and then a proof from right to left (R→L) for each equivalence. As it turns out, the proofs are in all cases perfectly straightforward, invoking only the standard introduction and elimination rules for $\wedge, \vee, \forall, \exists$, *except* in the one case of 3(*a*), R→L, which in fact cannot be proved in this way. (This point is established in Exercise 6.3.4. Meanwhile, see Exercises 2.5.1 and 2.5.3 for the standard introduction and elimination rules for $\wedge$ and $\vee$.)

Proof of 2(a)

L→R. By $\forall$-elimination we have $\forall\xi\phi \models \phi(\alpha/\xi)$. Here we choose α so that it does not occur in ψ or in ϕ, and we note that $\phi(\alpha/\xi)(\xi/\alpha)$ is therefore just ϕ. Employing principles for $\wedge$, it easily follows that $\psi \wedge \forall\xi\phi \models \psi \wedge \phi(\alpha/\xi)$, and hence by $\forall$-introduction $\psi \wedge \forall\xi\phi \models \forall\xi(\psi \wedge \phi(\alpha/\xi))(\xi/\alpha)$. But the consequent here is $\forall\xi(\psi \wedge \phi)$, as required.

R→L. By $\forall$-elimination we have $\forall\xi(\psi \wedge \phi) \models (\psi \wedge \phi)(\alpha/\xi)$. We choose α so that it does not occur in ϕ or in ψ, and by hypothesis ξ does not occur in ψ, so that $(\psi \wedge \phi)(\alpha/\xi)$ is $\psi \wedge \phi(\alpha/\xi)$. Employing principles for $\wedge$, this entailment can be split up into two, namely $\forall\xi(\psi \wedge \phi) \models \psi$ and $\forall\xi(\psi \wedge \phi) \models \phi(\alpha/\xi)$. We apply $\forall$-introduction to the second, to obtain $\forall\xi(\psi \wedge \phi) \models \forall\xi\phi$, and then we put the two entailments back together again to obtain our result.

Proof of 2(b)

L→R. By $\wedge$-introduction we have $\psi, \phi(\alpha/\xi) \models \psi \wedge \phi(\alpha/\xi)$, and by $\exists$-introduction we have $\psi \wedge \phi(\alpha/\xi) \models \exists\xi(\psi \wedge \phi(\alpha/\xi))(\xi/\alpha)$. Choosing α so that it does not occur in ϕ or in ψ, and applying CUT to these entailments, we therefore have $\psi, \phi(\alpha/\xi) \models \exists\xi(\psi \wedge \phi)$. We have only to apply $\exists$-elimination to this, and conjoin the two antecedents, and we have what we want.

R→L. The argument is similar to 2(*a*), R→L. Choosing α so that it does not occur in ψ or in ϕ, we have both $\psi \wedge \phi(\alpha/\xi) \models \psi$ and $\psi \wedge \phi(\alpha/\xi) \models \phi(\alpha/\xi)$. Applying $\exists$-introduction to the second, we obtain $\psi \wedge \phi(\alpha/\xi) \models \exists\xi\phi$. Then we add the two entailments together, to get $\psi \wedge \phi(\alpha/\xi) \models \psi \wedge \exists\xi\phi$, and finally we apply $\exists$-elimination to this to get our result.

Proof of 3(a)

L→R. The proof is exactly similar to 2(*a*), L→R.

R→L. Expressing $\vee$ in terms of $\neg$ and $\rightarrow$, it is sufficient to show that $\forall\xi(\neg\psi \rightarrow \phi) \models \neg\psi \rightarrow \forall\xi\phi$, and for this in turn it is sufficient to show that $\forall\xi(\neg\psi \rightarrow \phi), \neg\psi \models \forall\xi\phi$. Now we have $\forall\xi(\neg\psi \rightarrow \phi) \models \neg\psi \rightarrow \phi(\alpha/\xi)$ by $\forall$-elimination (and the fact that ξ does not occur free in ψ), and by our principle for the conditional we therefore have $\forall\xi(\neg\psi \rightarrow \phi), \neg\psi \models \phi(\alpha/\xi)$. Choosing α so that it does not occur in ϕ or ψ, we may apply $\forall$-introduction to this, and so complete the argument.

Proof of 3(b)

This is left as an exercise.

Having established our lemmas, we may now proceed to the main theorem. But it is convenient to establish this stronger version, which holds for the limited language we are presently considering:[23]

> For every formula ϕ there is a logically equivalent formula ϕ^P in PNF, and no longer than ϕ.

The proof is by induction on the length of the formula ϕ. The inductive hypothesis is

> For every formula ψ shorter than ϕ, there is a logically equivalent formula ψ^P which is (*a*) in PNF and (*b*) no longer than the formula ψ.

Since our language contains only $\neg, \wedge, \vee, \forall, \exists$, we have six cases to consider, but $\wedge$ and $\vee$ can conveniently be treated together, and so can $\forall$ and $\exists$. So the six cases reduce to four.

Case (1): ϕ is atomic. Then ϕ is already in PNF, and there is nothing to prove.

Case (2): ϕ is $\neg\psi$. By inductive hypothesis there is a formula ψ^P in PNF, logically equivalent to ψ, and shorter than ϕ. So

$$\phi \dashv\vDash \neg\psi^P.$$

If ψ^P contains no quantifiers, then $\neg\psi^P$ is already in PNF, and we have our result. Otherwise ψ^P begins with some quantifier, say Q, and we have

$$\phi \dashv\vDash \neg Q\xi\chi.$$

Hence by lemma 1, taking Q' to be $\forall$ if Q is $\exists$, and $\exists$ if Q is $\forall$, we have

$$\phi \dashv\vDash Q'\xi\neg\chi.$$

But $\neg\chi(\alpha/\xi)$ is the same length as $Q\xi\chi$, i.e. as ψ^P, and so by inductive hypothesis is shorter than ϕ. Hence, using the inductive hypothesis again, there is a formula $(\neg\chi(\alpha/\xi))^P$ in PNF, no longer than $\neg\chi(\alpha/\xi)$, such that

$$\neg\chi(\alpha/\xi) \dashv\vDash (\neg\chi(\alpha/\xi))^P.$$

Hence

$$Q'\xi\neg\chi \dashv\vDash Q'\xi(\neg\chi)^P.$$

---

[23] I owe this suggestion to Rowland Stout.

But then $Q'\xi(\neg\chi)^P$ is in PNF, and equivalent to ϕ, and no longer than ϕ, as desired.

Case (3): ϕ is $\psi_1*\psi_2$, where $*$ is either $\wedge$ or $\vee$. By inductive hypothesis there are formulae $(\psi_1)^P$ and $(\psi_2)^P$ in PNF, equivalent to ψ_1 and ψ_2, and no longer than they are. So

$$\phi =\!\Vdash (\psi_1)^P * (\psi_2)^P,$$

where the right-hand formula is no longer than ϕ. If neither of $(\psi_1)^P$ nor $(\psi_2)^P$ contains a quantifier, then this formula is already in PNF, as desired. Otherwise one of them, say $(\psi_2)^P$, contains an initial quantifier, say Q, and we have

$$\phi =\!\Vdash (\psi_1)^P * Q\xi\chi.$$

Since ϕ is a closed formula, so is $(\psi_1)^P$, and therefore ξ does not occur free in $(\psi_1)^P$. Hence by lemma 2 or 3, as appropriate,

$$\phi =\!\Vdash Q\xi((\psi_1)^P * \chi).$$

But $(\psi_1)^P * \chi(\alpha/\xi)$ is shorter than ϕ, so applying the inductive hypothesis again there is a logically equivalent formula $((\psi_1)^P * \chi(\alpha/\xi))^P$, also shorter than ϕ, and in PNF. Hence by interchange of equivalents

$$\phi =\!\Vdash Q\xi((\psi_1)^P * \chi)^P.$$

This is the formula desired, since it is in PNF and no longer than ϕ.

Case (4): ϕ is $Q\xi\psi$, where Q is either $\forall$ or $\exists$. By inductive hypothesis there is a formula $(\psi(\alpha/\xi))^P$ in PNF, no longer than $\psi(\alpha/\xi)$, and logically equivalent to it. Hence by interchange of equivalents

$$Q\xi\psi =\!\Vdash Q\xi(\psi)^P$$

and the right-hand formula is in PNF, and no longer than ϕ, as desired.

This completes the proof.

It may be remarked that we needed to use the point that the PNF equivalent of a formula is the same length as it in order to apply the inductive hypothesis twice over within a single case (in Cases (2) and (3)). This point is correct for a language with $\neg,\wedge,\vee$ as its only truth-functors. It would also be correct if we added some further truth-functors such as $\rightarrow$ and $\uparrow$. But it would not hold in all cases, in particular not if a truth-functor such as $\leftrightarrow$ was included. For example, there is no PNF equivalent of

$$P \leftrightarrow \forall xFx$$

that contains no more than one occurrence of a quantifier and one of a truth-functor. In order to find a PNF equivalent for this formula one must first express $\leftrightarrow$ in other terms, for example in terms of $\neg,\wedge,\vee$, as

$$(P \wedge \forall x Fx) \vee (\neg P \wedge \neg \forall x Fx).$$

Successive transformations on this then yield

$$(P \wedge \forall x Fx) \vee (\neg P \wedge \exists x \neg Fx)$$
$$\forall x(P \wedge Fx) \vee \exists x(\neg P \wedge \neg Fx)$$
$$\forall x((P \wedge Fx) \vee \exists x(\neg P \wedge \neg Fx))$$
$$\forall x((P \wedge Fx) \vee \exists y(\neg P \wedge \neg Fy))$$
$$\forall x \exists y((P \wedge Fx) \vee (\neg P \wedge \neg Fy)).$$

Two distinct quantifiers are essential (and, incidentally, the truth-functional part cannot be expressed just in terms of $\leftrightarrow$). The general result, then, is just this: whatever the truth-functors in a formula, it always has an equivalent in PNF, and we can always find such an equivalent by first expressing its truth-functors in terms of more straightforward ones. But the PNF equivalent may have to be longer than the formula we began with.

I also remark that once all the quantifiers have been placed at the front, then the quantifier-free part of the formula that follows them may, of course, be manipulated in the same way as in truth-functional logic. For example, it may be reworked into DNF, or CNF, or any other form that seems useful for the purpose at hand.

EXERCISES

3.7.1. Restore the missing proof of lemma 3(b). [You will need to use the basic principle for disjunction (2.5.G), and the introduction and elimination rules for $\exists$.]

3.7.2. For each of the following formulae, find an equivalent formula in PNF:

(a) $\exists x Fx \vee \neg \forall x Fx$.
(b) $(\forall x(Fx \rightarrow Gx) \wedge \exists x(Fx \wedge Hx)) \rightarrow \exists x(Gx \wedge Hx)$.
(c) $\forall x(Fx \wedge Gx) \leftrightarrow (\forall x Fx \wedge \forall x Gx)$.
(d) $\exists x \forall y \exists z Fxyz \rightarrow \exists x \forall y \exists z Fyzx$.

3.7.3. Our lemmas show that in any formula the quantifiers can always be driven *out*, so that no truth-functor has any quantifier in its scope. Why do they not also show that all quantifiers can be driven *in*, so that no quantifier has any truth-functor in its scope?

3.7.4.(*a*) The text asserts that there is no formula which contains just one occurrence of a (two-place) truth-functor, just one occurrence of a quantifier ($\forall$ or $\exists$), and is in PNF and equivalent to

$P \leftrightarrow \forall xFx.$

Verify this assertion. [A tedious method is to verify it one by one for each of the sixteen possible two-place truth-functors. Can you think of any short cuts?]
(*b*) What other two-place truth-functors are there, in place of $\leftrightarrow$ above, for which the same result holds?
(*c*) Can you generalize the result to truth-functors of three or more places?

3.8. Decision Procedures I: One-Place Predicates

In the logic of truth-functors the procedure of drawing up a full truth-table is a *decision procedure* for validity. This means that it is a procedure you can apply to any formula whatever, to determine whether it is valid, and it will always provide the answer in a finite number of steps. There is no such decision procedure for the general logic of quantifiers—a point which we shall explore more fully in Section 3.10. There are, however, *decision procedures for special cases*, i.e. for formulae of this or that special kind. The most generally known of these special cases is the case of one-place (or monadic) predicate-letters. There is a procedure one can apply to any formula in which the only predicate-letters to appear are one-place letters, and which will determine, in a finite number of steps, whether that formula is valid or not.

The procedure has two stages, and the first of them is the reverse of the procedure for forming PNF. To form PNF one 'drives the quantifiers *out*' so that they all end up at the beginning of the formula. Our decision procedure begins by 'driving the quantifiers *in*', so that at the end of the process no quantifier is in the scope of any other quantifier, but on the contrary in the scope of a quantifier one finds only open formulae with their free variable bound by that quantifier. Let us call this an *elementary* quantification. An elementary quantification, then, is a closed formula with one quantifier at the beginning and no other quantifiers. Examples would be

$\forall x(Fx \to Gx) \quad \exists x(Fx \wedge \neg Gx) \quad \forall y((Fy \wedge Gy \wedge \neg Hy) \to \neg Fy).$

It is clear that if two-place predicates are present, there need not be any way of paraphrasing a formula so that it contains only elementary quantifications. For example, the formula

$\forall x \exists yFxy$

is not elementary, since the first quantifier, $\forall x$, has another quantifier in its scope. (Also the second quantifier, $\exists y$, has a free x within its scope.) Moreover, there is clearly no way of finding a formula that is equivalent to this one and that does contain only elementary quantifications. The procedure of 'driving the quantifiers in', then, is not generally applicable. Of course, there are many formulae in which quantifiers can be 'driven in' to some extent, and it is nearly always useful to do so for increased comprehensibility. But it is only when predicate-letters of two (or more) places are absent that we can guarantee to drive the quantifiers in so far that only elementary quantifications remain.

For simplicity let us suppose that our language contains only $\neg, \wedge, \vee, \forall, \exists$. (Other truth-functors must therefore be re-expressed in these terms.) The relevant laws that we need for driving quantifiers in are then lemmas $2(a)$–$3(b)$ of the previous section (in particular $2(b)$ and $3(a)$) and in addition

$4(a)$ $\forall\xi\phi \wedge \forall\xi\psi \dashv\vDash \forall\xi(\phi \wedge \psi)$ (b) $\exists\xi\phi \vee \exists\xi\psi \dashv\vDash \exists\xi(\phi \vee \psi).$

Proof of these laws is left as an exercise. (It may be noted that $2(a)$ is actually a special case of $4(a)$, for when ψ does not contain ξ free then $\psi \dashv\vDash \forall\xi\psi$. Similarly $3(b)$ is a special case of $4(b)$.) Since our object now is to drive the quantifiers in rather than to drive them out, we shall apply these equivalences from right to left. Looked at in this way, $4(a)$ tells us that a universal quantifier may be 'distributed through' a conjunction, and then law $2(b)$ of the previous section tells us that it may be 'confined to' the relevant part of a disjunction, i.e. that part in which its variable occurs free. (This may involve reordering the disjuncts, so as to bring together those that contain the relevant free variable.) It follows that if we have a universal quantifier which is followed by a quantifier-free open formula in CNF, then by these two operations the universal quantifier may be driven in as far as it will go, so that in the resulting quantifications the atomic formulae within the scope of a quantifier all contain its variable free. If, then, these atomic formulae contain only one-place predicates, and hence no *other* names or variables, the resulting quantifications must be elementary. In a similar way, if we have an existential quantifier followed by a quantifier-free formula in DNF, then by law $4(b)$ we may distribute the existential quantifier through the disjunction so that each of the resulting quantifiers governs a conjunction, delete any occurrences that then become vacuous, and by law $3(a)$ confine the remaining quantifiers to that part of the conjunction that contains the relevant variables.

Here is a very simple example. Suppose we begin with the open formula

$\exists x(Fx \leftrightarrow Gy)$.

We first express the quantifier-free part in DNF, e.g. thus:

$\exists x((Fx \land Gy) \lor (\neg Fx \land \neg Gy))$.

Distributing the quantifier through the disjunction yields

$\exists x((Fx \land Gy) \lor \exists x(\neg Fx \land \neg Gy))$.

Then we confine each resulting quantifier to the relevant part of its conjunction, to obtain

$(\exists x Fx \land Gy) \lor (\exists x \neg Fx \land \neg Gy)$.

This is the desired result, since each of the quantifications shown is now elementary.

It is now simple to describe a recipe by which quantifiers can always be driven in to form elementary quantifications. We may suppose that the formula we begin with is in PNF. Then we start with the rightmost quantifier, i.e. the quantifier which has no other quantifier in its scope, but is followed by a quantifier-free formula. If this quantifier is $\forall$, we express what follows it in CNF, and if it is $\exists$ we express what follows it in DNF. Then we go through the operations just described, to move that quantifier in as far as it will go, which will result in the formation of one or more elementary quantifications. Next we go back to the rightmost quantifier that is still left in the prefix. Its scope will not be quantifier-free, but all the quantifications that it contains will be elementary. Henceforth we treat these elementary quantifications as if they were atomic formulae. That is, if the quantifier we are now considering is $\forall$, then we express what follows it in a form which *would be* CNF, if the elementary quantifications were atomic formulae. Similarly with $\exists$ and DNF. The operation of distributing the quantifier through, and then confining its scope to the open formulae which contain its variable, is evidently not affected by the presence of other elementary quantifications already formed. For we have noted that an elementary quantification must be a *closed* formula, and therefore cannot interfere with the rearrangement of any remaining open formulae. Having dealt in this way with the second quantifier in the prefix (counting from the right), we can then go back and deal with the third, and so on until all are exhausted. At each stage, when expressing the scope of a quantifier in CNF or in DNF, as appropriate, we treat all the elementary quantifications in it as if they were atomic formulae, and we take the quantifiers in such an order that the only quantifications to be found within the scope of the quantifier that we are dealing with are elementary. Clearly any formula can be transformed in this way, so long as it does not contain predicate-letters of two (or more) places. So this completes the first stage of our operation.

The recipe just given can be extremely tedious to apply in practice, so for practical purposes it pays to be familiar with more ways of driving quantifiers in than I have mentioned, and to think all the time whether some step can usefully be abridged. I illustrate this point with the quite complex example

$$\exists x \forall y \forall z(((Fx{\to}Gy){\to}Hx) \to ((Fz{\to}Gx){\to}Hz)).$$

According to the recipe, our first task is to eliminate $\to$ in favour of $\neg, \wedge, \vee$. Using the definition of $\to$ in terms of $\neg$ and $\vee$, this leads to

$$\exists x \forall y \forall z(\neg(\neg(\neg Fx \vee Gy) \vee Hx) \vee (\neg(\neg Fz \vee Gx) \vee Hz)).$$

Applying some obvious simplifications, so that the negation sign comes to govern only atomic formulae, we can rewrite this as

$$\exists x \forall y \forall z(((\neg Fx \vee Gy) \wedge \neg Hx) \vee ((Fz \wedge \neg Gx) \vee Hz)).$$

We now look at the first quantifier to be moved in, namely $\forall z$. A glance at the formula shows that z is not free in the first main disjunct, so the quantifier could be shifted at once to the second main disjunct, to form

$$\exists x \forall y(((\neg Fx \vee Gy) \wedge \neg Hx) \vee \forall z((Fz \wedge \neg Gx) \vee Hz)).$$

Then the next problem would be to put into CNF the now reduced scope of the quantifier $\forall z$. To continue with this line of thought, for the moment, one would notice next that y is not free in the second disjunct, so the scope of the quantifier $\forall y$ can be restricted to the first disjunct only, and by a couple of further moves it can in fact be confined to the atomic formula Gy without more ado. But let us come back to the directions of the recipe. It says that, before we do anything with the quantifier $\forall z$, we must first put into CNF the *whole* of the long formula that follows it. This is a tedious operation, involving several applications of the law of distribution, but if we persevere with it we come up with

$$\exists x \forall y \forall z[(\neg Fx \vee Gy \vee Fz \vee Hz) \wedge (\neg Fx \vee Gy \vee \neg Gx \vee Hz)$$
$$\wedge (\neg Hx \vee Fz \vee Hz) \wedge (\neg Hx \vee \neg Gx \vee Hz)].$$

We now distribute $\forall z$ through this whole conjunction, to get

$$\exists x \forall y[\forall z(\neg Fx \vee Gy \vee Fz \vee Hz) \wedge \forall z(\neg Fx \vee Gy \vee \neg Gx \vee Hz)$$
$$\wedge \forall z(\neg Hx \vee Fz \vee Hz) \wedge \forall z(\neg Hx \vee \neg Gx \vee Hz)].$$

Finally, the several occurrences of $\forall z$ are confined to the relevant parts of their disjunctions, yielding

$$\exists x \forall y [((\neg Fx \lor Gy \lor \forall z(Fz \lor Hz)) \land (\neg Fx \lor Gy \lor \neg Gx \lor \forall zHz)$$
$$\land (\neg Hx \lor \forall z(Fz \lor Hz)) \land (\neg Hx \lor \neg Gx \lor \forall zHz)].$$

This has dealt with the quantifier $\forall z$, according to the recipe, so we now turn our attention to the next quantifier to be moved in, namely $\forall y$. This requires to be followed by a formula in CNF, if we count elementary quantifications as atomic formulae, and mercifully that is what we already have. So we distribute $\forall y$ through the conjunction, deleting its occurrences where it would be vacuous, thus obtaining

$$\exists x [\forall y(\neg Fx \lor Gy \lor \forall z(Fz \lor Hz)) \land \forall y(\neg Fx \lor Gy \lor \neg Gx \lor \forall zHz)$$
$$\land (\neg Hx \lor \forall z(Fz \lor Hz)) \land (\neg Hx \lor \neg Gx \lor \forall zHz)].$$

Then we confine this quantifier to the relevant parts of the disjunctions it governs, to get

$$\exists x [(\neg Fx \lor \forall yGy \lor \forall z(Fz \lor Hz)) \land (\neg Fx \lor \forall yGy \lor \neg Gx \lor \forall zHz)$$
$$\land (\neg Hx \lor \forall z(Fz \lor Hz)) \land (\neg Hx \lor \neg Gx \lor \forall zHz)].$$

Finally, we turn our attention to the quantifier $\exists x$. To deal with this, we must now re-express the whole of its scope in DNF, treating the elementary quantifications within it as atomic formulae. After some considerable labour, we come up with this result:

$$\exists x [(\neg Fx \land \neg Hx) \lor (\forall yGy \land \neg Hx) \lor (\forall z(Fz \lor Hz) \land \forall zHz)$$
$$\lor (\forall z(Fz \lor Hz) \land \neg Gx)].$$

Distributing the existential quantifier through this disjunction, and deleting it where it is vacuous, we get

$$\exists x(\neg Fx \land \neg Hx) \lor \exists x(\forall yGy \land \neg Hx) \lor (\forall z(Fz \lor Hz) \land \forall zHz)$$
$$\lor \exists x(\forall z(Fz \lor Hz) \land \neg Gx).$$

Finally, we confine the quantifier $\exists x$ to the relevant parts of the conjunctions that it governs, and we reach

$$\exists x(\neg Fx \land \neg Hx) \lor (\forall yGy \land \exists x \neg Hx) \lor (\forall z(Fz \lor Hz) \land \forall zHz)$$
$$\lor (\forall z(Fz \lor Hz) \land \exists x \neg Gx).$$

This completes the first stage of our procedure, following the recipe.

At the start of this example of how to follow the recipe, I pointed out some simplifications that could be made. You are invited to follow these through. But I here introduce a further kind of simplification, whereby we do not bother (until we have to) to re-express our formula in terms of $\neg, \land, \lor$. For quantifiers can be moved in and out directly over $\rightarrow$, without any initial paraphrasing. Answering to laws 2–3 of the previous section, we have, *provided ξ is not free in ψ,*

$$\psi\to\forall\xi\phi \ \ =\!\!\models\ \ \forall\xi(\psi\to\phi) \qquad \psi\to\exists\xi\phi \ \ =\!\!\models\ \ \exists\xi(\psi\to\phi)$$
$$\forall\xi\phi\to\psi \ \ =\!\!\models\ \ \exists\xi(\phi\to\psi) \qquad \exists\xi\phi\to\psi \ \ =\!\!\models\ \ \forall\xi(\phi\to\psi).$$

And answering to law 4 of this section, we have

$$\exists\xi(\phi\to\psi) \ \ =\!\!\models\ \ \forall\xi\phi\to\exists\xi\phi.$$

Applying these laws to our formula, without any prior transformation into DNF or CNF, we may at once carry out the following reductions:

$$\exists x\forall y\forall z[((Fx\to Gy)\to Hx) \to ((Fz\to Gx)\to Hz)]$$
$$\exists x\forall y[((Fx\to Gy)\to Hx) \to \forall z((Fz\to Gx)\to Hz)]$$
$$\exists x[\exists y((Fx\to Gy)\to Hx) \to \forall z((Fz\to Gx)\to Hz)]$$
$$\exists x[(\forall y((Fx\to Gy)\to Hx) \to \forall z((Fz\to Gx)\to Hz)]$$
$$\exists x[(Fx\to\forall y Gy)\to Hx) \to \forall z((Fz\to Gx)\to Hz)]$$
$$[\forall x((Fx\to\forall y Gy)\to Hx) \to \exists x\forall z((Fz\to Gx)\to Hz)].$$

To make further progress we must now do something along the lines of introducing a CNF to follow the two universal quantifiers $\forall x$ and $\forall z$. Here is a suitable equivalence to apply:

$$(\phi\to\psi)\to\xi \ \ =\!\!\models\ \ (\neg\phi\to\xi) \wedge (\psi\to\xi).$$

Making use of this, and distributing the universal quantifiers through the conjunctions thus formed, we can then continue with the previous laws in order to complete our task:

$$\forall x((\neg Fx\to Hx) \wedge (\forall y Gy\to Hx)) \to \exists x\forall z((\neg Fz\to Hz) \wedge (Gx\to Hz))$$
$$(\forall x(\neg Fx\to Hx) \wedge \forall x(\forall y Gy\to Hx)) \to \exists x(\forall z(\neg Fz\to Hz)$$
$$\wedge \forall z(Gx\to Hz))$$
$$(\forall x(\neg Fx\to Hx) \wedge (\forall y Gy\to\forall x Hx)) \to (\forall z(\neg Fz\to Hz)$$
$$\wedge \exists x(Gx\to\forall z Hz))$$
$$(\forall x(\neg Fx\to Hx) \wedge (\forall y Gy\to\forall x Hx)) \to (\forall z(\neg Fz\to Hz)$$
$$\wedge (\forall x Gx\to\forall z Hz)).$$

This is the required result, since all the quantifications are now elementary. At first sight, it may not look very like the result that we first reached by following the recipe, but in fact only a little calculation is needed to show that the two are equivalent, the first being, in fact, the natural DNF transform of the second.

The moral is that there are *many* ways of moving the quantifiers into a formula. For practical purposes, it is best to be familiar with a number of relevant laws, and to apply them in whatever order best promises to reduce labour. But a set of rules, which one should always follow, and which will always minimize labour, would have to be very complex indeed.

We now come to the second stage of the decision procedure, which aims to decide the validity of formulae in which all the quantifications are elementary. It will simplify matters if we begin by supposing that the formula does not contain either name-letters or sentence-letters, so that its only atomic formulae are those formed from a one-place predicate and a variable. Different atomic formulae may contain different variables, but in fact there is no need for this, since each quantification is isolated from every other. So clarity is introduced by relettering all the variables in the same way, say as x, and we will suppose this done. This in itself can often enable one to see at a glance that the formula we are concerned with is or is not valid. For example, the formula we reached in our second example of how to drive quantifiers in (i.e. not following the recipe) is at once seen to be a tautology when the variables are relettered in this way, since it has the overall form $\phi \to \phi$. The formula we reached by following the recipe is not quite a tautology under this treatment, but it would quickly become one as soon as we take the next step of the reductive procedure.

This next step is to rewrite all occurrences of the universal quantifier $\forall \xi$ as occurrences of $\neg \exists \xi \neg$, so that it is only the existential quantifier that appears. At the same time we can simplify the quantifier-free formula that is the scope of a quantifier so that it is a conjunction of atomic formulae or their negations. Let us call this a *basic* elementary quantification. If we have been following the recipe, any existential quantification reached at the end of the first stage will already be of this form, and any universal quantification reached then will have as its scope a disjunction of atomic formulae or their negations. So at the same time as converting the universal quantifier to an existential one, we need only apply De Morgan's law to obtain the desired result. For example, the clause

$$\forall z(Fz \lor Hz),$$

which forms part of the result we reached by applying the recipe, is transformed thus

$$\forall x(Fx \lor Hx)$$
$$\neg \exists x \neg (Fx \lor Hx)$$
$$\neg \exists x(\neg Fx \land \neg Hx).$$

If we have not been following the recipe, then a little more work may be needed at this stage. Once all the quantifiers have been made into existential quantifiers, we shall need to express the scope of each quantifier in DNF, and then distribute the existential quantifier through any disjunction signs that turn up. The result so far, then, is that our formula has been transformed into a truth-function of basic elementary quantifications, i.e. formulae which contain an existential quantifier governing a conjunction of atomic formulae or their negations.

The final transformations needed are analogous to those required to change a formula in ordinary DNF into *perfect* DNF, except that we are applying these transformations *within* the elementary quantifications. Within each quantification we order the atomic formulae alphabetically, and at the same time delete any repetitions. If a quantification contains both an atomic formula and its negation, then that whole quantification is replaced by $\perp$. Then we list all the predicate-letters that occur anywhere in our formula, and ensure that every basic elementary quantification contains every predicate-letter. If a quantification is missing some letter, then within the scope of the quantifier we apply the law of development, i.e.

$$\phi \quad =\!\!\mid\!\!= \quad (\phi\wedge\psi)\vee(\phi\wedge\neg\psi)$$

to add the missing letter, and immediately distribute the quantifier (which is existential) through the disjunction so formed. When this process is completed, and all the same predicate-letters appear in each basic elementary quantification, our transformations are finished. The formula is now written in a form which can be mechanically tested for validity.

The test is essentially a truth-table test, in which each basic elementary quantification is treated as an atomic formula. For example, if we are considering just three predicate-letters, say F, G, H, then our basic elementary quantifications will be such formulae as

$$\exists x(Fx \wedge Gx \wedge Hx)$$
$$\exists x(Fx \wedge Gx \wedge \neg Hx)$$
$$\exists x(Fx \wedge \neg Gx \wedge Hx).$$

It is convenient at this point (or, indeed, earlier) to adopt a shortened way of writing these basic elementary quantifications. For any predicate-letter Φ, let us write $\bar{\Phi}$ in place of $\neg\Phi$, and simply drop all occurrences of x and of $\wedge$ as no longer needed. So the three examples above would simply become

$$\exists(FGH)$$
$$\exists(FG\bar{H})$$
$$\exists(F\bar{G}H).$$

Our formula is thus a truth-function of basic elementary quantifications such as these. To evaluate the formula as a whole, then, we need only consider two possibilities for each such quantification: either it is true, or it is false. But we need to make one modification to a standard truth-table. If it so happens that our formula with the three letters F, G, H contains every one of the eight possible basic elementary quantifications, then in drawing up the truth-table we omit the very last line which represents the situation in which every one of these eight possible quantifications is false. For that situation would only be possible if nothing existed at all, i.e. if the domain of discourse was empty. But we have already said that this is not a situation we permit, and therefore the last line of the truth-table does not represent any genuine possibility. So we omit it.

The same applies when our formula contains some other number of predicate-letters. If it also contains the maximum number of basic elementary quantifications that can be formed from those letters, so that each one figures in the truth-table, then we ignore the last line of the truth-table when testing for validity. That is, the formula is valid if, on the truth-table test, it is true in every line except the last, and it is invalid if it is false in some line other than the last. The reason for this claim is, I hope, obvious; if the formula is false in some line (other than the last), then we can easily construct an interpretation in which it is false, for this only requires us to choose a domain, and extensions for the predicate-letters on that domain, which verify the elementary quantifications counted as true in that line, and falsify those counted false. This is entirely straightforward. (There will be one element in the domain for each elementary quantification that is to be true, and no others). On the other hand if the formula comes out true in every line, except possibly the last, then no such falsifying interpretation is possible. Consequently, the formula must be valid.

I remark at this point that truth-tables may be used to test not just single formulae but also any finite sequents (as was observed on pp. 25–6). The point still applies in the present context. Given any finite sequent to be tested for correctness, we can if we wish express it as a single formula to be tested for validity, since

$$\Gamma \vDash \phi \quad \text{iff} \quad \vDash C(\Gamma) \to \phi$$
$$\Gamma \vDash \quad \text{iff} \quad \vDash \neg C(\Gamma),$$

where $C(\Gamma)$ is the conjunction of all the formulae in Γ. But there is no need to invoke this roundabout procedure. All that we need to do is to re-express *each* formula in our sequent as a truth-function of basic elementary quantifications, and then the truth-table test can be applied directly to that whole sequent, with the same modification as before: if our sequent happens to contain all the possible basic elementary quantifications that can be formed

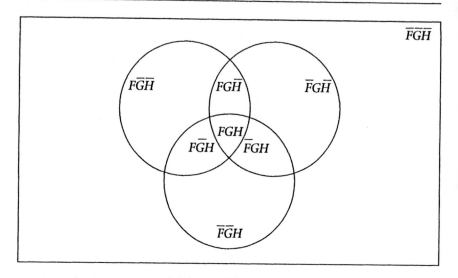

from its predicate-letters, then the last line of the truth-table, in which all of these are assigned F, is disregarded.

There is an interesting connection between the decision procedure just explained and the method of Venn diagrams, which is a traditional method for testing the validity of syllogisms. Syllogisms are arguments which involve three predicates, which we may represent by F, G, H, and a Venn diagram consists of three interlocking circles—one for F, one for G, and one for H—which between them divide the universe into eight compartments, answering to the eight possible basic elementary quantifications with three predicate-letters, as in the figure. The top left circle represents the things that are F, the top right circle the things that are G, and the bottom circle the things that are H. A syllogism is made up of three propositions, i.e. two premisses and one conclusion, which each take a very simple form: either 'All F are G' or 'No F are G' or 'Some F are G' or 'Some F are not G'. Consequently, one can test a syllogism by mapping onto the diagram the information contained in its premisses, and then observing whether this includes the information contained in the conclusion. The information is written on the diagram by marking suitable compartments of the universe as empty or non-empty, and that is exactly what we do when we consider the case of a basic elementary quantification being false or being true. But there are two significant ways in which our procedure is more general than this traditional use of Venn diagrams. First, even if we confine our attention to sequents which use only three predicate-letters, still many of them are much more complicated than syllogisms, and there need not be any way of mapping these more complicated statements onto the diagram. Truth-tables suffer from no such limitation. Second, our method is, of course, applicable no matter how many predicate-letters are involved, whereas diagrams for larger numbers of predicate-letters do become very unwieldy. (But they are not impossible, as Lewis Carroll (1896) showed.)

I end by remarking that a different version of this decision procedure will be given in the next chapter (Section 4.8), which is altogether simpler to apply in practice. The first stage of the procedure is the same in each case, namely to drive the quantifiers in until no quantifier is within the scope of any other. But in the next chapter there will be no need for any further manipulation of the formula; it can then be tested directly.

EXERCISES

3.8.1.(*a*) Supply proofs for lemmas 4(*a*) and 4(*b*) on p. 116.
(*b*) Verify the lemmas for → stated on p. 120. [Method: express → in terms of ¬ and ∨, and use lemmas already established.]

3.8.2. The four valid syllogistic moods in what Aristotle called 'the first figure' are these:

(*a*) All *F* are *G*	(*b*) All *F* are *G*
All *G* are *H*	No *G* are *H*
All *F* are *H*	No *F* are *H*
(*c*) Some *F* are *G*	(*d*) Some *F* are *G*
All *G* are *H*	No *G* are *H*
Some *F* are *H*	Some *F* are not *H*.

Express each of these as a sequent in a suitable language for quantifiers, and test it for validity. [Note that the sequents to be tested already have all their quantifiers driven in, so only the second stage of the procedure of this section is required. For practice, carry this stage out in full, even though it is already clear what the result must be.]

3.8.3. Test the following formulae for validity:

(*a*) $\forall z \exists y \exists x [\neg Fx \lor Gy \lor Hy \lor (Fz \land \neg Gz \land \neg Hz)]$.
(*b*) $\exists w \forall z \exists y \forall x [(Fw \rightarrow Gz) \rightarrow (Fx \rightarrow Gy)]$.
(*c*) $\forall x (Fx \rightarrow \forall y (Fy \rightarrow ((Gx \rightarrow Gy) \lor \forall z Fz)))$.
(*d*) $\exists z \forall y \forall x [Fx \rightarrow (Fy \rightarrow (Gz \rightarrow (Hy \rightarrow Fx)))]$.

Use any convenient method of driving the quantifiers in. If at any point it becomes clear what the result of the test must be, you may stop at that point, giving a brief explanation of why the result is now clear.

3.8.4. In the text, the decision procedure was restricted to formulae lacking sentence-letters and lacking name-letters. Show how these restrictions can be removed. [Sentence-letters are easy to accommodate; name-letters are more difficult. The simple idea of treating the atomic formula '*Fa*' as just another sentence-letter will not do. Why not? (A solution for name-letters will automatically emerge from the methods of the next section.)]

3.9. Decision Procedures II: ∀∃-Formulae

There are various special decision procedures for special classes of formulae. In this section I give another, which applies to all formulae in PNF where the quantifiers in the prefix are arranged in a special way, namely with all universal quantifiers preceding all existential quantifiers. These are called ∀∃-formulae. This new procedure is more general than the one given in the last section, for any formula which contains only one-place predicate-letters is equivalent to an ∀∃-formula (Exercise 3.9.1), but there are other ∀∃-formulae as well. Besides, the method of argument in this case is rather different from the last, being more closely related to the semantics for these formulae.

I begin with a lemma on the semantics of quantifier-free closed formulae, i.e. formulae which are built up just from predicate-letters and name-letters:

> *Lemma on quantifier-free formulae.* If φ is a closed formula without quantifiers which is not a tautology, then there is an interpretation in which φ is false, and which has in its domain just one element for each distinct name-letter in φ, and nothing else.

Proof. If φ is not a tautology, then there is a way of assigning truth-values to the atomic formulae in φ which makes φ false. Let $\mathcal{A}$ be such an assignment. Then we can construct an interpretation I to mirror $\mathcal{A}$ as follows. We select a domain with as many elements as there are name-letters in φ.[24] We interpret each name-letter in φ as denoting one of these elements, assigning a different denotation to each different letter. We interpret each predicate-letter Φ^n in φ on this domain, by setting $\langle x_1,...,x_n \rangle \in |\Phi^n|$ iff there are name-letters $\alpha_1,...,\alpha_n$, in φ such that $x_1 = |\alpha_1|,...,x_n = |\alpha_n|$, and the atomic formula $\Phi^n \alpha_1...\alpha_n$ is true in the assignment $\mathcal{A}$. (This is unambiguous, since no two names in φ name the same element.) Then I is so specified that it must

---

[24] If φ contains no name-letters (because all of its predicate-letters are zero-place letters), then select any one-element domain. But I shall generally ignore this degenerate case in what follows.

assign to each atomic formula the same value as A does, and hence φ is false in I. This completes the proof.

An evident corollary of this lemma is that a quantifier-free closed formula is valid (i.e. true in every interpretation) iff it is a tautology. For our lemma tells us that if it is not a tautology, then it is not valid, and it is easy to see that if it is a tautology, it must be valid. Consequently, there is certainly a decision procedure for determining the validity of such quantifier-free formulae, for example the truth-table test. The technique of the procedure to be developed in this section is to *reduce* the question of the validity of an ∀∃-formula to the question of the validity of a related quantifier-free formula. We shall build up to this step by step, making further use of the initial lemma, which allows us to restrict our attention to interpretations with nice small domains.

Our first step concerns formulae which begin just with a string of existential quantifiers. As a useful abbreviation, let us agree to write such a string by just writing the first occurrence of ∃ and suppressing all the others. For example, we shall abbreviate

$$\exists x \exists y \exists z \quad \text{to} \quad \exists xyz$$

and similarly,

$$\forall x \forall y \forall z \quad \text{to} \quad \forall xyz.$$

Any string of existential quantifiers, then, may be represented by $\exists x_1...x_n$. Using this abbreviation, our first step is

(1) If φ is quantifier-free, contains no name-letters, and only the variables $x_1,...,x_m$, then

$$\vDash \exists x_1...x_n\varphi \quad \text{iff} \quad \vDash \varphi(a/x_1,...,a/x_n).$$

Proof. L→R. Assume $\nvDash \varphi(a/x_1,...,a/x_n)$. Then as we have observed this formula is not a tautology, so by our lemma there is an interpretation I with a domain of just one element in which it is false. Suppose that $\exists x_1...x_n\varphi$ is true in I. By the semantics for ∃, applied n times, this means that there are (distinct) name-letters $\alpha_1,...,\alpha_n$, and an interpretation I^* which is just like I except perhaps in the denotation it assigns to these names, such that $\varphi(\alpha_1/x_1,...,\alpha_n/x_n)$ is true in I^*. But in fact I^* must assign the same denotation to all these names as I assigns to the name a, since I and I^* have the same domain, and there is only one element in that domain. Moreover, I^* interprets the name a, either because a is one of the names $\alpha_1,...,\alpha_n$, or if not because it inherits the interpretation of a from I. Thus by the lemma on extensionality we may substitute a for each of $\alpha_1,...,\alpha_n$, and deduce that $\varphi(a/x_1,...,a/x_n)$ is true in I^*. But this is impossible. For the same formula is now false in I and true in I^*, though those interpretations agree with one another on all the letters in that formula, which contradicts our lemma on interpretations. So the supposition must be rejected, and $\exists x_1...x_n\varphi$ is not true in I. Hence $\not\models \exists x_1...x_n\varphi$, as desired.

R→L. By repeated applications of ∃-introduction (3.6.F) we have

$$\varphi(a/x_1,...,a/x_n) \models \exists x_1...x_n\varphi.$$

From this the desired result follows by CUT.

This completes the proof of our first step, which shows how one very simple kind of quantified formula can be 'reduced' to a quantifier-free formula—not in the sense that the two formulae are logically equivalent, for that is certainly not the case here, but in the sense that the one is valid iff the other is, so that when we are testing for validity we can do so by applying a familiar test to the quantifier-free formula. I now proceed to the second step, which removes the restriction on name-letters that was imposed in step (1).

(2) If φ is quantifier-free, and contains only the name-letters $a_1,...,a_m$, and only the variables $x_1,...,x_n$, then

$$\models \exists x_1...x_n\varphi \quad \text{iff} \quad \models V(\varphi(a_i/x_j)),$$

where $V(\varphi(a_i/x_j)$ is the disjunction of *all* the ways of substituting the names $a_1,...,a_m$ for the variables $x_1,...,x_n$.

To illustrate, if φ contains just the variables x,y, and just the name-letters a,b, then $V(\varphi(a_i/x_j))$ is

$$\varphi(a/x,a/y) \vee \varphi(a/x,b/y) \vee \varphi(b/x,a/y) \vee \varphi(b/x,b/y).$$

If φ also contains the name-letter c, then we must add five more clauses to this disjunction, namely

$$\varphi(c/x,a/y) \vee \varphi(c/x,b/y) \vee \varphi(c/x,c/y) \vee \varphi(b/x,c/y) \vee \varphi(a/x,c/y).$$

Similarly, for yet more name-letters, or more variables.

Proof. L→R. Assume $\not\models V(\varphi(a_i/x_j))$. Then this formula is not a tautology, so by our lemma there is an interpretation I in which it is false, which has a domain of just m elements, with each different name a_i denoting a different element of this domain. Suppose also that $\exists x_1...x_n\varphi$ is true in I. Then this yields a contradiction, just as in step (1). For it implies that there are names

$\alpha_1,...,\alpha_n$ and an interpretation I^* which is like I except perhaps for the denotations of these names, such that $\varphi(\alpha_1/x_1,...,\alpha_n/x_n)$ is true in I^*. But every element of the domain is denoted by one of the names $a_1,...,a_m$, so by the lemma on extensionality it must be possible to replace each name α_i by one of the original names a_i, while preserving truth-value in I^*. But this means that I^* interprets some disjunct of $V(\varphi(a_i/x_j))$ as true, whereas I interprets each disjunct as false, which is impossible. We conclude, then, that $\exists x_1...x_n\varphi$ is not true in I, and hence $\not\models \exists x_1...x_n\varphi$.

R→L. By several applications of ∃-introduction, for each disjunct of $V(\varphi(a_i/x_j))$ we have

$$\varphi(a_i/x_j) \models \exists x_1...x_n\varphi.$$

It follows by our principle for disjunction that

$$V(\varphi(a_i/x_j)) \models \exists x_1...x_n\varphi.$$

From this the desired result follows by CUT.

Step (2) just established is in effect the result that we are aiming at, for a universally quantified formula is valid iff the result of replacing the universally quantified variables by new name-letters, not already occurring in that formula, is also valid. Our final step (3) applies this point to the question at hand:

(3) If the name-letters $a_1,...,a_m$ do not already occur in φ, then
$$\models \forall y_1...y_m\exists x_1...x_n\varphi \quad \text{iff} \quad \models \exists x_1...x_n\varphi(a_1/y_1,...,a_m/y_m).$$

Proof. L→R. By repeated applications of ∀-elimination we have

$$\forall y_1...y_m\exists x_1...x_n\varphi \models \exists x_1...x_n\varphi(a_1/y_1,...,a_m/y_m).$$

From this the result follows by CUT.

R→L. This follows by repeated applications of ∀-introduction, for the special case where Γ is null.

As step (3) states, then, an ∀∃-formula is valid iff the ∃-formula which results from it, upon replacing its universally quantified variables by new names, is also valid. And as step (2) states, this ∃-formula is valid iff a certain quantifier-free disjunction is also valid, namely one formed by substituting the names already in it for its existentially quantified variables, in all possible ways. And as we began by remarking, a quantifier-free formula can always be tested for validity in a mechanical way, e.g. by a truth-table. As special cases we note that where only universal quantifiers are present, step

(3) by itself gives us a 'reduction' to a quantifier-free formula, and where only existential quantifiers are present, we have a similar 'reduction' using either step (1) or step (2), depending on whether our formula is also free of name-letters.

Here is a simple example to illustrate how this test works in practice. Consider the formula

$$\forall x \forall y \exists z \exists w (((Rxy \wedge Fy \wedge \neg Fz) \vee (Rxy \wedge Fy \wedge Gz)) \rightarrow (Rxw \wedge Gw)).$$

To test this for validity we first replace the universally quantified variables x,y by new names, not already occurring in the formula, to obtain

$$\exists z \exists w (((Rab \wedge Fb \wedge \neg Fz) \vee (Rab \wedge Fb \wedge Gz)) \rightarrow (Rxw \wedge Gw)).$$

We next consider whether there is any way of replacing the remaining existentially quantified variables z, w by the names already present, so that the resulting formula is a tautology. In this case there is, namely by putting b both for z and for w, to obtain

$$((Rab \wedge Fb \wedge \neg Fb) \vee (Rab \wedge Fb \wedge Gb)) \rightarrow (Rab \wedge Gb).$$

We can therefore stop our test at this point, for since this formula is valid by a truth-table test, it follows, by the reasoning we have rehearsed, that the original formula is also valid. If, however, there had been no one way of substituting our existing names for the variables z, w to yield a tautology, the next step would have been to consider whether the disjunction of two or more ways of substituting names for the variables would yield a tautology. If it had turned out that the disjunction of *all four* possible ways of substituting a, b for z, w failed to yield a tautology, then we could have concluded that the original formula was not valid. But it has to be admitted that the final formula to be tested would have been uncomfortably long. In general, if this method is going to yield a positive result, then by taking a little thought one can usually obtain that result quite quickly, but to establish a negative result is generally rather tedious.

EXERCISES

3.9.1.(a) Show that, if φ is a formula with ¬,∧,∨ as its only truth-functors, and with all its quantifiers fully driven in (i.e. so that no quantifier has any other in its scope), then the quantifiers in φ can be brought to the front in any desired order. [Method: show first that any *one* quantifier can be brought to the front, leaving the others where they were. Then generalize this result.]

(*b*) Deduce that for any formula which contains only one-place predicate-letters there is an equivalent ∀∃-formula.

3.9.2. Test the following formulae for validity by first finding an equivalent ∀∃-formula:

(*a*) $\forall xyz(Rxy \wedge Ryz \to Rxz) \wedge (\forall xy(Rxy \to Ryx) \to \forall xRxx$.

(*b*) $\forall xyz(Rxy \wedge Ryz \to Rxz) \wedge \forall x\neg Rxx \to \forall xy(Rxy \to \neg Ryx)$.

(*c*) $\forall xy(Rxy \to Ryx) \to \exists x\neg\forall y(Ryx \to \neg Rxy)$.

(*d*) $\exists x\forall y(\exists zRzz \to Rxy) \to \forall x\exists y(Ryx \to \exists zRzz)$.

3.9.3. In the previous section it was observed that the decision procedure there discussed, for formulae with only one-place predicates, could automatically be extended to all finite *sequents* with only one-place predicates. Formulate a similar extension, to finite sequents, of the present procedure for ∀∃-formulae.

3.9.4.(*a*) Prove by any available means (e.g. by using the rules 3.6.F–G for ∀-introduction and ∀-elimination) that for any formula $\varphi(x,y)$ containing just x and y free

$$\forall x\exists y\varphi(x,y) \vDash \forall x(\exists y\varphi(x,y) \to Fx) \to \forall xFx.$$

(*b*) Show that, if F does not occur in $\varphi(x,y)$, then

If $\vDash \forall x(\exists y\varphi(x,y) \to Fx) \to \forall xFx$ then $\vDash \forall x\exists y\varphi(x,y)$.

[Note that the entailment in part (*a*) is not an equivalence. (This can be checked by testing a suitable ∀∃-formula.) So part (*b*) does not follow in this way, and some other method of argument is needed. (You may go back to first principles, invoking the semantics given in Section 3.4; but a quicker method is to consider a substitution for the predicate-letter F.)]

(*c*) Deduce from parts (*a*) and (*b*) that if ψ contains only two quantifiers (and only ¬,∧,∨,→ as truth-functors), then there is an ∃∀-formula ψ* such that $\vDash$ ψ iff $\vDash$ ψ*. (An ∃∀-formula is a formula in PNF with all existential quantifiers preceding all universal quantifiers.) [Method: find an ∃∀-formula that is equivalent to the longer formula above.]

(*d*) Generalize your result in (*c*) to show that for any formula ψ, no matter how many quantifiers it contains, there is an ∃∀-formula ψ* such that $\vDash$ ψ iff $\vDash$ ψ*. [Note. An ∃∀-formula is also said to be a formula in Skolem normal form. The result (*d*) was used by Gödel (1930) in his original completeness proof for the logic of quantifiers.]

3.10. The General Situation: Proofs and Counter-examples

When we were concerned just with languages for truth-functors, there was a simple and effective procedure, applicable to any formula whatever, which would determine in a finite number of steps whether that formula was valid or not. The process of drawing up a truth-table is just such a procedure. It is mechanical, in the sense that it needs no intelligence to apply it, for one could easily programme a machine to go through all the steps required. And it must yield a verdict, one way or the other, after some calculable number of steps. There is no such procedure which works for all the formulae of our languages for quantifiers. In the previous two sections we have given procedures for certain special cases, dealing only with restricted classes of formulae, but these cannot be extended to deal with all the formulae now available. In a word: there is no decision procedure for this class of formulae, as was first proved by Church (1936). (The proof, however, uses techniques which go beyond anything treated in this book, so it will not be reproduced here.)

Consequently, when faced with an arbitrary formula, we need to consider separately (*a*) whether there is a proof that it is valid, and (*b*) whether there is a proof that it is not, and there is no guarantee that we shall find either the one or the other in any specifiable number of steps. In fact, as we shall see in the next chapter, it is possible to give a procedure which searches for a proof of the validity of any desired formula, and which can be guaranteed to find a proof if the formula is in fact valid. But we do not know before we start how many steps of the procedure may be required. So after we have taken 1,000 steps—or even 10,000—we still do not know whether perhaps the next step will find a proof, or whether after all there is no proof, since the formula simply is not valid. In practice, therefore, it pays to consider also how to prove that a formula is not valid, i.e. how to find an interpretation in which that formula is false. (This is called finding a *counter-example* to the formula.) But here there is no routine that we can follow, even in principle. That is, there is no mechanical procedure which can be guaranteed to find a counter-example if there is one. The only technique that we can follow is to think about what the formula means, and hence to think up a situation in which it would be false.

The construction of counter-examples is easily illustrated in simple cases. For example, consider the formula

$$\forall x(Fx \lor Gx) \rightarrow (\forall xFx \lor \forall xGx).$$

To show that this is not a valid formula, all that we have to do is to point to the interpretation *I* in which the domain consists of just two objects *a* and *b*, and *F* is interpreted as true of one of them, while *G* is interpreted as true of the other. That is

$$\mathcal{D} = \{a,b\}$$
$$|F| = \{a\}$$
$$|G| = \{b\}.$$

On this interpretation it is stipulated that $Fx \vee Gx$ is true of a, since Fx is true of a, and that it is true of b, since Gx is true of b. Hence $Fx \vee Gx$ is true of all members of this domain, which is to say that $\forall x(Fx \vee Gx)$ is interpreted as true. But $\forall xFx$ is not interpreted as true, since Fx is not true of b, and similarly $\forall xGx$ is not interpreted as true, since Gx is not true of a. Hence $\forall xFx \vee \forall xGx$ is not true in this interpretation. Thus we have the left-hand side true and the right-hand side false, which is to say that the whole formula is interpreted as false. Since, then, there is an interpretation in which this formula is false, we conclude that it is not valid.

Many other simple formulae will yield to a similar approach, for example

$$\forall x\exists yFxy \rightarrow \exists y\forall xFxy.$$

Again, we need only a two-membered domain, and our interpretation of F can be that it relates each member of that domain to itself and to nothing else. Thus

$$\mathcal{D} = \{a,b\}$$
$$|F| = \{\langle a,a\rangle, \langle b,b\rangle\}.$$

Letting the name-letter a denote the object a of the domain, and similarly for b, we thus have Faa and Fbb both interpreted as true. Hence we also have as true both $\exists yFay$ and $\exists yFby$, and therefore in addition $\forall x\exists yFxy$. But on the other hand $\forall xFxa$ is not interpreted as true (since Fba is not true) and similarly $\forall xFxb$ is not true (since Fab is not). So in this interpretation $\exists y\forall xFxy$ is not true, and we therefore have our counter-example. For the left-hand side of our formula is true and the right-hand side is false.

In simple examples such as these we need only consider interpretations with a domain of just two elements to provide a counter-example. (You should verify that a domain of just one element will not provide a counter-example in either case.) With slightly more complex formulae it may be necessary to consider domains of three or four elements, as the exercises will show. But sometimes we need to take an interpretation with an infinite domain in order to specify a counter-example, and it is this which prevents there being a mechanical procedure for searching for a counter-example. (For we can easily devise a procedure which searches for a *finite* counter-example, and can be guaranteed to find one if one exists, namely by running through all the possibilities. A more practical procedure of this kind is given in the next chapter.) Yet the formulae which only have infinite counter-examples need not be very complicated.

Here is a simple example

$$\forall xyz(Rxy \wedge Ryz \rightarrow Rxz) \wedge \forall x\neg Rxx \rightarrow \neg\forall x\exists yRxy.$$

This formula says that if a relation R is transitive and irreflexive then it cannot also be serial, so a counter-example must construct a transitive and irreflexive relation that is serial. Now suppose that we have any element a_1 in the domain. Since R is to be serial, we must then have $\langle a_1,a_2\rangle$ in the extension of R, for some element a_2 of the domain; and since R is to be irreflexive, a_2 cannot be the same element as a_1. But then, since R is to be serial, we must also have $\langle a_2,a_3\rangle$ in the extension of R, for some element a_3 of the domain; and since R is to be transitive, that means that we must also have $\langle a_1,a_3\rangle$ in its extension; and then, for the same reason as before, a_3 cannot be the same element as a_1 or as a_2. Generalizing upon this argument, for any element a_i in the domain there must be another, a_{i+1}, which is not the same as a_i or as any of the predecessors of a_i. But that evidently implies that the domain must be infinite, and it must contain an element a_i for every natural number i. Given such a domain, we do, of course, have a falsifying interpretation. For example, we may take the domain simply to be the natural numbers (which I abbreviate to $\mathbb{N}$), and the relation to be the 'less than' relation on that domain. Thus

$$\mathcal{D} = \{x : x \in \mathbb{N}\}$$
$$|R| = \{\langle x,y\rangle : x<y\}.$$

On this interpretation R is transitive and irreflexive and serial, as required.

The skill of finding counter-examples in this way must simply be acquired by practice. Although in some cases there is a recipe that can be applied, as with the $\forall\exists$-formulae of the last section, there is no recipe that covers all the cases, as I have said. (It is worth noting, incidentally, that our last two examples are each formulae which have no $\forall\exists$-equivalent.) In practice much the same applies to the skill of finding proofs. Although in this case there *are* recipes that one could follow, it is extremely tedious to do so, and only a machine will tolerate this tedium. To find proofs with reasonable facility it is again necessary to think about what the formulae mean, and to employ one's intuitive grasp of what follows from what, and why. Thus, intelligence is needed in either case. But let us now turn our attention from counter-examples, which show that a formula is not valid, to proofs, which establish the opposite result.

From now on our proofs will be 'formal' proofs, belonging to some specified system of proofs. The system will lay down particular rules of proof, and a proof in that system must use just those rules and no others. It will be a requirement on any system of proof that there is an effective way of telling whether what we have *is* a proof in that system, i.e. a mechanical test to determine whether any particular array of formulae is or is not to count as a proof. It is for this reason that such systems of proof are called 'formal' systems: one does not need any understanding of the formulae involved in order to say what counts as a proof in the system, or to check whether this or that is an example. For the same reason, it used to be customary to count the rules of proof as part of the 'syntax' of a language, as opposed to its 'semantics', namely because one could in principle operate these rules without knowing what the language was supposed to mean. But, as we have said, that is not how it works in practice, and in any case it is quite wrong to suggest that a system of proof is constitutive of the language it applies to. On the contrary, we shall see in the following chapters that there are several systems of proof, quite different from one another, that each apply to the same languages, namely our schematic languages for quantifiers.

The decision procedures that we have given in this chapter (Sections 3.8 and 3.9) and in the last (Sections 2.4 and 2.11) are themselves systems of proof, or could easily be presented as such. But our topic from now on will be proof systems that aim to be adequate for all formulae of our languages for quantifiers without exception. So we shall want them to provide proofs of *all* the formulae that are in fact valid, and *only* of those. Where S is any such system of proof, we shall write $\vdash_S \varphi$ to mean that there is a proof of the formula φ in the system S. Then to say that only the formulae which are valid can be proved in S is to say

If $\vdash_S \varphi$ then $\vDash \varphi$.

A system S which satisfies this condition is said to be *sound*. Conversely, to say that all the formulae which are valid can be proved in S is to say

If $\vDash \varphi$ then $\vdash_S \varphi$.

A system which satisfies this condition is said to be *complete*. As it will turn out, all the systems that we shall consider will be both sound and complete, as desired. But whereas it is usually a simple matter to prove that a given system is sound, the proof of completeness is more complicated.

I remark here that in fact complete systems of proof have already been introduced in the treatment so far. As we shall see more fully later (in

Chapters 5–7), the basic principles for the truth-functors given in Section 2.5, together with the principles for the quantifiers given in Section 3.6, can easily be given a 'formal' presentation in which they do form a complete proof procedure for the languages that concern us. But that will emerge in due course. The proof procedure that I begin with in the next chapter will take a different line—one where it is more easy to see that any formula that has no proof, as specified in this procedure, must be an invalid formula.

Throughout this section so far I have simplified the discussion by concentrating on just one kind of sequent, namely a sequent $\models \varphi$ with no formula on the left and one on the right. Such a sequent says that its one formula is a valid formula, i.e. true in every interpretation of its vocabulary. Thus I have spoken simply of proving formulae to be valid, and of proving them to be invalid, as if validity were the only property to be considered. But in fact we have other sequents to consider too, namely those sequents $\Gamma \models \varphi$ which also have formulae on the left, and assert an entailment; and those $\Gamma \models$, which have no formulae on the right, and assert an inconsistency. It is obvious that the strategy of providing a counter-example to disprove a sequent can equally well be applied to these sequents too. It is also the case that a proof may be directly aimed at establishing the correctness of one or other of these kinds of sequents, rather than the simple kind of sequent considered so far. (In fact the system of proof to be studied in Chapter 4 focuses on sequents of the form $\Gamma \models$, the system studied in Chapter 5 focuses on sequents $\models \varphi$, and the system in Chapter 6 on sequents $\Gamma \models \varphi$.) We therefore have alternative ways of formulating the conditions for soundness and completeness, namely for soundness:

$$\text{If } \Gamma \vdash_S \varphi \text{ then } \Gamma \models \varphi,$$
$$\text{If } \Gamma \vdash_S \text{ then } \Gamma \models,$$

and for completeness

$$\text{If } \Gamma \models \varphi \text{ then } \Gamma \vdash_S \varphi,$$
$$\text{If } \Gamma \models \text{ then } \Gamma \vdash_S.$$

Now provided that we may restrict our attention to the case where Γ is a *finite* set of formulae, these various conditions are likely to be equivalent to one another. As we have already remarked (p. 123), where Γ is finite we may consider the single formula $C(\Gamma)$, which is the conjunction of all the formulae in Γ, and clearly

$$\Gamma \models \varphi \quad \text{iff} \quad \models C(\Gamma) \rightarrow \varphi$$
$$\Gamma \models \quad \text{iff} \quad \models \neg C(\Gamma).$$

This shows that entailment and inconsistency can both be defined in terms of validity. Conversely, validity can, of course, be defined in terms of entailment, since it is a special case of entailment (with Γ null), and it can also be defined in terms of inconsistency, since

$$\vDash \varphi \quad \text{iff} \quad \neg\varphi \vDash.$$

We may add that entailment and inconsistency can be defined in terms of one another, since

$$\Gamma \vDash \varphi \quad \text{iff} \quad \Gamma, \neg\varphi \vDash$$
$$\Gamma, \varphi \vDash \quad \text{iff} \quad \Gamma \vDash \neg\varphi.$$

(The last defines Γ ⊨ for all cases where Γ is non-empty. If we are relying on it as a definition, then we also need the supplementary information that where Γ is empty the sequent Γ ⊨ is false (see p. 12) above).) Thus all the various kinds of sequents using the turnstile ⊨ (which is called the semantic turnstile) may be defined in terms of one another, so long as we are confining our attention to finite sequents.

One would expect that, if S is any satisfactory system of proof, then the same relationships between different kinds of sequent will also hold for sequents using the turnstile ⊢$_S$ (which is called the syntactic turnstile, for reasons already mentioned and deplored). For example, one expects that

$$\Gamma \vdash_S \varphi \quad \text{iff} \quad \vdash_S C(\Gamma) \to \varphi,$$
$$\Gamma \vdash_S \quad \text{iff} \quad \vdash_S \neg C(\Gamma),$$

and so on. Whether this is so will depend upon the features of the system S being considered. For example, if S is a system for a language which does not contain a conjunction sign, or a conditional, or a negation, then obviously the two relations just noted cannot hold in S. But if we set aside this kind of consideration, assuming that our system contains all the usual logical vocabulary, then it is reasonable to say that a satisfactory system S must either contain these relations already, or allow us to introduce them by defining the turnstile ⊢$_S$ for new contexts not already considered in S. In that case it will not matter whether soundness and completeness are defined for S in terms of one kind of sequent rather than another, for all the definitions will be equivalent. At any rate, this equivalence will certainly hold for the major systems of proof that we shall be considering in what follows.

But all this depends upon the point that we are assuming a restriction to finite sequents, and discounting those in which the set Γ on the left is an infinite set. But why should this be a reasonable assumption? This is a problem that we shall tackle in the next chapter.

EXERCISES

3.10.1. Find counter-examples to the following sequents:

(a) $\forall xyz(Rxy \wedge Ryz \rightarrow Rxz) \models \forall xyz(\neg Rxy \wedge \neg Ryz \rightarrow \neg Rxz)$.

(b) $\forall xyz(Rxy \wedge Ryz \rightarrow Rxz), \forall xy(Rxy \rightarrow Ryx) \models \forall xyz(\neg Rxy \wedge \neg Ryz \rightarrow \neg Rxz)$.

(c) $\exists xFx, \forall x(Fx \rightarrow \exists y(Rxy \wedge Fy)), \forall x(Fx \rightarrow \exists y(Rxy \wedge \neg Fy)) \models \forall xy(Rxy \rightarrow (Fx \vee Fy)) \vee \forall x(Fx \rightarrow \exists yRyx)$.

[Note: for (a) and (b) you may *if you wish* use the method of finding an equivalent $\forall\exists$-formula; but this method is unnecessarily long-winded, and anyway is not available for (c).]

3.10.2. Consider the following axioms:

(1) $\exists xyRxy$.

(2) $\forall x\neg Rxx$.

(3) $\forall xyz(Rxy \wedge Ryz \rightarrow Rxz)$.

(4) $\forall xy(Rxy \rightarrow \forall z(Rxz \vee Rzy))$.

(5) $\forall xy(Rxy \rightarrow \exists z(Rxz \wedge Rzy))$.

(*a*) Show that any interpretation in which all these axioms are true must have an infinite domain.

(*b*) Let 'Axx' abbreviate the conjunction of axioms (1)–(5), and consider the following sequents:

(i) $Axx \models \forall x\exists yRxy$.

(ii) $Axx \models \neg\forall x\exists yRxy$.

(iii) $Axx \models \neg\forall x\exists y\neg Rxy$.

(iv) $Axx \models \forall x(\exists yRxy \vee \exists yRyx)$.

(v) $Axx \models \forall xy(\forall z(Rxz \rightarrow Ryz) \vee \forall z(Ryz \rightarrow Rxz))$.

In each case, either provide a counter-example to show that the sequent is not correct, or argue (informally) that the sequent is correct. [Hint: it helps to notice that, with R as 'less than', the axioms are true of the rational numbers, and of several subsets of the rationals.]

3.10.3. Argue that there can be no decision procedure for the validity of an arbitrary $\exists\forall$-formula. [Compare Exercise 3.9.4.]

Part II

PROOFS

4

Semantic Tableaux

4.1. The Idea

A tableau proof is a proof by *reductio ad absurdum*. One begins with an assumption, and one develops the consequences of that assumption, seeking to derive an impossible consequence. If the proof succeeds, and an impossible consequence is discovered, then, of course, we conclude that the original assumption was impossible. If the proof does not succeed, and no impossible consequence comes to light, then *in some cases* we can conclude that there is nothing wrong with the opening assumption. These are the cases where it can be shown that the search for an impossible consequence has been exhaustive, and would have found such a consequence if one existed. But not all cases are like this. Sometimes all that can be said is that the proof has not yet succeeded, and we do not know whether it would succeed if carried further.

The assumptions that are investigated in this way are assumptions that certain formulae have certain truth-values. The simplest case is when we assume that all the formulae in question are true. If this assumption turns out to be impossible, then what we have shown is that the formulae are together inconsistent. But we can also consider the assumption that all the formulae are false, or that some are true and others false. For example, to show that a suggested entailment '$\phi_1, \phi_2, \phi_3, \models \psi$' is correct, one would assume that ϕ_1, ϕ_2, and ϕ_3, are all true, and that ψ is false, and then show that this combination of truth-values leads to an impossible consequence. The impossible consequence that we seek to derive, in this case and in all others too, is that one and the same formula would have to be both true and false. (Compare pp. 53–4.)

The general method is to argue in this way: if such and such a formula is to be true (or false), then also such and such *shorter* formulae must be true (or false), and that in turn requires the truth (or falsehood) of *yet shorter* formulae, and so on, until in the end we can express the requirement in terms of the truth or falsehood of the shortest possible formulae, i.e. atomic formulae. So we need a number of particular rules which state how the truth-conditions for longer formulae carry implications for the truth or falsehood of their shorter components. For example, it is obvious that if $\phi \wedge \psi$ is to be true, then ϕ must be true, and so must ψ. It is also obvious that if $\phi \wedge \psi$ is to be false, then *either* ϕ must be false, *or* ψ must be. So if the original assumption is that $\phi \wedge \psi$ is true, then we 'develop' that assumption by adding that in that case ϕ and ψ are true too. But if the original assumption is that $\phi \wedge \psi$ is false, then the 'development' of that assumption requires us to distinguish cases: *one* possibility is that ϕ is false, and we can further pursue this way of developing the original assumption; *another* possibility is that ψ is false, and we can pursue this case too. If *both* cases lead to an impossible consequence, then we can infer that the original assumption was also impossible, i.e. that $\phi \wedge \psi$ cannot be false. But of course it is necessary to consider both cases.

Initially, we shall express the assumption that the formula ϕ is true by writing out '$|\phi| = T$', and similarly the assumption that it is false by '$|\phi| = F$'. (Later, we shall introduce a more succinct style.) So the rule just noted for the functor $\wedge$ may be graphically described in this way:

$$
\begin{array}{ccc}
|\phi \wedge \psi| = T & \quad & |\phi \wedge \psi| = F \\
| & & | \\
|\phi| = T & & \\
|\psi| = T & |\phi| = F \quad & |\psi| = F
\end{array}
$$

We may add to this the dual rules for the functor $\vee$, namely

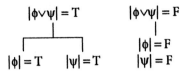

For each functor, one of the rules is a 'branching' rule, introducing two distinct cases to be considered, while the other rule is a straightforward 'non-branching' rule, which simply adds consequences of the assumption we begin with.

To give some idea of how a tableau proof works, let us at once proceed to an example. Suppose that we wish to prove one of the laws of distribution, namely

$$P \wedge (Q \vee R) \models (P \wedge Q) \vee (P \wedge R).$$

Our initial assumption is that the formula on the left is true and that on the right false. So we begin by writing down these assumptions, and adding a line underneath them to show where the assumptions end. We then develop these assumptions by using the rules for $\wedge$ and $\vee$ just noted. The result is tableau (P1) ('P' is for 'proof'). Lines (1) and (2) contain the initial assumptions. In lines (3) and (4) we apply to line (1) the sole rule that applies to it, namely the rule for $|\phi \wedge \psi| = T$. In line (3) we have already reached an atomic formula, so nothing more can be done with this, but we can apply a further rule to line (4). So in line (5) we do this, and at this point the tableau divides into two branches, each of which must now be separately pursued. At this point also, the information contained in line (1) has been exhausted: it has been broken down into a single consequence at line (3) and what is in effect the disjunction of two 'consequences' at line (5). So we now turn our attention to the information contained in line (2). The relevant rule here is the rule for $|\phi \vee \psi| = F$, which entitles us to draw the two consequences $|\phi| = F$ and $|\psi| = F$. These are therefore written in lines (6) and (7), and we have written them in each of the two branches. One does not have to treat each branch of a tableau in the same way; it is perfectly legitimate to apply one rule in one branch and a different rule in another branch. With this particular example, however, there were no alternatives to choose between at lines (6) and (7), though we now do have a choice at line (8). There is only one rule that we can use, namely that for $|\phi \wedge \psi| = F$, but we can choose whether to apply it to line (6) or to line (7). And here it pays to treat each branch differently, applying the rule to line (6) in the left branch and to line (7) in the right branch, so that is what we have done in line (8). This saves labour, because in fact we need go no further, as we have already reached the desired

143

Tableau (P1)

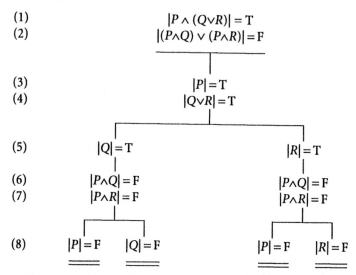

result. In line (8) each of our two branches has been split once again, so that the tableau now contains four branches, but at the same time each of the four branches comes to contain a contradiction, and thus shows itself to be impossible. The leftmost branch contains both $|P| = T$ in line (3) and $|P| = F$ in line (8); the next left contains both $|Q| = T$ in line (5) and $|Q| = F$ in line (8); the case is entirely similar with the two right-hand branches. Each branch therefore concludes with a double underline, meaning that that branch is *closed*, because, for some formula ϕ, it contains both $|\phi| = T$ and $|\phi| = F$. A closed branch therefore represents an impossible assignment of truth-values, and where every branch of a tableau is closed we can conclude that the assumptions from which the tableau begins must themselves be impossible. Thus in the present case it is not possible to find an interpretation for the letters P, Q, and R in which the formula $P \wedge (Q \vee R)$ comes out true and the formula $(P \wedge Q) \vee (P \wedge R)$ comes out false. That is to say, the entailment we set out to test has been shown to be correct.

Let us look at another example, namely the other half of the distribution law we began with:

$$(P \wedge Q) \vee (P \wedge R) \vDash P \wedge (Q \vee R).$$

A suitable tableau is (P2). Again we begin in lines (1) and (2) with the assumptions to be developed, and in line (3) we have applied to line (1) the rule appropriate to it, namely that for $|\phi \vee \psi| = T$. This splits the tableau into two branches right from the beginning. In each branch lines (4) and (5) are

Tableau (P2)

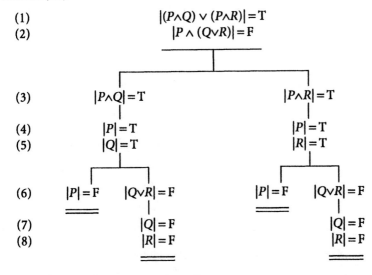

|(P∧Q) ∨ (P∧R)| = T
|P ∧ (Q∨R)| = F

obtained by applying the appropriate rule to line (3), and at this point the first assumption has been developed as far as possible. So on each branch we obtain line (6) by beginning to develop the assumption in line (2), and this splits each branch into two, so that we now have four branches to consider. But two of them can be closed off at once, since they each contain both $|P| = T$ and $|P| = F$, so we have only two that still need further development. And that development, in lines (7) and (8), allows us to close both those branches too, the one on the left because it contains both $|Q| = T$ and $|Q| = F$, the one on the right because it contains both $|R| = T$ and $|R| = F$.

Finally, let us look at a tableau that does not close. Suppose we wish to test the alleged entailment

$$(P∧Q) ∨ R \vDash (P∨Q) ∧ R.$$

An appropriate tableau is (P3). Here we have first developed the assumption in line (1), and this leads to a tableau with two branches, the left branch ending in lines (4) and (5) with $|P| = T$ and $|Q| = T$, the right branch ending in line (3) with $|R| = T$. We then add to this the development of the assumption in line (2), which divides the tableau further, so that we end with four branches. Of course the leftmost branch is closed—indeed, closed 'twice over', as it were—since it assigns contradictory truth-values both to P and to Q; and the rightmost branch is also closed. But the two middle branches are unclosed (and therefore they do not end in a double-underline). Both of these branches represent ways in which the original assumptions can be

Tableau (P3)

(1)
(2)

$$|(P \wedge Q) \vee R| = T \quad (1)$$
$$|(P \vee Q) \wedge R| = F \quad (2)$$

(3) $|P \wedge Q| = T$ $|R| = T$ (3)

(4) $|P| = T$ $|P \vee Q| = F$ $|R| = F$ (4)
(5) $|Q| = T$

                  $|P| = F$ (5)

(6) $|P \vee Q| = F$ $|R| = F$ $|Q| = F$ (6)

(7) $|P| = F$
(8) $|Q| = F$

satisfied, i.e. either by the interpretation which sets $|P| = T$, $|Q| = T$, $|R| = F$ or by the interpretation which sets $|P| = F$, $|Q| = F$, $|R| = T$.

The general structure of a semantic tableau is therefore this. It is a (finite) array of propositions assigning truth-values to formulae, arranged in a tree structure, where the tree has its 'root' at the top, and the 'branches' grow downwards. At the root are the basic assumptions that the tableau will develop. There must be at least one of these, if we are to have a tableau at all, but there may be any (finite) number of them. These assumptions at the root of the tableau will constitute an initial segment of every branch of the tableau, and the rest of the tableau will be developed from them by applying the tableau rules. The rules are of two kinds, branching rules and non-branching rules. The non-branching rules take this form: if a branch of the tableau, as developed so far, contains a line assigning a truth-value to such and such a kind of formula, then it may be extended by adding further lines assigning such and such values to certain further formulae. The branching rules, however, permit one to extend a branch, as developed so far, only by splitting that branch into two (or more) branches, showing the same initial segment up to that point, but then diverging, as a value is assigned to one formula (or formulae) on the one branch, and to another on the other. Finally, a branch which assigns contradictory values to the same formula may be closed (by writing a double-underline at its end), and once a branch is closed it is not developed any further. A tableau in which *every* branch is closed is called a closed tableau. The significance of a closed tableau is straightforward: it shows that the assumptions at its root cannot be jointly satisfied. The significance of an unclosed tableau is less straightforward: in some cases, as with the one example that we have seen so far, it shows that the assumptions at its root can be jointly satisfied. But this is not so in all cases. The question will receive further attention as we proceed.

EXERCISES

4.1.1. The tableau rules may be applied in any order. For example, we could always have begun by developing the assumption in line (2), instead of that in line (1). Experiment by varying the order in which the rules are applied in the tableaux already given for the two laws of distribution. Do you notice anything useful? (For the answer, see Section 4.4.)

4.1.2. Draw up two tableaux to verify the remaining two laws of distribution, namely

$$P \lor (Q \land R) \quad =\!\Vdash \quad (P \lor Q) \land (P \land R).$$

4.2. The Tableau Rules

Rules for the truth-functors are extremely simple to discover. In effect, they can just be read off the truth-tables, which tell us under what conditions a compound formula is true or is false. I list the rules for the five commonest truth-functors:

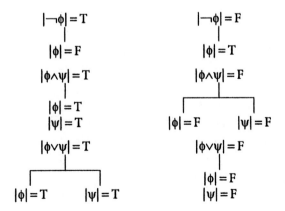

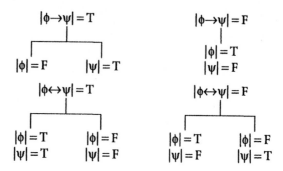

To illustrate the principle, let us consider a functor which is less common, for example $\nleftarrow$ (Exercise 2.7.1). The truth-table is

ϕ	ψ	$\phi\nleftarrow\psi$
T	T	F
T	F	F
F	T	T
F	F	F

We see from this table that the one case in which $\phi\nleftarrow\psi$ is true is the case in which ϕ is false and ψ is true, so that is no problem. There are three cases in which $\phi\nleftarrow\psi$ is false, so one might perhaps expect to find that we need a rule here which splits one branch into three. (There would be nothing wrong with such a rule.) But in fact the three cases can be summed up in this way: either ϕ is true or ψ is false. So the appropriate tableau rules are

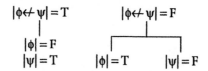

I say no more, then, about finding appropriate tableau rules for the truth-functors. Let us turn instead to the more difficult question of the quantifiers.

The rules for the truth-functors rely on facts of this kind: if a compound formula receives such and such a value in some interpretation, then its components must also receive certain values in the *same* interpretation. By contrast, the semantics for the quantifiers tell us that if a quantified formula receives such and such a value in some interpretation, then there will be *another* interpretation—related to the first but not identical to it—in which a singular instance of that formula has a certain value. We have to be careful to ensure that changing from one interpretation to another does not upset the working of the tableau.

For example, suppose that a formula $\exists\xi\phi$ is true in some interpretation I. This means that there will be some name α that is not in ϕ, and some α-variant interpretation I_α, in which the instance $\phi(\alpha/\xi)$ is true. The α-variant interpretation I_α will be just like the original interpretation I, except that it assigns to α some denotation which may be different from the denotation (if any) assigned to α by I. Now we have seen (pp. 95–6) that it follows from this criterion that if $\exists\xi\phi$ is true in I then for *every* name α that is not in ϕ there will be some α-variant interpretation in which $\phi(\alpha/\xi)$ is true. But we must confine attention to names that are not in ϕ, for all the symbols that actually occur in ϕ must be held to their existing interpretation in I, if the criterion is to do the work intended. This also has the consequence that in the variant interpretation I_α we have as true not only the desired instance $\phi(\alpha/\xi)$ but also the original formula $\exists\xi\phi$.

Now let us consider this in the context of a semantic tableau. The tableau begins at its root with a number of assumptions, each stating that some formula has a certain truth-value. But what is being assumed is, in fact, that all of these formulae can *simultaneously* receive the specified truth-values, i.e. that there is some *one* interpretation which satisfies all these assumptions at once. As the tableau is developed, we argue that if there is such an interpretation, then it must satisfy certain further constraints, so that the hypothesis being investigated, along each branch of the tableau, is that there is some one interpretation that satisfies every one of the claims made on that branch. Suppose, then, that one of these claims is that $\exists\xi\phi$ is true. If there is an interpretation which verifies $\exists\xi\phi$, then we know that there is also an interpretation which verifies both $\exists\xi\phi$ and $\phi(\alpha/\xi)$, for any name α that does not occur in ϕ. But why should we be entitled to assume that this latter interpretation *also* satisfies all the other claims made along that branch? Well, the answer is that we can assume this as long as the name α does not occur in *any* of the claims already made on that branch. For the hypothesis is that we have an interpretation I which satisfies claims about various other formulae, and at the same time makes $\exists\xi\phi$ true. So we pick any name α that does not occur either in the other formulae, or in ϕ. Then we know that there is some interpretation I_α which makes $\phi(\alpha/\xi)$ true. But I_α differs from I only in the interpretation that it assigns to α, and in no other way, so by our lemma on interpretations (3.5.A), I_α assigns the same values as I to all the formulae already on the branch. Thus, if I satisfies all claims made so far, then I_α also satisfies them, and in addition makes $\phi(\alpha/\xi)$ true. This at once gives us the following rule of development:

$$|\exists\xi\phi| = T \qquad \text{provided } \alpha \text{ does not already occur in any formula on the}$$
$$\qquad\qquad\qquad\qquad \text{branch in question}$$
$$|\phi(\alpha/\xi)| = T \qquad (\text{briefly: provided } \alpha \text{ is new})$$

Let us now turn to the universal quantifier, where things are rather more straightforward. Our first statement of the truth-condition for $\forall\xi\phi$ was this: $\forall\xi\phi$ is true in an interpretation I iff for every name α not in ϕ, and every α-variant interpretation I_α, $\phi(\alpha/\xi)$ is true in I_α. But we have already noted that this has as a consequence: if $\forall\xi\phi$ is true in I, then also for every name α that *is* in ϕ, $\phi(\alpha/\xi)$ will also be true in I. In fact $\phi(\alpha/\xi)$ will be true in I for any name α in the language of I, while for names α that are not in the language of I there will be α-variant interpretations in which $\phi(\alpha/\xi)$ is true. So we evidently have a suitable tableau rule which goes like this: suppose that there is an interpretation which satisfies all the claims made along a certain branch, including the claim that $\forall\xi\phi$ is true; then there is also an interpretation which satisfies all these claims and the claim that $\phi(\alpha/\xi)$ is true too, for any name α whatever. It will be the same interpretation if α is in the language of that interpretation (as it must be if α already occurs in some formula along the branch), and otherwise it will be an α-variant interpretation, adding α to the language. In brief, then, we may say

$$|\forall\xi\phi| = T$$
$$|\phi(\alpha/\xi)| = T$$

and there are no conditions on the name α at all.

The appropriate rules for a quantified formula assumed to be false may now be deduced, by relying on the relationship between the two quantifiers. For example, if $\exists\xi\phi$ is false, then $\forall\xi\neg\phi$ will be true, so we may develop the assumption by adding, for any name α, that $\neg\phi(\alpha/\xi)$ is true, i.e. that $\phi(\alpha/\xi)$ is false. Similarly, if $\forall\xi\phi$ is false, then $\exists\xi\neg\phi$ will be true, so we may develop the assumption by adding, for some new name α that has not yet occurred on the branch, that $\neg\phi(\alpha/\xi)$ may be assumed to be true, i.e. that $\phi(\alpha/\xi)$ may be assumed to be false. For ease of reference, I therefore set down here the four quantifier rules:

$$|\forall\xi\phi| = T \qquad\qquad |\forall\xi\phi| = F$$
$$|\phi(\alpha/\xi)| = T \qquad\qquad |\phi(\alpha/\xi)| = F$$
$$\text{for any } \alpha \qquad\qquad\quad \text{provided } \alpha \text{ is new}$$

$$|\exists\xi\phi| = T \qquad\qquad |\exists\xi\phi| = F$$
$$|\phi(\alpha/\xi)| = T \qquad\qquad |\phi(\alpha/\xi)| = F$$
$$\text{provided } \alpha \text{ is new} \qquad\quad \text{for any } \alpha$$

150

The justification of these rules for the quantifiers is a little more complex than the justification of rules for the truth-functors at the beginning of this section. But the rules themselves are simple enough to state and to apply. There is, however, an important difference between the two kinds of rules, which is this. The rules for the truth-functors reflect entailments which in fact hold in both directions. For example, if $\phi \rightarrow \psi$ is to be true, then ϕ must be false or ψ must be true, and conversely if ϕ is false or ψ true, then $\phi \rightarrow \psi$ must be true. So one may say that this rule is a correct entailment, whether it is read from top to bottom (as intended) or from bottom to top. But with the rules for the quantifiers this is not so. The formula $\exists \xi \phi$ certainly does not entail the formula $\phi(\alpha/\xi)$, for it is easy to see how the first may be true and the second false. One has to remember here the condition that α is to be a new name, and the change of interpretation from I to I_α. On the other hand, in this case the rule does hold as an entailment when read upside-down, from bottom to top. For if $\phi(\alpha/\xi)$ is true, then clearly $\exists \xi \phi$ must be true too. But with the universal quantifier it is the other way about, for $\forall \xi \phi$ does entail $\phi(\alpha/\xi)$, but not conversely. Thus $\phi(\alpha/\xi)$ does not by any means exhaust the information in $\forall \xi \phi$. This leads to complications, as we shall see.

EXERCISES

4.2.1.(*a*) There are two zero-place truth-functors, namely $\top$ and $\bot$. What are the appropriate tableau rules for them?
(*b*) There are four one-place truth-functors. What are the appropriate rules for them?
(*c*) Every truth-functor (except for the zero-place functors) can be expressed by a formula in DNF. (See Section 2.7.) Show how, if we permit branching rules which introduce many branches simultaneously, this yields a method for finding suitable tableau rules for any arbitrary truth-functor.

4.2.2. Let S and T each be systems of tableau proof, differing just in this way: S has the rule that a branch may be closed if it contains both $|\phi| = T$ and $|\phi| = F$ for *any* formula ϕ, whereas T adopts this rule only for *atomic* formulae. Otherwise the two share all the same rules, let us say just the rules for $\neg, \wedge, \vee$ given on p. 147.
(*a*) Show that, for any formula ϕ whose only truth-functors are $\neg, \wedge, \vee$, a tableau with assumptions $|\phi| = T$ and $|\phi| = F$ closes according to the rules of T. [Method: use induction on the length of ϕ.]
(*b*) Hence show that a tableau closes according to the rules of S iff it closes according to the rules of T.

4.3. A Simplified Notation

The notation we have used so far is more long-winded than it needs to be, so before the method is put to serious use I shall introduce a simplification. The notation so far uses explicitly semantical vocabulary, employing both 'T' and 'F'. This shows very clearly how it is related to the truth-tables of Section 2.4, and in particular how it carries to completion the short-cut method of truth-tables introduced on pp. 27–9. It also indicates how what is essentially the same method can be extended to deal with quantifiers. At the same time, because both 'T' and 'F' are in play, the method can treat each truth-functor and quantifier independently, with a pair of rules for each. This gives us an elegant set of rules, and in fact contains a flexibility that will be useful later on, in Chapter 7. So we shall later come back to what I shall call the 'original' notation for semantic tableaux. But now I introduce a briefer notation, which in practice saves a lot of writing, though at the cost of some loss of elegance.

The leading idea behind the new notation is that we do not need to consider both the truth and the falsehood of formulae, since a formula is false iff its negation is true. This, of course, will lead to some rephrasing of the rules. For example, the rule

$$|\phi \wedge \psi| = F$$

$$|\phi| = F \qquad |\psi| = F$$

will now be rephrased as

$$|\neg(\phi \wedge \psi)| = T$$

$$|\neg\phi| = T \qquad |\neg\psi| = T$$

Once all the rules are rephrased in this way, every line of the tableau will take the form $|\phi| = T$, and this can then be abbreviated simply to ϕ. So we shall rephrase the same rule once more, to

$$\neg(\phi \wedge \psi)$$

$$\neg\phi \qquad \neg\psi$$

By eliminating the explicitly semantical vocabulary in this way we obtain a tableau that is very much more compact. For example, tableau (P1) with

152

Tableau (P4)

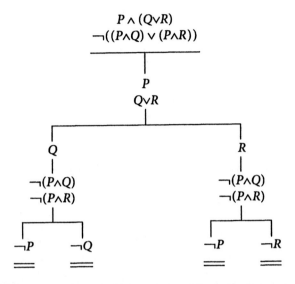

which we began will now be written as in tableau (P4). It is instructive to compare the two, for ease of writing and for ease of reading. I note also that in practice one very often omits the vertical lines that do not lead to branching, but merely indicate a new step of development, applying a new rule. This saves a little space, though it then becomes less easy to reconstruct, when reading the tableau, the rules that have been applied at each step. To simplify this task of reconstruction, one might not only retain the vertical lines, but also label each with the rule being applied at that step. ('∨' will indicate the rule for $\phi \vee \psi$, '¬∨' the rule for $\neg(\phi \vee \psi)$, and so on.) So (P4) might be expanded to (P4'). Alternatively it might be contracted just to (P4").

Perhaps one who is just beginning an acquaintance with tableau proofs might be helped by the longer form, but after a little practice you will find that the shortest form offers no problems.

I add further that in practice it helps, when constructing a tableau, to 'tick off' any formula to which a rule is being applied, so that one does not waste time by applying the same rule to the same formula twice over. At least, this can safely be done for all the rules for truth-functors, and for applications of the rules for ∃ and ¬∀, *provided* that the rule has been applied in every (unclosed) branch on which the formula lies. But it *cannot* be done with applications of the rules for ∀ and ¬∃, since in these cases—but in these cases only—one may *need* to apply the same rule to the same formula more than once. (These points will be proved in what follows.) This 'ticking-off'

153

Tableau (P4′)

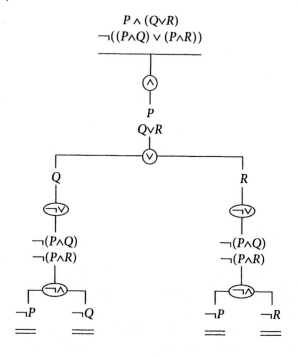

Tableau (P4″)

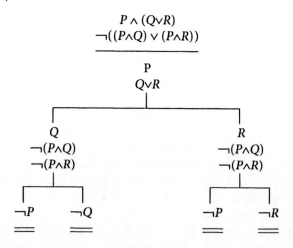

procedure does indeed help when you are in the process of constructing a tableau, for at each stage it shows you what you have dealt with and what is still unused. But I have not illustrated it in this book, for it is of no significance when you are looking at a completed tableau. If I had added suitable ticks to the finished examples here given, the result would simply be this: atomic formulae and their negations are never ticked (since no rule can be applied to them); all other formulae are ticked (since my examples contain nothing superfluous); except that formulae beginning with $\forall$ or $\neg\exists$ are never ticked, because—as I have said—in these cases the same rule may need to be applied more than once.

For convenience I collect together below all the rules for developing a tableau, in the new notation. (There is also, of course, a new rule for closing branches: a branch may be closed if it contains both ϕ and $\neg\phi$, for any formula ϕ.) It will be seen that the position of negation has now become rather peculiar. In the case of all other truth-functors, and of the quantifiers, there is now one rule for that functor (or quantifier) by itself, and one in which it is preceded by a negation sign. But there is no rule for the negation sign by itself, for the rule for $|\neg\phi| = T$, changing it to $|\phi| = F$, has now become a rule to replace $\neg\phi$ by $\neg\phi$, which is evidently pointless. The pleasing symmetry of the rules when stated in the original notation has thus been destroyed, and so has this rather nice feature: on the original rules the assumption that a particular formula was true, or false, led to a consequence concerning the truth or falsehood of its *subformulae*, in the case of a truth-functor, or of its *instances*, in the case of a quantifier. But this feature is not preserved in the new notation, because (for example) $\neg\phi$ is not a subformula of $\phi\rightarrow\psi$, and $\neg\phi(\alpha/\xi)$ is not an instance of $\neg\forall\xi\phi$. The new notation, then, destroys several elegant features of the original notation, but it is easy to check that the two have just the same effect. That is, any tableau which is closed according to the one set of rules is also closed according to the other.

It should be noted that in all cases these rules apply only to whole formulae standing alone, and not to formulae which are merely parts of longer formulae. Thus the rules in the left column can be used only to eliminate the *main* functor, or quantifier, of a formula; and similarly the rules in the right column can be used only to eliminate an *initial* negation sign, with all the rest of the formula in its scope, and then the main functor in what follows it.

We now introduce the notation $\Gamma \vdash$ to mean that there is a closed tableau, drawn according to the rules here listed, whose initial formulae are all members of the set Γ. This is our basic notion of a tableau proof. But in terms of it we can also define further notions, e.g.

$$\Gamma \vdash \phi \quad \text{for} \quad \Gamma, \neg\phi \vdash$$

and hence

$$\vdash \phi \quad \text{for} \quad \neg\phi \vdash$$

Rules for developing a tableau

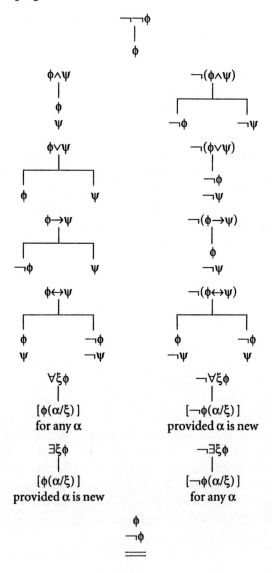

EXERCISES

4.3.1. Any tableau in the original notation has a unique translation into the new notation, namely, for any formula ϕ,

$|\phi| = T$ translates to ϕ,

$|\phi| = F$ translates to $\neg\phi$.

Verify that under this translation a correct tableau in the old notation must become a correct tableau in the new notation. [Method: check that each individual rule in the old notation becomes a correct rule in the new notation.]

4.3.2. A tableau in the new notation does not have a unique translation into the old notation. Given a formula ϕ which does not begin with a negation sign, then we do have a unique translation, namely

ϕ translates to $|\phi| = T$.

But with a formula $\neg\phi$ that does begin with a negation sign we have two alternatives, namely

$\neg\phi$ translates to $|\neg\phi| = T$
   or to $|\phi| = F$.

Show that, if we always choose the second alternative, then our tableau in the new notation translates into something that *either* is a correct tableau in the original notation *or* can be transformed into one by adding lines $|\neg\phi| = T$ above lines $|\phi| = F$, and/or adding lines $|\phi| = T$ below lines $|\neg\phi| = F$. [Notice that if $\neg\phi$ occurs as premiss to a rule of development, it must there be replaced by $|\phi| = F$. If $\neg\phi$ occurs as conclusion to a rule, it may have to be replaced instead by $|\neg\phi| = T$. So where we have an occurrence that is used in both ways we may need to replace it by $|\neg\phi| = T$ above $|\phi| = F$. The other point to think about is where a branch is closed because it contains both $\neg\neg\phi$ and $\neg\phi$.]

4.4. Constructing Proofs

When we are concerned only with quantifier-free formulae, the construction of tableau proofs is a mechanical task, like truth-tables or truth-value analysis. The essential point here is that, for any formula, there is only one rule that can be applied to it, and we never need to apply that rule to it more than once. The information contained in a formula is fully used up when the rule applicable to it has been applied to it, in every branch on which it lies, so once this has happened we never need to consider that formula again in the development of the tableau, but can concentrate instead upon the shorter formulae obtained from it. Continuing in this way, we must eventually reach the shortest possible formulae, i.e. sentence-letters or their negations, to which no further rules can be applied. That is to say, we must reach a situation where the tableau is *completed*, i.e. nothing more can be done, in accordance with the rules, which is not a mere repetition of what has been done already. Given a completed tableau, either it is closed, in which case the set of formulae at its root is inconsistent, or it is not closed, in which case (as the next section will demonstrate) the set of formulae at its root is consistent. The tableau proofs thus provide us with a *decision procedure* for finite sets of quantifier-free formulae, as do truth-tables and truth-value analysis.

There is therefore little scope for a display of ingenuity in the construction of such proofs, but perhaps it is worth mentioning one or two simple ways of avoiding unnecessary work. Nothing is laid down about the order in which the tableau rules are to be applied, so the freedom that one has in proof-construction is just the freedom to choose one order rather than another. The general principle is to minimize the number of branches in the tableau, and the number of formulae in each branch. So one sensible rule of thumb is to postpone the introduction of new branches by always applying a non-branching rule before a branching rule, where that is possible. Sometimes the gain is hardly appreciable. For example, tableau (P5) is another proof of the entailment

$$P \wedge (Q \vee R) \quad \models \quad (P \wedge Q) \vee (P \wedge R)$$

Tableau (P5)

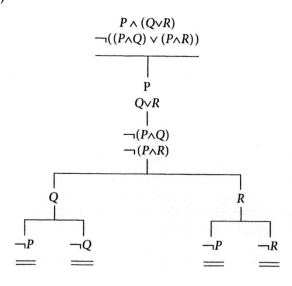

already demonstrated several times. (P5) obeys the suggested maxim, and may be compared with (P4), which does not. The only difference is that the formulae $\neg(P \wedge Q)$ and $\neg(P \wedge R)$ are written only once in this proof, but twice in the earlier proof. That is not much of an advantage, but it is something. But let us change to another example, the entailment

$$P \rightarrow Q, Q \rightarrow R, R \rightarrow S \models P \rightarrow S.$$

Here are two proofs, (P6) obeying the suggested maxim, and (P7) flouting it. Each is a perfectly satisfactory proof of the desired result, but clearly the second demands more ink and more wristpower.

Another proof of this same sequent will illustrate a further point: where it is necessary to apply several branching rules, the order in which they are applied may make a difference. It is a good general principle that one should, if possible, choose to apply first any rule that will lead to a branch that can be closed at once. Obviously this minimizes the effect of branching. In tableaux (P6) and (P7) the rule for $\rightarrow$ was applied to the three formulae

$$P \rightarrow Q, Q \rightarrow R, R \rightarrow S$$

in the order in which they are here listed, and this obeys the maxim. The reverse order would have been equally good, as you are invited to check. But if we disregard this maxim we again cover more paper, as you may see by comparing (P6) with the further tableau (P8).

Tableau (P6)

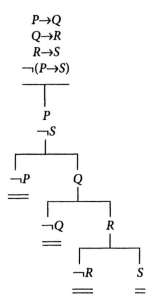

Tableau (P7)

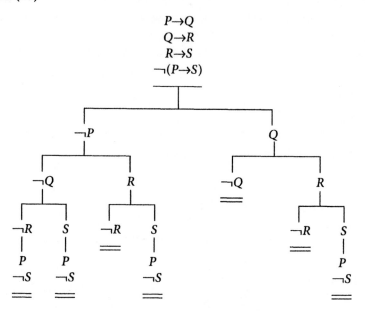

Tableau (P8)

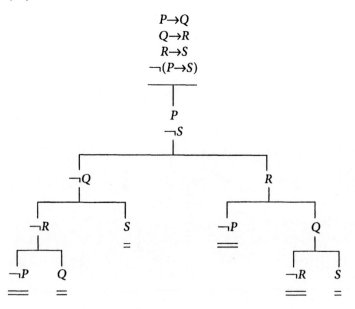

Tableau (P9)

(1)	$\exists x \forall y Fxy$
(2)	$\neg \forall y \exists x Fxy$
(3)	$\forall y Fay$
(4)	$\neg \exists x Fxb$
(5)	Fab
(6)	$\neg Fab$

These examples have illustrated how we may obtain quite different-looking tableaux by applying the same rules in a different order. All the different tableaux will in fact lead to the same result, provided that they are all completed tableaux, in the sense explained. (This will be proved in the next section.) So the choice of one order rather than another is simply a matter of elegance and economy; nothing important will depend upon it. But when we come to deal with quantified formulae, the case is rather different. This is for two reasons: first, there is more than one way of applying the same quantifier rule to the formula, for we may choose now this name-letter and now that, when forming our singular instance; second, we may *need* to apply the same rule more than once to the same formula, in order to get a closed tableau. As a matter of fact we never do need to use the rule for $\exists$, or for $\neg\forall$, more than once on the same formula in the same branch; but this can happen with the rule for $\forall$, and for $\neg\exists$. Moreover, we cannot, in advance, set any upper limit to the number of times that the same rule may need to be applied to the same formula. This means that we cannot guarantee that a completed tableau will ever be reached, and for that reason the tableau method no longer provides a decision procedure when quantifiers are involved.

Let us start with a simple proof of the entailment

$$\exists x \forall y Fxy \vDash \forall y \exists x Fxy.$$

The tableau is (P9), in which I have (for brevity) omitted the vertical lines marking each new step of development. In lines (1) and (2) we write down the two formulae that are to be shown inconsistent. In line (3) the rule for $\exists$ is applied to the formula in line (1), introducing the name a that has not occurred earlier. In line (4) the rule for $\neg\forall$ is applied to the formula in line (2), and since this rule again requires that the name to be introduced has not occurred earlier, we cannot use a again, but must choose a new letter. So here the name introduced is b. Then in line (5) the rule for $\forall$ is applied to the formula in line (3), and in line (6) the similar rule for $\neg\exists$ is applied to the formula in line (4). In either of these rules we may use any name that we wish, so in line (5) one might have put *Faa* or (e.g.) *Fac* in place of *Fab*; similarly, in line (6) one might have put ¬*Fbb* or ¬*Fcb*. If we had made any of these choices, then, of course, the tableau would not have closed at this point, so the choice of *b* in the first case and *a* in the second was made simply with a view to producing the required contradiction. This illustrates how finding a proof can depend upon choosing the right names.

Now let us look at something more difficult. The converse entailment

$$\forall y \exists x Fxy \vDash \exists x \forall y Fxy$$

is not correct, as was noted earlier (Exercise 3.6.3(*b*)). But there are some special cases of it that are correct, for example this one:

$$\forall y \exists x (Fx \wedge Gy) \vDash \exists x \forall y (Fx \wedge Gy).$$

(This is because both premiss and conclusion are equivalent to $\exists x Fx \wedge \forall y Gy$, as we may see by driving the quantifiers in.) A tableau proof of its correctness must apply the ∀-rule twice to the same formula, as in tableau (P10). In lines (3) and (4) we apply first the ∀-rule and then the ∃-rule to line (1). The name *a* chosen in line (3) is arbitrary; it could have been any other name. The name *b* chosen in line (4) must be new; it could not have been *a* again. Then lines (5) and (6) simply unpack the information in line (4). In lines (7) and (8) we apply first the ¬∃-rule then the ¬∀-rule to line (2). In line (7) we can choose whatever name we like, and we choose *b* because that

Tableau (P10)

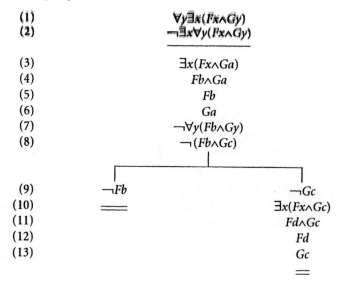

(1)	$\forall y \exists x(Fx \wedge Gy)$
(2)	¬$\exists x \forall y(Fx \wedge Gy)$
(3)	$\exists x(Fx \wedge Ga)$
(4)	$Fb \wedge Ga$
(5)	Fb
(6)	Ga
(7)	¬$\forall y(Fb \wedge Gy)$
(8)	¬$(Fb \wedge Gc)$
(9)	¬Fb $\quad$ ¬Gc
(10)	$=\!=$ $\quad$ $\exists x(Fx \wedge Gc)$
(11)	$\quad$ $Fd \wedge Gc$
(12)	$\quad$ Fd
(13)	$\quad$ Gc
	$\quad$ $=\!=$

gives us some chance of finding a contradiction with what has gone before. But in line (8), when for the same reason we should want to choose the name *a* to put in place of *y*, we are not permitted to do so. A name introduced by the ¬∀-rule must be a new one, and so can be neither *a* nor *b*. At first sight, one might think that this would block the proof, for evidently ¬(*Fb*∧*Gc*) in line (8) does not contradict *Fb*∧*Ga* in line (4). But it turns out that the proof is not blocked, for when we look back to see how the letter *a* first entered the proof we find that it was arbitrarily chosen, as a result of applying the ∀-rule to line (1). We therefore go back and apply the ∀-rule to line (1) *again*, this time using *c* instead of *a*, to obtain ∃*x*(*Fx*∧*Gc*) in line (10). This does give us the required contradiction, but only after a few more steps in which yet another (and irrelevant) name has to be introduced in line (11), as a result of applying the ∃-rule to line (10). By comparison with other methods of proof, which we shall come to later, the tableau system must, I think, count as the simplest. But even so it can turn out that proofs are not always simple to discover, as this example illustrates.

Some general advice can be given. First, it generally pays to apply the rules for ∃ and for ¬∀ before applying those for ∀ and ¬∃, wherever this is possible. For wherever the introduction of a new name is required, it helps to get that name onto the tableau at an early stage, so that we can take it into account when it comes to applying an ∀ rule or an ¬∃ rule. Remember, too, that there is never any need to apply the rules for ∃ or ¬∀ more than once in the same branch to the same formula; one new name is always enough. (This will be proved in the next section.) Second, when one is choosing what name to use when applying the rules for ∀ and for ¬∃, one can confine attention to names that are already on the tableau, so long as there are some. If there are none, and if we cannot introduce one by applying a rule for ∃ or ¬∀, then one must use the rule for ∀ or ¬∃ with a new name in order to get started. But there is never any need to introduce more than one new name in this way. (This too will be proved in the next section.) Beyond this, there is little one can say, by way of general advice, except to reiterate that the object is to derive a contradiction in every branch, and names should be chosen in whatever way seems likely to contribute to this. In the next section I give a recipe for finding proofs which will always succeed if there is a proof to be found. But in practice this recipe can lead to long and cumbersome proofs, which a judicious choice of names would avoid. The best way of learning how to find reasonably neat proofs is practice. I end this section with one more 'worked example', which again involves applying the same rule—in this case the ¬∃ rule—twice to the same formula. You should first provide your own commentary on this proof, before turning to the exercises to acquire some of the needed practice.

The proof shows that

$$\vdash \exists x(Fx \to \forall xFx),$$

and it runs as follows

Tableau (P11)

(1)	$\neg\exists x(Fx \to \forall xFx)$

(2)	$\neg(Fa \to \forall xFx)$
(3)	Fa
(4)	$\neg\forall xFx$
(5)	$\neg Fb$
(6)	$\neg(Fb \to \forall xFx)$
(7)	Fb
(8)	$\neg\forall xFx$

EXERCISES

4.4.1. Find tableau proofs to verify the following claims:

(a) $P \;\dashv\vdash\; (P{\to}Q){\to}P$.

(b) $P{\vee}Q \dashv\vdash (P{\to}Q){\to}Q$.

(c) $P{\leftrightarrow}Q \;\dashv\vdash\; (P{\vee}Q){\to}(P{\wedge}Q)$.

(d) $\exists x(P \wedge Fx) \;\dashv\vdash\; P \wedge \exists xFx$.

(e) $\exists x(P \vee Fx) \;\dashv\vdash\; P \vee \exists xFx$.

(f) $\exists x(Fx \vee Gx) \;\dashv\vdash\; \exists xFx \vee \exists xGx$.

(g) $\forall xy(Rxy \to \neg Ryx) \;\vdash\; \forall x\neg Rxx$.

(h) $\forall xyz(Rxy \wedge Ryz \to \neg Rxz) \;\vdash\; \forall x\neg Rxx$.

(i) $\forall xyz(Rxy \wedge Ryz \to Rxz), \forall xy(Rxy \to Ryx)$
    $\vdash \forall x(\exists y(Rxy \vee Ryx) \to Rxx)$.

(j) $\forall x\exists y(Fx{\to}Gy) \;\vdash\; \exists y\forall x(Fx{\to}Gy)$.

(k) $\forall x\exists y(Fx{\leftrightarrow}Gy) \;\vdash\; \exists y\forall x(Fx{\to}Gy) \wedge \exists y\forall x(Gy{\to}Fx)$.

(l) $\forall x\exists y(Fx{\leftrightarrow}Gy) \;\dashv\vdash\; \exists yz\forall x((Fx{\to}Gy) \wedge (Gz{\to}Fx))$.

[Note. It is difficult to find from scratch a proof for (l) from left to right. The search will be assisted by considering first a proof for (k), and asking how it could be modified. A proof for (k) in turn should result readily enough from a proof for (j), which may be modelled on the proof already given on p. 162 for the related sequent

$$\forall x\exists y(Fx{\wedge}Gy) \vdash \exists y\forall x(Fx{\wedge}Gy).]$$

4.4.2. In place of the rules $\neg\forall$ and $\neg\exists$ cited in the main text, one sometimes finds these rules instead:

$$\neg\forall\xi\phi \qquad \neg\exists\xi\phi$$
$$| \qquad\qquad |$$
$$\exists\xi\neg\phi \qquad \forall\xi\neg\phi$$

(*a*) Explain why these alternative rules should be counted as less elegant than those in the text. [Compare p. 152.] You may, for all that, find them easier to use.

(*b*) Suppose that we confined attention to languages whose only logical symbols are $\neg, \wedge, \vee, \forall, \exists$; that we adopted the alternative rules $\neg\forall$ and $\neg\exists$ above; and also these alternative rules for $\neg\wedge$ and $\neg\vee$.

$$\neg(\phi\wedge\psi) \qquad \neg(\phi\vee\psi)$$
$$| \qquad\qquad\qquad |$$
$$\neg\phi\vee\neg\psi \qquad \neg\phi\wedge\neg\psi$$

Discuss the elegance of this alternative tableau system. Could the same principle be applied to deal with a wider range of languages? [Hint: compare Section 2.10.]

(*c*) Show that wherever a tableau can be closed using the rules in the main text, it can also be closed using these alternative rules instead.

(*d*) Show that wherever a tableau can be closed using the alternative rules it can also be closed using the rules in the main text. [Hint: consider just the alternative rule $\neg\wedge$. This introduces a formula $\neg\phi\vee\neg\psi$ which was not present before. Now *either* this formula is further developed in the course of the tableau, by using the $\vee$-rule, in which case we can get the same effect by using the original $\neg\wedge$ rule; *or* it is not further developed. But in the latter case it may nevertheless be used to close the tableau, if its negation $\neg(\neg\phi\vee\neg\psi)$ is also on the tableau. Consider how, with the original rules, one could close a branch containing both $\neg(\phi\wedge\psi)$ and $\neg(\neg\phi\vee\neg\psi)$.]

4.5. **Soundness**

Recall that, for the purposes of the present chapter, '$\Gamma\vdash$' means 'there is a closed tableau, conforming to the rules of development listed on p. 156, in which every formula at the root is a formula in the set Γ'. Recall also that, as always, '$\Gamma\vDash$' means 'Γ is a set of closed formulae, and there is no (standard) interpretation in which all of the formulae in Γ are true'. We abbreviate this last to 'Γ is inconsistent'. Our tableau system of proof is sound iff

    If $\Gamma\vdash$ then $\Gamma\vDash$.

It is complete iff

    If $\Gamma\vDash$ then $\Gamma\vdash$.

The purpose of this section and the next two is to prove that the system is both sound and complete.

The soundness of the system has in effect been proved in Section 4.2, when its various rules were stated and justified, but let us now set out this argument a little more formally. The tableau begins by assuming that the formulae at its root are jointly consistent, so this is an assumption of the form

$\quad \Gamma \nvdash.$

The tableau is developed by applying rules which say: if the set of formulae on the branch so far is consistent, then (in the case of a non-branching rule) so is the set that results by adding such and such a further formula, or (in the case of a branching rule) so is one or other of two sets that result in this way. For example, the rules for $\wedge$ are:

$\quad$ If $\Gamma, \phi \wedge \psi \nvdash$ then $\Gamma, \phi \wedge \psi, \phi, \psi \nvdash.$
$\quad$ If $\Gamma, \neg(\phi \wedge \psi) \nvdash$ then either $\Gamma, \neg(\phi \wedge \psi), \neg\phi \nvdash$
$\quad\quad\quad\quad\quad\quad\quad\quad\quad\quad\quad\quad$ or $\Gamma, \neg(\phi \wedge \psi), \neg\psi \nvdash.$

And the rules for $\forall$ are:

$\quad$ If $\Gamma, \forall \xi \phi \nvdash$ then $\Gamma, \forall \xi \phi, \phi(\alpha/\xi) \nvdash$ for any α.
$\quad$ If $\Gamma, \neg\forall \xi \phi \nvdash$ then $\Gamma, \neg\forall \xi \phi, \neg\phi(\alpha/\xi) \nvdash$ provided α
$\quad$ is not in Γ or in ϕ.

(Γ represents all the other formulae on the branch, besides the one to which the rule is being applied.) To show that the system is sound we have to show that each of these rules is indeed a correct rule. To verify this point for the truth-functors we need only consult their truth-tables, which is simple; to verify it for the quantifiers requires a little more discussion, but that discussion has been provided in Section 4.2. Let us take it, then, that this step is accomplished. It follows, then, that if the set of formulae at the root of the tableau is consistent, then there is at least one branch of the tableau such that the set of all formulae on that branch is consistent. But suppose also that the tableau closes. Then on every branch there occurs both some formula and its negation, and a set containing both of these is not consistent. That is

$\quad \Gamma, \phi, \neg\phi \vDash.$

Thus, if the tableau closes, the set of formulae at its root cannot be consistent, which is the required result

$\quad$ If $\Gamma \vdash$ then $\Gamma \vDash.$

I note, incidentally, that what our argument shows could be more fully spelled out in this way: if there is *at least one* closed tableau for a given set of formulae, that set is inconsistent. This will be important in what follows.

Meanwhile, I end this section with a brief remark on the notion of consistency, as applied to systems of proof. There are two familiar ways of explaining this notion. If S is any system of proof, then S is said to be *negation-consistent* iff there is no formula φ such that

$$\vdash_S \phi \text{ and } \vdash_S \neg\phi.$$

And S is said to be *absolutely consistent* (or: consistent in the sense of Post (1921)) iff it is not the case that for *every* formula φ we have

$$\vdash_S \phi.$$

For most systems of proof it is quite easy to show that if they are consistent in the one sense then they must also be consistent in the other, but tableau systems in general are interesting examples of systems of proof in which the two notions genuinely diverge. (This is shown in Exercise 4.5.1.) But it is easy to see that any system that is sound must also be consistent in both senses. Consistency is of independent interest only when we are dealing with a system that is not sound (or not known to be sound). But such systems do, of course, exist.

EXERCISE

4.5.1. Let S^+ be a tableau system of proof, which includes all the rules listed in Section 4.3, and in addition these two further rules to deal with the new two-place sentence-functor 'tonk'

$$
\begin{array}{cc}
\phi \text{ tonk } \psi & \neg(\phi \text{ tonk } \psi) \\
| & | \\
\phi & \neg\phi \\
\psi & \neg\psi
\end{array}
$$

(a) Show that S^+ is not negation-consistent. [Hint: consider the formula (P tonk $\neg P$).]
(b) Show that S^+ is absolutely consistent. [Hint: consider the formula $\neg P$.]
(c) Deduce from (a) and (b) that this simple case of CUT does not hold for S^+:

If $\vdash_{S+} \phi$ and $\phi \vdash_{S+} \psi$ then $\vdash_{S+} \psi$.

(d) Show that, if the above rules are to hold for 'tonk', then it cannot be a truth-functor. Could it be any other kind of sentence-functor?

4.6. **Completeness I: Truth-Functors**

To show that the tableau system of proof is a complete system, we have to show that

If $\Gamma \models$ then $\Gamma \vdash$.

The argument in this case is rather more complex, and I shall present it in three stages. In this section we shall confine attention to the rules for the truth-functors, and so we may assume that our language contains only sentence-letters as schematic letters. The first stage of the argument will also confine attention to sets Γ of formulae that are finite. The second stage will then show how to extend the argument to cover infinite sets of formulae, and the third stage (in the following section) will show how the argument may be extended to take account of the quantifiers.

It is helpful to begin by slightly modifying the definition of a completed tableau. Let us say that a branch on a tableau is *fully developed* iff no rule can be applied to any formula on the branch to generate a new formula not already on the branch. Then we may count a tableau as *completed* iff every branch on it is either closed or fully developed. (The point is that we are not requiring closed branches to be fully developed.) Now, as we have observed (pp. 157–8), for any finite set of quantifier-free formulae, there will always be a completed tableau. We shall now argue that if there is *at least one* completed tableau for the set which is not closed, then the set is consistent. Hence, if the set is inconsistent (i.e. if $\Gamma \models$), then *every* completed tableau for it will be closed (i.e. $\Gamma \vdash$). Recall here that the soundness proof of the last section also yielded the result that if the set of formulae is consistent, then *every* tableau for it will be open. So this gives us our proof of a point that has simply been assumed so far, namely that all the different completed tableaux for the same set of formulae will give the same result, i.e. that either all of them will be closed or none of them will be. But, at the present stage, this point will be established only for quantifier-free formulae.

Let us turn to the proof. Suppose that we are given a completed tableau with an open branch. (There may be several such branches, but just fix attention on one.) We can then define an interpretation for the language of the formulae on that branch under which all the formulae on that branch are true, namely by stipulating, for each atomic formula P_i in the language

$$|P_i|_I = T \quad \text{iff} \quad P_i \text{ is on the selected branch.}$$

This is a possible stipulation, for since the branch is open it does not contain both P_i and $\neg P_i$; if it contains P_i, then P_i is stipulated to be true; if it does not contain P_j, but P_i is in the relevant language, then P_i is stipulated to be false, so $\neg P_i$ will be true. Now this interpretation verifies every formula on the branch. We have just seen that it verifies both the atomic formulae that are on the branch and any negations of atomic formulae that are on the branch. Every other formula on the branch will have had a rule of development applied to it, since the branch is fully developed. But, as we noted earlier (p. 151), the rules of development for the truth-functors all have this feature: when the rule is applied to a complex formula, the simpler formulae that result entail the complex formula they descend from. So if the simpler formulae on the branch are all true, the complex formulae above them on the branch must be true too. It follows that all the formulae on the branch are true. (You are invited to set out this argument as a proper argument by induction on the length of an arbitrary formula on the branch, and to do so before you get to p. 172, where the task is done for you.) In particular, then, the initial formulae at the root of the tableau are all true in this interpretation, and hence they form a consistent set. This completes the argument. Any completed open tableau has a consistent set of formulae at its root. Any finite set of quantifier-free formulae has a completed tableau. Hence any such set which is inconsistent has a completed and closed tableau. That is

If $\Gamma \models$ then $\Gamma \vdash$.

Reflection on this argument shows that there will be two difficulties in extending it to cover quantified formulae as well: one is that when a formula $\forall \xi \phi$ is developed, the simpler formulae that result do *not* entail it; the other is that we cannot guarantee that a completed tableau will be available. (Indeed, we shall have to redefine 'completed tableau' in order to make it *possible* to have them, once quantifiers are included.) I shall deal with the second problem first, showing how we can still push through the same *kind* of argument even without a completed tableau. For this problem can be raised, and solved, while we are still at the level of truth-functors. Let us still suppose, then, that we have no quantifiers to deal with, but let us lift the restriction to *finite* sets of formulae. Suppose that Γ is an infinite set of formulae, and is inconsistent. Does it then follow that there is a closed tableau for it? Since a tableau is itself a finite structure, by definition, this must mean: does it follow that there is a closed tableau which has at its root some finite subset of the whole set Γ? The answer is yes. But in reaching this answer we need *in effect* to consider an 'infinite tableau', in so far as we do consider an *infinite series* of finite tableaux, each extending the last.

Assume, then, that Γ is an infinite set of formulae, each built up from truth-functors and sentence-letters. We may further assume that the formulae in Γ may be ordered in an infinite list as the 1st, 2nd, 3rd, ... nth ... formula, and every formula in Γ is, for some finite number n, the nth formula in this list.[1] We begin by considering just the first formula in Γ, and we construct a completed tableau for this in the ordinary way; call this the first tableau. Any branches in this tableau that are closed are closed for ever, and we never add anything more to them. But if there are some open branches, then we add to the root of the first tableau the second formula in Γ—think of it as being added above the formula that is already there—and we extend the open branches so that we again have a completed tableau. This is the second tableau. Again, any branch in this tableau that is closed is left undisturbed in further operations, but if there are some open branches then the third formula from Γ is added at the root and the open branches are developed further so that they form the third tableau, which is a completed tableau for all three of the formulae at its root. And so on. For each n, the nth tableau (if there is one) contains the previous tableau as a part, and all its open branches are fully developed. Now *either* at some stage in this series of tableaux there is a closed tableau (in which case the series halts there) *or* at no stage is there a closed tableau, and the series goes on for ever. In the first case the set of formulae at the root of the closed tableau is an inconsistent set (by the soundness proof given earlier), and since this set is a subset of the set Γ then Γ is inconsistent. In the second case we must show that the set Γ is consistent, i.e. that there is an interpretation which verifies every formula in Γ.

Looking at the matter intuitively, what we need is this. Consider our series of tableaux as together forming one infinite tableau. Any closed branch in this tableau is, of course, closed at some finite stage in the construction of the tableau, and so contains only finitely many formulae after those in the root. But if there was never a stage at which all branches closed, then there must be some branch which contains infinitely many formulae after the root, and it must be open. We can then use this infinite open branch to define an interpretation which will verify all the formulae on the branch, including those at the root, just as we did previously in the finite case.

Looking at the matter more precisely, let us say that a branch of the nth tableau is *satisfactory* iff, for every $m \geqslant n$, there is an open branch of the mth tableau of which it is a part. Then we have to show

---

[1] This is the assumption that Γ is a countably infinite set. This must be so, since each formula in Γ contains only finitely many occurrences of truth-functors and sentence-letters, and there is only a countable infinity of truth-functors and sentence-letters to begin with. It follows that the list of all formulae in Γ can be constructed lexicographically.

(1) There is a branch of the first tableau that is satisfactory.

(2) For each n, if there is a branch of the nth tableau that is satisfactory, then there is a branch of the $(n+1)$th tableau that is satisfactory and contains it as a part.

Proof of (1). Suppose not. Then for each branch of the first tableau there is an m such that no open branch of the mth tableau contains it. Let us say, in that case, that all descendants of that branch are closed by the mth tableau. But each individual tableau is finite. So there are only finitely many branches of the first tableau, say $\mathcal{B}_i...\mathcal{B}_k$. Each of these has all its descendants closed by some stage, say stages $m_i...m_k$ respectively. Let m_j be the maximum of $m_i...m_k$. Then each branch of the first tableau has all its descendants closed by stage m_j. But that is just to say that the m_jth tableau is closed, and this contradicts the original hypothesis.

Proof of (2). Suppose not. So some branch $\mathcal{B}$ of the nth tableau is satisfactory, but no branch of the $(n+1)$th tableau containing $\mathcal{B}$ is satisfactory. That is, every branch of the $(n+1)$th tableau containing $\mathcal{B}$ has all its descendants closed by some stage. But, as before, there are only finitely many branches of the $(n+1)$th tableau containing $\mathcal{B}$, so we can take the maximum m_j of these stages, and every branch of the $(n+1)$th tableau containing $\mathcal{B}$ has all its descendants closed by m_j. But that means that $\mathcal{B}$ itself has all its descendants closed by m_j, contradicting the hypothesis that $\mathcal{B}$ is satisfactory.

We are now in a position to specify our infinite series of finite branches, which will serve as the intuitive 'infinite branch'. We pick some satisfactory branch $\mathcal{B}_1$, of the first tableau, for we have shown that there is one. (One could make this definite by specifying a definite order in which the tableau rules were to be applied, and then saying that we are to pick the first satisfactory branch counting from the left.) We similarly pick some satisfactory branch $\mathcal{B}_2$ of the second tableau containing $\mathcal{B}_1$, as a part, for again we have shown that there is one. In general, for each n we pick a satisfactory branch $\mathcal{B}_{n+1}$ of the $(n+1)$th tableau, containing as a part the branch $\mathcal{B}_n$ already selected from the previous tableau. So we have an infinite set of selected branches $\mathcal{B}_n$, each contained in the next, and each open.

The proof then proceeds exactly as before. We specify an interpretation I, for all the formulae in the language of Γ, by stipulating that for each sentence-letter P_i in that language

$$|P_i|_I = T \quad \text{iff} \quad P_i \text{ is on one of the selected branches } \mathcal{B}_n.$$

For each branch $\mathcal{B}_n$ this interprets all the formulae on that branch as true, including therefore the first n formulae of Γ, which form its root. I give the argument in more detail this time.

Let ϕ be an arbitrary formula on the branch $\mathcal{B}_n$. The inductive hypothesis is

If ψ is shorter than ϕ, and occurs on $\mathcal{B}_n$, then $|\psi|_I = T$.

To abbreviate labour, I assume that the language under consideration contains $\rightarrow$ and $\neg$ as its only truth-functors. This gives us three cases to consider, one of them with three subcases.

Case (1): ϕ is atomic. Then, by definition of I, if ϕ occurs on $\mathcal{B}_n$, $|\phi|_I = T$.

Case (2): ϕ is $\neg\psi$.

Subcase (*a*): ψ is atomic. Assume $\neg\psi$ occurs on $\mathcal{B}_n$. Then ψ does not occur on any of the selected branches $\mathcal{B}_i$. (For suppose ψ occurs on $\mathcal{B}_k$, and let $\mathcal{B}_l$ be whichever is the longer of the two branches $\mathcal{B}_n$ and $\mathcal{B}_k$. Then both ψ and $\neg\psi$ occur on $\mathcal{B}_l$, so $\mathcal{B}_l$ is a closed branch, contrary to hypothesis.) So, by the definition of I, $|\psi|_I = F$. Hence $|\phi|_I = |\neg\psi|_I = T$.

Subcase (*b*): ψ is $\neg\chi$. Assume ϕ, i.e. $\neg\neg\chi$, occurs on $\mathcal{B}_n$. Then, since $\mathcal{B}_n$ is fully developed, χ also occurs on $\mathcal{B}_n$. Hence, since χ is shorter than $\neg\neg\chi$, by inductive hypothesis $|\chi|_I = T$. Therefore $|\phi|_I = |\neg\neg\chi|_I = T$.

Subcase (*c*): ψ is $\chi_1 \rightarrow \chi_2$. Assume ϕ, i.e. $\neg(\chi_1 \rightarrow \chi_2)$, occurs on $\mathcal{B}_n$. Then, since $\mathcal{B}_n$ is fully developed, both χ_1 and $\neg\chi_2$ occur on $\mathcal{B}_n$. So by the inductive hypothesis $|\chi_1|_I = |\neg\chi_2|_I = T$. Hence $|\phi|_I = |\neg(\chi_1 \rightarrow \chi_2)|_I = T$.

Case (3): ϕ is $\psi \rightarrow \chi$. Assume ϕ occurs on $\mathcal{B}_n$. Then, since $\mathcal{B}_n$ is fully developed, either $\neg\psi$ or χ occurs on $\mathcal{B}_n$. So, by inductive hypothesis, either $|\neg\psi|_I = T$ or $|\chi|_I = T$. In either case $|\phi|_I = |\psi \rightarrow \chi|_I = T$.

This completes the induction, and thereby establishes our result. For every formula in Γ is in the root of one of our tableaux (in fact the nth formula in Γ is in the root of the nth tableau and all later ones); thus every formula in Γ is true in I, and hence Γ is a consistent set. If Γ is inconsistent, then, it must be because some finite subset of Γ is inconsistent, in which case it can be proved inconsistent by a finite tableau, as we have seen.

I observe here that we have made use of the tableau system of proof to establish a result that can be stated without reference to that system, namely

If $\Gamma \models$ then, for some finite subset Γ' of Γ, $\Gamma' \models$.

(For we showed that if $\Gamma \models$, then $\Gamma \vdash$. But from the nature of a tableau proof it is clear that if $\Gamma \vdash$, then, for some finite subset Γ' of Γ, $\Gamma' \vdash$. And, from the soundness of the tableau system, if $\Gamma' \vdash$, then $\Gamma' \models$.) I shall comment on the significance of this result in Section 4.8, when it has been extended to include languages with quantifiers. Meanwhile I add that, for quantifier-free languages, it is relatively straightforward to prove the result directly, without reference to any system of proof. The following exercise shows how.[2]

EXERCISE

4.6.1.(*a*) Show that, if $P_1,...,P_n$ are all the letters in a formula φ, and if $\pm P_i$ is either P_i or $\neg P_i$, then

either $\pm P_1,...,\pm P_n \models \varphi$ or $\pm P_1,...,\pm P_n \models \neg\varphi$.

[Simple consideration of truth-tables should suffice.]

(*b*) Let '$\Gamma \models$' mean 'for some finite set Γ', included in Γ, $\Gamma' \models$'. Show that, for any sentence-letter P_i,

If $\Gamma,P_i \models$ and $\Gamma,\neg P_i \models$ then $\Gamma \models$.

[Hint: if Γ' and Γ'' are both finite subsets of Γ, then so is their union $\Gamma' \cup \Gamma''$.]

(*c*) Let Γ be any set of formulae, possibly infinite, and let $P_1, P_2,...,P_n,...$ be a list, possibly infinite, of all the letters in the formulae in Γ. Define a series of sets of formulae Γ_i, one for each letter P_i on the list, by

$$\Gamma_0 = \Gamma$$
$$\Gamma_{n+1} = \begin{cases} \Gamma_n \cup \{P_{n+1}\} & \text{if } \Gamma_n, \neg P_{n+1} \models \\ \Gamma_n \cup \{\neg P_{n+1}\} & \text{otherwise} \end{cases}$$

(In words: begin with the given set Γ as Γ_0, and then extend it by running through the series of all the letters occurring in it. For each letter P_n, add either P_n or $\neg P_n$ to the set of all formulae formed so far, by adding P_n if the set formed so far (namely Γ_{n-1}), together with $\neg P_n$, has a finite subset that is inconsistent; otherwise by adding $\neg P_n$.)

Assume $\Gamma \not\models$. Using part (*b*), prove that, for each n, $\Gamma_n \not\models$. [Method: use ordinary induction on n.]

(*d*) Define an interpretation I by stipulating that, for each letter P_n,

$$|P_n|_I = T \quad \text{iff} \quad P_n \in \Gamma_n.$$

Prove that for any formula φ in Γ we have $|\varphi|_I = T$. [Method: let φ be a formula in Γ, containing just the letters $P_j,...,P_k$. Then by our construction, for some choice of $\pm P_i$ as P_i or $\neg P_i$, we have

---

[2] I owe to Lawrence Fumagalli the form of the proof given here.

$\{\pm P_j,...,\pm P_k,\varphi\} \in \Gamma_k.$

This is a finite subject of Γ_k. Hence, using the result of part (c), it is consistent. Hence, using the result of part (a) we have

$\pm P_j,...,\pm P_k \vDash \varphi.$

It is easy to argue that this implies the desired result.]

(e) Observe that what is proved in (c)–(d) is

If $\Gamma \nVdash$ then $\Gamma \nvDash$.

Or in other words,

If $\Gamma \vdash$ then $\Gamma \vDash$.

4.7. **Completeness II: Quantifiers**

When the language contains quantifiers, and the tableau rules include the rules for quantifiers already given, it is easily seen that there cannot be any completed tableaux in the sense of the previous section. For the quantifier rules allow one to go on introducing new names *ad infinitum*. I begin then by stipulating a special and restricted way in which those rules are to be applied, namely in a cycle of three stages, thus:

(1) Apply the rules for the truth-functors until each branch is either closed or as fully developed as it can be by using those rules, without repetition.

(2) Apply the rules $\exists$ and $\neg\forall$, introducing new names, as many times as they can be applied to the formulae already on the tableau, except that neither rule is ever to be applied more than once on the same branch to the same formula.

(3) Apply the rules $\forall$ and $\neg\exists$ as many times as they can be applied to the formulae already on the tableau, but using only the names already on the tableau, and never writing the same formula more than once in the same branch. However, if there are no names already on the tableau, then one new name, say a, may be introduced on the first occasion that either $\forall$ or $\neg\exists$ is used.

We are to think of the rules as being applied in cycles: first the rules for truth-functors, as in (1); then $\exists$ and $\neg\forall$, as specified in (2); then $\forall$ and $\neg\exists$, as specified in (3). Then we go back to the beginning again and apply the rules for truth-functors once more; then for $\exists$ and $\neg\forall$, to any new formulae that have appeared since the first stage; then for $\forall$ and $\neg\exists$, to any new names that have appeared; then the truth-functors again; and so on. Naturally, we close off any branches as soon as it becomes possible to do so, and if at any stage all branches are closed, then, of course, work stops: we have reached our goal. But it may also be that work stops because no tableau rule can be applied, compatibly with the restrictions noted in (1)–(3). In either case we shall say in a new sense that we have a *completed* tableau, this being one in which every branch is either closed or fully developed, but where 'fully developed' now means 'developed as far as it can be by applying the rules in the stipulated cycle, and conforming to the restrictions imposed on the quantifier rules'.

Here is a simple example of a tableau that is open but completed in this new sense. Suppose someone proposes the following as an entailment:

$$\exists x(Fx \rightarrow Gx) \vDash \exists xFx \rightarrow \exists xGx.$$

We test this in tableau (P12), using the rules in the order suggested.

Tableau (P12)

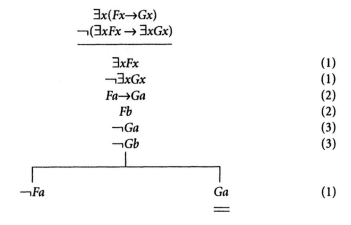

At this stage we stop. The tableau has not closed, but no more rules can be applied, compatibly with our restrictions. (I have noted on the right which kind of rule is being applied at each step.) Now we notice that the open branch of the tableau in fact provides a counter-example to the suggested entailment, i.e. an interpretation in which both of the formulae at the root of the tableau are true. It is an interpretation in which the domain has just two members, say A and B, one denoted by a and the other by b, those being the only names that occur on the tableau. We interpret the predicate-letters on the open branch so as to make true the atomic formulae, or their negations, on that branch. Thus F is to be true of the object denoted by b, but not of the object denoted by a, while G is to be true of neither of these objects. So our interpretation is

$$\mathcal{D} = \{A,B\}$$
$$|a| = A$$
$$|b| = B$$
$$|F| = \{A\}$$
$$|G| = \emptyset.^3$$

It is easy to check, reading up the open branch, that on this interpretation every formula on that branch is true, including the two formulae at its root.

Here is another example. It is easy to fall into the error of supposing that a relation which is both transitive and symmetrical must also be reflexive, i.e. that

$$\forall xyz(Fxy \wedge Fyz \rightarrow Fxz), \forall xy(Fxy \rightarrow Fyx) \models \forall xFxx.$$

We draw up a suitable tableau (P13), using the rules in the order suggested.

Tableau (P13)

$\forall xyz(Fxy \wedge Fyz \rightarrow Fxz)$	
$\forall xyz(Fxy \rightarrow Fyx)$	
$\neg\forall xFxx$	

$\neg Faa$	(2)
$\forall yz(Fay \wedge Fyz \rightarrow Faz)$	(3)
$\forall z(Faa \wedge Faz \rightarrow Faz)$	(3)
$Faa \wedge Faa \rightarrow Faa$	(3)
$\forall y(Fay \rightarrow Fya)$	(3)
$Faa \rightarrow Faa$	(3)

$\neg Faa \qquad\qquad Faa$	(1)
$\neg(Faa \wedge Faa) \qquad\qquad Faa$	(1)
$\neg Faa \qquad\qquad \neg Faa$	(1)

This tableau is completed, according to the restrictions we have imposed. It has two open branches, but both are alike in requiring the falsehood of the atomic formula Faa, and no other atomic formulae appear. So it evidently

---

³ '$\emptyset$' is a variation on '{ }'. Both are symbols for the empty set.

yields the following interpretation, in which all the formulae on its open branches are true

$$\mathcal{D} = \{\text{A}\}$$
$$|a| = \text{A}$$
$$|F| = \varnothing.$$

Again it is easy to check that this interpretation yields the required result: all three formulae at the root are true in it, the first two 'vacuously', because their antecedent clauses are true of nothing.

In these two examples it was simple enough to obtain a completed tableau. Often it is extremely tedious. Here is just a slight variation on the last example. Someone might suggest that if we add to the premisses of that sequent the statement that the relation F is not empty, then the counter-example just given will be ruled out, and perhaps the entailment will hold after all. That is, he proposes the entailment

$$\forall xyz(Fxy \wedge Fxz \to Fyz), \forall xy(Fxy \to Fyx), \exists xyFxy \vDash \forall xFxx.$$

This is not in fact a correct entailment, as a completed tableau would show. But the tedium of writing out a completed tableau is now very considerable. In the first two lines three names will be introduced, so there will then be 3^2 ways of applying the $\forall$ rule to the second premiss, and 3^3 ways of applying it to the first premiss, which adds thirty-six lines to the tableau. Each of those thirty-six lines then has to be broken down by rules for the truth-functors, and the tableau is quite unwieldy. In practice it is very much simpler to use one's wits to find a counter-example, rather than rely on this very cumbersome procedure. (You are invited to do so.[4]) The only points that it may be useful to note are (a) that there will be a completed tableau in this case, and (b) that it will contain only three names. This tells us that if the entailment is not correct, then there will be a counter-example to it in a domain of only three objects, so we need not try to think about larger domains.

In these last remarks I have, of course, been simply assuming the general principle that an open branch in a completed tableau will always yield an interpretation that verifies every formula on the branch. It is time to prove this. The interpretation is specified in this way. The domain is to have as many members as there are names on the open branch, and each different name is interpreted as denoting a different member of the domain. The predicate-letters are interpreted so that if F is an n-place predicate-letter, it is taken to be true of just those n-tuples $\langle |a_1|,...,|a_n| \rangle$ that correspond to

---

[4] It may be useful to recall that the correct form of this entailment is as given in Exercise 4.4.1(i).

atomic formulae $Fa_1...a_n$ which occur on the branch in question. The result then is that the atomic formulae which occur on the branch are all interpreted as true, and the atomic formulae which do not occur on the branch are all interpreted as false, just as in the earlier case when our only atomic formulae were sentence-letters. So the inductive argument showing that on this interpretation all the formulae on the branch are true begins as before, with cases (1)–(3) on p. 172. We need to add two new cases for the quantifiers, thus:

> *Case (4):* ϕ is $\exists\xi\psi$. Assume ϕ, i.e. $\exists\xi\psi$, occurs on the branch. Then, since the branch is fully developed, $\psi(\alpha/\xi)$ also occurs on the branch, for some name α. So, by the inductive hypothesis, it is true in I. But $\psi(\alpha/\xi)$ $\models \exists\xi\psi$. Hence $|\phi|_I = |\exists\xi\psi|_I = T$.
>
> *Case (5):* ϕ is $\forall\xi\psi$. Assume ϕ, i.e. $\forall\xi\psi$, occurs on the branch. Then for every name α on the branch, $\psi(\alpha/\xi)$ also occurs on the branch, since the branch is fully developed. So, by the inductive hypothesis, $\psi(\alpha/\xi)$ is true in I for every such name. But every object in the domain of the interpretation is the denotation of some such name, so it follows that ψ is true of every object in the domain. Hence $\forall\xi\psi$ is true in I.

We also need to add two new subcases under case (2), to cover $\neg\forall$ and $\neg\exists$. I leave these as an exercise. When they are added the induction is completed. On the new definition of a fully developed branch in a tableau, designed to suit the case where quantifiers are present, it remains true that all the formulae on a fully developed and open branch are true in some interpretation.

Notice that it does not yet follow that if Γ is an inconsistent set of formulae, true in no interpretation, then there must be a closed tableau for it. What follows is that any fully developed branch of a tableau for it will be closed, but we have not shown that there is a tableau for it in which all branches are fully developed. The trouble is that there are some (finite) sets of formulae for which there is no completed tableau, even in the new sense. Here is a very simple example, a tableau (P14) with one formula at its root, namely $\forall x\exists yFxy$. It is clear that, however far this tableau is continued, there is no finite stage at which it will be completed. The key to the difficulty is to think of what happens when this tableau is *infinitely* developed, for then it is clear that we can read off an interpretation which verifies all the formulae on it. As before, it will be an interpretation in which each name on the tableau names a distinct member of the domain, so the domain will be infinite. But it is easy to see that we can interpret F on this domain so that all the atomic statements on the tableau are true, and therefore $\exists yFxy$ will be true for each name in place of x, and so $\forall x\exists yFxy$ will be true too. Thus, if we allow ourselves to

Tableau (P14)

$$\forall x \exists y F x y$$

$\exists y F a y$	(3)
$F a b$	(2)
$\exists y F b y$	(3)
$F b c$	(2)
$\exists y F c y$	(3)

$$\vdots$$

think in terms of infinite tableaux, the problem over there being no finite tableau that is completed is easily overcome.

To prevent misunderstanding at this point, I pause to observe that we do not *have* to invoke an infinite domain in order to find an interpretation in which $\forall x \exists y F x y$ is true. On the contrary, there is a very simple interpretation with a domain of *one* element that will serve this purpose, namely where F is interpreted as true of that one element and itself. But we shall not find that interpretation by applying the tableau rules and then trying to read off an interpretation in the way proposed. One might, therefore, introduce a more complicated way of trying to read off an interpretation, roughly along these lines: develop each branch of the tableau until either it closes or it is fully developed or it begins to repeat itself, in the way that our example clearly does. When this happens, seek for an interpretation in which two or more of the names on the branch are taken to denote the *same* object. With this kind of method, but much more carefully specified, one could find a verifying interpretation with a finite domain wherever one exists. But as we have seen (p. 134), there are cases where all the verifying interpretations have infinite domains, so we must be able to take infinite domains into account somehow. Provided that we do do this, it turns out that the simple method of reading an interpretation off a fully developed branch, finite or infinite, is all that we need. So I shall not introduce any more complicated method.[5]

The argument that we now need is just a matter of putting together the ideas that we have developed so far. We wish to show that if Γ is an inconsistent set of formulae—and for the moment we shall still assume Γ to be finite—then there is a closed tableau with the formulae in Γ at its root. We consider a tableau grown from the root Γ by applying our rules in cycles, as specified at the start of this section. We shall speak of the 1st, 2nd, ..., nth, ... stage of developing the tableau, each stage to contain one full cycle of

---

[5] I briefly indicate just the initial steps towards such a method at the end of the chapter.

applications of the rules. It may be noted that if a formula first appears on a branch during the nth stage (including the case $n = 0$, for a formula at the root of the tableau), then the appropriate rule is applied to it either during the nth stage or during the $n+1$th stage, so that, in all cases except the rules for $\forall$ and for $\neg\exists$, by the end of the $n+1$th stage there is on the branch a shorter formula that entails it. And where the relevant rule is $\forall$ or $\neg\exists$ then by the end of the $n+1$th stage the rule has been applied using every name that is then on the branch. At subsequent stages, new names may be introduced (by the rules for $\exists$ and $\neg\forall$), but by the end of each stage the $\forall$ rule and the $\neg\exists$ rule will have been applied, using those names too, to any appropriate formula on the branch. Now, we have these possibilities. It may be that at some stage of developing the tableau we form a closed tableau. Then we can infer that the set Γ is inconsistent. Or it may be that at some stage we form a completed tableau with an open branch. Then we can infer that the set Γ is consistent, since a fully developed open branch always yields a verifying interpretation, as we have seen. If neither of these proves to be the case, then we may say—looking at the matter from an intuitive point of view—that the development of the tableau will go on for ever, and will result in the formation of an infinite branch. In that case also the set Γ is consistent, since again an infinite branch also yields a verifying interpretation, when it is developed in the stages we have specified. What we still have to prove is this last point.

We show that there is an infinite branch by the same technique as at the end of the previous section. We can say that a branch of the tableau formed at stage n is *satisfactory* if at each stage $m \geqslant n$ it has some descendant branch which is neither closed nor fully developed. Exactly as before we then show that if the tableau is not completed at any stage then (*a*) there is a branch of the tableau formed at stage 1 that is satisfactory, and (*b*) for each n, if there is a satisfactory branch in the tableau formed at stage n, then there is also a satisfactory branch, extending it, in the tableau formed at stage $n+1$. So it follows that there is an infinite series of such satisfactory branches, each extending the previous one, and we select some such series. Our interest is now in the formulae that occur in the selected series of branches.

The language of those formulae will contain infinitely many names, and to interpret it we take a domain which has one object for each name—different objects for different names—and no other objects. We then interpret the predicate-letters on that domain so that all the atomic formulae that occur on a branch of the selected series are interpreted as true, and all the other atomic formulae as false. It then follows that *all* the formulae occurring on the selected series of branches are interpreted as true. We have only to note that any formula in the series must first appear at some stage, and will be developed by the end of the next stage, and all cases except that for $\forall$ and $\neg\exists$ fall into place at once. For in all these other cases the shorter formulae which result from development entail the original. Moreover, no new principle is needed for $\forall$ and for $\neg\exists$, for if the formula $\forall\xi\phi$ appears at some stage, then for *every* name α the instance $\phi(\alpha/\xi)$ will appear at some stage (namely at the stage when α first appears, if that was after the stage at which $\forall\xi\phi$ appeared, and otherwise at the stage after the one which introduced $\forall\xi\phi$). Hence $\phi(\alpha/\xi)$ is interpreted as true for every name α, and every object in the domain is named by some name α, from which it follows that $\forall\xi\phi$ is also interpreted as true. The case is exactly similar for $\neg\exists$.

I do not delay to elaborate this proof more precisely, since no new principle is involved. It follows that there is an interpretation which verifies every formula occurring on any branch of the selected series. *A fortiori* there is an interpretation which verifies the formulae at the root of the branch, namely the formulae of the set Γ with which we began. So Γ is consistent. Thus, if Γ is *inconsistent*, then it cannot be that the tableau for Γ goes on for ever, and it cannot be that the tableau stops with an open branch. Accordingly, the tableau must stop with all branches closed. That is,

If $\Gamma \models$ then $\Gamma \vdash$,

which was to be proved.

One last point should be made, before this section ends. In the last section, we began with a completeness proof for the truth-functional case with Γ finite, and then extended this to the case with Γ infinite, and in fact it was the second case which took most of the work. In this section, where quantifiers are also being considered, we have now achieved the result that we want on the assumption that Γ is finite, but we have not yet said anything about the case with Γ infinite. So let us finally deal with this case, which can actually be done very briefly indeed. We combine the techniques of both sections by developing a series of tableaux in this way: The first tableau has the first formula in Γ at its root, and employs just one cycle of our cycle of rules. The second tableau adds to the root the second formula of Γ, and adds a second cycle of our cycle of rules. And so on indefinitely. The nth tableau will have the first n formulae in Γ at its root, and will result from having applied the cycle of rules once to the nth formula in Γ, twice to the $n-1$th formula in Γ,...,n times to the first formula in Γ. There is one trifling change to be made to the previous argument: since the set Γ is presumed to be infinite, we shall never be able to stop the development of the tableau on the ground that we have reached a fully developed open branch. For when we add the next formula in Γ to the root, that branch (probably) will not remain both open and fully developed. So there are only two possibilities to be considered: either we find a closed tableau at some stage, or the tableau goes on for ever. But the proof that, in the second case, the set Γ must be consistent, is exactly the same as before. I leave it to you to think through the detail.

EXERCISES

4.7.1. Complete the inductive argument on p. 178 by adding the new subcases under case (2) to cover $\neg\forall$ and $\neg\exists$.

4.7.2. Set out in greater detail the argument of the last paragraph above.

4.7.3.(a) Show that the number of non-equivalent formulae that can be constructed from truth-functors and a given finite stock of sentence-letters is finite. [Hint: for each n, how many n-place truth-functions are there?]
(b) Show that the same holds of the number of non-equivalent formulae that can be constructed from truth-functors, quantifiers, variables, and a given finite stock of one-place predicate-letters. [Hint: reflect on the implications of Section 3.8.]
(c) Show that the point no longer holds when we include a single two-place predicate-letter. [Hint: for each number n let us write

R^1xy for Rxy
$R^{n+1}xy$ for $\exists z(R^nxz \wedge Rzy)$.

Consider the infinitely many formulae $\exists xy R^nxy$.]

4.8. Further Remarks on Completeness, Compactness, and Decidability

Completeness   The fact that our tableau system is both sound and complete shows us that this method of proof does achieve all that we want it to achieve, and no more. It also allows us to take over for the notion of provability by a tableau (i.e. for $\vdash$) all those results that were established in Part I for semantic entailment (i.e. for $\models$). For example, we can now take it for granted that the Cut principle holds for tableau proofs, in the sense that

If $\Gamma \vdash \phi$ and $\phi, \Delta \vdash \psi$ then $\Gamma, \Delta \vdash \psi$.

It is actually quite tricky to prove this directly for the tableau system, because it is not in any straightforward way a consequence of the basic method of proof (as Exercise 4.5.1 reveals).[6] We can also take it for granted that for each formula there is a tableau proof that it has an equivalent in DNF, in CNF, in PNF, and so on. But it was not for the sake of such results as these that we originally needed this method of proof, for proof is not an end in itself. Our ultimate concern is with the semantic notions of entailment, consistency, validity, and so on, and proof is of value because it helps us to recognize these, or to recognize them more simply. As you will have discovered, in most ordinary cases a tableau proof is really quite simple to construct, and certainly simpler than arguing directly from the specified semantics. Nevertheless, there are some by-products of our completeness proof which it is worth elaborating in this section.[7]

Compactness Our completeness proof shows that both the logic of truth-functors and the logic of quantifiers have this property:

If $\Gamma \vDash$ then for some finite subset Γ' of Γ, $\Gamma' \vDash$.

Since inconsistency and entailment are interdefinable, an equivalent formulation is

If $\Gamma \vDash \phi$ then for some finite subset Γ' of Γ, $\Gamma' \vDash \phi$.

A logic with this property is said to be *compact*.[8] This means that if we have an inconsistency or an entailment which holds just because of the truth-functors and quantifiers involved, then it is always due to a finite number of the propositions in question. For example, no consequence can be drawn from an infinite set of assumptions that could not have been drawn from a finite subset of them. This is surprising, for it is easy to mention examples where all of infinitely many assumptions would be needed in order to justify some consequence. Here is a very simple one. Consider the infinite set of assumptions

(1) a is not a parent of b;
(2) a is not a parent of a parent of b;
(3) a is not a parent of a parent of a parent of b;
etc.

---

[6] For the curious, I outline a direct proof in the appendix to this chapter.

[7] Here is one by-product which I shall not elaborate: our proof shows incidentally that any consistent set of formulae has a verifying interpretation in which the domain has no more than denumerably many members. This is of some significance when we are concerned with axioms whose *intended* interpretation has a non-denumerably infinite domain (as with axioms for the real numbers). But the present book is not concerned with such axioms. (The remarks below on second-order logic are relevant to this point too, for the point does not hold in second-order logic.)

[8] The word 'compact', in this use, is inherited from topology, where it is used with a somewhat similar meaning.

From all these assumptions together there follows

a is not an ancestor of b.

But the conclusion is not entailed by any finite subset of the assumptions.

The explanation, of course, is that this inference does not depend just on the truth-functors and quantifiers in the premises and the conclusion, but also on the special relation between being a parent of and being an ancestor of. But it should be noted that this explanation brings with it an interesting consequence: the relation between being a parent of and being an ancestor of cannot *itself* be defined by using only the truth-functors and the quantifiers. For, if it could be so defined, then the definition could be added to the set of assumptions, and we should have an impossible situation. (If the definition is adequate, then the conclusion should follow from it, together with all the infinitely many other assumptions. But then, by compactness, the conclusion would also have to follow from a finite subset of those assumptions, which is absurd.) As a matter of fact the relation in question *can* be defined in what is called *second-order* logic, where we have not only the familiar quantifiers, binding variables which take the place of names, but also quantifiers which bind variables taking the place of predicates. This gives the language a greater expressive power, and consequently second-order logic is not compact. But elementary logic is compact, and so there are many notions that we understand perfectly well but cannot express in its vocabulary. Indeed, as things are at present, we cannot even define identity (though a second-order logic can). Later, in Chapter 8, we shall add identity as a new primitive notion, and this will allow us to distinguish between the different finite numbers while still preserving compactness. But, if I may put the position roughly, and in very general terms, we cannot express the distinction between what is finite and what is infinite without moving essentially beyond the resources available in elementary logic.

Decidability   In any case where we can tell in advance that the formulae we are concerned with will yield a completed tableau (according to the revised definition on pp. 174–5), we know that we can get a definite decision, one way or the other, by constructing that tableau in full. If we apply a little thought, then the full tableau can almost certainly be abbreviated, but even without thought the result can eventually be obtained just by plodding through the cycles of moves specified by our recipe. And there are several cases where we can tell in advance that there must be a completed tableau.

One such case is the case of formulae which have only one-place predicate-letters, as explored in Section 3.8. The decision procedure given there had two main stages: first, the quantifiers were to be driven in so that no quantifier was in the scope of any other, and second, the elementary quantifications so formed were to be simplified in such a way that truth-tables could then be applied. From our present position we still need the first part of this procedure: begin by driving the quantifiers in. But thereafter all that we need to do is to draw up a tableau in accordance with our suggested recipe. For such a tableau must terminate. In fact any tableau formed in accordance with this recipe will terminate unless on some branch it comes to contain an ∀∃-formula, i.e. a formula which has a universal quantifier preceding an existential quantifier. That sort of formula will yield an infinite tableau, as the example on p. 179 shows, but where no quantifier occurs within the scope of any other it is easy to see that our recipe must yield a completed tableau.

To prevent confusion, let me at once note that in Section 3.9 we gave a decision procedure for testing ∀∃-formulae. But that test was a test for *validity*. The tableau technique is in the first instance a test for *inconsistency*. Now to test a formula for validity is the same as to test its negation for inconsistency, and the negation of an ∀∃-formula is of course (equivalent to) an ∃∀-formula. So the discussion of Section 3.9 showed that there is a way of deciding on the inconsistency of any ∃∀-formula, and in fact our recipe for constructing tableau proofs provides such a way. (It hardly differs, in practice, from the recipe provided in Section 3.9.)

The two decision procedures provided in Chapter 3, for formulae of special kinds, are thus subsumed under the more general recipe for constructing tableau proofs provided here. In fact this recipe provides a useful framework for considering further decision procedures for further special kinds of formulae. I illustrate this point by considering an inconsistency test for one more special kind of formula, namely a formula which is in PNF and which contains just one universal quantifier, and after that just one existential quantifier. Let us begin by supposing that the quantifier-free part following these two quantifiers contains only one two-place predicate-letter, say F, and no other schematic letters. So our formula is

$$\forall x \exists y f(Fxx, Fxy, Fyx, Fyy),$$

when 'f' indicates some quantifier-free combination of the formulae that follow it. We apply the quantifier rules for ∀ and for ∃ once each, to obtain the quantifier-free formula

$$f(Faa, Fab, Fba, Fbb).$$

The truth-functional rules are then applied to this. If the tableau closes, then of course the original formula is inconsistent. If not, we distinguish cases.

In case (1) there is an open branch on which *Faa* and *Fbb* may be assigned the *same* value. In that case, we are through, for the tableau will never close. (*a*) There must be an interpretation with an infinite domain which verifies our formula, and which would be given by continuing to apply the tableau recipe *ad infinitum*. For if *Faa* and *Fbb* can be given the same value in an interpretation which verifies

$$f(Faa,Fab,Fba,Fbb),$$

then also *Fbb* and *Fcc* can be given that same value again in an interpretation which verifies

$$f(Fbb,Fbc,Fcb,Fcc),$$

and so on for ever. There is therefore no chance of the second step, or any subsequent step, introducing a contradiction. Also (*b*), there must in fact be an interpretation with a finite domain which verifies our formula. For if all four of the atomic formulae can be given the same value in a verifying interpretation, then we may identify *a* and *b* to obtain a one-element domain. If *Fab* and *Fba* can be given the same value as one another (but not the same value as *Faa* and *Fbb*), then we may identify *a* and *c* to obtain a two-element domain. And finally if *Fab* and *Fba* need to be given different values, we may still identify *a* and *d* (introduced in the next cycle of quantifier rules) to obtain a three-element domain.

In case (2) every open branch at the end of the first cycle of development is one on which *Faa* and *Fbb* need to be assigned different values. In that case, we proceed to a second cycle, adding as above

$$f(Fbb,Fbc,Fcb,Fcc).$$

If this tableau closes, then, of course, the original formula is inconsistent. If it does not, then the formula is consistent. For (*a*), there must be a verifying interpretation with an infinite domain, obtained by growing the tableau *ad infinitum*, which assigns alternating values to *Faa*, *Fbb*, *Fcc*, *Fdd*, etc. Also (*b*), there must be one with a finite domain, which need not contain more than four elements (identifying *a* and *e*, introduced in the fourth cycle of the tableau rules), and which may contain less than four, given suitable truth-values for *Fab*, *Fba*, *Fbc*, and *Fcb*.

In general, then, with formulae of this special kind all that we need are two cycles of the tableau rules, and if the tableau has not closed by then, it never will close, so our formula is consistent. But it is a rather special kind of formula that we have been concerned with. Some generalizations will be indicated in the exercises that follow, but a full treatment of this topic is beyond the scope of this book.

EXERCISE

4.8.1.(*a*) Show that it makes no difference to the argument of the last two pages if we take the single predicate-letter to have some number of places other than two.
(*b*) Investigate in the same way the case of a formula made up of a single universal quantifier, then a single existential quantifier, then a quantifier-free part containing two predicate-letters, and no other schematic letters. [The answer is that if the tableau has not closed after four cycles of the rules, then it never will close. In general, if there are *n* predicate-letters then 2^n cycles of the rules need to be investigated.]
(*c*) Experiment with the case of a formula made up of a single universal quantifier, then two existential quantifiers, then a quantifier-free part. (Begin, as before, by assuming that it contains just one predicate-letter.)

....

4.9. Appendix: A Direct Proof of the Cut Principle

....

For the tableau system, the most convenient form in which to consider the Cut principle is this:

If $\Gamma, \phi \vdash$ and $\Gamma, \neg\phi \vdash$ then $\Gamma \vdash$.

(You are invited to check that this is equivalent to the more familiar version cited on p. 182). The proof will be by induction on the length of the formula ϕ, so to save labour I shall assume that we are dealing with a language containing $\neg, \wedge, \forall$ as its only logical symbols. As a minor convenience I shall assume too that the rule for closing branches is applied only to atomic formulae and their negations (cf. Exercise 4.2.2). We shall need the following lemmas:

(1) If $\Gamma, \neg\neg\psi \vdash$ then $\Gamma, \psi \vdash$.
(2) If $\Gamma, \phi \wedge \psi \vdash$ then $\Gamma, \phi, \psi \vdash$.
(3) If $\Gamma, \neg(\phi \wedge \psi) \vdash$ then $\Gamma, \neg\phi \vdash$ and $\Gamma, \neg\psi \vdash$.
(4) If $\Gamma, \neg\forall\xi\psi \vdash$ then $\Gamma, \neg\psi(\alpha/\xi) \vdash$ for all names α.

Lemmas (1)–(3) are very easily proved by considering the relevant tableau rules, and I say no more about them. Lemma (4) is rather more tricky, and I set it at the end as an assisted exercise. Meanwhile, I assume that the lemmas are all available, so that we can turn to the main proof.

The proof is by induction on the length of ϕ, and the hypothesis of induction is

for all ψ shorter than ϕ, and for all sets Δ, if $\Delta,\psi \vdash$ and $\Delta,\neg\psi \vdash$ then $\Delta \vdash$.

We have four cases to consider:

Case (1): ϕ is an atomic formula. We are given a closed tableau with Γ,ϕ at its root, and another with $\Gamma,\neg\phi$ at its root. We remove ϕ from the closed tableau for Γ,ϕ, and consider what remains. If this is still a closed tableau, we have our result. If it is not, then any branches that have become open must contain $\neg\phi$. So we append to each of them the closed tableau for $\Gamma,\neg\phi$, and the result must be a closed tableau for Γ, as desired.

Case (2): ϕ is $\neg\psi$. So we are given that $\Gamma,\neg\psi \vdash$ and $\Gamma,\neg\neg\psi \vdash$. By lemma (1) the latter implies that $\Gamma,\psi \vdash$. So by the inductive hypothesis we have $\Gamma \vdash$, as desired.

Case (3): ϕ is $\psi\wedge\chi$. So we are given that $\Gamma,\psi\wedge\chi \vdash$ and $\Gamma,\neg(\psi\wedge\chi) \vdash$. By lemmas (2) and (3) it follows that $\Gamma,\psi,\chi \vdash$ and that $\Gamma,\neg\psi \vdash$. It is obvious from the structure of tableaux that thinning applies, so from the latter we also have $\Gamma,\neg\psi,\chi \vdash$. Hence by the inductive hypothesis $\Gamma,\chi \vdash$. But also, applying lemma (3) again to our premiss, we have $\Gamma,\neg\chi \vdash$. Hence by the inductive hypothesis once more we have $\Gamma \vdash$, as desired.

Case (4): ϕ is $\forall\xi\psi$. So we are given that there is a closed tableau for $\Gamma,\forall\xi\psi$, and (applying lemma (4)) that $\Gamma,\neg\psi(\alpha/\xi) \vdash$ for all names α. We take the closed tableau for $\Gamma,\forall\xi\psi$, remove $\forall\xi\psi$ from its root, and consider what remains. If it is still a closed tableau, then we are through. If not, then that is because one or more branches contain one or more occurrences of $\psi(\alpha/\xi)$ for one or more names α. We consider any such branch which has an occurrence of such a formula $\psi(\alpha/\xi)$ with no further occurrence below it. Letting Δ be the set of formulae on this branch between Γ and this occurrence of $\psi(\alpha/\xi)$, omitting $\forall\xi\psi$, we consider the branch as a tableau with all the formulae $\Gamma,\Delta,\psi(\alpha/\xi)$ in its root. So considered, it is clear that it must be a closed tableau. Thus $\Gamma,\Delta,\psi(\alpha/\xi) \vdash$. But we also have by lemma (4) that $\Gamma,\neg\psi(\alpha/\xi) \vdash$, and hence by thinning that $\Gamma,\Delta,\neg\psi(\alpha/\xi) \vdash$. So by inductive hypothesis $\Gamma,\Delta \vdash$, i.e. there is a closed tableau with Γ,Δ at its root. We therefore substitute this for all the branch below Γ,Δ, and the occurrence of $\psi(\alpha/\xi)$ has been eliminated. Continuing the same procedure, we work up the tableau, from the bottom, eliminating in turn each occurrence of a formula $\psi(\alpha/\xi)$ for some name α. The result is to form a closed tableau for Γ, as desired.

This completes the induction, and so provides the required proof.

EXERCISE

4.9.1.(*a*) Let $\Gamma(\beta/\alpha)$ be the result of substituting the name β uniformly for all occurrences of α throughout all the formulae in Γ. Show that

If $\Gamma \vdash$ then $\Gamma(\beta/\alpha) \vdash$.

[If we assume the soundness and completeness of the tableau system, then, of course, this is just an application of 3.6.I(*a*). But we can also argue that point directly, from the structure of the tableau rules. First, if β already occurs in Γ, it is easy to see that substituting β for α throughout the closed tableau for Γ cannot upset the operation of the quantifier rules, and so must still leave a correct closed tableau. Second, the same applies if β does not already occur in Γ or anywhere else in the closed tableau for Γ. So the substitution might upset the quantifier rules only in case β does occur somewhere in the tableau, but not in Γ, and the problem is to say what to do in this case.]

(*b*) Prove lemma (4) above, i.e.

If $\Gamma, \neg\forall\xi\psi \vdash$ then $\Gamma, \neg\psi(\alpha/\xi) \vdash$ for all names α.

[In the closed tableau with $\Gamma, \neg\forall\xi\psi$ at its root the $\neg\forall$ rule may have been applied several times to $\neg\forall\xi\psi$, yielding various instances, say $\neg\psi(\beta_1/\xi)$, $\neg\psi(\beta_2/\xi)$,...., $\neg\psi(\beta_n/\xi)$. Removing $\neg\forall\xi\psi$ from the root, and adding these various instances instead, we evidently obtain a closed tableau showing that $\Gamma, \neg\psi(\beta_1/\xi)$, $\neg\psi(\beta_2/\xi)$, ...,$\neg\psi(\beta_n/\xi) \vdash$. Recalling that each of the names β_i must be new, and hence do not occur in Γ, the desired result then follows by part (*a*).]

(*c*) Show that the converse of lemma (4) is also correct, i.e. that

If $\Gamma, \neg\psi(\alpha/,\xi) \vdash$, for all names α, then $\Gamma, \neg\forall\xi\psi \vdash$.

5

Axiomatic Proofs

5.1. The Idea

The idea of using semantic tableaux to provide a proof procedure is a recent invention. (In effect it stems from work done by Gentzen (1934), but the main ideas were first clearly presented by Beth (1955). The tree format used in the last chapter is due to Jeffrey (1981).) Originally proofs in elementary logic were quite differently conceived.

One of the great achievements of Greek mathematics was the introduction of 'the axiomatic method', most famously in Euclid's *Elements*, but by no means confined to that work. The method results quite naturally from reflection upon the idea of a proof. For in an ordinary proof one shows that some proposition is true by showing that it follows from premises that are already accepted as true, and this will lead the theoretician to ask whether those premises could be proved in their turn. Pressing this question, one is led to the idea of the 'basic premises' of the subject, from which all other propositions must be proved, but which must themselves be accepted without proof. These, then, are the axioms of the subject. It was recognized by Aristotle that there must be such axioms for any subject that could be 'scientifically' pursued; and it was Euclid's achievement to have found a set of axioms from which almost all the mathematics then known could be deduced. In fact the axioms need some supplementation if the deduction is to confirm to modern standards of rigour, but that is of small importance. The Greeks had, apparently, supplied mathematics with a clear 'foundation'.

Over the succeeding centuries mathematics grew and developed in many ways, but it was not until the nineteenth century that interest turned once more to the question of 'foundations'. By then it was quite clear that Euclid's work would no longer suffice, and this led to a renewed search for the basic premisses of the subject. At the same time some mathematicians became interested in the principles of logic, which governed the deductions from these premisses, and an interest in both topics at once led Frege to the 'logicist' theory of the foundations of mathematics. This theory is that mathematics has no special axioms of its own, but follows just from the principles of logic themselves, when augmented by suitable definitions. To argue in detail for this theory Frege had first to supply an adequate account of the principles of logic, which he did in his *Begriffsschrift* of 1879. This epoch-making work was the first presentation of what we now think of as modern logic, and in it Frege supplied a set of axioms, i.e. basic premisses, for logic itself. No doubt he was led to present the foundations of logic in this way at least partly because it was a well-known way of presenting the foundations of other disciplines, especially parts of mathematics. But nowadays it does not strike us as at all natural for logic.

Logic has always been regarded as concerned with correct inference, and so it is natural to expect that it will take as its basic notion the relation of entailment between premisses and conclusion. In fact the proof technique of the last chapter did not conform to that expectation entirely. For the original version aims to show, quite generally, that certain combinations of truth-values are impossible, and while this includes entailment as a special case, it is not directly focused upon it. And the revised version, which one uses in practice, is naturally seen just as a technique for proving inconsistency. Equally a proof technique that is founded on axioms does not conform, since an axiom is basically a claim that something is true. More particularly, an axiom of logic claims that something is logically true, and hence a necessary truth. So when we employ 'formal' (i.e. schematic) languages in our logic, an axiom will claim that some formula is such that all its instances are logically true, i.e. that the formula comes out true under all (possible) interpretations of its non-logical symbols, which is to say that it is a valid formula. So here the basic use of the turnstile has one formula on the right and none on the left. Of course, facts about entailment will follow from this, for, as we know,

$$\varphi_1,...,\varphi_n \vDash \psi \quad \text{iff} \quad \vDash (\varphi_1 \rightarrow ...(\varphi_n \rightarrow \psi)..)$$

But we do not work with entailment from the beginning. Our axioms are single formulae, not sequents of several formulae.

We shall lay down infinitely many axioms, which we do by using axiom-schemas. For example, our first axiom-schema will be

$$\varphi \rightarrow (\psi \rightarrow \varphi),$$

and to say that this is an axiom-schema is to say that every formula that can be obtained from it, by substituting some definite formula for φ and some definite formula for ψ, is an axiom. Clearly, there are infinitely many such formulae, and we count them all as axioms. But despite this prodigality with the axioms, we must also lay down at least one rule of inference, to allow us to make deductions from the axioms. Since the axioms state that certain selected formulae are valid, the sort of rule that we need will be a rule telling us that if such and such formulae are valid, then so also is such and such another formula. By tradition, axiomatic systems almost always adopt here a version of Modus Ponens, which in this context is also called the rule of *detachment*, namely

$$\text{If } \vDash \varphi \text{ and } \vDash \varphi \rightarrow \psi \text{ then } \vDash \psi.$$

An axiomatic system may also adopt other rules, but the general idea is to keep the rules of inference to a minimum, so that it is the axioms rather than the rules which embody the substantial assumptions. Finally, a proof in such a system is just a finite sequence of formulae, each of which is either an axiom or a consequence of preceding formulae by one of the stated rules of inference. It is a proof of the last formula in the sequence. (Note that it follows at once that there is a proof of each axiom, namely the 'sequence' of formulae which consists just of that axiom and nothing else.)

The syntactic turnstile is used in the context

$$\vdash \varphi$$

to mean 'There is a proof of φ' (i.e. in the system currently being considered). Another way of saying the same thing is 'φ is a theorem'. When the proof system is being formally presented, independently of any semantic considerations, we use '$\vdash$' in place of '$\vDash$' to state the axioms and the rules of inference.

EXERCISE

5.1.1. Older axiom systems proceeded not from axiom-schemas but from single axioms, but in addition they adopted as a further rule of proof the principle of uniform substitution for schematic letters (2.5.D and 3.6.I). Now to lay down an axiom-schema is the same as to lay down a single axiom together with a licence to apply the principle of substitution to it. (Why, exactly?) So one could say that the difference between the two approaches is that older systems allowed one to apply substitution at any point in a proof, whereas our approach confines its application to axioms. Consider how one might try to show that the two approaches are equivalent, in the sense that each yields exactly the same theorems. [In effect one has to show that a proof containing a step of substitution applied to a non-axiom can always be replaced by one which eliminates that step, and instead applies substitution only to axioms. The obvious suggestion is: make the same substitution in every formula earlier in the proof. In fact this gives the right answer for formulae that lack quantifiers, but complications can arise when quantifiers are present. Explain. (Recall Exercise 4.9.1.)]

5.2. Axioms for the Truth-Functors

One of the interests in an axiomatic presentation of elementary logic is the economy that can be achieved in the rules and axioms. When combined with the very simple and straightforward structure of proofs in such a system, this can be a considerable help in the investigation of what can and cannot be proved in the system. But economy can be carried too far. For example, it is possible to take a language which contains just one truth-functor, e.g. one of the stroke functors, and to set down just one axiom and one rule for that language, and nevertheless to provide thereby a complete basis for all of truth-functional logic. (See the appendix to this chapter.) But it is horribly difficult to learn to manipulate such a system. We shall, then, aim for a compromise, seeking to economize where it is relatively simple to do so, but not at the cost of losing intelligibility. We may economize on the language, by taking just $\neg, \rightarrow, \forall$ as our logical symbols ($\rightarrow$ because of its connection with Modus Ponens, $\neg$ because it is the natural partner to $\rightarrow$, and $\forall$ for a reason which will become clear in Section 5.6). We shall adopt two axiom-schemas which concern $\rightarrow$ alone, and are deliberately chosen so as to simplify a crucial proof (Section 5.3); one further axiom-schema for $\neg$ (somewhat arbitrarily chosen); and two more axiom-schemas for $\forall$, of which one is very natural and the other is chosen to simplify a crucial proof. Some other possible axiomatizations will be mentioned in the course of the chapter. But I postpone the axioms for ∀ to Section 5.6, so that we can begin by confining attention just to the logic of truth-functors.

We shall take, then, a language with ¬ and → as its only logical symbols. For this language there will be three axiom-schemas, each generating infinitely many axioms, namely

(A1) ⊢ φ→(ψ→φ).
(A2) ⊢ (φ→(ψ→χ)) → ((φ→ψ) → (φ→χ)).
(A3) ⊢ (¬φ→¬ψ) → (ψ→φ).

and there will be one rule of inference:

DET: If ⊢ φ and ⊢ φ→ψ then ⊢ ψ.

It is very easily seen that this system is *sound*, i.e. that every provable formula is valid:

If ⊢ φ then ⊨ φ.

In effect we have only to observe that each axiom is valid, and that the one rule of inference preserves validity, and that yields the result at once. To put this argument more fully, we argue by induction on the length of a proof to show that every proof has a valid formula as its last line. Consider, then, any arbitrary proof 𝒫, with a formula φ as its last line. The hypothesis of induction is

Every proof shorter than 𝒫 has a valid last line,

and we have to show that φ must therefore be a valid formula. Since 𝒫 is a proof, we have two cases to consider.

Case (1): φ is an axiom. It is easily checked by the tables that every axiom is valid, and this yields our result at once.

Case (2): φ is a consequence, by detachment, of two earlier lines in 𝒫. From the definition of a proof it is clear that any initial segment of a proof is itself a proof, and of course a (proper) initial segment of 𝒫 is a proof shorter than 𝒫. Hence any line in 𝒫, other than the last line, is the last line of some proof shorter than 𝒫. So, by the hypothesis of induction, it is valid. But it is easily checked that the rule of detachment, applied to valid formulae, yields only valid formulae as results. Hence φ must be valid.

This completes the argument.

I remark at this point that our system is also *complete*, i.e. that for any formula φ of the language,

If $\vDash \varphi$ then $\vdash \varphi$.

But I postpone a proof of this claim to Section 5.4. Meanwhile, I turn to a different topic, the *independence* of our three axiom-schemas.

Clearly, our axiom-schemas will not be economically chosen if one of the axiom-schemas is superfluous, in that all the axioms generated from it could be obtained as theorems by using only the other axioms. We have to show that this is not the case. In other words we have to show (*a*) that from axiom-schemas (A1) and (A2) together one cannot deduce all the instances of axiom-schema (A3); in particular one cannot deduce the instance

$(\neg P \to \neg Q) \to (Q \to P).$

(If one could deduce this instance, then one could also deduce every other. Why? Consider Exercise 5.1.1.) Similarly, we have to show (*b*) that there is an instance of axiom-schema (A2) that cannot be deduced from (A1) and (A3) together; and (*c*) that there is an instance of axiom-schema (A1) that cannot be deduced from axioms (A2) and (A3) together. Now one can show that some formula can be deduced by actually producing the deduction. But how are we to show that a given formula cannot be deduced? The general method is this: one finds some property possessed by every permitted axiom, and preserved by the rule of inference, but not possessed by the formula in question.

The independence of axiom-schema (A3) is easily established in this way. We have observed that, on the standard interpretations of $\neg$ and $\to$, every axiom is valid and the rule of inference preserves validity. Evidently, this need not be true for non-standard interpretations of these symbols. In particular, consider this non-standard interpretation: $\to$ is to be interpreted as usual, but $\neg$ is to be interpreted so that $\neg\varphi$ always has the same truth-value as φ. (In other words, we interpret $\neg$ as we standardly interpret $\neg\neg$.) Under this interpretation it is clear that all instances of (A1) and (A2) remain 'valid', and that the rule of inference preserves 'validity', since $\to$ is not affected. But a typical instance of (A3), such as

$(\neg P \to \neg Q) \to (Q \to P)$

is now given the same interpretation as

$(P \to Q) \to (Q \to P)$

and so it is not 'valid'. (It takes the value F when $|P| = $ F and $|Q| = $ T.) It follows that this instance of (A3) cannot be deduced from (A1) and (A2) by the rule of inference. For everything that can be so deduced is not only valid under the standard interpretation of $\rightarrow$ and $\neg$, but also 'valid' under the non-standard interpretation just given.

A slightly different way of putting the same argument is this. Consider a transformation f which transforms each formula of our language into another, by erasing all the negation signs. That is, f is a function from formulae to formulae which obeys these conditions

(1) $f(P_i) = P_i$, for P_i an atomic formula.
(2) $f(\varphi \rightarrow \psi) = (f(\varphi) \rightarrow f(\psi))$.
(3) $f(\neg \varphi) = f(\varphi)$.

Then we argue as follows: if φ is an instance of (A1) or (A2), then $f(\varphi)$ is valid (under the *standard* interpretation of all the signs involved). (This is because $f(\varphi)$ is also an instance of the same axiom-schema.) Also, if $f(\varphi)$ is valid, and $f(\varphi \rightarrow \psi)$ is valid, then $f(\psi)$ is valid too. So it follows that if φ is any formula deducible, by the rule of inference, from (A1) and (A2), then $f(\varphi)$ is valid. But we have seen that if φ is a typical instance of axiom-schema (A3), then $f(\varphi)$ is not valid. It follows that φ cannot be so deduced.

It was relatively easy to show the independence of (A3), because this schema contains a new symbol, $\neg$, that is not present in the other schemata. It is rather more difficult to show the independence of (A1) and (A2). We may begin by looking for some non-standard interpretation of $\rightarrow$, on which (A2) is not counted as 'valid', but (A1) and (A3) are still 'valid', and the rule of inference still preserves 'validity'; or vice versa (A1) is not 'valid' but (A2) and (A3) still are. However, if we confine our attention to the interpretations that can be given in terms of the usual two-valued truth-tables, we shall not find one. (And this remains true even if (A3) is ignored. On the usual two-valued truth-tables, any interpretation of $\rightarrow$ that verifies one of (A1) and (A2) also verifies the other.) We must, then, look to a non-standard interpretation which goes beyond the usual, two-valued, truth-tables.

The usual ploy here is to introduce three-valued tables. These can be thought of in various ways, but for present purposes this approach will be adequate: we shall retain the familiar values T and F, but we shall add another value, which we shall think of as 'between' those two, and which we shall call N (for 'Neither'). (This is intended simply as a helpful prop for thought. But for the formal technique to work it does not matter in the slightest whether the supposed 'values'—T,F,N—can be given an interpretation which makes any kind of sense. Compare the tables given in Exercise 5.2.2(c).) As before, a formula will count as 'valid' iff it always takes the value T, on our tables, whatever the values of its sentence-letters. It follows from this that when φ and ψ both take the value N then $\varphi \rightarrow \psi$ must not take the value N (for if it did neither of (A1) and (A2) would be valid). To deal with this point, it is natural to say that even when we have three values to consider we shall preserve the principle that $\varphi \rightarrow \psi$ takes the value T whenever φ and ψ take the same value. It is also fairly natural to preserve the principles that $\varphi \rightarrow \psi$ takes the value T whenever ψ takes the value T, and whenever φ takes the value F, and that it takes the value F when φ is T and ψ is F. These decisions have already filled in *most* of the places in our new three-valued tables. In fact we have

$\varphi \rightarrow \psi$	ψ				$\rightarrow$	T	N	F
	T	N	F					
T	T		F	which I	T	T		F
φ N	T	T		abbreviate to	N	T	T	
F	T	T	T		F	T	T	T

(The table on the left is, I hope, self-explanatory, and thus explains the briefer table on the right that I shall use henceforth.) We still have two questions to consider, namely the value of $\varphi \rightarrow \psi$ (1) when $|\varphi| = T$ and $|\psi| = N$, (2) when $|\varphi| = N$ and $|\psi| = F$. There is a further restriction to be observed in case (1), namely that we cannot here have $|\varphi \rightarrow \psi| = T$. For if we do have T here, then the rule of inference will not preserve validity. We may observe also that there is no point in considering tables with T in case (2), for such tables will be equivalent to the standard two-valued tables, with N and F taken to be the *same* value.

With so much by way of initial scene-setting, we now have to resort to tedious experiment. The four tables left for consideration are:

(I) $\rightarrow$	T	N	F
T	T	N	F
N	T	T	N
F	T	T	T

(II) $\rightarrow$	T	N	F
T	T	F	F
N	T	T	F
F	T	T	T

(III) $\rightarrow$	T	N	F
T	T	N	F
N	T	T	F
F	T	T	T

(IV) $\rightarrow$	T	N	F
T	T	F	F
N	T	T	N
F	T	T	T

We first try these tables simply on typical instances of (A1) and (A2), namely

(1) $P \rightarrow (Q \rightarrow P)$

(2) $(P \rightarrow (Q \rightarrow R)) \rightarrow ((P \rightarrow Q) \rightarrow (P \rightarrow R))$.

We find that on table I we have (1) valid and (2) invalid (for if $|P| = |Q| = N$ and $|R| = F$, then (2) takes the value N); on table II we have (1) invalid and (2) valid (for if $|P| = N$ and $|Q| = T$, then (1) takes the value N); on table III both (1) and (2) are valid; on table IV both (1) and (2) are invalid (for if $|P| = N$ and $|Q| = T$, then (1) takes the value N, and if $|P| = |Q| = N$ and $|R| = F$, then (2) takes the value F). For present purposes, then, the tables of interest are I and II, since the other two do not discriminate between our first two axioms.

We must now add a suitable three-valued table for the negation sign. The natural candidates to consider are these three:

(V) $\neg$		(VI) $\neg$		(VII) $\neg$	
T	F	T	F	T	F
N	N	N	F	N	T
F	T	F	T	F	T

It turns out that V will serve our purpose perfectly well, for a typical instance of (A3), namely

(3) $(\neg P \rightarrow \neg Q) \rightarrow (Q \rightarrow P)$,

is valid both on tables I and V and on tables II and V. Thus axiom-schema (A1) is independent of (A2) and (A3), since on tables II and V together both (A2) and (A3) are valid while (A1) is not; and (A2) is independent of (A1) and (A3), since on tables I and V together both (A1) and (A3) are valid while (A2) is not. The argument requires us also to observe that on any of these tables the rule of detachment preserves validity. (I remark, incidentally, that our tables give us another proof that (A3) is independent of (A1) and (A2), since on tables III and VI both (A1) and (A2) are valid while (A3) is not. The same applies to tables III and VII.)

Unfortunately, there is little that one can say by way of advice on finding independence proofs such as these. For the most part, it is a tedious matter of experiment by trial and error. Moreover, there are, in principle, no limits on the complexity of the tables that may be needed: one cannot guarantee that if axioms are independent, then this can be shown by n-valued tables for any specified n, and it may be much more effective to use a different kind of semantics altogether. I give only a very brief indication here of how this might be done. The interpretations for $\rightarrow$ that we have been considering have been, in an extended sense, truth-functional. But there is no need to limit attention to such interpretations. For example, suppose that $P \rightarrow Q$ is to be interpreted as 'it is a *necessary* truth that if P then Q'. Then it should be possible to see that axiom-schema (A1) is not correct for this interpretation, while (A3) certainly is correct (given the standard interpretation for $\neg$), and (A2) is somewhat difficult to think about, but might be correct. Moreover, the rule of detachment preserves correctness. So here is a different way of trying to show that (A1) is independent of (A2) and (A3). But some knowledge of modal logic would be required to carry this line of argument through with full rigour.[1]

I end this section with one further application of our three-valued tables. One might have expected that axioms (A1) and (A2) between them would be enough for the deduction of every theorem in which $\rightarrow$ is the sole logical symbol, and that (A3) would have to be used only for theorems containing $\neg$. This is not the case. For a counter-example, consider the thesis known as Peirce's law:

$$((P \rightarrow Q) \rightarrow P) \rightarrow P.$$

As a truth-table check will show, this thesis is valid on the standard interpretation of $\rightarrow$. As will be proved in Section 5.4, our system is complete, so this thesis is provable in it. But it cannot be proved from axiom-schemas (A1) and (A2) alone. For we have noted that whatever can be proved just from those schemas must also be 'valid' on the three-valued table III, but Peirce's law is not. On those tables, it has the value N when $|P| = N$ and $|Q| = F$. I shall come back to the significance of this point on several occasions hereafter.

EXERCISES

5.2.1. Prove the assertion (p. 196) that any interpretation of $\rightarrow$ on the usual two-valued truth-tables will verify either both or neither of axiom-schemas (A1) and (A2). [Of course, this can be done by tediously trying each of the sixteen possible interpretations in turn. But see if you can find a shorter method of argument.]

5.2.2. As will be shown in Section 5.4, in place of our axiom-schema (A3) we could have used this alternative (A3') instead:

(A3'): $(\neg \varphi \rightarrow \psi) \rightarrow ((\neg \varphi \rightarrow \neg \psi) \rightarrow \varphi)$.

---

[1] The fact is that, under the suggested interpretation for $\rightarrow$, (A2) and (A3) are valid in the modal logic S4, and so is anything that can be deduced from them by the rule of detachment, while (A1) is not valid in any modal logic.

(*a*) Show that (A3′) is independent of (A1) and (A2). [The same argument as works for (A3) will also work for (A3′).]

(*b*) Show that (A1) is independent of (A2) and (A3′). [Use table VII in place of table V.]

(*c*) Show that no combination of tables I–VII will demonstrate that (A2) is independent of (A1) and (A3′), but that the following unexpected tables will do the trick:

$\rightarrow$	T	N	F		$\neg$	
T	T	F	F		T	N
N	T	F	T		N	N
F	T	T	T		F	N

5.3. **The Deduction Theorem**

So far, we have established various results about what *cannot* be proved from this or that set of axioms, but we have not shown that anything *can* be proved. This will now be remedied. As we have observed, the most straightforward way of showing that something can be proved is by actually giving a proof of it, and we will begin with an example. Here is a proof of the simple theorem $P \rightarrow P$.

$\vdash P \rightarrow P$

    1. $(P \rightarrow ((P \rightarrow P) \rightarrow P)) \rightarrow ((P \rightarrow (P \rightarrow P)) \rightarrow (P \rightarrow P))$ A2

    2. $P \rightarrow ((P \rightarrow P) \rightarrow P)$ A1

    3. $P \rightarrow (P \rightarrow P)$ A1

    4. $(P \rightarrow (P \rightarrow P)) \rightarrow (P \rightarrow P)$ 1,2

    5. $P \rightarrow P$ 3,4

On the right we have noted the justification for each line of the proof. Thus the first line is an instance of axiom-schema (A2) and the second and third are instances of axiom-schema (A1). The fourth line follows by the rule of detachment from lines (1) and (2) earlier, and the fifth line follows similarly from lines (3) and (4). It is standard practice always to furnish a justification for each line of a proof, so that it can easily be checked that indeed it is a proof. Now let us note two things about this proof.

First, it is obvious that by the same proof as we have used to prove $P \rightarrow P$ one could also prove any substitution-instance of that theorem, e.g.

$Q \rightarrow Q$
$(P \rightarrow Q) \rightarrow (P \rightarrow Q)$
$\neg(P \rightarrow Q) \rightarrow \neg(P \rightarrow Q)$
etc.

All one has to do to find a proof of the substitution-instance is to make the same substitutions all the way through the original proof. It is clear that this argument holds quite generally, so we can say that in our axiomatic system uniform substitution for schematic letters preserves provability, i.e.

A substitution-instance of a theorem is itself a theorem.

To save having to cite this principle explicitly every time that we wish to use it, in future we shall very seldom cite actual theorems of the system, or give actual proofs of them, but will cite theorem-*schemas* (like our axiom-schemas), and give proof-schemas to establish them. So the above proof would be given with the schematic φ in place of the definite formula P throughout, and would be taken as establishing the theorem-schema

Lemma. $\vdash \varphi \rightarrow \varphi$.

(But, to avoid prolixity, we shall often in practice refer to theorem-schemas simply as theorems, and to axiom-schemas as axioms).

A second point to note about the proof just given is that it is remarkably roundabout. When seeking for a proof of the simple theorem $P \rightarrow P$, how would one know that anything as complicated as line (1) would be needed? What principles are there that can guide one to the right axioms to use in the first place? Well, the answer is that the problem of finding proofs can be very much simplified if we begin by looking for a different *kind* of proof altogether, namely a *proof from assumptions*.

We shall use '$\Gamma \vdash \varphi$' to mean 'there is a proof of φ from the set of assumptions Γ', and we define this as short for 'there is a finite sequence of formulae such that each of them is either an axiom, or a member of Γ, or a consequence of previous formulae by one of the specified rules of inference; and the last formula in the sequence is φ'. It is worth noting at once that from this definition there follow without more ado the three 'structural' principles of Assumptions, Thinning, and Cutting, namely

ASS: $\varphi \vdash \varphi$
THIN: If $\Gamma \vdash \varphi$ then $\Gamma, \psi \vdash \varphi$
CUT: If $\Gamma \vdash \varphi$ and $\phi, \Delta \vdash \psi$ then $\Gamma, \Delta \vdash \psi$.

These follow independently of how the rules of inference are specified. For example, to verify the principle of Assumptions we have only to note that the sequence consisting of the single formula φ and nothing else is, by the definition, a proof of φ from the assumption φ. The other two principles are proved equally simply. But let us now come to the question of specifying rules of inference.

Rules of inference for use in proofs from assumptions need not be the same as those specified for axiomatic proofs, but they should have the axiomatic rules as a special case, namely the case where there are no assumptions. Thus at present our axioms are (A1)–(A3) as specified in the last section, and as our rule of inference we now take Modus Ponens in its most general form, which is usually written as

$$\varphi, \varphi \to \psi \vdash \psi.$$

But since we are licensed to apply this rule within proofs from assumptions, a more precise formulation is

If $\Gamma \vdash \varphi$ and $\Gamma \vdash \varphi \to \psi$ then $\Gamma \vdash \psi$.

It is therefore not the *same* rule as the rule of detachment that we began with, but a more general rule. For the rule of detachment is the special case of this rule in which Γ is null, i.e. in which there are no assumptions. Consequently, proofs in the axiomatic system that we began with are special cases of proofs from assumptions in general, namely the cases in which there are no assumptions.

Now, it is very much easier to look for proofs from assumptions than it is to look for proper axiomatic proofs. Yet also, every proof from assumptions can be transformed into a proper axiomatic proof in this sense: a proof of ψ from the assumptions $\varphi_1,...,\varphi_n$, showing that

$$\varphi_1,...,\varphi_n \vdash \psi$$

can be transformed to a proof showing that

$$\varphi_1,...,\varphi_{n-1} \vdash \varphi_n \to \psi,$$

and this in turn can be transformed to show that

$$\varphi_1,...,\varphi_{n-2} \vdash \varphi_{n-1} \to (\varphi_n \to \psi)$$

and by repeating such transformations as often as necessary we eventually get a proof from no assumptions showing that

$$\vdash \varphi_1 \to (\varphi_2 \to (...(\varphi_n \to \psi)..)).$$

This last is called the *conditionalization* of the sequent with which we began. To establish the claim, we prove what is called the *Deduction Theorem*, which states that

If $\Gamma,\varphi \vdash \psi$ then $\Gamma \vdash \varphi \rightarrow \psi$.

(Compare 2.5.H.)

The argument is by induction on the length of the proof showing that $\Gamma,\varphi \vdash \psi$. So let $\mathcal{P}$ be such a proof. The hypothesis of induction is

Any proof shorter than $\mathcal{P}$ showing that $\Gamma,\varphi \vdash \chi$ can be transformed into a proof showing that $\Gamma \vdash \varphi \rightarrow \chi$, for any formula χ.

We have three cases to consider, according to the three possible justifications for the line ψ in the proof.

Case (1): ψ is an axiom. Then $\psi \rightarrow (\varphi \rightarrow \psi)$ is also an axiom. So by Modus Ponens $\varphi \rightarrow \psi$ is provable on no assumptions. So we have (by Thinning) a proof that $\Gamma \vdash \varphi \rightarrow \psi$.

Case (2): ψ is an assumption.

Subcase (*a*): ψ is φ. Then $\varphi \rightarrow \psi$ is $\varphi \rightarrow \varphi$, and so is provable on no assumptions. (Lemma, proved above.) So we have (by Thinning) a proof that $\Gamma \vdash \varphi \rightarrow \psi$.

Subcase (*b*): ψ is in Γ. Then there is a proof (by Assumptions, and Thinning) that $\Gamma \vdash \psi$. Add to this proof the lines $\psi \rightarrow (\varphi \rightarrow \psi)$ and $\varphi \rightarrow \psi$. The first adds an axiom, and the second a consequence by Modus Ponens of two previous lines. So the result is a proof showing that $\Gamma \vdash \varphi \rightarrow \psi$.

Case (3): ψ is a consequence by Modus Ponens of two previous lines χ and $\chi \rightarrow \psi$. Then by inductive hypothesis there are proofs showing that $\Gamma \vdash \varphi \rightarrow \chi$ and $\Gamma \vdash \varphi \rightarrow (\chi \rightarrow \psi)$. Put these proofs together and add the lines $(\varphi \rightarrow (\chi \rightarrow \psi)) \rightarrow ((\varphi \rightarrow \chi) \rightarrow (\varphi \rightarrow \psi))$, $(\varphi \rightarrow \chi) \rightarrow (\varphi \rightarrow \psi)$, and $\varphi \rightarrow \psi$. The first adds an axiom, and the second and third add consequences of previous lines by Modus Ponens. So the result is a proof showing that $\Gamma \vdash \varphi \rightarrow \psi$.

This completes the argument. It may be noted that axioms (A1) and (A2), together with their consequence $\varphi \rightarrow \varphi$, are exactly the premises needed to push the argument through. The axioms were chosen precisely for this purpose.

Let us illustrate the use of the deduction theorem by proving, with its help, some simple sequents. A nice easy example is

$\varphi \to \psi, \psi \to \chi \vdash \varphi \to \chi$

  1. $\varphi \to \psi$ ASS
  2. $\psi \to \chi$ ASS
  3. φ A̶S̶S̶[6]
  4. ψ 1,3,MP
  5. χ 2,4,MP
  6. $\varphi \to \chi$ 3–5,Deduction theorem

The citation 'ASS' as a justification is short for 'Assumption'. We begin the proof by writing as the first two lines the assumptions in the sequent we are trying to prove. Then in line (3) we introduce an *auxiliary* assumption, which will be *discharged* (i.e. will no longer be an assumption) by the time we have got to the end of this proof. When we introduce it, we simply write 'ASS' in justification; the line through 'ASS' will be added later, in fact when we come to line (6), at which the assumption is discharged. Lines (4) and (5) are then simple applications of Modus Ponens (abbreviated to MP) to previous lines. By the time that we have reached line (5) what we have shown is

$\varphi \to \psi, \psi \to \chi, \varphi \vdash \chi.$

At this stage we cite the deduction theorem, which tells us that our proof so far may be transformed into another proof which shows that

$\varphi \to \psi, \psi \to \chi \vdash \varphi \to \chi.$

We do not write that other proof out, but simply rely on the fact that that other proof does exist, as the deduction theorem has shown. Consequently, at line (6) we write the desired conclusion $\varphi \to \chi$, we discharge the assumption φ by putting a line through its original justification 'ASS', and we add the tag (6) to show at what point this assumption was discharged. Finally, in justification of line (6) we cite the line at which φ was introduced as an assumption, the line at which the conclusion χ was obtained, and the deduction theorem itself. (In future I shall abbreviate the citation 'Deduction theorem' simply to 'D'. In many books this important principle is called 'the rule of Conditional Proof', abbreviated to 'CP'. We shall meet another name for it in the next chapter.)

I remarked that when we apply the deduction theorem we do not write out a further proof, but just rely on the fact that it exists. Of course, the proof of the deduction theorem shows us how to write out such a proof if we wish to, but the proof found by that method is usually quite unnecessarily roundabout. I illustrate by applying the method to the proof just given, adding to each original assumption two extra lines, showing that it can be prefaced by $\varphi \to$, and replacing other lines by proofs which show that they too can be prefaced by $\varphi \to$. The result is this:

$\varphi{\rightarrow}\psi, \psi{\rightarrow}\chi \vdash \varphi{\rightarrow}\chi$

1.	$\varphi{\rightarrow}\psi$	ASS
1a.	$(\varphi{\rightarrow}\psi) \rightarrow (\varphi{\rightarrow}(\varphi{\rightarrow}\psi))$	A1
1b.	$\varphi{\rightarrow}(\varphi{\rightarrow}\psi)$	1,1a,MP
2.	$\psi{\rightarrow}\chi$	ASS
2a.	$(\psi{\rightarrow}\chi) \rightarrow (\varphi{\rightarrow}(\psi{\rightarrow}\chi))$	A1
2b.	$\varphi{\rightarrow}(\psi{\rightarrow}\chi)$	2,2a,MP
3a.	$\varphi{\rightarrow}\varphi$	Lemma
4a.	$(\varphi{\rightarrow}(\varphi{\rightarrow}\psi)) \rightarrow ((\varphi{\rightarrow}\varphi){\rightarrow}(\varphi{\rightarrow}\psi))$	A2
4b.	$(\varphi{\rightarrow}\varphi){\rightarrow}(\varphi{\rightarrow}\psi)$	1b,4a,MP
4c.	$\varphi{\rightarrow}\psi$	3a,4b,MP
5a.	$(\varphi{\rightarrow}(\psi{\rightarrow}\chi)) \rightarrow ((\varphi{\rightarrow}\psi){\rightarrow}(\varphi{\rightarrow}\chi))$	A2
5b.	$(\varphi{\rightarrow}\psi) \rightarrow (\varphi{\rightarrow}\chi)$	2b,5a,MP
5c.	$\varphi{\rightarrow}\chi$	4c,5b,MP

It is to be noted that lines (1a), (1b), (3a), (4a), (4b) were all added to the original proof in order to obtain $\varphi{\rightarrow}\psi$ in line (4c). This was all quite unnecessary, since $\varphi{\rightarrow}\psi$ is one of the assumptions to the proof anyway. So we may obviously simplify the proof in this way:

$\varphi{\rightarrow}\psi, \psi{\rightarrow}\chi \vdash \varphi{\rightarrow}\chi$

1.	$\varphi{\rightarrow}\psi$	ASS
2.	$\psi{\rightarrow}\chi$	ASS
3.	$(\psi{\rightarrow}\chi) \rightarrow (\varphi{\rightarrow}(\psi{\rightarrow}\chi))$	A1
4.	$\varphi{\rightarrow}(\psi{\rightarrow}\chi)$	2,3,MP
5.	$(\varphi{\rightarrow}(\psi{\rightarrow}\chi)) \rightarrow ((\varphi{\rightarrow}\psi){\rightarrow}(\varphi{\rightarrow}\chi))$	A2
6.	$(\varphi{\rightarrow}\psi){\rightarrow}(\varphi{\rightarrow}\chi)$	4,5,MP
7.	$\varphi{\rightarrow}\chi$	1,6,MP

This is the simplest proof of the result, *not* using the deduction theorem, that I am aware of. It is only one line longer than our original proof, which did use the deduction theorem. But it is much more difficult to find.

The point can be made yet more obvious if we introduce a further step of complication, and consider the sequent

$$\varphi{\rightarrow}\psi \vdash (\psi{\rightarrow}\chi){\rightarrow}(\varphi{\rightarrow}\chi).$$

If we may make use of the deduction theorem, then the proof of this is extremely simple. We repeat the original proof given on p. 204 and add one further use of the deduction theorem at the end, discharging assumption (2). This assures us that there is a proof of the sequent which does not use the deduction theorem. But when one tries to find such a proof, it turns out to be very complicated indeed, as you are invited to discover. One can, of course, continue the lesson yet further by considering proofs, with and without the deduction theorem, of the sequent

$$\vdash (\varphi \to \psi) \to ((\psi \to \chi) \to (\varphi \to \chi)).$$

Use of the deduction theorem greatly simplifies the search for proof (or, more strictly, the task of showing that there is a proof). Once this theorem is available, there is usually no difficulty in finding a proof (or, a proof that there is a proof) of any sequent whose proof depends simply on axioms (A1) and (A2). Some simple examples are suggested in the exercises to this section. I postpone to the next section the use of axiom (A3). Meanwhile, I bring this section to an end with some further reflections upon the content of our axioms (A1) and (A2).

We have seen that from axioms (A1) and (A2), together with the rule Modus Ponens, one can prove the deduction theorem:

If $\Gamma, \varphi \vdash \psi$ then $\Gamma \vdash \varphi \to \psi$.

The converse is also true. Given the deduction theorem (as stated here), and Modus Ponens, one can prove (A1) and (A2). Here is a proof of (A1):

$\vdash \varphi \to (\psi \to \varphi)$

1.	ψ	~~ASS~~(3)
2.	φ	~~ASS~~(4)
3.	$\psi \to \varphi$	1–2,D
4.	$\varphi \to (\psi \to \varphi)$	2–3,D

When the proof is set out like this, it may seem to be something of a cheat. In lines (1) and (2) we introduce two assumptions. Then in line (3) we infer that if the first is true, so is the second, and discharge the first, so that this conclusion depends only on the second. But, of course, we have not, in any intuitive sense, *deduced* the second assumption from the first, and so this step is certainly unexpected. It is, however, entirely in accordance with the deduction theorem as we have stated it. For the two-line proof which consists of first ψ and then φ, with each line entered as an assumption, is a proof showing that $\psi, \varphi \vdash \varphi$. (Compare the remark earlier on $\varphi \vdash \varphi$.) Since the order of the premises makes no difference, we can also say that it is a proof showing that $\varphi, \psi \vdash \varphi$. To this we apply the deduction theorem, as stated, to infer that $\varphi \vdash \psi \to \varphi$, and that is exactly what line (3) records. The further step of the deduction theorem in line (4) is then completely straightforward.

This shows that axiom (A1) does indeed follow from the deduction theorem, as stated. Axiom (A2) follows also, if we allow Modus Ponens to be used too, as this proof shows:

$\vdash (\varphi \to (\psi \to \chi)) \to ((\varphi \to \psi) \to (\varphi \to \chi))$

1.	$\varphi \to (\psi \to \chi)$	~~ASS~~(9)
2.	$\varphi \to \psi$	~~ASS~~(8)
3.	φ	~~ASS~~(7)
4.	$\psi \to \chi$	1,3,MP
5.	ψ	2,3,MP
6.	χ	4,5,MP
7.	$\varphi \to \chi$	3–6,D
8.	$(\varphi \to \psi) \to (\varphi \to \chi)$	2–7,D
9.	$(\varphi \to (\psi \to \chi)) \to ((\varphi \to \psi) \to (\varphi \to \chi))$	1–8,D

In the presence of Modus Ponens, then, (A1) and (A2) are together equivalent to the deduction theorem. It may also be noted that Modus Ponens is itself equivalent to the converse of the deduction theorem, namely

If $\Gamma \vdash \varphi \to \psi$ then $\Gamma, \varphi \vdash \psi$.

To see that Modus Ponens follows from this principle we have only to consider the special case in which Γ is the formula $\varphi \to \psi$. Then the left-hand side is simply a case of the principle of Assumptions, so we may infer the correctness of the right-hand side, which is Modus Ponens. As for the argument in the other direction, if we suppose that $\Gamma \vdash \varphi \to \psi$, and we also assume that $\varphi \to \psi, \varphi \vdash \psi$, then by an application of CUT it follows at once that $\Gamma, \varphi \vdash \psi$.

We may conclude that the assumptions about $\to$ that are stated in axioms (A1) and (A2) of the axiomatic system, together with the rule of inference Modus Ponens, are actually equivalent to this assumption (namely 2.5.H):

$\Gamma \vdash \varphi \to \psi$ iff $\Gamma, \varphi \vdash \psi$.

Whatever follows from the one will therefore follow from the other also. But we have observed (at the end of Section 5.2) that not all truths about $\to$ do follow from the assumptions in question. Even when our attention is focused just on $\to$, we cannot ignore the effect of our axiom (A3).

EXERCISES

5.3.1. Use the deduction theorem to prove the following:

(a) $\vdash \varphi \to \varphi$.

(b) $\varphi \to (\varphi \to \psi) \vdash \varphi \to \psi$.

(c) $\varphi \to (\psi \to \chi) \vdash \psi \to (\varphi \to \chi)$.

(d) $(\varphi \to \psi) \to \chi \vdash \psi \to \chi$.

(e) $((\varphi \to \psi) \to \psi) \to \chi \vdash \varphi \to \chi$.

5.3.2. Find a proof, not using the deduction theorem, of the sequent

$$\varphi \to \psi \vdash (\psi \to \chi) \to (\varphi \to \chi).$$

[Method: begin with the seven-line proof on p. 205, adding to it a use of the deduction theorem as a final step. Then eliminate that use by the method employed in proving the deduction theorem, and simplify the result by omitting superfluous detours. This should yield a proof of thirteen lines, using three instances of each axiom-schema.]

5.3.3. To axioms (A1) and (A2) add a further axiom:

(P) $\vdash ((\varphi \to \psi) \to \varphi) \to \varphi.$

(*a*) Observe that the proof of the deduction theorem is not affected by adding a new axiom.

(*b*) Using the new axiom (and the deduction theorem, and Modus Ponens) prove the sequent

$$(\varphi \to \psi) \to \psi \vdash (\psi \to \varphi) \to \varphi.$$

(*c*) Show that this sequent is not provable from (A1) and (A2) alone. [Hint: recall the last paragraph of Section 5.2.]

5.4. Some Laws of Negation

Our axiom (A3) for negation was somewhat arbitrarily chosen. There are many other useful and important laws for negation that might perfectly well be used in its place. To begin with, we may note that there are four laws which are together known as the laws of *contraposition*, namely

(i) $\varphi \to \psi \vDash \neg\psi \to \neg\varphi.$
(ii) $\varphi \to \neg\psi \vDash \psi \to \neg\varphi.$
(iii) $\neg\varphi \to \psi \vDash \neg\psi \to \varphi.$
(iv) $\neg\varphi \to \neg\psi \vDash \psi \to \varphi.$

It is easily seen that any of these can be deduced from any of the others, given in addition the two laws of double negation, namely

$$\varphi \vDash \neg\neg\varphi.$$
$$\neg\neg\varphi \vDash \varphi.$$

Now in fact our axiom (A3) corresponds to the fourth law of contraposition above, and—as we shall see—both the laws of double negation can be deduced from this. But in place of (A3) we could have had an axiom corresponding to the first law of contraposition, together with two further axioms corresponding to the two laws of double negation. Or we could have had axioms corresponding to the second law of contraposition plus the second law of double negation; or the third law of contraposition plus the first law of double negation. For in either case we should have been able to deduce from these the axiom that we do have, as may easily be checked. But on the other hand there was no need to start from any version of the laws of contraposition, as I now demonstrate. I first give a series of deductions from the axiom (A3) that we have in fact adopted, but I then point out how this series shows that quite different starting-points could have been adopted.

The deductions will assume as background both the rule Modus Ponens (cited as MP) and the deduction theorem (cited as D). In view of my remarks at the end of the last section, I shall count the sequents

$$\vdash \varphi \rightarrow \varphi$$
$$\varphi \vdash \psi \rightarrow \varphi$$

as following from the deduction theorem alone. I shall also suppose that our axiom (A3) may be cited without more ado in the form

$$\neg\varphi \rightarrow \neg\psi \vdash \psi \rightarrow \varphi.$$

With so much by way of preliminaries, let us now proceed to the deductions.

(T1) $\varphi, \neg\varphi \vdash \psi$ (EFQ)

1.	φ	ASS
2.	$\neg\varphi$	ASS
3.	$\neg\psi \rightarrow \neg\varphi$	2,D
4.	$\varphi \rightarrow \psi$	3,A3
5.	ψ	1,4,MP

I label the sequent proved '(T1)', short for 'theorem 1'. I also put in brackets the label 'EFQ', short for *ex falso quodlibet*, which is the usual name for this law.[2] The proof is, I think, perfectly straightforward. So let us proceed.

(T2) $\neg\varphi \rightarrow \varphi \vdash \varphi$ (CM*)

1.	$\neg\varphi \rightarrow \varphi$	ASS
2.	$\neg\varphi$	~~ASS~~(5)
3.	φ	1,2,MP
4.	$\neg(\neg\varphi \rightarrow \varphi)$	2,3,T1
5.	$\neg\varphi \rightarrow \neg(\neg\varphi \rightarrow \varphi)$	2–4,D
6.	$(\neg\varphi \rightarrow \varphi) \rightarrow \varphi$	5,A3
7.	φ	1,6,MP

---

[2] The label is inaccurate; it means 'from what is false there follows anything you like', but it should say 'from a contradiction', not 'from what is false'.

The label 'CM' stands for *consequentia mirabilis*; I have added an asterisk to distinguish this version from the perhaps more usual version proved as (T4) below. The proof is perhaps rather unexpected; in lines (2) and (3) we have reached a contradiction, so we may employ the result already established as (T1) to infer any formula that we like. We cunningly choose the negation of our first assumption. We then apply the deduction theorem, discharging our second assumption, and this allows us to bring the axiom to bear, so yielding the desired conclusion. Two points should be noted about the use of the result (T1) *within* the proof of (T2). First, we have taken a substitution-instance of (T1) as first stated, writing $\neg(\neg\varphi\to\varphi)$ in place of ψ. This is a perfectly legitimate procedure, as I have already remarked (p. 201). Second, since (T1) is not itself one of the initially stated rules of inference, the sequence of lines (1)–(4) does not satisfy the original definition of a proof from assumptions (p. 201). It should be regarded, rather, as a proof that there is a proof in the original sense, namely one got by inserting the original proof of (T1) into the proof of (T2) at this point. So, if the proof of (T2) were to be written out more fully, its first four lines would be replaced by

1. $\neg\varphi\to\varphi$	ASS	
2. $\neg\varphi$	~~ASS~~(5)	
3. φ	1,2,MP	
4a. $\neg\neg(\neg\varphi\to\varphi)\to\neg\varphi$	2,D	
4b. $\varphi\to\neg(\neg\varphi\to\varphi)$	4a,A3	
4c. $\neg(\neg\varphi\to\varphi)$	3,4b,MP	

The citation of one result already proved, within the proof of a further result, is therefore—like citations of the deduction theorem—an indication that there is a proof, but not itself part of that proof. When we are working from a small number of initial axioms, use of this technique is in practice unavoidable. It is also a convenient way of showing what can be proved from what; in the present case, it may be noted that axiom (A3) will never be cited again in this series of deductions. All the further results can be obtained just from (T1) and (T2) as 'basic premisses'.

(T3) $\neg\neg\varphi\vdash\varphi$ (DNE)

1. $\neg\neg\varphi$	ASS	
2. $\neg\varphi$	~~ASS~~(4)	
3. φ	1,2,T1	
4. $\neg\varphi\to\varphi$	2–3,D	
5. φ	4,T2	

('DN' abbreviates 'double negation' and 'DNE' is 'double negation elimination'.)

(T4) $\varphi \to \neg\varphi \vdash \neg\varphi$ (CM)

   1. $\varphi \to \neg\varphi$ ASS
   2. $\neg\neg\varphi$ ~~ASS~~(5)
   3. φ 2,T3
   4. $\neg\varphi$ 1,2,MP
   5. $\neg\neg\varphi \to \neg\varphi$ 2–4,D
   6. $\neg\varphi$ 5,T2

(T5) $\varphi \to \psi, \varphi \to \neg\psi \vdash \neg\varphi$ (RAA)

   1. $\varphi \to \psi$ ASS
   2. $\varphi \to \neg\psi$ ASS
   3. φ ~~ASS~~(7)
   4. ψ 1,3,MP
   5. $\neg\psi$ 2,3,MP
   6. $\neg\varphi$ 4,5,T1
   7. $\varphi \to \neg\varphi$ 3–6,D
   8. $\neg\varphi$ 7,T4

'RAA' abbreviates '*reductio ad absurdum*'. (For a strengthened form of RAA, as CM* is stronger than CM, see Exercise 5.4.2.) Note here that (T1), (T2), and (T4) will not be used again in the following proofs, which depend only on (T3) and (T5).

(T6) $\varphi \to \neg\psi \vdash \psi \to \neg\varphi$ (CON(ii))

   1. $\varphi \to \neg\psi$ ASS
   2. ψ ~~ASS~~(5)
   3. $\varphi \to \psi$ 2,D
   4. $\neg\varphi$ 1,3,T5
   5. $\psi \to \neg\varphi$ 2–4,D

('CON' abbreviates 'contraposition')

(T7) $\varphi \vdash \neg\neg\varphi$ (DNI)

   1. φ ASS
   2. $\neg\varphi \to \neg\varphi$ D
   3. $\varphi \to \neg\neg\varphi$ 2,T6
   4. $\neg\neg\varphi$ 1,3,MP

('DNI' abbreviates 'double negation introduction'.)

(T8) $\varphi \rightarrow \psi \vdash \neg\psi \rightarrow \neg\varphi$ (CON(i))

    1. $\varphi \rightarrow \psi$ ASS
    2. φ ~~ASS~~(5)
    3. ψ 1,2,MP
    4. $\neg\neg\psi$ 3,T7
    5. $\varphi \rightarrow \neg\neg\psi$ 2–4,D
    6. $\neg\psi \rightarrow \neg\varphi$ 5,T6

(T9) $\neg\varphi \rightarrow \psi \vdash \neg\psi \rightarrow \varphi$ (CON(iii))

    1. $\neg\varphi \rightarrow \psi$ ASS
    2. $\neg\psi$ ~~ASS~~(6)
    3. $\neg\varphi \rightarrow \neg\psi$ 2,D
    4. $\neg\neg\varphi$ 1,3,T5
    5. φ 4,T3
    6. $\neg\psi \rightarrow \varphi$ 2–5,D

(T10) $\varphi \rightarrow \psi, \neg\varphi \rightarrow \psi \vdash \psi$ (TND)

    1. $\varphi \rightarrow \psi$ ASS
    2. $\neg\varphi \rightarrow \psi$ ASS
    3. $\neg\psi \rightarrow \neg\varphi$ 1,T8
    4. $\neg\psi \rightarrow \neg\neg\varphi$ 2,T8
    5. $\neg\neg\psi$ 3,4,T5
    6. ψ 5,T3

'TND' abbreviates 'tertium non datur', which is another name for the law of excluded middle (LEM). (Literally 'TND' means 'A third (possibility) is not given'.) Properly speaking, LEM is $\vdash \varphi \vee \neg\varphi$, and so requires $\vee$ in its formulation, and is not yet available. What is here named TND is perhaps best viewed as a *consequence* of LEM, since it says in effect that if a conclusion ψ can be got both from φ as assumption and from $\neg\varphi$ as assumption then it must be true, which, of course, is because those two assumptions between them exhaust the possibilities. Given standard rules for $\vee$, as in Section 5.7 below, one can very swiftly deduce TND as stated here from LEM as properly formulated.

I now introduce some reverse deductions. First, CM, which was used in the proof of RAA, is in fact a special case of RAA, as the following proof shows:

CM: $\varphi\rightarrow\neg\varphi\vdash\neg\varphi$

   1. $\varphi\rightarrow\neg\varphi$ ASS
   2. $\varphi\rightarrow\varphi$ D
   3. $\neg\varphi$ 1,2,RAA(=T5)

In a similar way CM* is a special case of TND:

CM*: $\neg\varphi\rightarrow\varphi\vdash\varphi$

   1. $\neg\varphi\rightarrow\varphi$ ASS
   2. $\varphi\rightarrow\varphi$ D
   3. φ 1,2,TND(=T10)

This latter is rather more significant, since it shows that whatever can be deduced from CM* (=T2) can also be deduced from TND (=T10), and several important theses were deduced from CM*. Another quite significant reverse deduction is that EFQ, which was our first theorem, could have been obtained instead from the third law of contraposition, which was (T9):

EFQ: $\varphi,\neg\varphi\vdash\psi$

   1. φ ASS
   2. $\neg\varphi$ ASS
   3. $\neg\psi\rightarrow\varphi$ 1,D
   4. $\neg\varphi\rightarrow\psi$ 3,CON(iii) (=T9)
   5. ψ 2,4,MP.

I now add two of the points made at the outset of this section, that from CON(ii) with DNE, or from CON(iii) with DNI, it is possible to recover the original axiom (A3). Here are proofs.

(A3) $\neg\varphi\rightarrow\neg\psi\vdash\psi\rightarrow\varphi$

   1. $\neg\varphi\rightarrow\neg\psi$ ASS
   2. $\psi\rightarrow\neg\neg\varphi$ 1,CON(ii) (=T6)
   3. ψ ~~ASS~~(6)
   4. $\neg\neg\varphi$ 2,3,MP
   5. φ 4,DNE(=T3)
   6. $\psi\rightarrow\varphi$ 3–5,D

(A3) $\neg\varphi\rightarrow\neg\psi\vdash\psi\rightarrow\varphi$

   1. $\neg\varphi\rightarrow\neg\psi$ ASS
   2. $\neg\neg\psi\rightarrow\varphi$ 1,CON(iii) (=T9)
   3. ψ ~~ASS~~(6)
   4. $\neg\neg\psi$ 3,DNI(=T7)

5. φ 2,4,MP
6. $\psi \rightarrow \varphi$ 3–5,D

The results of all these deductions may conveniently be surveyed in the following diagram (where the arrows indicate that the sequent at the pointed end of the arrows may be proved from the sequents at the other end of those arrows, assuming the rules MP and D as background rules).

From this diagram one can at once read off that each of the following sets of basic axioms would be equivalent to the single axiom (A3):

(a) TND(=T10) + EFQ(=T1)

$$\varphi \rightarrow \psi, \neg \varphi \rightarrow \psi \vdash \psi$$
$$\varphi, \neg \varphi \vdash \psi$$

(b) CM*(=T2) + EFQ(=T1)

$$\neg \varphi \rightarrow \varphi \vdash \varphi$$
$$\varphi, \neg \varphi \vdash \psi$$

(c) TND(=T10) + RAA(=T5)

$$\varphi \rightarrow \psi, \neg \varphi \rightarrow \psi \vdash \psi$$
$$\varphi \rightarrow \psi, \varphi \rightarrow \neg \psi \vdash \neg \varphi$$

(d) DNE(=T3) + RAA(=T5)

$$\neg \neg \varphi \vdash \varphi$$
$$\varphi \rightarrow \psi, \varphi \rightarrow \neg \psi \vdash \neg \varphi$$

(e) DNE(=T3) + CON(ii)(=T6)

$$\neg \neg \varphi \vdash \varphi$$
$$\varphi \rightarrow \neg \psi \vdash \psi \rightarrow \neg \varphi$$

(f) CON(iii)(=T9) + DNI(=T7)

$$\neg \varphi \rightarrow \psi \vdash \neg \psi \rightarrow \varphi$$
$$\varphi \vdash \neg \neg \varphi$$

(g) CON(iii)(=T9) + CM*(=T2)

$$\neg \varphi \rightarrow \psi \vdash \neg \psi \rightarrow \varphi$$
$$\neg \varphi \rightarrow \varphi \vdash \varphi$$

(h) CON(iii)(=T9) + CON(ii)(=T6)

$$\neg \varphi \rightarrow \psi \vdash \neg \psi \rightarrow \varphi$$
$$\varphi \rightarrow \neg \psi \vdash \psi \rightarrow \neg \varphi$$

There are yet other combinations which are again equivalent, not only those that can be read off the diagram as it stands, but also some that would

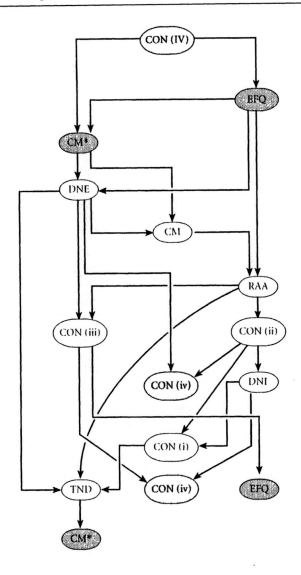

be revealed by complicating the diagram still further. This matter is further explored in the exercises.

EXERCISES

5.4.1. Many books choose DNE and RAA as their basic assumptions on negation. The diagram shows that all the theses we have considered can be obtained from this basis, but often the route suggested is rather indirect.

(*a*) Using DNE and RAA as basic assumptions, give direct proofs of EFQ, CM*, and CON(i), not relying on any other thesis.

(*b*) Using the same assumptions, give a proof of Peirce's law

$\vdash ((\varphi{\rightarrow}\psi){\rightarrow}\varphi) \rightarrow \varphi.$

5.4.2. Show that the single thesis RAA*, namely

$\vdash (\neg\varphi{\rightarrow}\psi) \rightarrow ((\neg\varphi{\rightarrow}\neg\psi) \rightarrow \varphi),$

is equivalent to the single axiom (A3) that we have adopted. [It is easy to deduce RAA* from RAA and DNE. For the converse deduction, perhaps the simplest plan is to deduce both EFQ and CM* directly from RAA*. The argument can then be concluded by relying on the results presented on the diagram.]

5.4.3. Suppose that we define negation by putting

$\neg\varphi$ for $\varphi{\rightarrow}\bot.$

(*a*) Without adding any extra assumptions about $\bot$, show that the following theses are immediate consequences of the definition: CM, RAA, CON(ii), DNI, CON(i).

(*b*) Adding a further assumption about $\bot$, namely

$\vdash \bot{\rightarrow}\psi,$

show that EFQ may then be counted a consequence of the definition.

(*c*) Independently of these suggestions for defining negation, show that if just EFQ and RAA are assumed as basic principles for negation, then CM, DNI, CON(i), CON(ii) can all be deduced.

5.4.4. What is called intuitionist logic differs from the classical two-valued logic primarily over its treatment of negation. At any rate, an intuitionist logic[3] for $\rightarrow$ and $\neg$ can be axiomatized by adding to our axiom-schemas (A1) and (A2) two further axiom-schemas for negation, corresponding to EFQ and RAA, i.e.

$\vdash \varphi{\rightarrow}(\neg\varphi{\rightarrow}\psi)$
$\vdash (\varphi{\rightarrow}\psi){\rightarrow}((\varphi{\rightarrow}\neg\psi){\rightarrow}\neg\varphi).$

Alternatively, it can be axiomatized by defining $\neg$ in terms of $\bot$, and adding to (A1) and (A2) the single axiom-schema

$\vdash \bot{\rightarrow}\psi.$

Thus intuitionist logic contains all the theses of the previous exercise (i.e. CM, DNI, CON(i)–(ii), in addition to EFQ and RAA).

Show that it does not contain any of the other theses on the diagram (i.e. CM*, DNE, CON(iii)–(iv), TND). [Argue first that it is sufficient to show that it does not contain DNE. Then show that tables III and VI of Section 5.2 verify all intuitionist axioms (and Modus Ponens), but do not verify DNE.]

---

[3] See also n. 8 in the Appendix to this chapter.

5.5. A Completeness Proof

We shall now show that the three axioms (A1)–(A3), together with the rule MP, form a complete basis for truth-functional logic. As we noted long ago, $\to$ and $\neg$ are together expressively adequate (p. 46), i.e. can express every truth-function. Also, as we showed in the last chapter, the logic of truth-functions is compact (pp. 173–4), so that sequents with infinitely many formulae on the left introduce nothing new. Moreover, if we are confining attention to finite sequents, then we can also confine our attention further to those with *no* formula on the left, since any finite sequent can be exchanged for its conditionalization (pp. 202–3). To prove the completeness of our system, then, it is sufficient to show that, for any formula φ,

If $\vDash \varphi$ then $\vdash \varphi$.

That is what we shall now show.

The idea of the proof is this. If the formula φ is valid then it is a truth-table tautology, i.e. it comes out true in every row of the truth-table. We shall show that our deductive system can *mirror* the truth-table calculations.[4] Suppose that we have a formula φ which contains just the sentence-letters $P_1,...,P_n$, and no others. Then a row of the truth-table says that, for a given assignment of truth-values to the letters $P_1,...,P_n$, the formula φ takes a certain value. We can say the same thing by means of a sequent of the form

$$\pm P_1,...,\pm P_n \vdash \pm\varphi,$$

where $\pm P_i$ is either P_i or $\neg P_i$, depending on whether P_i takes the value T or the value F in that row, and similarly $\pm\varphi$ is either φ or $\neg\varphi$, depending on whether φ then takes the value T or F in that row. Let us say that this sequent is the sequent that *corresponds* to that row of the truth-table. Our completeness proof will show as a first step that for each row of any truth-table the corresponding sequent is provable in our deductive system. Then as a second step it will show that a tautology, which comes out true in every row of its truth-table, is provable on no assumptions at all. For convenience I list here the lemmas that will be needed about our system. For the first part of the proof they are

(1) $\varphi \vdash \neg\neg\varphi$.
(2) $\varphi \vdash \psi\to\varphi$.
(3) $\neg\varphi \vdash \varphi\to\psi$.
(4) $\varphi, \neg\psi \vdash \neg(\varphi\to\psi)$.

---

[4] This proof is due to Kalmár (1934–5).

Of these, (1) was proved as (T7) of the previous section; (2) is an immediate consequence of the deduction theorem; (3) results by applying the deduction theorem to (T1) of the previous section; and the proof of (4) may safely be left as an exercise. In the second part of the proof we shall need a version of TND, and the most convenient form is this:

(5) If $\Gamma, \varphi \vdash \psi$ and $\Gamma, \neg\varphi \vdash \psi$ then $\Gamma \vdash \psi$.

This is obtained by applying the deduction theorem to (T10) of the previous section. I remark here that since lemmas (1)–(5) are the *only* features of the deductive system that are needed for this completeness proof, it follows that any other system which contains (1)–(5)—including the system which consists *just* of (1)–(5) and nothing else (except the structural rules)—is equally complete, in the sense that it suffices to yield a proof, on no assumptions, of every tautology. (But we would need to add the rule MP if we are to ensure that from a proof of the conditionalization of a sequent, we can always construct a proof of the sequent itself.)

As the first stage of the proof we need to show this. Let the letters $P_1,...,P_n$ be the letters in a formula φ. Consider any assignment of truth-values to those letters. Let $\pm P_i$ be P_i or $\neg P_i$ according as P_i is assigned the value T or the value F in that assignment. Then we must establish

(a) If φ is true on this assignment, then $\pm P_1,...,\pm P_n \vdash \varphi$.
(b) If φ is false on this assignment, then $\pm P_1,...,\pm P_n \vdash \neg\varphi$.

The proof is by induction on the length of the formula φ. We have three cases to consider:

Case (1): φ is atomic, say P_i. Then what has to be shown is

(a) $P_i \vdash P_i$
(b) $\neg P_i \vdash \neg P_i$.

This is immediate.

Case (2): φ is $\neg\psi$. Then the letters in φ are the same as those in ψ. (a) Suppose φ is true on the assignment. Then ψ is false, and by inductive hypothesis we have

$$\pm P_1,...,\pm P_n \vdash \neg\psi$$
i.e. $\pm P_1,...,\pm P_n \vdash \varphi$

as required. (b) Suppose φ is false. Then ψ is true, and by inductive hypothesis

$$\pm P_1,...,\pm P_n \vdash \psi.$$

Hence, by lemma (1)

$$\pm P_1,...,\pm P_n \vdash \neg\neg\neg\psi$$
i.e. $\pm P_1,...,\pm P_n \vdash \varphi$

as required.

Case (3): φ is $\psi \to \chi$. Then the letters in ψ and in χ are subsets of those in φ, say $P_i,...,P_j$ and $P_k,...,P_l$ respectively. (*a*) Suppose φ is true on the assignment. Then either ψ is false or χ is true, and by inductive hypothesis

$\pm P_i,...,\pm P_j \vdash \neg\psi$ or $\pm P_k,...,\pm P_l \vdash \chi$

$\therefore$ $\pm P_1,...\pm P_n \vdash \neg\psi$ or $\pm P_1,...,\pm P_n \vdash \chi$ (by THIN)

$\therefore$ $\pm P_1,...\pm P_n \vdash \psi \to \chi$ (by lemmas (2) and (3))

i.e. $\pm P_1,...\pm P_n \vdash \varphi$, as required.

(*b*) Suppose φ is false on the assignment. Then ψ is true and χ is false, and by inductive hypothesis

$\pm P_i,...,\pm P_j \vdash \psi$ and $\pm P_k,...,\pm P_l \vdash \neg\chi$

$\therefore$ $\pm P_1,...,\pm P_n \vdash \psi$ and $\pm P_1,...,\pm P_n \vdash \neg\chi$ (by THIN)

$\therefore$ $\pm P_1,...,\pm P_n \vdash \neg(\psi \to \chi)$ (by lemma (4))

i.e. $\pm P_1,...,\pm P_n \vdash \varphi$, as required.

This completes the induction, and therefore completes the first stage of our proof. So we now move on to the second stage.

Suppose that φ is a tautology. If there are n letters in φ, then there are 2^n rows in the truth-table for φ, and for each of them there is a corresponding sequent which is provable. We consider these sequents in the order of the corresponding rows of the truth-table, and take them in pairs. Each pair has the form

$\pm P_1,...,\pm P_{n-1}, P_n \vdash \varphi.$
$\pm P_1,...,\pm P_{n-1}, \neg P_n \vdash \varphi.$

Applying lemma (5) to each pair, we infer in each case

$\pm P_1,...,\pm P_{n-1} \vdash \varphi.$

This leaves us a set of 2^{n-1} provable sequents, covering every assignment of truth-values to the sentence-letters $P_1,...,P_{n-1}$, but no longer containing the letter P_n on the left. By taking these in pairs, and applying lemma (5) to each pair, as before, we obtain a set of 2^{n-2} provable sequents, covering every assignment of truth-values to the letters $P_1,...,P_{n-2}$, but no longer containing the letters P_n or P_{n-1} on the left. By continuing this manœuvre, as often as necessary, we eventually reach the provable sequent $\vdash \varphi$, with no sentence-letters on the left. This completes the argument.

EXERCISES

5.5.1. Let I be the intuitionist logic specified in Exercise 5.4.4, and let $\vdash_I$ mean provability in that logic.

(*a*) Establish the lemmas

$$\varphi \vdash_I \neg\neg\varphi.$$
$$\varphi \vdash_I \psi\to\varphi.$$
$$\neg\varphi \vdash_I \varphi\to\psi.$$
$$\varphi,\neg\psi \vdash_I \neg(\varphi\to\psi).$$

Deduce that the first stage of our completeness proof holds also for intuitionist logic.

(*b*) Establish the lemma

If $\Gamma,\varphi \vdash_I \neg\neg\psi$ and $\Gamma,\neg\varphi \vdash_I \neg\neg\psi$ then $\Gamma \vdash_I \neg\neg\psi$.

Deduce that the second stage of our completeness proof can be modified to yield this result:

If $\vDash \varphi$ then $\vdash_I \neg\neg\varphi$.

5.5.2.(*a*) Show that an axiomatic system S which contains EFQ is absolutely consistent iff it is negation-consistent, i.e.

for all $\varphi, \vdash_S \varphi$ iff   for some $\varphi, \vdash_S \varphi$ and $\vdash_S \neg\varphi$.

(*b*) Show that if we add to the axioms (A1)–(A3) any new axiom-schema of our language, not already provable from those axioms, then the result is an inconsistent system. (That is, the axioms (A1)–(A3) are 'complete in the sense of Post (1921)'.) [Since (A1)–(A3) are complete, any axiom-schema not provable from them must be non-tautologous. So it has to be shown that any non-tautologous schema has an inconsistent substitution-instance.]

5.6. Axioms for the Quantifiers

By being very generous over what to count as an axiom, it is *possible* to present a logic for the quantifiers which still contains no rule of inference other than the familiar rule Modus Ponens. (See the appendix to this chapter.) But it does complicate matters quite noticeably, since the Deduction Theorem is then much more difficult to establish. Consequently, the more usual way of extending axioms (A1)–(A3), so as to cover quantifiers as well as truth-functors, adds not only new axioms but a new rule of inference also. The simplest such rule to add is the rule of *generalization*, in this form:

GEN: If $\vdash \varphi$ then $\vdash \forall\xi\varphi(\xi/\alpha)$.

As well as this new rule, one adds also these two axiom-schemas:

(A4) $\vdash \forall\xi\varphi \rightarrow \varphi(\alpha/\xi)$.

(A5) $\vdash \forall\xi(\psi\rightarrow\varphi) \rightarrow (\psi\rightarrow\forall\xi\varphi)$, provided ξ is not free in ψ.

As we shall eventually see (but not until Chapter 7), this provides a complete basis for the logic of quantifiers.

There is room for some variation in the statement of the rule GEN and the axiom (A4). As I have just set down these theses, φ represents any formula, ξ any variable, and α any name-letter. This formulation evidently presumes that name-letters do occur in the language we are considering, and it also presumes that we are confining attention to closed formulae, so that no variables occur free in a finished formula. If open formulae are to be permitted too, then in (A4) α should be replaced by τ, standing in for any *term* (i.e. name-letter or variable). We may also write τ in place of α in the rule GEN, though in fact this will not make any difference to the theorems that can be proved, except when name-letters do *not* occur in the language. (For in that case the rule can only be applied where φ contains a free variable.) It should also be noted that GEN and (A4), as stated here, do allow for there to be vacuous quantifiers. For example, if φ lacks the letter α, but $\vdash \varphi$, then according to GEN we shall also have $\vdash \forall\xi\varphi$ for any variable ξ whatever. (Recall that if φ lacks α then $\varphi(\xi/\alpha)$ is φ.) If formulae with vacuous quantifiers are not wanted, then a restriction should be added to GEN to prevent this. But note also that if vacuous quantifiers are permitted, then it is easy to show, from the rules and axioms, that they add nothing. For if ξ is not free in φ, then from (A4) we have at once

$\vdash \forall\xi\varphi\rightarrow\varphi$.

Conversely, from GEN we have

$\vdash \forall\xi(\varphi\rightarrow\varphi)$,

and hence by (A5) and MP

$\vdash \varphi\rightarrow\forall\xi\varphi$.

Thus φ and $\forall\xi\varphi$ are provably equivalent, if the quantifier is vacuous.

The new axioms and rules are sound, as I shall show shortly; that is, they are all correct under the intended interpretation. We can also choose unintended interpretations which make some correct and some incorrect, in ways which will show their mutual independence. For example, if we interpret the universal quantifier so that $\forall\xi\varphi$ is always counted as false, for every formula φ, then the two axioms are correct, but the rule GEN is clearly incorrect. This shows that GEN is independent of the rest of the system, i.e. that there are formulae which cannot be proved on the basis of (A1)–(A5), with MP, but can be proved if GEN is added to this basis. (The formula $\forall x(Fx \to Fx)$ is an example.) Equally, if we interpret the quantifier so that $\forall\xi\varphi$ is always counted as true, then GEN and (A5) remain correct, but (A4) does not, and this shows the independence of (A4). Finally, if we take a as our only name-letter, and interpret $\forall\xi\varphi$ to mean the same as '$\varphi(a/\xi)$ is a necessary truth', then GEN and (A4) remain correct, but (A5) does not, since there is now no way in which the proviso on (A5) can be used to prevent unwanted inferences. I should perhaps add that the earlier arguments to show that (A1)–(A3) were independent of one another can easily be carried over to show that each of (A1)–(A3) is independent of all the rest of the enlarged system containing (A4)–(A5) and GEN in addition. To see this, we may again take a as our only name-letter and interpret $\forall\xi\varphi$ to mean just $\varphi(a/\xi)$, so that the quantifiers are doing no work at all. Then GEN is a triviality, and the axioms each take the form $\vdash \varphi \to \varphi$, which is verified by all the tables that we considered.

We shall naturally want to extend the deduction theorem so that we are entitled to use proofs from assumptions with formulae involving quantifiers. Now there is no problem here over the addition of two new axioms, (A4) and (A5). The proof given earlier in Section 5.2 relies upon the fact that the system does contain the axioms (A1) and (A2), but it does not matter to that proof what other axioms there might be in the system. So we can add as many more axioms as we like without in any way disturbing the deduction theorem. But with rules of inference the position is different, for the earlier proof relies on the fact that the system does have the rule MP, *and* on the fact that it has no other rule. For it presumes that in a proof from assumptions every line must be either an assumption or an axiom or a consequence of previous lines *by the rule MP*. If there are other rules to be considered too, for example GEN, then there are further cases that need to be considered.

As a matter of fact, the rule GEN cannot itself be used within proofs from assumptions. It is instructive here to bring out the contrast between generalization on the one hand and on the other hand the original rule of detachment. These rules are

DET: If $\vdash \varphi$ and $\vdash \varphi \to \psi$ then $\vdash \psi$.
GEN: If $\vdash \varphi$ then $\vdash \forall\xi\varphi(\xi/\alpha)$.

Each of them is framed as a rule for use in proofs from *no* assumptions, which is how axiomatic proofs were first conceived. But the rule of detachment can immediately be liberalized into Modus Ponens, which is designed to be used in proofs from assumptions:

MP: If $\Gamma \vdash \varphi$ and $\Gamma \vdash \varphi \rightarrow \psi$ then $\Gamma \vdash \psi$.

On the other hand, the rule of generalization certainly cannot be liberalized in a similar way, to

?: If $\Gamma \vdash \varphi$ then $\Gamma \vdash \forall \xi \varphi(\xi/\alpha)$.

To take a simple counter-example, the sequent

$Fa \vdash Fa$

is, of course, correct, but if we apply the suggested rule to it, then we obtain

$Fa \vdash \forall x Fx,$

which is certainly not correct. (From the assumption that a is F it evidently does not follow that everything else is F as well.) The reason why GEN, as first stated, is a correct rule could be put like this: if you can prove some formula containing the name a *on no assumptions*, then in particular you have made no assumptions about a, so a could be anything. That is, we could in the same way prove the same point about anything else. So our formula must hold of everything whatever, and that is what the rule GEN says. But the important premiss to this reasoning is not that the formula is proved on no assumptions *at all*, but rather that it is proved on no assumptions *about* a; that is what allows us to add 'a could be anything'. The right way, then, to liberalize the rule GEN, so that it can be used in proofs from assumptions, is this:

($\forall$I) If $\Gamma \vdash \varphi$, and if α does not occur in Γ, then $\Gamma \vdash \forall \xi \varphi(\xi/\alpha)$.

(The label '($\forall$I)' stands for 'universal quantifier introduction', cf. 3.6.G.) It will be seen that just as DET is a special case of MP, namely the case where there are no assumptions, so also GEN is the same special case of ($\forall$I). Consequently, a proof from no assumptions that uses the rule ($\forall$I) is at the same time a proper axiomatic proof using only the rule GEN.

We can now return to the deduction theorem. A proof from assumptions is now to be a finite sequence of formulae, each of which is either an assumption, or one of the axioms (A1)–(A5), or a consequence of previous formulae either by the rule MP or by the rule ($\forall$I). The deduction theorem states that if we have a proof from assumptions showing that $\Gamma, \varphi \vdash \psi$, then this can be transformed into another proof showing that $\Gamma \vdash \varphi \rightarrow \psi$. By repeated steps of this transformation, any proof from assumptions can therefore be transformed into a fully conditionalized proof, which is then an axiomatic proof as first defined. To prove the deduction theorem we must invoke axioms (A1) and (A2) to cover a case where the rule MP is applied, and axiom (A5) to cover a case where the rule ($\forall$I) is applied. The proof is just the same as before (p. 203), except for the extra case for the rule ($\forall$I), which is this:

> *Case (4)*: ψ is $\forall\xi\chi(\xi/\alpha)$, obtained from a previous line χ by the rule ($\forall$I). Note that, since ($\forall$I) was applicable, the name α does not occur either in Γ or in φ. By inductive hypothesis there is a proof showing that $\Gamma \vdash \varphi\rightarrow\chi$. Since α is not Γ, we may apply ($\forall$I) to this, to obtain a proof showing that $\Gamma \vdash \forall\xi(\varphi\rightarrow\chi)(\xi/\alpha)$. Since α is not in φ, this last formula is $\forall\xi(\varphi\rightarrow\chi(\xi/\alpha))$, where ξ is not free in φ. So we may add the axiom $\forall\xi(\varphi\rightarrow\chi(\xi/\alpha)) \rightarrow (\varphi\rightarrow\forall\xi\chi(\xi/\alpha))$, and apply MP to get $\varphi\rightarrow\forall\xi\chi(\xi/\alpha)$, i.e. $\varphi\rightarrow\psi$. The result is a proof showing that $\Gamma \vdash \varphi\rightarrow\psi$.

This establishes the deduction theorem.

I proceed at once to an illustration of its use. Given the rule ($\forall$I), all that was needed to establish the deduction theorem was an application of the axiom (A5). It is also true conversely that, given ($\forall$I) and the deduction theorem, we can now deduce (A5) (though we also need to call on (A4) in the proof).

(A5) $\vdash \forall\xi(\varphi\rightarrow\psi) \rightarrow (\varphi\rightarrow\forall\xi\psi)$, provided ξ is not free in φ

1. $\forall\xi(\varphi\rightarrow\psi)$	~~ASS~~(10)	
2. $\forall\xi(\varphi\rightarrow\psi) \rightarrow (\varphi\rightarrow\psi)(\alpha/\xi)$	A4; choose α so that it is not in φ or ψ.	
3. $(\varphi\rightarrow\psi)(\alpha/\xi)$	1,2,MP.	
4. $\varphi\rightarrow\psi(\alpha/\xi)$	This is line (3), assuming ξ is not free in φ.	
5. φ	~~ASS~~(9)	
6. $\psi(\alpha/\xi)$	4,5,MP	
7. $\forall\xi\psi(\alpha/\xi)(\xi/\alpha)$	6,$\forall$I; α is not in lines (1) or (5)	
8. $\forall\xi\psi$	This is line (7), since α is not in ψ	
9. $\varphi\rightarrow\forall\xi\psi$	5–8,D	
10. $\forall\xi(\varphi\rightarrow\psi) \rightarrow (\varphi\rightarrow\forall\xi\psi)$	1–9,D	

This proof-schema shows that, once we are given the deduction theorem, the basis consisting of the axiom (A4) with the rule ($\forall$I) is equivalent to our original basis consisting of (A4) and (A5) and the rule GEN. That is why I did not pause to prove the soundness of (A4), (A5), and GEN when they were first introduced, for the soundness of (A4) and (∀I) has been proved already, on pp. 97–9.

Some features of this proof-schema deserve comment. Since it is a *schema*, and not an actual proof of a particular formula, it contains things which would not appear in an actual proof. The most obvious example is that what is written on line (3) is different from what is written on line (4), though the actual formula represented is exactly the same in each case. The same applies to lines (7) and (8). Since this kind of thing can be very distracting to one who is not already familiar with proofs of this sort, it is better, to begin with, to practise on actual proofs with actual formulae. This also eliminates such things as the instruction 'choose α so that it is not in φ or ψ' attached to line (2), for instead of putting in the instruction, we simply conform to it. For example, here is something more like a genuine proof of an instance of (A5):

$\forall x(P{\rightarrow}Fx) \rightarrow (P{\rightarrow}\forall xFx)$

1.	$\forall x(P{\rightarrow}Fx)$	A̶S̶S̶(8)
2.	$\forall x(P{\rightarrow}Fx) \rightarrow (P{\rightarrow}Fa)$	A4
3.	$P{\rightarrow}Fa$	1,2,MP
4.	P	A̶S̶S̶(7)
5.	Fa	3,4,MP
6.	$\forall xFx$	5,∀I; a is not in lines (1) or (4)
7.	$P{\rightarrow}\forall xFx$	4–6,D
8.	$\forall x(P{\rightarrow}Fx) {\rightarrow} (P{\rightarrow}\forall xFx)$	1–7,D

Here lines (1)–(6) do constitute a genuine proof from assumptions, though, of course, lines (7) and (8) merely indicate that this can be transformed into a proof from no assumptions; they do not carry out that transformation. Nevertheless, the proof now looks more like the kind of examples that we have had earlier in this chapter, except that the justification for line (6) is untypically long. This is because the rule (∀I) is a *conditional* rule, for it allows you to introduce a universal quantifier *on the condition that* the name that is to be generalized does not occur in the assumptions to the proof. So whenever the rule is applied one must look back at all the previous lines labelled 'Assumption', and check that this condition is indeed satisfied. (Assumptions which have *already* been discharged can, of course, be ignored.) When one has grown used to checking in this way, then no doubt one can save time by not bothering to write in explicitly that the condition is satisfied, but still the check must, of course, be done.

I close this section with two more examples of proofs involving quantifiers, to establish a thesis first used earlier on p. 120, namely

$$\neg\forall x\neg(Fx{\rightarrow}Gx) \dashv\vdash \forall xFx \rightarrow \neg\forall x\neg Gx.$$

(But here I have to write '$\neg\forall x\neg$' in place of the shorter '$\exists x$' used earlier.)

(a) $\neg\forall x\neg(Fx{\rightarrow}Gx) \vdash \forall xFx \rightarrow \neg\forall x\neg Gx$

1.	$\neg\forall x\neg(Fx{\rightarrow}Gx)$	ASS
2.	$\forall xFx$	~~ASS~~(11)
3.	$\forall x\neg Gx$	~~ASS~~(8)
4.	Fa	2,A4,MP
5.	$\neg Ga$	3,A4,MP
6.	$\neg(Fa{\rightarrow}Ga)$	4,5,Exercise 5.5.1(a)
7.	$\forall x\neg(Fx{\rightarrow}Gx)$	6,$\forall$I; a is not in lines (1)–(3)
8.	$\forall x\neg Gx \rightarrow \forall x\neg(Fx{\rightarrow}Gx)$	3–7,D
9.	$\neg\forall x\neg(Fx{\rightarrow}Gx) \rightarrow \neg\forall x\neg Gx$	8,CON(i)
10.	$\neg\forall x\neg Gx$	1,9,MP
11.	$\forall xFx \rightarrow \neg\forall x\neg Gx$	2–10,D

(b) $\forall xFx \rightarrow \neg\forall x\neg Gx \vdash \neg\forall x\neg(Fx{\rightarrow}Gx)$

1.	$\forall xFx \rightarrow \neg\forall x\neg Gx$	ASS
2.	$\forall x\neg(Fx{\rightarrow}Gx)$	~~ASS~~(8)
3.	$\neg(Fa{\rightarrow}Ga)$	2,A4,MP
4.	Fa	3,Exercise 5.5.1(a)
5.	$\neg Ga$	3,Exercise 5.5.1(a)
6.	$\forall xFx$	4,$\forall$I; a is not in lines (1)–(2)
7.	$\forall x\neg Gx$	5,$\forall$I; a is not in lines (1)–(2)
8.	$\forall x\neg(Fx{\rightarrow}Gx) \rightarrow \forall x\neg Gx$	2→7,D
9.	$\neg\forall x\neg Gx \rightarrow \neg\forall x\neg(Fx{\rightarrow}Gx)$	8, CON(i)
10.	$\neg\forall x\neg Gx$	1,6,MP
11.	$\neg\forall x\neg(Fx{\rightarrow}Gx)$	9,10,MP.

These proofs should be studied before turning to the exercises that follow.

EXERCISES

5.6.1. Provide proofs of the following. (You may use in the proofs any sequent that has been proved earlier in this chapter—or indeed, in view of the completeness of the axioms for $\rightarrow$ and $\neg$, any sequent that can be established by truth-tables.)

(a) $\forall x(Fx{\rightarrow}Gx) \vdash \forall xFx \rightarrow \forall xGx$.

(b) $\forall x(Fx{\rightarrow}Gx) \vdash \neg\forall x\neg Fx \rightarrow \neg\forall x\neg Gx$.

(c) $\forall x(P{\rightarrow}Fx) \dashv\vdash P \rightarrow \forall xFx$.

(d) $\forall x(Fx \rightarrow P)$ ⊣⊢ $\neg\forall x\neg Fx \rightarrow P$.
(e) $\neg\forall x\neg\forall yFxy$ ⊢ $\forall y\neg\forall x\neg Fxy$.

[If (e) proves difficult, then try it again after reading the next section.]

5.6.2. (continuing 5.5.2). Assume (as is the case) that our axiom-schemas (A1)–(A5), together with MP and GEN, form a complete basis for the logic of quantifiers. Show that it is nevertheless *not true* that if we add to them any further axiom-schema of the language, not already provable from them, then the result is an inconsistent system. [Hint: consider the schema $\forall\xi\varphi \vee \forall\xi\neg\varphi$.]

5.7. Definitions of Other Logical Symbols

As we have noted (p. 46), the zero-place truth-functors $\top$ and $\bot$ cannot strictly be defined in terms of any other truth-functors. But usually one does not speak so strictly, and accepts definitions such as

$\top$ for $P \rightarrow P$.
$\bot$ for $\neg(P \rightarrow P)$.

It is easily seen that these definitions give rise to the rules characteristic of $\top$ and $\bot$, namely

$\varphi \vdash \top$.
$\bot \vdash \varphi$.

It may also be noted that if $\bot$ is available, then this gives us a simple way of defining sequents with no formula on the right, for we may abbreviate

$\Gamma \vdash$ for $\Gamma \vdash \bot$.

Putting these definitions together, we obtain the 'structural' rule of Thinning on the right

If $\Gamma \vdash$ then $\Gamma \vdash \varphi$.

We can also, if we wish, restrict EFQ to this

EFQ′: $\varphi, \neg\varphi \vdash \bot$.

And a rather nice form of *reductio ad absurdum* becomes available, namely

RAA′: If $\Gamma, \varphi \vdash \bot$ then $\Gamma \vdash \neg\varphi$.

This will be used in what follows. Notice that, like applications of the deduction theorem, this is a rule that *discharges* an assumption. For if φ was an assumption, and from it we obtain a contradiction $\bot$, then we can infer $\neg\varphi$ and drop φ from the assumptions. (The justification of this form of RAA is left as an exercise.)

The functors $\top$ and $\bot$ may be regarded as something of a luxury; at any rate they have little work to do in the usual applications of logical theory to test actual arguments. Here the functors $\wedge$ and $\vee$ are very much in demand, and we may, of course, define them in terms of $\rightarrow$ and $\neg$ by putting

$\quad\quad \varphi\wedge\psi \quad$ for $\quad \neg(\varphi\rightarrow\neg\psi)$.
$\quad\quad \varphi\vee\psi \quad$ for $\quad \neg\varphi\rightarrow\psi$.

But we shall not be able to do much with these functors until we have proved for them some suitable rules. In the case of $\wedge$, the rules are these:

$\quad\quad (\wedge\text{I}) \quad \varphi,\psi \vdash \varphi\wedge\psi \quad\quad (\wedge\text{E}) \quad \varphi\wedge\psi \vdash \varphi, \quad \varphi\wedge\psi \vdash \psi.$

(The labels '$(\wedge\text{I})$' and '$(\wedge\text{E})$' are short for '$\wedge$-introduction' and '$\wedge$-elimination'.) These rules (once we have proved them) are to be used in proofs from assumptions in just the way that the various rules for negation were used in Section 5.3. Proofs are as follows. (These proofs use RAA and EFQ in the new forms, and in addition DNE and the principle $\neg\varphi \vdash \varphi\rightarrow\psi$, for which I cite EFQ plus one step of the deduction theorem.)

$(\wedge\text{I}) \quad \varphi,\psi \vdash \varphi\wedge\psi$

1. φ	ASS
2. ψ	ASS
3. $\varphi\rightarrow\neg\psi$	~~ASS~~(6)
4. $\neg\psi$	1,3,MP
5. $\bot$	2,4,EFQ$'$
6. $\neg(\varphi\rightarrow\neg\psi)$	3–5,RAA$'$
7. $\varphi\wedge\psi$	6,Def$\wedge$

$(\wedge\text{E}) \quad \varphi\wedge\psi \vdash \varphi$

1. $\varphi\wedge\psi$	ASS
2. $\neg(\varphi\rightarrow\neg\psi)$	1,Def$\wedge$
3. $\neg\varphi$	~~ASS~~(6)
4. $\varphi\rightarrow\neg\psi$	3,EFQ,D
5. $\bot$	2,4,EFQ$'$
6. $\neg\neg\varphi$	3–5, RAA$'$
7. φ	6,DNE

(∧E) φ∧ψ ⊢ ψ

   1. φ∧ψ   ASS
   2. ¬(φ→¬ψ)   1,Def∧
   3. ¬ψ   ASS(6)
   4. φ→¬ψ   3,D
   5. ⊥   2,4,EFQ′
   6. ¬¬ψ   3–5,RAA′
   7. ψ   6,DNE

In the case of ∨, it is easy to state suitable introduction rules, namely

   (∨I) φ ⊢ φ∨ψ, ψ ⊢ φ∨ψ.

It is more difficult to frame a suitable 'elimination' rule to accompany these. For the moment, I shall put it in this way:

   (∨E) φ→χ,ψ→χ ⊢ φ∨ψ→χ.

(But a different version, which more clearly justifies the title '(∨E)', will be introduced shortly.) Here are proofs:

(∨I) φ ⊢ φ∨ψ

   1. φ   ASS
   2. ¬φ→ψ   1,EFQ,D
   3. φ∨ψ   2,Def∨

(∨I) ψ ⊢ φ∨ψ

   1. ψ   ASS
   2. ¬φ→ψ   1,D
   3. φ∨ψ   2,Def∨

(∨E) φ→χ,ψ→χ ⊢ φ∨ψ→χ

   1. φ→χ   ASS
   2. ψ→χ   ASS
   3. φ∨ψ   ASS(10)
   4. ¬φ→ψ   3,Def∨
   5. ¬φ   ASS(8)
   6. ψ   4,5,MP
   7. χ   2,6,MP
   8. ¬φ→χ   5–7,D
   9. χ   1,8,TND
   10. φ∨ψ→χ   3–9,D

This has shown that our axioms (A1)–(A3), together with suitable definitions of $\wedge$ and $\vee$, will allow us to deduce suitable rules for using those functors in proofs. The reverse is also true. That is, if we add to the original axioms the introduction and elimination rules for $\wedge$ and $\vee$, then we can deduce the defining equivalences. (The proof of this is left as an exercise.)

Finally in this chapter let us consider the definition of $\exists$, namely

$$\exists\xi \quad \text{for} \quad \neg\forall\xi\neg.$$

We shall show that this definition yields these rules:

($\exists$I) $\varphi(\alpha/\xi) \vdash \exists\xi\varphi$

($\exists$E) If $\Gamma,\varphi \vdash \psi$, and if α is not in Γ or in ψ, then $\Gamma,\exists\xi\varphi(\xi/\alpha) \vdash \psi$

Here are proofs:

($\exists$I) $\varphi(\alpha/\xi) \vdash \exists\xi\varphi$

1.	$\varphi(\alpha/\xi)$	ASS
2.	$\forall\xi\neg\varphi$	~~ASS~~(5)
3.	$\neg\varphi(\alpha/\xi)$	2,A4,MP
4.	$\bot$	1,3,EFQ$'$
5.	$\neg\forall\xi\neg\varphi$	2–4,RAA$'$
6.	$\exists\xi\varphi$	4,Def$\exists$

($\exists$E) If $\Gamma,\varphi \vdash \psi$ then $\Gamma,\exists\xi\varphi(\xi/\alpha) \vdash \psi$, provided α is not in Γ or in ψ

1.	Γ	ASS
2.	$\exists\xi\varphi(\xi/\alpha)$	ASS
3.	$\neg\forall\xi\neg\varphi(\xi/\alpha)$	2,Def$\exists$
4.	$\neg\psi$	~~ASS~~(11)
5.	φ	~~ASS~~(8)
6.	ψ	1,5,Hypothesis
7.	$\bot$	4,6
8.	$\neg\varphi$	5–7,RAA$'$
9.	$\forall\xi\neg\varphi(\xi/\alpha)$	8,$\forall$I; α is not in lines (1),(2),(4)
10.	$\bot$	3,9,EFQ$'$
11.	$\neg\neg\psi$	4–10, RAA$'$
12.	ψ	11,DNE

EXERCISES

5.7.1. Show that the deductions of this section can be reversed, i.e. that if we assume as premisses the rules $(\wedge I),(\wedge E),(\vee I),(\vee E),(\exists I),(\exists E)$, then we can deduce from them equivalences corresponding to the definitions of $\wedge,\vee,\exists$, namely

$$\varphi \wedge \psi \quad \dashv\vdash \quad \neg(\varphi \rightarrow \neg\psi).$$
$$\varphi \vee \psi \quad \dashv\vdash \quad \neg\varphi \rightarrow \psi.$$
$$\exists \xi \varphi \quad \dashv\vdash \quad \neg\forall\xi\neg\varphi.$$

5.7.2. Consider an axiomatic system which has $\rightarrow$ as its only truth-functor, the rule of detachment as its only rule, and the following three axiom-schemas:

1. $\varphi \rightarrow (\psi \rightarrow \varphi)$.
2. $(\varphi \rightarrow (\psi \rightarrow \chi)) \rightarrow ((\varphi \rightarrow \psi) \rightarrow (\varphi \rightarrow \chi))$.
3. $((\varphi \rightarrow \psi) \rightarrow \varphi) \rightarrow \varphi$.

You may assume that proof from assumptions is defined, and the deduction theorem proved (using axioms (1) and (2)). Introduce the functor $\vee$ by defining

$$\varphi \vee \psi \quad \text{for} \quad (\varphi \rightarrow \psi) \rightarrow \psi$$

and prove the following:

4. $\varphi \vdash \varphi \vee \psi$
5. $\varphi \vee \psi \vdash \psi \vee \varphi$ [See Exercise 5.3.3.]
6. $\varphi \rightarrow \psi, \varphi \vee \chi \vdash \psi \vee \chi$
7. $\varphi \rightarrow \chi, (\varphi \rightarrow \psi) \rightarrow \chi \vdash \chi$ [Use 3.]
8. $\varphi \rightarrow \chi, \psi \rightarrow \chi \vdash (\varphi \vee \psi) \rightarrow \chi$ [Use 7.]
9. $(\varphi \vee \psi) \vee \chi \vdash \varphi \vee (\psi \vee \chi)$ [Use 4,5,8.]
10. If $\Gamma, \varphi \vdash \chi$ and $\Gamma \vdash \varphi \vee \chi$ then $\Gamma \vdash \chi$
11. If $\Gamma, \varphi \vdash \chi$ then $\Gamma \vdash \chi \vee (\varphi \rightarrow \psi)$
12. If $\Gamma \vdash \chi \vee \psi$ then $\Gamma \vdash \chi \vee (\varphi \rightarrow \psi)$ [Use 6.]
13. If $\Gamma, \psi \vdash \chi$ and $\Gamma \vdash \varphi \vee \chi$ then $\Gamma, \varphi \rightarrow \psi \vdash \chi$ [Use 6,10.]

This is the beginning of a proof to show that axioms (1)–(3) form a complete basis for all valid sequents whose only truth-functor is $\rightarrow$. To assist comprehension, let us write '$\Gamma \vdash \Delta$' to mean 'from the set of formulae in Γ there is a proof of the disjunction of all the formulae in Δ'. Then (5) and (9) tell us that the order and grouping of the disjunction represented by Δ may be ignored, and (10)–(13) may be rewritten thus:

10' If $\Gamma, \varphi \vdash \Delta$ and $\Gamma \vdash \varphi, \Delta$ then $\Gamma \vdash \Delta$
11' If $\Gamma, \varphi \vdash \Delta$ then $\Gamma \vdash \varphi \rightarrow \psi, \Delta$
12' If $\Gamma \vdash \psi, \Delta$ then $\Gamma \vdash \varphi \rightarrow \psi, \Delta$
13' If $\Gamma, \psi \vdash \Delta$ and $\Gamma \vdash \varphi, \Delta$ then $\Gamma, \varphi \rightarrow \psi \vdash \Delta$.

(As usual we write φ, Δ as short for $\{\varphi\} \cup \Delta$.) To see how the proof continues from here, consult Exercise 7.4.5.

5.7.3. Add to the system of the previous exercise the truth-functor $\bot$, and a single axiom-schema for it, to give the following set of axiom-schemas:

1. $\varphi \rightarrow (\psi \rightarrow \varphi)$.
2. $(\varphi \rightarrow (\psi \rightarrow \chi)) \rightarrow ((\varphi \rightarrow \psi) \rightarrow (\varphi \rightarrow \chi))$.
3. $((\varphi \rightarrow \psi) \rightarrow \varphi) \rightarrow \varphi$.
4. $\bot \rightarrow \varphi$.

Define negation by putting

$\neg\varphi$ for $\varphi\rightarrow\perp$.

Show that this set of axioms is a complete basis for the logic of truth-functors. [Method: show that from (3) and (4) and the definition one can deduce both EFQ and CM*.]

5.8. Appendix: Some Alternative Axiomatizations

The first axiomatization of logic was in Frege's *Begriffsschrift* of 1879. His axioms for the truth-functors were[5]

1. $\varphi\rightarrow(\psi\rightarrow\varphi)$.
2. $(\varphi\rightarrow(\psi\rightarrow\chi)) \rightarrow ((\varphi\rightarrow\psi)\rightarrow(\varphi\rightarrow\chi))$.
3. $(\varphi\rightarrow(\psi\rightarrow\chi)) \rightarrow (\psi\rightarrow(\varphi\rightarrow\chi))$.
4. $(\varphi\rightarrow\psi) \rightarrow (\neg\psi\rightarrow\neg\varphi)$.
5. $\neg\neg\varphi\rightarrow\varphi$.
6. $\varphi\rightarrow\neg\neg\varphi$.

It was later shown that his third axiom was superfluous, since it can be derived from the first two (Łukasiewicz 1936). Another early axiomatization, which became widely known, was that of Russell and Whitehead's *Principia Mathematica* (vol. i, 1910), which takes $\neg$ and $\vee$ as its basic vocabulary, but at once introduces $\rightarrow$ by the usual definition. The axioms are

1. $\varphi\vee\varphi \rightarrow \varphi$.
2. $\psi \rightarrow \varphi\vee\psi$.
3. $\varphi\vee\psi \rightarrow \psi\vee\varphi$.
4. $\varphi\vee(\psi\vee\chi) \rightarrow (\varphi\vee\psi)\vee\chi$.
5. $(\psi\rightarrow\chi) \rightarrow (\varphi\vee\psi\rightarrow\varphi\vee\chi)$.

It was later shown that the fourth axiom was superfluous (Bernays 1926), and in fact with minor changes elsewhere both (3) and (4) can be rendered superfluous (Rosser 1953). But in any case this is an unsatisfying set of axioms, for their purport is reasonably clear only when (as here) one uses *both* $\rightarrow$ *and* $\vee$ in the formulation. But officially, the primitive notation is just $\neg$ and $\vee$, and when $\rightarrow$ is replaced by this primitive notation the axioms seem very arbitrary indeed.

In almost all cases,[6] axioms for the truth-functors are designed to be used with the rule of detachment as the sole rule of inference, and that rule is naturally

---

[5] Strictly speaking, Frege did not use axiom-schemas, as here, but single axioms and a rule of substitution. (The idea of an axiom-schema was due to J. von Neumann (1927).) I have consistently ignored this distinction in this appendix.

[6] An exception is noted below, where axioms and rules are designed for the stroke functor.

formulated with $\to$. One therefore expects to find $\to$ in the primitive vocabulary, and playing an important role in the axioms. If this is granted, then there are broadly speaking two approaches to choose between. One may aim for economy in the axioms, by restricting the language. In that case one will naturally choose a language with just $\to$ and $\neg$, or just $\to$ and $\bot$. Or one may say that it is much more convenient in practice to have a richer language, and a correspondingly rich set of axioms. I pursue each of these suggestions in turn.

The system in $\to$ and $\neg$ that we have used in this chapter is easily seen to be a descendant of Frege's original system. It retains his first two axioms for $\to$ alone, omitting his third as superfluous, and adds to these one further axiom for negation. We have already explored (in Section 5.4) various other possibilities for the negation axioms, and do not need to add anything more here. A variation is to add axioms for $\bot$ rather than for $\neg$, and here we find that a single axiom which will do by itself is

$$((\varphi \to \bot) \to \bot) \to \varphi.$$

This yields a nicely economical system (which is used by Church 1956).

There is nothing in this general approach that forces us to retain Frege's first two axioms. It is true that they are very convenient, since they are just what we need to prove the deduction theorem (which was not known to Frege),[7] and this is a great help in finding proofs. But (a) this theorem can of course be postponed, if other axioms prove more attractive, and (b) there is the objection that these two axioms for $\to$ are not strong enough as they stand, since they do not suffice by themselves for the proof of all correct sequents concerning $\to$ on its own (cf. Exercise 5.3.3). In response to (a) there are various sets of axioms known to be equivalent to Frege's first two, for example this set of three:

1. $\varphi \to (\psi \to \varphi)$.
2. $(\varphi \to (\varphi \to \psi)) \to (\varphi \to \psi)$.
3. $(\varphi \to \psi) \to ((\psi \to \chi) \to (\varphi \to \chi))$.

(See Exercise 5.8.2.) But I am not aware of any set that seems more simple or more attractive than Frege's own pair. In response to (b) the most straightforward suggestion is just to *add* to Frege's pair a further axiom, for example Peirce's law:

$$((\varphi \to \psi) \to \varphi) \to \varphi.$$

This provides a set of three axioms for $\to$ which do suffice for the deduction of all correct sequents whose only functor is $\to$. (See Exercises 5.7.2. and 7.4.5.) An alternative with the same effect is to allow Peirce's law to replace the second axiom in the trio just cited, to yield

1. $\varphi \to (\psi \to \varphi)$
2. $((\varphi \to \psi) \to \varphi) \to \varphi$
3. $(\varphi \to \psi) \to ((\psi \to \chi) \to (\varphi \to \chi))$

---

[7] It is due to Herbrand (1930).

(Łukasiewicz and Tarski 1930). As it turns out, we can provide a *single* axiom which is adequate on its own for all correct sequents whose only functor is $\rightarrow$, namely

$$((\varphi\rightarrow\psi_1)\rightarrow\chi) \rightarrow ((\chi\rightarrow\varphi)\rightarrow(\psi_2\rightarrow\varphi))$$

(Łukasiewicz 1948). But this does not exactly strike one as a perspicuous axiom, and it is not at all easy to work with. Finally I add here that if we do adopt axioms for $\rightarrow$ which suffice for the deduction of all valid sequents in $\rightarrow$, then we need add only one simple axiom for $\bot$ to obtain a complete system, namely

$$\bot\rightarrow\varphi.$$

The axiom system adopted in this chapter can obtain many results for $\rightarrow$ without calling upon its axiom for negation, but not all, as we have seen. One could shift this balance in the other direction by strengthening the negation axioms, relying even more upon them for results which concern $\rightarrow$ alone, and consequently weakening the axioms for $\rightarrow$. An interesting system which does just this is based on the three axioms

$$(\varphi\rightarrow\psi) \rightarrow ((\psi\rightarrow\chi) \rightarrow (\varphi\rightarrow\chi))$$
$$(\neg\varphi\rightarrow\varphi)\rightarrow\varphi$$
$$\varphi\rightarrow(\neg\varphi\rightarrow\psi)$$

(Łukasiewicz 1936). Pursuing this direction further, and making no attempt to distinguish between axioms for $\rightarrow$ and axioms for $\neg$, we can in fact make do with a single axiom, namely

$$((((\varphi_1\rightarrow\varphi_2)\rightarrow(\neg\psi_2\rightarrow\neg\psi_1))\rightarrow\psi_2)\rightarrow\chi) \rightarrow ((\chi\rightarrow\varphi_1)\rightarrow(\psi_1\rightarrow\varphi_1))$$

(Meredith 1953). Like all single axioms, it is neither perspicuous nor easy to work with.

(This is perhaps the place to mention that the first single axiom for the logic of truth-functors was found as long ago as 1917, by J. Nicod. His axiom is formulated for the Sheffer stroke (p. 58), and is

$$[\varphi_1\!\uparrow\!(\varphi_2\!\uparrow\!\varphi_3)]\!\uparrow\!([\chi\!\uparrow\!(\chi\!\uparrow\!\chi)]\!\uparrow\!\{(\psi\!\uparrow\!\varphi_2)\!\uparrow\![(\varphi_1\!\uparrow\!\psi)\!\uparrow\!(\varphi_1\!\uparrow\!\psi)]\}).$$

This axiom is designed to be used, not with the usual rule of detachment for $\rightarrow$, but with a special rule for the Sheffer stroke, namely

If $\vdash \varphi$ and $\vdash \varphi\!\uparrow\!(\psi\!\uparrow\!\chi)$ then $\vdash \chi$.

(This is a generalization of the usual rule, for Detachment itself corresponds to the special case of this where ψ and χ are identified.) Since Nicod, some other versions of his single axiom have been found, which are equally long but perhaps do have a marginally better claim to elegance. But in any case single axioms seem to me to be a mere curiosity.)

To sum up on $\rightarrow$ and $\neg$, or $\rightarrow$ and $\bot$, it will be seen that although there is plenty of choice on which axioms to adopt, there is no choice which stands out as the most simple and straightforward, or the most elegant, or the one that most reveals our understanding of the functors involved. There is nothing here to rival the simple and very obvious rules of the semantic tableaux:

$$
\begin{array}{cc}
|\varphi{\to}\psi| = T & |\varphi{\to}\psi| = F \\
& \\
\end{array}
$$

This awkward situation will gradually be improved during the next two chapters. I now turn to a brief account of the alternative approach to axiomatization.

We may wish to consider from the start a richer language with more truth-functors, and a correspondingly richer set of axioms for those functors. For example, the following rather nice set is used by Kleene (1952):

1. $\varphi{\to}(\psi{\to}\varphi)$.
2. $(\varphi{\to}(\psi{\to}\chi)) \to ((\varphi{\to}\psi){\to}(\varphi{\to}\chi))$.
3. $\varphi{\wedge}\psi{\to}\varphi$.
4. $\varphi{\wedge}\psi{\to}\psi$.
5. $\varphi{\to}(\psi{\to}\varphi{\wedge}\psi)$.
6. $\varphi{\to}\varphi{\vee}\psi$.
7. $\psi{\to}\varphi{\vee}\psi$.
8. $(\varphi{\to}\chi) \to ((\psi{\to}\chi) \to (\varphi{\vee}\psi{\to}\chi))$.
9. $(\varphi{\to}\psi) \to ((\varphi{\to}\neg\psi) \to \neg\varphi)$.
10. $\neg\neg\varphi{\to}\varphi$.

Here axioms (1) and (2) are our standard (but incomplete) axioms for $\to$, and axioms (9) and (10) are a standard pair of axioms for $\neg$. But (3)–(5) add new axioms for $\wedge$, and (6)–(7) add new axioms for $\vee$. (We could restore the symmetry between these two new sets of axioms by rewriting (5) as

5'. $(\varphi{\to}\psi) \to ((\varphi{\to}\chi) \to (\varphi{\to}\psi{\wedge}\chi))$.

This would make no difference to the resulting theorems.) Axioms in this style were first introduced by Hilbert and Bernays (1934). (Their version adopts the modification just suggested, and it also has different but equivalent versions of axioms (1)–(2) and (9)–(10).) I observe here merely that the proposed axioms for $\wedge$ and $\vee$ lead very directly into the methods pursued in the next chapter, so I reserve further comment until then.[8]

Turning to the quantifiers, almost all systems adopt our axiom (A4):

[8] The full version of intuitionist logic, without quantifiers, is given by axioms (1)–(9), with EFQ in place of (10). The version used earlier in Exercises 5.4.3 and 5.4.4 is a truncated version, since it does not include $\wedge$ and $\vee$, and in intuitionist logic these cannot be defined in terms of $\to$ and $\neg$.

$\vdash \forall \xi \varphi \rightarrow \varphi(\alpha/\xi).$

Then there is a choice, either to add also our axiom (A5) and the simple rule GEN, or to add a more complex rule from which both of these are deducible, namely

If $\vdash \varphi \rightarrow \psi$ then $\vdash \varphi \rightarrow \forall \xi \varphi(\xi/\alpha)$, provided that α is not in φ.

(Frege himself adopted both this and GEN, but in his system GEN is superfluous.) The existential quantifier can then be defined in terms of the universal one, or it can be introduced by a dual pair of one axiom and one rule:

$\vdash \varphi(\alpha/\xi) \rightarrow \exists \xi \varphi.$

If $\vdash \varphi \rightarrow \psi$ then $\vdash \exists \xi \varphi(\xi/\alpha) \rightarrow \psi$, provided that α is not in ψ.

This technique is again closely related to that which will be pursued in the next chapter.

A different approach altogether is taken by Quine in his *Mathematical Logic* (1951), ch. 2. Just as one may assume the rule of substitution for all theorems, or one may in effect confine it to axioms, i.e. by adopting axiom-schemata, so also one may adopt the rule of generalization for all theorems (as we did in Section 5.6), or one may in effect confine it to axioms. The broad idea is that all ways of applying generalization to one's initial axioms are taken to yield further axioms. The result is that many more formulae are accepted as axioms, but the only rule of inference is the familiar rule of detachment. As a matter of fact Quine is forced to proceed along these lines, because of two other decisions that he has taken for philosophical reasons: in his system there are no name-letters, and open formulae are not permitted to occur as axioms or as theorems. This means that there are not actually any formulae in the system to which one could apply the rule of generalization. So what Quine takes as axioms are, roughly speaking, the formulae you would have obtained by applying generalization to axioms containing name-letters, if only such axioms had been permitted.

In more detail, Quine dispenses with separate axioms for the truth-functors by simply adopting every truth-table tautology as an axiom. But also he allows an *open* formula to count as a truth-table tautology, and he adopts as further axioms the *universal closures* of all such formulae. To state this economically, let us temporarily take over Quine's special usage of $\vdash$, whereby for any formula φ, open or closed, '$\vdash \varphi$' means 'the *closure* of φ is a theorem'. (Of course, if φ is already closed, then the closure of φ is φ itself.) Then we may say that in Quine's system there are four kinds of axioms, as follows

1. If φ is tautologous, $\vdash \varphi$.
2. $\vdash \forall \xi (\varphi \rightarrow \psi) \rightarrow (\forall \xi \varphi \rightarrow \forall \xi \psi).$
3. $\vdash \varphi \rightarrow \forall \xi \varphi$, provided ξ is not free in φ.
4. $\vdash \forall \xi \varphi \rightarrow \varphi(\zeta/\xi).$

($\varphi(\zeta/\xi)$ must contain ζ free wherever φ contains ξ free). And the sole rule of inference is detachment, which we can state in this way.

If φ and ψ are *closed* formulae, then if ⊢ φ and ⊢ φ→ψ, then ⊢ ψ.

Quine goes on to prove that the rule also holds where φ and ψ are open, but this takes some proving, as is clear when we remember the special meaning here attached to ⊢. But I cannot here describe how his deductions go.

EXERCISES

5.8.1. Consider Church's system for → and ⊥, which has these three axioms:

1. φ→(ψ→φ).
2. (φ→(ψ→χ)) → ((φ→ψ)→(φ→χ)).
3. ((φ→⊥)→⊥) → φ.

Show how to modify the completeness proof of Section 5.5 to prove that in this system every valid formula whose only truth-functors are → and ⊥ is a theorem.

5.8.2. Consider the system given by these three axioms:

1. φ→(ψ→φ).
2. (φ→(φ→ψ)) → (φ→ψ).
3. (φ→ψ) → ((ψ→χ) → (φ→χ)).

In this system, prove the following theorems:

4. φ→((φ→ψ)→ψ).
5. (φ→(ψ→χ)) → (ψ→(φ→χ)).
6. (ψ→χ) → ((φ→ψ) → (φ→χ)).
7. (φ→(ψ→χ)) → ((φ→ψ)→(φ→χ)).

Deduce that this system is equivalent to that given by our axioms (A1) and (A2). [Hints: we cannot assume that the deduction theorem applies to this system until we have proved (7), so this exercise calls for genuinely axiomatic proofs to be constructed. Since this is far from easy, I give some help. Here is a proof of (4) in a much abbreviated form:

φ→((φ→ψ)→φ)	from (1)
→ ((φ→ψ) → ((φ→ψ)→ψ))	from (3)
→ ((φ→ψ)→ψ)	from (2)

Show how to reconstruct the full proof from this sketch. To construct a similar sketch for (5) you will need to use

[φ→(ψ→χ)] → [((ψ→χ)→χ) → (φ→χ)]	from (3)
[((ψ→χ)→χ) → (φ→χ)] → [ψ→(φ→χ)]	from (4) and (3)

Given (5), it is easy to prove (6) from (3). The proof of (7) begins by stating (5) and then using this instance of (6):

[ψ→(φ→χ)] → [(φ→ψ) → (φ→(φ→χ))].

5.8.3. Consider the system given by these three axioms:

1. $\varphi \rightarrow (\psi \rightarrow \varphi)$.
2. $((\varphi \rightarrow \psi) \rightarrow \varphi) \rightarrow \varphi$.
3. $(\varphi \rightarrow \psi) \rightarrow ((\varphi \rightarrow \chi) \rightarrow (\varphi \rightarrow \chi))$.

In this system, prove the theorem

4. $(\varphi \rightarrow (\varphi \rightarrow \psi)) \rightarrow (\varphi \rightarrow \psi)$.

Deduce, using the previous exercise, that the deduction theorem holds for this system. [Hint: you will need this instance of axiom (2)]:

$$[((\varphi \rightarrow \psi) \rightarrow \psi) \rightarrow (\varphi \rightarrow \psi)] \rightarrow (\varphi \rightarrow \psi).$$

5.8.4. Consider the system got by adding, to any basis that is adequate for the truth-functors, these two further rules of inference:

1. If $\vdash \varphi \rightarrow \psi$ then $\vdash \forall \xi \varphi(\xi/\alpha) \rightarrow \psi$, provided that ξ is not free in φ.
2. If $\vdash \varphi \rightarrow \psi$ then $\vdash \varphi \rightarrow \forall \xi \psi(\xi/\alpha)$, provided that α does not occur in φ.

Show that this system is equivalent to the system of Section 5.6, which instead adds the two axioms (A4) and (A5) and the rule GEN.

6

Natural Deduction

6.1. The Idea

Axiomatic proofs are hard to construct, and often very lengthy. So in practice one does not actually construct such proofs; rather, one proves that *there is* a proof, as originally defined. One way in which we make use of this technique is when we allow ourselves to use, in a proof, any theorem that has been proved already. For officially this is short for writing out once more, as part of the new proof, the whole of the original proof of that theorem. Another way is when we are explicitly relying on the deduction theorem, and so are actually concerned with a proof from assumptions, and not an axiomatic proof as first defined. Proofs from assumptions are much easier to find, and much shorter. A third way is when we introduce new symbols by definition, for in practice one will go on at once to derive new rules for the new symbols, and these will usually be rules for use in proofs from assumptions. So it comes about that, after a few initial moves, the development of an axiomatic system will scarcely ever involve writing out real axiomatic proofs, but will rely on a number of short cuts.

The main idea behind what is called 'natural deduction' is to abandon the axiomatic starting-point altogether, and instead to *begin* with what I have just been calling the 'short cuts'. The most important point is that in natural deduction one takes the notion of a proof from assumptions as a basic notion, and works simply with it. Such proofs are not thought of as abbreviating some other and more basic kind of proofs, but are the primary objects of study. So from the beginning our basic rules will be rules for use in proofs from assumptions, and axioms (as traditionally understood) will have no role to play. That is the most crucial feature of all systems of natural deduction. But there are several other features too that are nowadays expected and desired.

First, the truth-functor $\to$ will no longer have any special prominence. In axiomatic treatments it almost always does, both because the main rule of inference, namely detachment, is a rule for $\to$, and because there are only a very few formulae that one might naturally think of adopting as axioms and that do not have $\to$ (or $\leftrightarrow$) as their main functor. (The only obvious exceptions are the laws of excluded middle and non-contradiction, i.e. $\vdash \varphi \vee \neg\varphi$ and $\vdash \neg(\varphi \wedge \neg\varphi)$.) But we shall now have no axioms, and put no special weight on detachment (or Modus Ponens). Instead, we shall have separate rules for each truth-functor of the language to be employed, so that there will not only be rules for $\to$, but also for $\neg, \wedge, \vee$, and any other functor that is desired. To illustrate, a very natural principle for $\wedge$ is this: given both φ and ψ as premisses, one may infer $\varphi \wedge \psi$. If we try to phrase this as an axiom, then probably the simplest way is this:

$$\vdash \varphi \to (\psi \to \varphi \wedge \psi).$$

Here, of course, we use $\to$ as well as $\wedge$. But evidently the principle can also be formulated as a rule of inference which does not use $\to$. As a rule for use in axiomatic systems it would be

If $\vdash \varphi$ and $\vdash \psi$ then $\vdash \varphi \wedge \psi$.

(In this form it is called 'the rule of adjunction'.) But for use in proofs from assumptions we shall adopt the more general version

If $\Gamma \vdash \varphi$ and $\Delta \vdash \psi$ then $\Gamma, \Delta \vdash \varphi \wedge \psi$.

Given the structural rules ASS and CUT in the background, it is easy to show that this is actually equivalent to the simpler version

$\varphi, \psi \vdash \varphi \wedge \psi$.

Let us come back to the task of giving a general characterization of what is nowadays called 'natural deduction'. I have said so far (1) that the basic notion is that of a proof from assumptions, (2) that there will accordingly be no axioms (as traditionally understood) but a number of rules of inference for use in such proofs, and (3) that we shall expect to find, for each truth-functor or quantifier in the language being considered, rules that specifically concern it, and no other truth-functor or quantifier. Now (3) is more a requirement of elegance than a condition on what can be counted as natural deduction, and certainly systems have been proposed which one would wish to call systems of natural deduction even though they do not entirely conform to it. The same applies to this further elaboration of (3): for each truth-functor or quantifier concerned, there will be one or two rules that are counted as its *introduction* rules, and one or two that are counted as its *elimination* rules, and no other rules. Again, there are well-known systems which do not entirely conform to this, but it is what one expects nowadays. We can illustrate by continuing with our example of the functor $\wedge$. This has just one introduction rule, henceforward called $(\wedge I)$, namely the rule already stated

$(\wedge I)$ $\varphi, \psi \vdash \varphi \wedge \psi$.

It has a pair of elimination rules, each (for brevity) called $(\wedge E)$, namely

$(\wedge E)$ $\varphi \wedge \psi \vdash \varphi$, $\varphi \wedge \psi \vdash \psi$.

And there are no other rules for $\wedge$. Moreover, we may add here a fourth requirement on systems of natural deduction, which is certainly a requirement of elegance and nothing more, for in fact I know of no system which succeeds in conforming to it without exception. This is (4)(*a*) that the introduction and elimination rules for any one sign be complete for that sign, in the sense that all correct sequents involving only that sign be provable from those rules alone; and (*b*) that combining the introduction and elimination rules for any two or more signs yields a system complete for those signs together, again in the sense that all correct sequents containing only those signs be provable from those rules alone.

Finally, I add two more requirements, of which it is evident that there is no fully objective way of telling whether they are satisfied or not. These are: (5) that the rules for each sign be 'natural', in the sense that inferences drawn in accordance with them strike us as 'natural' ways of arguing and inferring; and (6) that so long as the sequent that we are trying to prove is 'not too complicated', there should be a proof of it which is 'reasonably short' and uses only the rules initially adopted. As we observed earlier, in an axiomatic system it is necessary in practice to proceed in a cumulative fashion: after a brief initial development, one's proofs seldom go back to the original axioms, but rely instead on other results that have been proved already. Consequently, the tools that one has available for use in constructing proofs will vary, depending on how far the development of the system has gone. But the idea is that in natural deduction this should not be necessary, and *every* proof should rely just on the handful of rules first given as the rules of the system, even in practice. In other words, the initial rules should themselves be natural, and it should be natural to use them, and *only* them, in all one's deductions. That is primarily what we mean by 'natural' deduction.

As we shall see, there is some conflict between these requirements of naturalness and the requirements of elegance noted earlier.

EXERCISE

6.1.1. Using just the rules (∧I) and (∧E), and setting out proofs as in Chapter 5, give proofs of

(a) $P \wedge Q \dashv\vdash Q \wedge P$.
(b) $P \wedge (Q \wedge R) \dashv\vdash (P \wedge Q) \wedge R$.
(c) $P \dashv\vdash P \wedge P$.

6.2. Rules of Proof I: Truth-Functors

There are several different ways of setting out proofs in a natural deduction system. I begin with an approach which is likely to be unfamiliar, but which has been claimed to be specially 'natural', whereby a proof is not a linear sequence of formulae but a two-dimensional array of them, arranged in a tree structure. The structure has just one formula at its root, which is at the bottom. (This time, trees do not grow upside-down, as they did in Chapter 4.) The formula at the root is the formula that is proved by that proof, i.e. it is the conclusion to the sequent established by the proof. The branches spread upwards from it, representing the trains of reasoning needed to reach the conclusion, and each branch has as its topmost formula an assumption to the proof. So, as we follow the proof downwards, we begin with assumptions at the top, and whenever a one-premiss rule of inference is applied (such as (∧E)) the conclusion is written directly below the premiss, whereas when we apply a two-premiss rule (such as (∧I)) we take one premiss from one branch and the other from another, and bring the two branches together at that point. A proof, then, is a finite array of formulae with just one at the bottom, having none below it, and one or more at the top, having none above them. Apart from these topmost formulae, every formula is placed under one or two others, and follows from them by one of the stated rules of inference. And the whole structure is a tree, which means that for each occurrence of a formula in the structure, except the lowest, there is one and only one formula that is directly below it. Consequently, any occurrence of a formula in the structure is linked with the lowest occurrence by one and only one route.

This is only a preliminary description of our two-dimensional proofs, for further complications will be added as we proceed, concerning the discharging of assumptions. But already we can see (*a*) that this definition automatically satisfies the principle of Assumptions

$$\varphi \vdash \varphi,$$

since the single formula φ is a proof of itself from itself; and (*b*) that it also satisfies the Cut principle

If $\Gamma \vdash \varphi$ and $\varphi, \Delta \vdash \psi$ then $\Gamma, \Delta \vdash \psi$.

For suppose that we have a tree, formed according to the rules, which has φ at its root and only members of Γ at its topmost positions; and suppose that we have another tree, formed according to the rules, with ψ at its root and at its topmost positions only the formula φ and otherwise members of Δ. Then we have only to place the first tree on top of the second, at any point where the second had φ as a topmost formula, and the result is a tree with ψ at its root and only formulae in Γ or in Δ at its topmost positions. And if the original trees conformed to the stated rules of inference, then so must the new tree formed from them both.[1]

The remaining 'structural' principle is the principle of Thinning, and this is not automatically satisfied by the present definition of what a proof is. If we think of the principle in its usual form, namely

If $\Gamma \vdash \varphi$ then $\Gamma, \psi \vdash \varphi$,

then apparently we can argue that it *is* satisfied in this way: a proof which has as assumptions only formulae in Γ must automatically be a proof which has as assumptions only formulae which are either ψ or in Γ. But in fact this does not give us what we want, since it does not allow us to use the principle *within* proofs, or in other words it does not give us a way of actually adding a further assumption ψ to an existing proof. For if the proof is to remain a tree structure, then the added assumption ψ must actually be linked, via some rule of inference, to the rest of the structure, and the argument just suggested gives us no way of doing this. I shall therefore add Thinning as a basic rule of inference to all natural deduction systems. As is easily checked, since we do have both ASS and CUT in the background, the rule can be simply stated in this form:

---

[1] At least, this must be so when the only rules concerned are rules for the truth-functors, as may be verified by inspection of those rules, as they are introduced. But the position with quantifiers is more complex. See Exercise 6.3.3.

THIN: $\varphi, \psi \vdash \varphi$.

In some systems that we shall consider, this rule will be deducible from the other rules, and in some it will not. (For example, if we are given the rules for $\wedge$, then we may easily deduce it by one step of ($\wedge$I) followed by one step of ($\wedge$E).) But I shall assume that it is always present.

Let us now look at some examples of proofs in this two-dimensional structure. First let us restate the rules for $\wedge$ in a vertical form, with the premiss or premisses written above a horizontal line, and the conclusion below it. For that is how the rules will actually appear in these structures, i.e. as

$$(\wedge\text{I}) \frac{\varphi \quad \psi}{\varphi \wedge \psi} \qquad (\wedge\text{E}) \frac{\varphi \wedge \psi}{\varphi}, \qquad (\wedge\text{E}) \frac{\varphi \wedge \psi}{\psi}.$$

Then if we wish to show that $\wedge$ is associative, i.e. that

$$\varphi \wedge (\psi \wedge \chi) \vdash (\varphi \wedge \psi) \wedge \chi,$$

all that we need to do is to fit the rules together in this way

$$
(\wedge\text{I}) \frac{(\wedge\text{E}) \dfrac{\varphi \wedge (\psi \wedge \chi)}{\varphi} \qquad (\wedge\text{E}) \dfrac{(\wedge\text{E}) \dfrac{\varphi \wedge (\psi \wedge \chi)}{\psi \wedge \chi}}{\psi}}{\varphi \wedge \psi} \qquad (\wedge\text{E}) \frac{(\wedge\text{E}) \dfrac{\varphi \wedge (\psi \wedge \chi)}{\psi \wedge \chi}}{\chi}
$$
$$(\wedge\text{I}) \frac{}{(\varphi \wedge \psi) \wedge \chi}$$

This is a proof with three branches, but each begins with the same formula as assumption, so it nevertheless proves a sequent which has just one premiss.

I remark here that in this proof each application of a rule has been labelled, to the left of the line separating premisses and conclusion, to show which rule it is that is being applied at each point. When one is not yet familiar with proofs constructed in this style, it is probably helpful if such labels are put in explicitly, and so I shall do so in this section and the next. But in fact they are superfluous, for if we do have a correctly constructed proof, then there cannot be any doubt about which rule is being applied at any given stage. So, since these labels do clutter up the page quite noticeably, one soon learns to omit them in practice.

The rules for $\wedge$ are extremely simple to work with, so let us at once move on to something a little more tricky, namely the rules for $\vee$. There is no problem over the two introduction rules, which mirror the two elimination rules for $\wedge$ in an obvious way, namely

$$(\vee I) \, \frac{\varphi}{\varphi \vee \psi}, \quad (\vee I) \, \frac{\psi}{\varphi \vee \psi}.$$

But we have (at present[2]) no way of stating an elimination rule for $\vee$ which is at all similar to the simple introduction rule for $\wedge$. Instead, our rule is in effect this:

If $\Gamma, \varphi \vdash \chi$ and $\Delta, \psi \vdash \chi$ then $\Gamma, \Delta, \varphi \vee \psi \vdash \chi$.

It is not unreasonably counted as an 'elimination' rule because, when you present it in a form suitable for our two-dimensional proof trees, it looks like this:

$$(\vee E) \, \frac{\varphi \vee \psi \quad \quad \overset{\displaystyle \frac{\quad}{\varphi}(n)}{\underset{\displaystyle \chi}{\vdots}} \quad \quad \overset{\displaystyle \frac{\quad}{\psi}(n)}{\underset{\displaystyle \chi}{\vdots}}}{\chi} (n)$$

Think of it in this way. Suppose that we are given a premiss $\varphi \vee \psi$, stated on the left, and we wish to know what can be deduced from it. Then we introduce the extra assumption φ, in the middle of the diagram, and see what can be deduced from that. We also introduce the extra assumption ψ, on the right of the diagram, and see what can be deduced from that. Suppose that we find a conclusion χ that can be deduced from each of these assumptions. Then we write the proof of χ from φ, and the proof of χ from ψ, in place of the vertical dots of the diagram, and we are ready to apply our step of $(\vee E)$. The rule tells us that, since χ can be obtained both from φ and from ψ, it can also be obtained from $\varphi \vee \psi$. So we now write χ once more, but beneath the line representing this step of $(\vee E)$, i.e. beneath $\varphi \vee \psi$, and at the same time we *discharge* the two assumptions φ and ψ by drawing a horizontal line *above* each of them. From this point onwards, φ and ψ are no longer assumptions to the proof. Instead the assumptions are: first, $\varphi \vee \psi$, which we are imagining to be given as a premiss; next, any further assumptions Γ which may have been used, in addition to φ itself, in the deduction of χ from φ; and finally, any further assumptions Δ that may have been used, in addition to ψ itself, in the deduction of χ from ψ. (Of course, $\varphi \vee \psi$ might not have been given as a premiss, but deduced from some further assumptions,

---

[2] The situation will alter in the next chapter.

say Θ. In that case the whole proof is a deduction of χ from all the assumptions Θ,Γ,Δ.) Finally, when we discharge the assumptions φ and ψ by drawing lines above them, we label those lines (on the right) with a numeral n, to show that this is the nth set of assumptions to be discharged in the proof, and at the same time we attach the same label to the line representing the step of $(\vee E)$, which shows *when* those assumptions were discharged. Thus the part of the proof that is *between* two lines labelled n does depend on the assumptions labelled n—i.e. either on φ or on ψ, as the case may be—but what comes below the second such line does not. (I remark incidentally that whereas one soon learns to omit the labels to the left of each line, one must *not* omit the labels on the right showing which assumptions are discharged when; it is essential to keep this feature of the proof firmly in mind.)

Here is an example of how to use these rules for $\vee$, namely a proof to show that $\vee$, like $\wedge$, is associative:

$$(\varphi\vee\psi)\vee\chi \vdash \varphi\vee(\psi\vee\chi)$$

Notice that this begins with three proofs, using only $(\vee I)$, to show that the desired conclusion follows from each of φ, ψ, χ taken singly. Then at the first step of $(\vee E)$, labelled (1), it is inferred that the conclusion also follows from $\varphi\vee\psi$, and the assumptions φ and ψ are discharged, while $\varphi\vee\psi$ is introduced in their place. Finally, at the second step of $(\vee E)$, labelled (2), it is inferred that the conclusion follows from the desired assumption $(\varphi\vee\psi)\vee\chi$, and the assumptions $\varphi\vee\psi$ and χ are discharged, so that this is the only remaining assumption.

Before leaving $\wedge$ and $\vee$, here are two further examples of proofs, using all four of the rules introduced so far, to establish one of the laws of distribution

$$\varphi\vee(\psi\wedge\chi) \dashv\vdash (\varphi\vee\psi)\wedge(\varphi\vee\chi).$$

These proofs should be studied before proceeding. Notice that in the first of them we used the assumption φ twice when showing that the desired conclusion followed from it and similarly the assumption $\psi\wedge\chi$. But that

(a) $\varphi \vee (\psi \wedge \chi) \vdash (\varphi \vee \psi) \wedge (\varphi \vee \chi)$

$$
\cfrac{\varphi \vee (\psi \wedge \chi) \qquad
\cfrac{\cfrac{\overline{\varphi}^{(1)}}{\varphi \vee \psi}(\vee\mathrm{I}) \quad \cfrac{\overline{\varphi}^{(1)}}{\varphi \vee \chi}(\vee\mathrm{I})}{(\varphi \vee \psi) \wedge (\varphi \vee \chi)}(\wedge\mathrm{I}) \qquad
\cfrac{\cfrac{\cfrac{\overline{\psi \wedge \chi}^{(1)}}{\psi}(\wedge\mathrm{E})}{\varphi \vee \psi}(\vee\mathrm{I}) \quad \cfrac{\cfrac{\overline{\psi \wedge \chi}^{(1)}}{\chi}(\wedge\mathrm{E})}{\varphi \vee \chi}(\vee\mathrm{I})}{(\varphi \vee \psi) \wedge (\varphi \vee \chi)}(\wedge\mathrm{I})}
{(\varphi \vee \psi) \wedge (\varphi \vee \chi)}(\vee\mathrm{E})^{(1)}
$$

(b) $(\varphi \vee \psi) \wedge (\varphi \vee \chi) \vdash \varphi \vee (\psi \wedge \chi)$

$$
\cfrac{\cfrac{(\varphi \vee \psi) \wedge (\varphi \vee \chi)}{\varphi \vee \psi}(\wedge\mathrm{E}) \qquad
\cfrac{\overline{\varphi}^{(1)}}{\varphi \vee (\psi \wedge \chi)}(\vee\mathrm{I}) \qquad
\cfrac{\cfrac{\cfrac{\overline{\psi}^{(1)} \quad \overline{\chi}^{(2)}}{\psi \wedge \chi}(\wedge\mathrm{I})}{\varphi \vee (\psi \wedge \chi)}(\vee\mathrm{I}) \qquad \cfrac{\cfrac{(\varphi \vee \psi) \wedge (\varphi \vee \chi)}{\varphi \vee \chi}(\wedge\mathrm{E})}{\varphi \vee (\psi \wedge \chi)}\overline{\varphi}^{(2)} (\vee\mathrm{E})^{(2)}}{\varphi \vee (\psi \wedge \chi)}(\vee\mathrm{E})^{(1)}}
{\varphi \vee (\psi \wedge \chi)}(\vee\mathrm{E})
$$

does not matter: at the final step of (∨E) we discharge *both* occurrences of each assumption. Notice also that in the second we can obtain our conclusion readily enough from φ as assumption, but we cannot obtain it from ψ as assumption without using χ as a further assumption. Consequently, at the first step of (∨E), labelled (1), we can discharge φ and ψ, but χ is still outstanding. So at this stage the desired conclusion is obtained from the given premiss (on the left) *and* from χ as a further assumption. But χ is discharged at the second step of (∨E), labelled (2).

Let us come now to → and ¬. It is usual to adopt for → the two rules which in the previous chapter were called the deduction theorem and Modus Ponens. They are now given new names, i.e. (→I) and (→E) respectively, and may be stated as

$$\begin{array}{c} \underline{} \ (n) \\ \varphi \end{array}$$

$$\cdot$$
$$\cdot$$
$$\cdot$$

$$(\to I) \ \frac{\psi}{\varphi \to \psi} \ (n) \qquad\qquad (\to E) \ \frac{\varphi \quad \varphi \to \psi}{\psi}$$

Note that the first is a rule that discharges an assumption, so the same technique applies as with (∨E). When the assumption is discharged, we draw a line over it, labelling it with the numeral *n* to show that it is the *n*th assumption discharged in the proof, and we attach the same label to the line of (→I) to show where that assumption is discharged. (If φ was used several times as an assumption in the proof of ψ, then we discharge all of those occurrences of φ at once.)

Since the task of constructing proofs from these two rules is essentially the same as that practised extensively in the previous chapter, it need not be illustrated here. As we have noted, these rules (→I) and (→E) are together equivalent to what was called in Chapter 2 the basic principle for →, namely

$$\Gamma, \varphi \vdash \psi \quad \text{iff} \quad \Gamma \vdash \varphi \to \psi.$$

As we have also noted (p. 199), the two rules together do *not* actually suffice for the deduction of all correct sequents whose only truth-functor is →, and from our present perspective there is no very obvious way of putting this right. We could, of course, add a further rule, but the simplest suggestion here seems to be to add Peirce's law, e.g. in the form

$$\frac{\qquad}{\varphi \rightarrow \psi} (n)$$

.

.

.

$$(P) \frac{\varphi}{\varphi} (n)$$

No one can pretend, however, that this is a very *natural* rule to add. The situation here is essentially the same as it was in the last chapter.

Very much the same applies to rules for negation. All the axioms for negation that we considered in the last chapter can be rewritten as rules for negation in the new style of this chapter, with the occurrences of $\rightarrow$ eliminated. For example, our single axiom for negation, namely

$$\vdash (\neg\varphi \rightarrow \neg\psi) \rightarrow (\psi \rightarrow \varphi),$$

can be rephrased as a rule for natural deduction in this way:

$$\frac{\qquad}{\neg\varphi} (n)$$

.

.

.

$$(CON\ iv) \frac{\neg\psi \qquad\qquad \psi}{\varphi} (n)$$

This says: suppose you have a deduction of $\neg\psi$ from $\neg\varphi$; then if you add the premiss ψ, you may discharge the premiss $\neg\varphi$ of this deduction, and infer φ as conclusion. The relation between this version and the original axiom is, I hope, clear: if you do have a deduction of $\neg\psi$ from $\neg\varphi$, then by $(\rightarrow I)$ you have a deduction of $\neg\varphi \rightarrow \neg\psi$ which no longer has φ as a premiss.

Clearly the other versions of contraposition may also be rephrased in the same way. I add here suitable rephrasings of the other laws of negation that were mentioned in Section 5.4.

$$\frac{\qquad}{\varphi} (n) \qquad\qquad\qquad \frac{\qquad}{\neg\varphi} (n)$$

.

.

.

$$(CM) \frac{\neg\varphi}{\neg\varphi} (n) \qquad\qquad (CM^*) \frac{\varphi}{\varphi} (n)$$

$$
\text{(RAA)} \quad \frac{\displaystyle \frac{\rule{1.5em}{0.4pt}}{\varphi}(n) \quad\vdots\quad \psi \qquad\qquad \frac{\rule{1.5em}{0.4pt}}{\varphi}(n) \quad\vdots\quad \neg\psi}{\neg\varphi}(n)
\qquad
\text{(RAA*)} \quad \frac{\displaystyle \frac{\rule{1.5em}{0.4pt}}{\neg\varphi}(n) \quad\vdots\quad \psi \qquad\qquad \frac{\rule{1.5em}{0.4pt}}{\neg\varphi}(n) \quad\vdots\quad \neg\psi}{\varphi}(n)
$$

$$
\text{(EFQ)} \quad \frac{\varphi \qquad\qquad \neg\varphi}{\psi}
\qquad
\text{(TND)} \quad \frac{\displaystyle \frac{\rule{1.5em}{0.4pt}}{\varphi}(n) \quad\vdots\quad \psi \qquad\qquad \frac{\rule{1.5em}{0.4pt}}{\neg\varphi}(n) \quad\vdots\quad \psi}{\psi}(n)
$$

$$
\text{(DNI)} \quad \frac{\varphi}{\neg\neg\varphi}
\qquad
\text{(DNE)} \quad \frac{\neg\neg\varphi}{\varphi}
$$

Against the background of the standard structural rules (including THIN), all the deductive relations between these principles that were diagrammed on p. 215 continue to hold when they are rephrased in this way, *but with one important exception.* On p. 209 I gave a proof of CM* from CON(iv) and EFQ, and when we try to repeat this proof in the new format the best that we can do is this:

$$
\text{(CON iv)} \cfrac{\text{($\to$I)} \cfrac{\dfrac{\rule{1.5em}{0.4pt}}{\neg\varphi}(1) \quad\vdots\quad \varphi}{\neg\varphi\to\varphi}(1)}{\varphi}
\qquad
\text{(EFQ)} \cfrac{\dfrac{\dfrac{\rule{1.5em}{0.4pt}}{\neg\varphi}(2) \quad\vdots\quad \varphi \qquad \dfrac{\rule{1.5em}{0.4pt}}{\neg\varphi}(2)}{\neg(\neg\varphi\to\varphi)}(2)}{}
$$

But this proof uses ($\to$I) in addition. As it happens, reliance on the rules for $\to$ can be eliminated from all the other deductions given in Section 5.4, as you are invited to check. But in this particular case the use of a negated conditional resists elimination, and so far as I am aware there is no alternative deduction which would avoid the difficulty.

The result, then, is that in the new setting our original axiom CON(iv) will no longer serve as the sole rule for negation, for it needs help from the rules for →. If we wish for a single rule, the obvious one to choose is RAA*, for this is still adequate by itself. But, as I have said, the usual procedure in natural deduction is to look for a pair of rules, with one as 'introduction' rule and the other as 'elimination' rule. Consequently, many books adopt RAA and DNE in these respective roles, though RAA is not at all naturally described as an introduction rule. My own preference is for the pair TND and EFQ, with TND counted as the 'introduction' rule. For I have already observed (p. 212) that it is the nearest that we can get, without using ∨, to what is a clear introduction rule, namely the law of excluded middle ⊢ φ∨¬φ.[3] Moreover, EFQ forms a natural pair with this, since it is again the nearest that we can get to the dual law of non-contradiction in the form φ∧¬φ ⊢. But whatever pair of rules we choose for negation, and however 'natural' we find them as rules for use in inferring one thing from another, still there will inevitably be this 'unnatural' feature of the system: there are *many* rules for negation which are very useful in constructing proofs, and to be confined to just two of these—one for 'introducing' and one for 'eliminating'—will certainly not seem to be a 'natural' restriction.

To summarize: the standard rules for ∧ are a shining example of how the ideal of natural deduction may be met, and the standard rules for ∨ are not far behind. It is true that the rule (∨E) strikes one at first as rather complex, but familiarity breeds contentment, and the rule does do exactly the job that is required (Exercise 6.2.2). But with → and ¬ the situation is less appealing. The trouble with the suggested rules for ¬ is that we have too many to choose from, that no choice stands out as specially 'natural', and that whatever we do choose it will be 'unnatural' to be deprived of the others. By contrast, with → there is a pair of rules which it is very natural to choose, but then it turns out that those two are not strong enough to do all the work required of them. Either, then, we must add some further and rather 'unnatural' rule for →, or we must put up with the inelegance that the theory of → must rely upon that of ¬ if it is not to remain incomplete.

For ease of reference, I end this section with a summary statement of the rules for the truth-functors that I shall assume in what follows. They are:

---

[3] Also, in the terminology of the next chapter, TND is a rule for eliminating on the left, and such rules correspond quite naturally to rules for introducing on the right.

$$(\wedge I)\ \frac{\varphi \quad \psi}{\varphi \wedge \psi} \qquad\qquad (\wedge E)\ \frac{\varphi \wedge \psi}{\varphi},\quad (\wedge E)\ \frac{\varphi \wedge \psi}{\psi}$$

$$(\vee I)\ \frac{\varphi}{\varphi \vee \psi},\quad (\vee I)\ \frac{\psi}{\varphi \vee \psi} \qquad (\vee E)\ \frac{\varphi \vee \psi \quad \displaystyle{\overline{\quad}(n) \atop \varphi} \quad \displaystyle{\overline{\quad}(n) \atop \psi} \atop \chi \qquad\quad \chi}{\chi}\ (n)$$

$$(\to I)\ \frac{\displaystyle{\overline{\quad}(n) \atop \varphi} \atop \vdots \atop \psi}{\varphi \to \psi}\ (n) \qquad\qquad (\to E)\ \frac{\varphi \qquad \varphi \to \psi}{\psi}$$

$$(\text{TND})\ \frac{\displaystyle{\overline{\quad}(n) \atop \varphi} \quad \displaystyle{\overline{\quad}(n) \atop \neg\varphi} \atop \psi \qquad\quad \psi}{\psi}\ (n) \qquad (\text{EFQ})\ \frac{\varphi \qquad \neg\varphi}{\psi}$$

EXERCISES

6.2.1.(*a*) Devise suitable natural deduction rules for $\leftrightarrow$, first allowing yourself to use $\to$ in formulating the rules, and then eliminating $\to$ so that only $\leftrightarrow$ appears in the rules.

(*b*) Prove from these rules

(1) $\vdash \varphi \leftrightarrow \varphi$.
(2) $\varphi \leftrightarrow \psi \dashv\vdash \psi \leftrightarrow \varphi$.
(3) $\varphi \leftrightarrow (\psi \leftrightarrow \chi) \dashv\vdash (\varphi \leftrightarrow \psi) \leftrightarrow \chi$.

(*c*) Deduce that, if the only truth-functor in φ is $\leftrightarrow$, then $\vdash \varphi$, according to these rules, iff $\vDash \varphi$. [Hint: recall pp. 60–1 of Chapter 2.]

6.2.2. Let S be the system for natural deduction which contains just $\wedge$ and $\vee$ as truth-functors, and the standard rules $(\wedge I),(\wedge E),(\vee I),(\vee E)$.

(*a*) Show that, if $\Gamma \models \varphi$, and the only truth-functor in Γ or in φ is $\wedge$, then $\Gamma \vdash_S \varphi$. [Hint: you will need to show that the premiss implies that every sentence-letter in φ occurs in some formula in Γ.]

(*b*) Show that, if $\Gamma \models \varphi$, and the only truth-functor in Γ or in φ is $\vee$, then $\Gamma \vdash_S \varphi$. [Hint: you will need to show that the premiss implies that there is some formula in Γ such that every sentence-letter in it occurs in φ.]

(*c*) Prove

$$\varphi \vee (\psi \wedge \chi) \; {}_S\!\dashv\vdash_S \; (\varphi \vee \psi) \wedge (\varphi \vee \chi).$$

(*d*) Let $\delta(\psi)$ result from $\delta(\varphi)$ upon substituting ψ for one or more occurrences of φ in $\delta(\varphi)$. Prove

If $\varphi \; {}_S\!\dashv\vdash_S \psi$ then $\delta(\varphi) \; {}_S\!\dashv\vdash_S \delta(\psi)$.

[Use induction on the number of truth-functors in $\delta(\varphi)$ but not in φ. Compare pp. 101–2.]

(*e*) Deduce from (*c*) and (*d*) that for every formula φ whose only truth-functors are $\wedge$ and $\vee$ there is a formula φ' in CNF such that

$$\varphi \; {}_S\!\dashv\vdash_S \varphi'.$$

(*f*) Using parts (*b*) and (*e*), show that, if $\Gamma \models \varphi$, and the only truth-functors in Γ or in φ are $\wedge$ and $\vee$, then $\Gamma \vdash_S \varphi$. [Hint: $\varphi_1 \wedge \varphi_2 \models \psi_1 \wedge \psi_2$ iff $\varphi_1, \varphi_2 \models \psi_1$ and $\varphi_1, \varphi_2 \models \psi_2$.]

6.2.3. Lets S be a system for natural deduction which contains just $\wedge$ and $\neg$ as truth-functors, and just the rules $(\wedge I),(\wedge E),(DNE),(DNI),(EFQ)$.

(*a*) Show that, if $\Gamma \models \varphi$, and the only truth-functor in Γ or in φ is $\neg$, then $\Gamma \vdash_S \varphi$. [For the method, compare parts (*a*) and (*b*) of the previous exercise.]

(*b*) Despite part (*a*), and the previous exercise, show that it is *not* true that if $\Gamma \models \varphi$, and the only truth-functors in Γ or in φ are $\wedge$ and $\neg$, then $\Gamma \vdash_S \varphi$. [Hint: note that no rule in S discharges assumptions, and consider the fact that $\models \neg(P \wedge \neg P)$.]

6.2.4.(*a*) Let S contain just the rules $(\wedge I),(\wedge E),(TND),(EFQ)$. Show that, if $\Gamma \models \varphi$, and the only functors in φ are $\wedge$ and $\neg$, then $\Gamma \vdash_S \varphi$. [Method: mimic the completeness proof of Section 5.5.]

(*b*) Do the same for a system S' which contains just the rules $(\vee I),(\vee E),(TND)$, (EFQ), *and* THIN. [Method as before.] Was it necessary to be given THIN in addition to the other rules?

6.2.5.(*a*) Let S_1 contain just the rules $(\wedge I),(\wedge E),(\vee I),(\vee E)$ and in addition

$$\vdash_{S_1} \varphi \vee \neg\varphi, \quad \vdash_{S_1} \neg(\varphi \wedge \neg\varphi).$$

Show that S_1 is *not* complete. [Hint: interpret $\neg\varphi$ as always true.]

(*b*) Let S_2 contain the rules $(\wedge I),(\wedge E),(\vee I),(\vee E)$, the structural rule for Thinning on the right (p. 227), and in addition

$$\vdash_{S_2} \varphi \vee \neg \varphi, \quad \varphi \wedge \neg \varphi \vdash_{S_2}$$

Show that S_2 *is* complete. [Use Exercise 6.2.4.]

6.3. **Rules of Proof II: Quantifiers**

The rules for the quantifiers $\forall$ and $\exists$ are essentially those reached in the last chapter (Sections 5.6 and 5.7). For the universal quantifier we have

($\forall$I) If $\Gamma \vdash \varphi$ then $\Gamma \vdash \forall \xi \varphi(\xi/\alpha)$, provided α is not in Γ.
($\forall$E) $\forall \xi \varphi \vdash \varphi(\alpha/\xi)$.

And for the existential quantifier,

($\exists$I) $\varphi(\alpha/\xi) \vdash \exists \xi \varphi$.
($\exists$E) If $\Gamma,\varphi \vdash \psi$ then $\Gamma,\exists \xi \varphi(\xi/\alpha) \vdash \psi$, provided α is not in Γ or in ψ.

When we restate these in a form suited for our two-dimensional proofs, the rules for $\forall$ are entirely straightforward:

$$(\forall I) \frac{\varphi}{\forall \xi \varphi(\xi/\alpha)} \qquad (\forall E) \frac{\forall \xi \varphi}{\varphi(\alpha/\xi)}$$

provided α is not in any
assumption on which φ rests

But the elimination rule for $\exists$ takes a form which may be somewhat unexpected; it resembles $(\vee E)$:

$$(\exists I) \frac{\varphi(\alpha/\xi)}{\exists \xi \varphi} \qquad (\exists E) \frac{\exists \xi \varphi(\xi/\alpha) \qquad \begin{array}{c} \overline{\quad}\,(n) \\ \varphi \\ \cdot \\ \cdot \\ \cdot \\ \psi \end{array}}{\psi}\,(n)$$

provided that α is not in ψ, nor in
any assumption used in the derivation of ψ from φ, except for φ itself.

When using these rules it is essential to observe the restrictions in ($\forall$I) and ($\exists$E), stating that a name-letter that is to be generalized upon must not occur in any of the assumptions of the proof. For this purpose, an 'assumption' means, of course, an *undischarged* assumption, i.e. one not discharged at the stage of the proof at which ($\forall$I) or ($\exists$E) is being applied. Note also that, by the definition of our substitution-notation (pp. 80–1), α cannot occur in $\forall\xi\varphi(\xi/\alpha)$ or in $\exists\xi\varphi(\xi/\alpha)$, except in the trivial case when $\varphi(\xi/\alpha)$ is φ.

Let us at once illustrate these rules with some examples. Here are two very simple proofs concerning $\forall$ and $\wedge$, to demonstrate the law

$\forall x(P\wedge Fx)$ ⊣⊢ $P \wedge \forall xFx$:

(*a*) $\forall x(P\wedge Fx) \vdash P \wedge \forall xFx$

$$
\begin{array}{cc}
(\forall\text{E})\dfrac{\forall x(P\wedge Fx)}{P\wedge Fa} & (\forall\text{E})\dfrac{\forall x(P\wedge Fx)}{P\wedge Fa} \\[2ex]
(\wedge\text{E})\dfrac{}{P} & (\wedge\text{E})\dfrac{}{Fa} \\[2ex]
(\wedge\text{I})\dfrac{}{P \wedge \forall xFx} & (\forall\text{I})\dfrac{}{\forall xFx}
\end{array}
$$

(*b*) $P \wedge \forall xFx \vdash \forall x(P\wedge Fx)$

$$
\begin{array}{cc}
(\wedge\text{E})\dfrac{P \wedge \forall xFx}{P} & (\wedge\text{E})\dfrac{P \wedge \forall xFx}{\forall xFx} \\[2ex]
(\wedge\text{I})\dfrac{}{} & (\forall\text{E})\dfrac{}{Fa} \\[2ex]
& (\wedge\text{I})\dfrac{P\wedge Fa}{} \\[2ex]
& (\forall\text{I})\dfrac{}{\forall x(P\wedge Fx)}
\end{array}
$$

In each case the proof begins by using ($\forall$E) and ($\wedge$E) to remove the occurrences of $\forall$ and $\wedge$ in the premiss, and then it continues by using ($\forall$I) and ($\wedge$I) to put them back again, but in a different order. Notice that in each case the name *a* is introduced by ($\forall$E), so it does not occur in the assumptions of the proof, and there is therefore no obstacle to applying ($\forall$I).

Now let us consider the analogous law with $\exists$ in place of $\forall$, i.e.

$\exists x(P\wedge Fx)$ ⊣⊢ $P \wedge \exists xFx$.

The general tactic of the proof is entirely the same, but the proof looks more complicated, because of the more complex form of the rule ($\exists$E):

(a) $\exists x(P \wedge Fx) \vdash P \wedge \exists xFx$

$$
(\exists E) \cfrac{\exists x(P \wedge Fx) \qquad (\wedge I)\cfrac{(\wedge E)\cfrac{\cfrac{P \wedge Fa}{\quad}(1)}{P} \qquad (\exists I)\cfrac{(\wedge E)\cfrac{\cfrac{P \wedge Fa}{\quad}(1)}{Fa}}{\exists xFx}}{P \wedge \exists xFx}}{P \wedge \exists xFx}(1)
$$

(b) $P \wedge \exists xFx \vdash \exists x(P \wedge Fx)$

$$
(\exists E)\cfrac{(\wedge E)\cfrac{P \wedge \exists xFx}{\exists xFx} \qquad (\exists I)\cfrac{(\wedge I)\cfrac{(\wedge E)\cfrac{P \wedge \exists xFx}{P} \qquad \cfrac{\quad}{Fa}(1)}{P \wedge Fa}}{\exists x(P \wedge Fx)}}{\exists x(P \wedge Fx)}(1)
$$

Proof (a) is entirely straightforward: there are no extra assumptions used in the proof of $P \wedge \exists xFx$ from $P \wedge Fa$, so when we apply ($\exists$E) in the last step we only need to check that a is not in the conclusion. Proof (b) is a little more interesting, for here we do have an extra assumption, $P \wedge \exists xFx$, used in the proof of our conclusion from Fa. So when applying ($\exists$E) in the last step we have to check that a is not in either the extra assumption or the conclusion. Notice here that this means that we have to apply ($\exists$I) *before* we can apply ($\exists$E); if we had tried to use these rules the other way round, the check would not be satisfied.

To bring out the necessity of these various restrictions on name-letters, I here give three little examples of *incorrect* proofs, the first two purporting to establish the sequent

$\exists xFx \vdash \forall xFx,$

and the third purporting to establish, what comes to the same thing,

$$\exists xFx, \exists x\neg Fx \vdash \bot.$$

(a) $\exists xFx \vdash \forall xFx$ (b) $\exists xFx \vdash \forall xFx$

$$(\exists E) \frac{\exists xFx \quad (\forall I)\dfrac{\overline{Fa}^{\,(1)}}{\forall xFx}}{\forall xFx}\,(1)$$

$$(\exists E)\dfrac{\exists xFx \quad \overline{Fa}^{\,(1)}}{(\forall I)\dfrac{Fa}{\forall xFx}}\,(1)$$

(c) $\exists xFx, \exists x\neg Fx \vdash \bot$

$$(\exists E)\dfrac{(\exists E)\dfrac{\exists xFx \quad (EFQ)\dfrac{\overline{Fa}^{\,(1)} \quad \overline{\neg Fa}^{\,(2)}}{\bot}}{\bot}\,(1) \quad \exists x\neg Fx}{\bot}\,(2)$$

In proof (a) the step of ($\forall$I) is wrong, for it generalizes upon the name a in
Fa at a stage when Fa is itself an undischarged assumption. Consequently,
the condition for ($\forall$I) is not satisfied. (But the following step of ($\exists$E) is perfectly correct.) In proof (b) the step of ($\exists$E) is wrong. The proof has set up
the assumption Fa, and deduced from it, in a one-line proof, the conclusion
Fa. That in itself is perfectly all right. But if ($\exists$E) is to be applied, then the
name a introduced in the assumption Fa must not occur in the conclusion
derived from it, which in this case it manifestly does. (But the following step
of ($\forall$I) is in this example perfectly correct.) Finally, in proof (c) the first step
of ($\exists$E), labelled (1), is wrong. When this step occurs, the proof of $\bot$ from Fa
has used an extra assumption, $\neg Fa$, which at this stage is *not* yet discharged.
Consequently, the condition for applying ($\exists$E) requires that a should not
occur in $\neg Fa$, but of course it does. (By contrast, the second step of ($\exists$E) is
perfectly correct, for the extra assumption Fa *has* been discharged by the
time that this second step is taken.)

Let us now look at a rather more complicated proof, designed to establish
the thesis

$$\forall x\exists y(Fx \wedge Gy) \vdash \exists y\forall x(Fx \wedge Gy)$$

(compare p. 162). The proof is this:

$$
\cfrac{
(\exists E)\ \cfrac{
(\forall E)\ \cfrac{\forall x\exists y(Fx\wedge Gy)}{\exists y(Fa\wedge Gy)}
\qquad
(\wedge E)\ \cfrac{\overline{Fa\wedge Gb}\ ^{(1)}}{Fa}
}{
(\wedge I)\ \cfrac{Fa \qquad (\wedge E)\ \cfrac{\overline{Fc\wedge Gb}\ ^{(2)}}{Gb}}{
(\forall I)\ \cfrac{Fa\wedge Gb}{
(\exists I)\ \cfrac{\forall x(Fx\wedge Gb)}{\exists y\forall x(Fx\wedge Gy)}}}
}\ ^{(1)}
\qquad
(\forall E)\ \cfrac{\forall x\exists y(Fx\wedge Gy)}{\exists y(Fc\wedge Gy)}
}{\exists y\forall x(Fx\wedge Gy)}\ ^{(2)}
$$

The first application of (∃E), in the top left corner, establishes that $\forall x\exists y(Fx\wedge Gy) \vdash Fa$. It should be noted here that it was necessary to choose a new name b, other than the name a already occurring in $\exists y(Fa\wedge Gy)$, when setting up our assumption $Fa\wedge Gb$. For if we had used the same name a again, and had set up the assumption $Fa\wedge Ga$, then this would be a formula that is not properly related to $\exists y(Fa\wedge Gy)$. That is, there is no name α such that $Fa\wedge Gy$ is the result of substituting y for α in $Fa\wedge Ga$. Moreover, since we did choose the new name b in our assumption, then all that we had to ensure was that that name b did not also occur in the conclusion derived from it. It does not matter at all that there is a different name a that occurs both in the assumption and in the conclusion derived from it, for it is b and not a that is taking the place of the existentially quantified variable y. I remark also that after this first step of (∃E) the assumption $Fa\wedge Gb$ is discharged, so after this step the name a no longer occurs in the assumptions of the proof. Consequently, we may apply (∀I) to it at any time we like. We could indeed have applied (∀I) at once, to prove the sequent $\forall x\exists y(Fx\wedge Gy) \vdash \forall xFx$.

Just as the argument in the top left part of our proof could easily be modified to show that $\forall xFx$ follows from our premiss, so equally the argument in the bottom right part could easily be modified to show that $\exists yGy$ also follows. We have only to alter it in this way:

$$(\land E)\ \dfrac{\overline{Fc \land Gb}\ ^{(2)}}{Gb}$$
$$(\exists I)\ \dfrac{}{\exists y Gy}$$
$$(\forall E)\ \dfrac{\forall x \exists y (Fx \land Gy)}{\exists y (Fc \land Gy)}\ ^{(2)}$$
$$(\exists E)\ \dfrac{}{\exists y Gy}$$

Then the result that we want could be obtained by adding to these two proofs a proof of the sequent

$$\forall x Fx,\ \exists y Gy \vdash \exists y \forall x (Fx \land Gy).$$

You may like to work out this version of the proof, which is more long-winded but conceptually simpler. Meanwhile, let us return to the proof as first given.

We have Fa from the left side of the proof and Gb from the right, so we bring them together before applying ($\forall$I). Notice that, to legitimize this application, it was necessary for us to choose some letter other than a to substitute for x when applying ($\forall$E) in the right side of the proof. For at the stage when ($\forall$I) is applied, the earlier assumption $Fa \land Gb$ has been discharged, as we have said, but the later assumption $Fc \land Gb$ has not. So if this had contained a instead of c, the proof would have failed at this point. Of course, we could also have chosen a new letter, say d, to substitute for y, rather than the same letter b as we had used earlier. But in this case there was no need. For all that is necessary is to ensure that the letter chosen for the assumption is not the letter a, does not already occur in $\exists y (Fc \land Gy)$, does not occur in the conclusion to be derived from that assumption, namely $\exists y \forall x (Fx \land Gy)$, and does not occur in the auxiliary assumption used in the derivation, namely $\forall x \exists y (Fx \land Gy)$ at the top left corner of the proof.

You will notice that in these examples of proofs with quantifiers the sequents to be proved have contained only the functor $\land$, and the quantifiers, and the proofs have used only the rules for $\land$, and for the quantifiers. In fact the point holds generally: any correct sequent which contains only $\land$ and the quantifiers can be proved by these rules, as will be shown in Section 7.5. You would not expect the same point to hold for $\rightarrow$ and the quantifiers, since, as we have noted, the usual rules for $\rightarrow$ are not complete, even for sequents which contain only $\rightarrow$. You might have expected the point to hold for $\lor$ and the quantifiers, but the expectation is disappointed. There are correct sequents whose only logical symbols are $\vee$ and $\forall$ which cannot be proved just from the rules for $\vee$ and $\forall$. A simple example is

$$\forall x(P \vee Fx) \vdash P \vee \forall x Fx.$$

Here is a simple proof of the sequent which in addition makes use of the negation rules (EFQ) and (TND):

$$
(\text{TND}) \cfrac{
  (\vee\text{I}) \cfrac{
    (\forall\text{I}) \cfrac{
      (\vee\text{E}) \cfrac{ (\forall\text{E}) \cfrac{\forall x(P\vee Fx)}{P\vee Fa} \qquad (\text{EFQ})\cfrac{\overline{}^{(1)}_{P} \quad \overline{}^{(2)}_{\neg P}}{Fa} \qquad \overline{}^{(1)}_{Fa} }{Fa}^{(1)}
    }{\forall x Fx}
  }{P\vee \forall x Fx} \qquad\qquad
  (\vee\text{I})\cfrac{\overline{}^{(2)}_{P}}{P\vee \forall x Fx}
}{P\vee \forall x Fx}{}^{(2)}
$$

Here is another proof, which this time makes use of the definition of $\vee$ in terms of $\rightarrow$ and $\neg$, and otherwise only the rules for $\rightarrow$ and $\forall$. (Of course, to prove the definition one would have to use a negation rule.)

$$
(\text{Def})\cfrac{
  (\rightarrow\text{I}) \cfrac{
    (\forall\text{I}) \cfrac{
      (\rightarrow\text{E}) \cfrac{ \overline{}^{(1)}_{\neg P} \qquad (\text{Def})\cfrac{(\forall\text{E})\cfrac{\forall x(P\vee Fx)}{P\vee Fa}}{\neg P\rightarrow Fa} }{Fa}
    }{\forall x Fx}
  }{\neg P\rightarrow \forall x Fx}{}^{(1)}
}{P\vee \forall x Fx}
$$

But there is no proof which uses only the four rules $(\vee\text{I}),(\vee\text{E}),(\forall\text{I}),(\forall\text{E})$ (Exercise 6.3.4). Indeed, so far as I know, there are no natural deduction rules for $\vee$ alone, and for $\forall$ alone, which are individually sound and jointly sufficient for the proof of this sequent.

EXERCISES

6.3.1. Give natural deduction proofs of the following sequents:

    (*a*) $\forall x(Fx \wedge Gx)$ ⊣⊢ $\forall xFx \wedge \forall xGx$.
    (*b*) $\exists x(Fx \vee Gx)$ ⊣⊢ $\exists xFx \vee \exists xGx$.
    (*c*) $\exists x(Fx{\rightarrow}Gx)$ ⊣⊢ $\forall xFx{\rightarrow}\exists xGx$.
    (*d*) $\forall x\exists y(Fx \vee Gy)$ ⊣⊢ $\exists y\forall x(Fx \vee Gy)$.

[Warning: you will need to use a negation rule in the proofs of (*c*) R→L and (*d*) L→R. Feel free to use any such rule you find convenient.]

6.3.2.(*a*) Let $\varphi(a)$ be the result of substituting a for some occurrences of x in $\varphi(x)$, not excluding bound occurrences of x. Show by means of an example that the following rule is not sound:

$$\varphi(a) \vdash \exists x\varphi(x).$$

(*b*) Let $\varphi(x)$ be the result of substituting x for some, but not necessarily all, occurrences of a in $\varphi(a)$. Show by means of an example that the following rule is not sound:

    If $\Gamma,\varphi(a) \vdash \psi$ then $\Gamma,\exists x\varphi(x) \vdash \psi$, provided that a does not occur in Γ or in ψ.

(*c*) Let $\varphi(x)$ be the result of substituting x for all occurrences of a in $\varphi(a)$, but without regard to whether the substituted occurrences of x are free in $\varphi(x)$. Show that the rule in part (*b*) is still not sound.

6.3.3. Show that the Cut principle holds for natural deduction proofs using the quantifier rules. [Hint: see the argument on p. 243, with its footnote, and recall Exercise 4.9.1(*a*).]

6.3.4. Consider the following unexpected interpretation for formulae containing just $\vee$ and $\forall$. There are to be two 'worlds', which we call w_1 and w_2. (If it helps, you may think of the formulae true in w_1 as representing what we know now, and the formulae true in w_2 as representing what we will know later.) The worlds may contain different domains of objects, and a formula containing a name is interpreted at a world only if the name is interpreted as denoting some object in the domain of that world. We stipulate that any object in the domain of w_1 must also be in the domain of w_2, and that any atomic formula that is interpreted as true at w_1 must also be interpreted as true at w_2, but not vice versa. For $\vee$, we further stipulate that, for either world w_i,

    $\varphi\vee\psi$ is true at w_i iff φ is true at w_i or ψ is true at w_i.

For $\forall$, we have a more complicated clause:

    $\forall\xi\varphi$ is true at w_2 iff for any name α not in φ, and for any interpretation of α on the domain of w_2, $\varphi(\alpha/\xi)$ is true at w_2.

$\forall\xi\varphi$ is true at w_1 iff (1) for any name α not in φ, and for any interpretation of α on the domain of w_1, $\varphi(\alpha/\xi)$ is true at w_1; *and* (2)$\forall\xi\varphi$ is true at w_2.

(So, if you like to think of it this way, $\forall\xi\varphi$ is taken to mean (1) everything we now know of satisfies φ, *and* (2) everything we will know of will also satisfy φ.) Finally, we say that $\Gamma \vDash \varphi$ iff, for any way of interpreting φ and all the formulae in Γ at each world w_i, if all the formulae in Γ are interpreted as true at w_i, then φ is interpreted as true at w_i.

(*a*) Prove as a lemma that, for any formula φ, if φ is true at w_1, then φ is true at w_2. [Method: use induction on the length of φ.]

(*b*) Verify that the four rules ($\vee$I),($\vee$E),($\forall$I),($\forall$E) are all sound on this interpretation. [Hint: you will need to use part (*a*) when verifying ($\forall$I).] Deduce that any sequent that is provable from these four rules must be sound on this interpretation.

(*c*) Hence show that the sequent

$$\forall x(P\vee Fx)\vdash P \vee \forall xFx$$

is not provable from these four rules. [Hint: consider an interpretation in which the domain of w_1 is $\{a\}$ and the domain of w_2 is $\{a,b\}$. Let Fa be true at w_1, and hence also at w_2. Let P be true at w_2, but not at w_1. Let Fb be not true at w_2.]

[Note. The method of this exercise is a very special case of a much more general result proved by Kripke (1965) for intuitionist logic.]

6.4. **Alternative Styles of Proof**

The two-dimensional proofs pursued so far are only one of many possible styles of proof using the rules of natural deduction. They have the advantage that the overall structure of the proof is easily seen, except perhaps that the places where assumptions are first introduced and then discharged do not stand out quite as clearly as they might. (Ideally, one might draw in different colours each pair of lines marking the discharge of an assumption and the place where it is discharged.) But, as you will have discovered, it can often be tedious to write out such a proof, since one often finds that the same premiss, and the same initial deductions from it, have to be written out again and again at the top of a number of different branches. This sort of thing is never needed when a proof is taken to be a linear sequence of formulae as in the last chapter.

Even a fully axiomatic proof, with no assumptions, can be given a two-dimensional presentation in a tree structure, if we desire it. In this case, the topmost formula of each branch would be required to be an axiom, and all the rest of the proof would consist of pairs of branches being brought together by a step of Modus Ponens. Again it might be said that such a presentation clarifies the structure of the proof, and again it can be replied that it increases the labour of writing the proof out. Since in this case the labour is already very considerable, and since tree structures for axiomatic proofs would quickly become very unwieldy, they are never adopted in practice. Much the same applies to the proofs from assumptions that were employed in the last chapter. They could have been defined as tree structures, but were in fact defined as linear sequences of formulae, since such proofs are in practice easier to write out. When the only rule of inference is Modus Ponens, the branches of a tree proof soon spread too wide for comfort.

Now the official position in the last chapter was indeed that Modus Ponens, and later Generalization, were the only rules of inference, and that there was no such thing as a proof which discharges assumptions. The deduction theorem was not officially regarded as a rule for use *in* proofs, but as a theorem *about* proofs, telling us that if there is a proof of some formula from a certain set of assumptions, then there is also a proof of a related formula from a reduced set of assumptions. But although this was the official position, we did in practice use this theorem as if it were a rule for discharging assumptions within a proof, and that was why our deductions could be so nice and compact. Yet our proofs still remained linear sequences of formulae, and not two-dimensional arrays. Could we not generalize this approach? The answer is that so long as the rules for the quantifiers are not yet added there is no difficulty. The procedure that we used before, of labelling a line with 'ASS' when it is introduced as an assumption, and then crossing out that label when the assumption is discharged, could perfectly well be written into the definition of what is to count as a proof. But there is also an alternative procedure, used in several elementary books, which appears to be an improvement on this. For the proof is given just a little more structure than a straightforward linear sequence of formulae, and as a result it certainly contains more information.[4]

To begin with, let us simplify by supposing that we have just one rule discharging assumptions, say ($\rightarrow$I). Then the idea is that when a formula is introduced as an assumption, and is later to be discharged, that formula is written at the head of a new column in the proof, slightly to the right of the existing column of formulae. (The new column can be set off by drawing a vertical line to its left.) All subsequent deductions are then written in the new column, until the assumption that heads it (say φ) is discharged. When this happens the new column is closed, and we revert to the original column,

---

[4] This style of proof is used in Quine (1952).

beginning with the formula (say $\varphi \to \psi$) which results upon discharging that assumption. The idea is that what is written in the new column depends upon the assumption that heads it, whereas what is written in the original column does not, so that we can see at a glance what parts of the proof depend upon that assumption. The procedure may be iterated. As the proof proceeds, a new column may be opened, then brought to a close, and later another new column may be opened. More interestingly, a new column may be opened, to the right of the original, and then *before* it is closed another new column may be opened to its right, and so on indefinitely. This, of course, represents the introduction of several assumptions, the second being introduced before the first is discharged. But in that case one must be careful to introduce the assumptions in the right order, so that the last to be introduced is the first to be discharged, and so on. Thus on each discharge work shifts back to the left by just one column.

Here is a simple example. Suppose (for variety) that we wish to verify the rule of inference cited for the Sheffer stroke on p. 234, namely

$$\varphi, \varphi \uparrow (\psi \uparrow \chi) \vdash \psi.$$

Suppose also that we wish to do this in a system whose rules are given in terms of $\to$ and $\neg$, say as $(\to I), (\to E), EFQ, CM^*$, where this last is formulated as in the previous chapter (p. 209). We therefore regard the stroke functor as defined in terms of $\to$ and $\neg$, by abbreviating

$$\varphi \uparrow \psi \quad \text{for} \quad \varphi \to \neg \psi.$$

Then we can set out a simple proof in the new style like this:

$\varphi, \varphi \uparrow (\psi \uparrow \chi) \vdash \chi$

1. φ		ASS
2. $\varphi \uparrow (\psi \uparrow \chi)$		ASS
3. $\varphi \to \neg(\psi \to \neg \chi)$		2,Def $\uparrow$
4. $\neg(\psi \to \neg \chi)$		1,3,$\to$E
5. $\neg \psi$		ASS
6. ψ		ASS
7. $\neg \chi$		5,6,EFQ
8. $\psi \to \neg \chi$		6–7,$\to$I
9. ψ		4,8,EFQ
10. $\neg \psi \to \psi$		5–9,$\to$I
11. ψ		10,CM*

This notation for proofs is only very slightly different from that used in the last chapter, and it is very easy to rewrite all the proofs of that chapter in the new style, as you may check. But there is certainly some gain in clarity. The new style is only partly linear, because its 'line' of formulae is further distinguished into various 'sublines', but it shares with fully linear proofs the advantage that one does not have to keep writing out the same premiss over and over again. At the same time, it also has something of the advantage of a two-dimensional proof, in that it shows more clearly what assumptions are being used in any part of the proof.

There is no serious difficulty in extending this style of proof to allow for several rules which discharge assumptions. At any rate, there is no problem over further rules which discharge just one assumption, for example CM* as formulated in this chapter (p. 249). (In the example just given, this would allow one to omit line (10), for the subdeduction in lines (5)–(9) would then justify the conclusion in line (11) without any intermediate step.) As another example, for this style of proof the rule RAA would be formulated as follows: if in a column headed by an assumption φ there occurs both a formula ψ and its negation ¬ψ, then φ may be discharged, i.e. the column may be closed, and ¬φ entered in the column next to the left. When we turn to consider rules which discharge two assumptions at once, such as (∨E) or TND, the situation is not quite so tidy, for the proper method would be to allow for two parallel right-hand columns to be opened and closed simultaneously. But this does, of course, destroy the close approximation to a genuinely linear structure, and one might therefore be tempted to avoid such rules altogether. (For example, (∨E) might be formulated as on p. 229.) In any case, I shall not pursue this problem further, for when quantifier rules are added we soon discover that this style of setting out proofs is really only a half-way house.

The source of the trouble is that the technique does not really give us, as at first it seems to, all the information we need about what assumptions are being relied on at any stage of the proof. This is because the convention is that, at any line, one may invoke as a premiss any formula above that line, *either* in the same column *or* in any column to the left. And you cannot tell, just by looking at the proof-diagram, which columns to the left of a given column have been used in the deductions in that column. Thus, to go back to the very simple example just given, you cannot tell, from the structure of the proof as displayed, that the conclusion of the third column does rest upon the assumption heading the second column, but does not rest upon either of the assumptions introduced in the first column. By contrast, the conclusion of the second column does rest upon both the assumptions of the first column. This kind of thing would be perfectly clear if our proof had been given as a two-dimensional tree structure, in this way:

$$\text{(EFQ)} \cfrac{\text{(}\rightarrow\text{E)} \cfrac{\varphi \qquad \text{(Def)} \cfrac{\varphi\uparrow(\psi\uparrow\chi)}{\varphi\rightarrow\neg(\psi\rightarrow\neg\chi)}}{\neg(\psi\rightarrow\neg\chi)}}{\text{(CM*)} \cfrac{\text{(}\rightarrow\text{I)} \cfrac{\text{(EFQ)} \cfrac{\text{(}\rightarrow\text{I)} \cfrac{\overline{\psi}^{(1)} \qquad \overline{\neg\psi}^{(2)}}{\neg\chi}}{\psi\rightarrow\neg\chi}^{(1)} \qquad \overline{\psi}^{(2)}}{\neg\psi\rightarrow\psi}}{\psi}}$$

For, with this kind of proof, if you wish to know what assumption a given formula rests on, all that you have to do is to trace its ancestry upwards, and the answer appears at once.

One does not really notice this lack of information in the (quasi-)linear proofs until the quantifier rules are added, because until then it never matters. That is, so far as the rules for truth-functors are concerned, you can suppose that *every* line in the proof rests on *all* the (undischarged) assumptions above it, and no problem will appear. But with the rules (∀I) and (∃E) the situation changes; these rules impose conditions upon the names occurring in the assumptions on which a given line rests, and it is just *those* assumptions that need to be checked, and not any other assumptions that may be used somewhere in the proof but not here. Consequently, we do need to know just what the assumptions are that are used in the proof of this or that particular line. Proofs set out as tree structures yield this information at once, but the linear or quasi-linear structures considered so far do not. (I mean that they do not yield this information at a glance; of course, one can always recover it by actually tracing through all the details of the proof.)

I think, then, that the best way of setting out natural deduction proofs in a linear form is one in which each line of the proof is accompanied by an explicit statement of the assumptions on which it rests.[5] We can do this by writing, to the left of the line number, the numbers of those lines that contain the relevant assumptions. To illustrate, here is a proof of the same sequent once more, this time with the assumptions of each line explicitly noted.

$\varphi, \varphi\uparrow(\psi\uparrow\chi) \vdash \chi$

1	(1) φ	ASS
2	(2) $\varphi\uparrow(\psi\uparrow\chi)$	ASS
2	(3) $\varphi\rightarrow\neg(\psi\rightarrow\neg\chi)$	2,Def ↑
1, 2	(4) $\neg(\psi\rightarrow\neg\chi)$	1,3,→E

[5] This style of proof is used in Lemmon (1965).

5	(5) $\neg\psi$	ASS
6	(6) ψ	ASS
5, 6	(7) $\neg\chi$	5,6,EFQ
5	(8) $\psi\rightarrow\neg\chi$	6–7,$\rightarrow$I
1, 2, 5	(9) ψ	4,8,EFQ
1, 2	(10) ψ	5–9,CM*

You will observe: (1) that an assumption is always entered as resting on itself; (2) that when we apply a rule which does not discharge assumptions, the conclusion is entered as resting upon all of the assumptions that any of its premises rest on; (3) that when we apply a rule which does discharge an assumption, that assumption is dropped from what is entered on the left. In the light of these comments it should be clear how to formulate each natural deduction rule as a rule for use in proofs of this kind. I give just one example in detail, namely the rule ($\vee$E), which is the most complex of all the rules for truth-functors:

> ($\vee$E). Given a line $\varphi\vee\psi$, and a line χ which has φ amongst its assumptions, and another line χ which has ψ amongst its assumptions, we may enter a further line χ whose assumptions are (1) those of the line $\varphi\vee\psi$, (2) those of the line χ which has φ as assumption, minus the assumption φ itself, (3) those of the line χ which has ψ as assumption, minus the assumption ψ itself. (And in justification for this step we cite, on the right, (1) the line $\varphi\vee\psi$, (2) the lines in which χ is derived from φ, (3) the lines in which χ is derived from ψ, and finally ($\vee$E).)

I end this section with two further examples of proofs presented in this style, with all assumptions explicitly noted on the left. They rewrite in this linear form the two proofs of a law of distribution given earlier in tree form on p. 247. You should carefully compare the two versions, and make sure that you see how to translate any proof written in the one style into a corresponding proof written in the other style.

Henceforth, when I speak of *the* linear style of proof for natural deduction, I shall mean this last style of proof, with all the assumptions noted explicitly on the left. When *looking for* a proof you may find it helpful to use the quasi-linear style introduced earlier, for that style does reveal something of the structure of the proof, and it is conveniently succinct. Or you may prefer to work explicitly with the two-dimensional tree structures that we began with, where the full structure is evident at a glance. But once the proof is found it can always be written out, for official purposes, in this last, and fully explicit, linear form. We shall build upon this point in the next chapter.

267

(a) $\varphi\vee(\psi\wedge\chi) \vdash (\varphi\vee\psi)\wedge(\varphi\vee\chi)$

1	(1)	$\varphi\vee(\psi\wedge\chi)$	ASS
2	(2)	φ	ASS
2	(3)	$\varphi\vee\psi$	2,$\vee$I
2	(4)	$\varphi\vee\chi$	2,$\vee$I
2	(5)	$(\varphi\vee\psi)\wedge(\varphi\vee\chi)$	3,4,$\wedge$I
6	(6)	$\psi\wedge\chi$	ASS
6	(7)	ψ	6,$\wedge$E
6	(8)	$\varphi\vee\psi$	7,$\vee$I
6	(9)	χ	6,$\wedge$E
6	(10)	$\varphi\vee\chi$	9,$\vee$I
6	(11)	$(\varphi\vee\psi)\wedge(\varphi\vee\chi)$	8,10,$\wedge$I
1	(12)	$(\varphi\vee\psi)\wedge(\varphi\vee\chi)$	1,2–5,6–11,$\vee$E

(b) $(\varphi\vee\psi) \wedge (\varphi\vee\chi) \vdash \varphi\vee(\psi\wedge\chi)$

1	(1)	$(\varphi\vee\psi)\wedge(\varphi\vee\chi)$	ASS
1	(2)	$\varphi\vee\psi$	1,$\wedge$E
1	(3)	$\varphi\vee\chi$	1,$\wedge$E
4	(4)	φ	ASS
4	(5)	$\varphi\vee(\psi\wedge\chi)$	4,$\vee$I
6	(6)	ψ	ASS
7	(7)	χ	ASS
6,7	(8)	$\psi\wedge\chi$	6,7,$\wedge$I
6,7	(9)	$\varphi\vee(\psi\wedge\chi)$	8,$\vee$I
1,7	(10)	$\varphi\vee(\psi\wedge\chi)$	2,4–5,6–9,$\vee$E
1	(11)	$\varphi\vee(\psi\wedge\chi)$	3,4–5,7–10,$\vee$E

EXERCISES

6.4.1.(*a*) Rewrite your answers to Exercise 5.7.1 as proofs in the two-dimensional tree style for natural deduction.

(*b*) Rewrite your answers to Exercise 6.3.1 as proofs in the linear style for natural deduction.

6.4.2.(*a*) First using the pair of negation rules DNE and RAA, and then using instead the pair TND and EFQ, give proofs in the linear style of

(1) $\forall x Fx \dashv\vdash \neg\exists x\neg Fx.$
(2) $\exists x Fx \dashv\vdash \neg\forall x\neg Fx.$

(*b*) Using any negation rules you find convenient, give proofs in the linear style of

   (1) $\forall xFx \rightarrow \forall xGx \vdash \exists x(Fx \rightarrow Gx)$.
   (2) $\exists xFx \rightarrow \exists xGx \vdash \exists x(Fx \rightarrow Gx)$.
   (3) $\exists xFx \rightarrow \forall xGx \vdash \forall x(Fx \rightarrow Gx)$.
   (4) $\vdash \exists x(Fx \rightarrow \forall yFy)$.

6.4.3.(*a*) Give a full definition of 'a proof in the linear style for natural deduction'. [The definition starts 'A proof is a finite sequence of formulae which . . .'. After this general characterization, which must say something about how the assumptions are recorded, it goes on to state the particular rules of inference in a form suited to this style of proof. For this purpose, take the rules to be those given in a different form on p. 252 for the truth-functors, and on p. 254 for the quantifiers.]
(*b*) Verify that, on your definition of a proof in part (*a*), the Cut principle and the principle of Assumptions are automatically satisfied, whatever rules are adopted for the truth-functors. (Ignore here any complications that may be introduced by the quantifier rules (Exercise 6.3.3).)

6.4.4. Give an explicit recipe for rewriting any proof given in the two-dimensional tree structure as a linear proof.

6.5. Interim Review

I think that a majority of elementary books on logic written in the last twenty or thirty years have used some form of natural deduction as their proof procedure. The prevalence of this method is understandable, given that the very first treatments of logic from a modern point of view were axiomatic treatments. For, as we have seen, these are very unwieldy as they stand, but much simplified by the deduction theorem, allowing us to use proofs from assumptions in place of full axiomatic proofs. Given this breakthrough, the main ideas behind natural deduction then come quite readily to mind, as one tries to simplify yet further the complexities involved in the original way of doing things. In any case, it is easy to see that the two methods are closely related to one another. If we begin from axioms, we shall at once wish to develop from them what are in effect the methods of natural deduction; and if we begin from natural deduction it is extremely easy to re-establish the original axioms. But how do they each compare with the method of semantic tableaux, which we began with in Chapter 4?

The first contrast that strikes one is that with semantic tableaux there are recipes for proof-construction that we can operate, whereas with natural deduction there are not. To take first the logic of truth-functors, we know in advance that this is decidable by truth-tables, and we have also seen how the semantic tableaux yield another decision procedure for it. For, so long as we are dealing only with quantifier-free formulae, there can be only finitely many steps before a completed tableau is reached, and a completed tableau must provide either a proof or a counter-example. By contrast, the rules for natural deduction do not at first seem to yield any decision procedure. When looking for a proof of a sequent, the best that we can do is to work simultaneously in both directions, thinking forward from the premisses, to see what can be deduced from them, and thinking backwards from the conclusion, to see what it can be deduced from. Pursuing both these procedures at once, we hope that they will meet in the middle and so provide the desired proof. But failure to find a proof in this way certainly does not imply that there is no proof, and even if in fact there is no proof, still our failure to find one need not be of any help in the search in the other direction, i.e. for a counter-example.

Now in fact there are decision procedures that one can extract from the natural deduction rules for the truth-functors, or indeed from the original axioms for those functors. One of them is given by our completeness proof for the axioms, in Section 5.5. It can easily be adapted to a completeness proof for the natural deduction rules instead (cf. Exercise 6.2.4). The strategy of the argument here was to show how to mimic, with our rules of proof, just the same steps as one would use when drawing up an ordinary truth-table. So it would certainly be possible to devise a recipe for applying the natural deduction rules which was bound to lead to a decision, one way or the other, namely by following through all the steps of the completeness proof, one by one, until we had in effect constructed the truth-table. But that would be a complete waste of time, since it is much simpler just to write out the truth-table directly. Much the same applies to other recipes that one might construct, using the natural deduction rules, for determining the correctness or otherwise of any quantifier-free sequent. This can certainly be done (Exercises 6.5.1 and 6.5.2), but the recipes are quite cumbersome in practice, and one might just as well draw up a truth-table in the ordinary way. By contrast, the decision procedure given by the semantic tableaux is worth having on its own account, for it is often shorter than a full truth-table would be.

Similar remarks apply to the logic of quantifiers. Here the method of semantic tableaux does offer a recipe *of a kind*, i.e. one which will give a definite result, one way or the other, for many simple sequents, and which is at least a guide to the construction of proofs or counter-examples in other cases. (This is all that one can ask of a recipe for the logic of quantifiers.) So far, no such recipe has emerged for the method of natural deduction. Nor can we say in this case that one has only to look to a completeness proof to provide one. For (*a*) it will be noted that I have not yet given any completeness proof in this case; I add (*b*) that the kind of completeness proof that is usually offered these days (due to Henkin 1949) is highly non-constructive, and so gives us no hint of how a practical recipe might be discovered;[6] and finally (*c*) I shall in fact offer a different completeness proof in the next chapter, but that will merely show how the methods of natural deduction can be made to do all the work that semantic tableaux are capable of. In so far as it does provide something by way of a recipe, then, it merely tells us how to mimic in natural deduction what we can already do more conveniently in semantic tableaux.

I conclude that on this question of how to find proofs the semantic tableaux allow us to offer much more by way of guidance than does natural deduction. You may perhaps reply that natural deduction has a different but compensating advantage: because its methods really do reflect how we 'naturally' think, it allows us to construct very 'natural' proofs, and it is easier to find a 'natural' proof than an 'unnatural' one. But here I suspect that 'natural' just means 'familiar', and *any* method will become familiar if you practise it enough.

The next chapter will bring about a reconciliation between the methods of natural deduction pursued in this chapter and the method of semantic tableaux pursued earlier. It will do so by showing how each can be reformulated as what is called a 'sequent calculus', and by showing the relation between these sequent calculi. At the same time, the various problems of elegance affecting our rules for natural deduction will be easily overcome in the new setting.

EXERCISES

6.5.1. Consider a system S which has $\neg, \wedge, \vee$ as its only logical symbols, and rules of natural deduction for them as on p. 252.
(*a*) Show that for each formula φ of S there is a formula φ' in CNF such that $\varphi \; _S\!\dashv\vdash_S \varphi'$. [Recall Exercise 6.2.2(*c*)–(*e*).]
(*b*) Hence show that S is complete, in the sense that if φ is any formula of S, and

---

[6] Gödel's original completeness proof of 1930 was rather more constructive. The same might be said, even more warmly, of some of its more modern descendants (e.g. Kleene 1952). But they will not be explored in this book.

if $\models \varphi$, then $\vdash_S \varphi$. [Hint: complete this sentence 'A formula in CNF is a tautology iff
...'.]
(c) Hence show that S is also complete in the sense that if φ and all the formulae
in Γ are formulae of S, and if $\Gamma \models \varphi$, then $\Gamma \vdash_S \varphi$. [You may confine attention to the
case where Γ is finite.]

6.5.2. Show how to modify the argument of 6.5.1 so that it uses DNF rather than
CNF. [Hint: use *perfect* DNF. (Incidentally, what would have happened if we had
tried to use *perfect* CNF in 6.5.1?).]

6.5.3. Let S be a system for $\neg, \wedge, \vee, \forall, \exists$, with the usual natural deduction rules for
these signs, but with only one-place predicate letters and no name-letters. Outline
an argument to show that S is complete. [Recall Section 3.8.]

7

Sequent Calculi

7.1. The Idea

Let us think, in a general way, about what happens in a natural deduction proof. As a whole the proof is an array of formulae, which we say establishes some sequent (namely the sequent which has on its left all the formulae which are undischarged assumptions in the proof, and on its right the single formula proved at the bottom of the proof). Moreover, the rules of inference too are rules about sequents. A proof always starts with an assumption, say φ, and if we add nothing more, then this itself counts as the proof of a sequent, namely

$\varphi \vdash \varphi$.

So the rule which allows us to get started is a rule which tells us directly that all sequents of this kind are correct. The other rules are all conditional, for they tell us that if certain sequents are correct, then so also is a further sequent, for example Modus Ponens in the form

If $\Gamma \vdash \varphi$ and $\Delta \vdash \varphi \rightarrow \psi$ then $\Gamma, \Delta \vdash \psi$.

So what happens in a proof is that we begin with certain sequents known to be correct, and we deduce that certain other sequents must therefore be correct. The proof proceeds by establishing one sequent after another, for at every step there is some sequent which is there established.

The idea of a sequent calculus is that it keeps an explicit record of just what sequent is established at each point of a proof. It does this by means of a new kind of proof in which every line is *itself* the sequent proved at that point in the proof. So a proof in a sequent calculus is not a linear sequence or other array *of formulae*, but a matching array *of whole sequents*. That is the basic idea.

Now we are familiar with sequents which have the (syntactic) turnstile ⊢ as their main verb; these are interpreted as claiming the existence of a proof, in whatever system of proof is currently being considered. We are also familiar with sequents which have the semantic turnstile ⊨ as their main verb; these make a claim about interpretations, namely that there is no interpretation which makes what is on the left true and what is on the right false. But neither of these signs has been allowed to occur *in* a proof. By convention, when we do have whole sequents occurring in a proof they are written not with ⊨ as their main verb, nor with ⊢, but instead with the new sign ⇒. But the *intended* interpretation is that in which ⇒ is taken to mean the same as the familiar turnstile ⊨. Consequently, ⇒ has the same syntax as ⊨; it cannot occur within a formula but only between formulae, i.e. with some (or none) to the left and at the moment with just one to the right. There are, however, a couple of small changes that we must now make in our account of what a sequent is, and it is convenient to associate them with the change of notation.

The changes are required because it is a generally accepted condition on what can be counted as a proof that there must always be a mechanical decision procedure which can be applied to tell us whether or not an array of symbols is a proof.[1] An evident corollary of this is that a proof must be finite. Now a finite array of formulae is as a whole a finite structure, to which a decision procedure can be applied, because each formula is itself finite. But in a sequent calculus a proof is an array of sequents, not of formulae, so we must now insist that the sequents to be considered are themselves finite. That is the first change. Hitherto a sequent has been regarded as having a *set* of formulae on the left, and there has been no bar on infinite sets, but for the purposes of the present chapter they are debarred. As we saw in Chapter 4, nothing is actually lost thereby. For the compactness theorem (Section 4.8)

---

[1] In more *advanced* logic this condition is sometimes relaxed; but in elementary logic it is universally obeyed.

tells us that if we do have an infinite set of formulae which entails some formula φ, that is always because it has a finite subset which entails φ. The second change is a further elaboration of the first. While we regard a sequent as having a set of formulae on its left, we must accept that there are all kinds of ways of specifying such sets. For example, one could specify the set as: 'all formulae which will ever be written down by any person born on a Thursday'. No doubt that is a finite set, so a sequent given in this way would pass our first condition. But if proofs are to be certifiable as such by a mechanical decision procedure, then they clearly cannot be allowed to contain sequents given in this kind of way. We must instead require that what occurs to the left of ⇒ is to be a finite list, consisting of zero or more formulae, written out in full and separated by commas. In this chapter, the Greek letters 'Γ,Δ,...' will be used to represent such lists.

We may continue, if we like, to think of these lists of formulae as tacitly surrounded by curly brackets {. . .}, so that their role is still to specify a set. But now that we have come so far why should we not go one step further, and say that what is to the left of the ⇒ is not a set at all, but simply a finite sequence of zero or more formulae separated by commas? The answer is that we can perfectly well take this further step, though it does bring with it the need for an explicit statement of two further rules of inference. When a set is specified by listing its members, then the order in which the members are listed makes no difference, and any repetitions in the list may automatically be discounted. This is because sets are the same iff their members are the same, and different listings may yet list the same members. But if we are no longer thinking in terms of sets, and are working with lists directly, then we cannot continue with the attitude that it simply goes without saying that order and repetition are irrelevant. This is not a problem. It just means that we have to say it, instead of letting it go without saying. So we shall need two new rules of inference, the rule of Interchange (INT), which allows us to change the order of the formulae in the list, and the rule of Contraction, (CONTR), which allows us to delete a repetition.

It is customary to present a sequent calculus as a system in which proofs have the structure of trees, in the same way as we did first present natural deduction (in Section 6.2). At the topmost position on each branch there will therefore be a sequent which, according to the rules, can be asserted outright. This will therefore be an instance of the rule of assumptions. Every other position in the proof will be occupied by a sequent which is deduced from other sequents, the sequents that it is deduced from being written immediately above it, and separated from it by a horizontal line. We may therefore set out our basic rules of inference in the same way. Here, then, are the so-called 'structural' rules of inference, i.e. rules which do not concern any particular truth-functors or quantifiers.

$$(\text{ASS}) \frac{}{\varphi \Rightarrow \varphi}$$

$$(\text{THIN}) \frac{\Gamma \Rightarrow \varphi}{\Gamma, \psi \Rightarrow \varphi}$$

$$(\text{CUT}) \frac{\Gamma \Rightarrow \varphi \qquad\qquad \varphi, \Delta \Rightarrow \psi}{\Gamma, \Delta \Rightarrow \psi}$$

$$(\text{INT}) \frac{\Gamma, \varphi, \psi, \Delta \Rightarrow \chi}{\Gamma, \psi, \varphi, \Delta \Rightarrow \chi}$$

$$(\text{CONTR}) \frac{\Gamma, \varphi, \varphi \Rightarrow \chi}{\Gamma, \varphi \Rightarrow \chi} \;.$$

Whether one lists INT and CONTR explicitly as rules, or whether one lets them go without saying, is very much a matter of taste. (My own taste is to say that they should be listed as rules that are needed in theory, but then to let them go without saying in practice, since it is so very tedious to put in a separate step each time that one of them should, in theory, be invoked.) In any case, every sequent calculus will certainly conform to INT and CONTR, whether or not they are officially listed. But of the other rules one can only say that you would *expect* a sequent calculus to contain each of them (either as a basic rule or as derived from other basic rules). They all are basic rules in the system to be considered in the next section. But, as we shall see later on, there are sequent calculi in which they are either modified or lacking altogether.

EXERCISES

7.1.1.(*a*) Starting with an instance of ASS, and using suitable steps of THIN and INT, given in full, establish the sequent

$$P, Q, \neg P, \neg Q, R \Rightarrow \neg Q.$$

(*b*) By suitable steps of INT and CONTR, given in full, establish the following rule of inference

$$\frac{\varphi,\psi,\varphi,\chi,\psi \Rightarrow \neg\varphi}{\chi,\psi,\varphi \Rightarrow \neg\varphi} \, .$$

(c) Generalize your arguments in parts (a) and (b) to show that, however the formulae to the left of $\Rightarrow$ may be listed initially, (1) the order of the list may be rearranged in any desired way, and (2) repetitions may be introduced or eliminated in any desired way, still leaving a sequent that is interdeducible with the one initially given.

7.1.2. A rule such as ($\wedge$I) is sometimes formulated in this way.

$$\frac{\Gamma \Rightarrow \varphi \quad \Gamma \Rightarrow \psi}{\Gamma \Rightarrow \varphi\wedge\psi}$$

and sometimes in this way

$$\frac{\Gamma \Rightarrow \varphi \quad \Delta \Rightarrow \psi}{\Gamma,\Delta \Rightarrow \varphi\wedge\psi}$$

Show that, if Γ and Δ are both finite, then each of these formulations may be deduced from the other. [For the argument in one direction you will need THIN and INT; for the other direction you will need INT and CONTR.]

7.2. Natural Deduction as a Sequent Calculus

It is very simple to rewrite the natural deduction rules given in the last chapter as rules for a sequent calculus. We may adopt all the structural rules just noted, and then we may reproduce the rules for truth-functors and quantifiers, as given on pp. 252–4, in this form:[2]

$$(\wedge I)\frac{\Gamma \Rightarrow \varphi \quad \Delta \Rightarrow \psi}{\Gamma,\Delta \Rightarrow \varphi\wedge\phi} \qquad (\wedge E)\frac{\Gamma \Rightarrow \varphi\wedge\psi}{\Gamma \Rightarrow \varphi}, \quad \frac{\Gamma \Rightarrow \varphi\wedge\psi}{\Gamma \Rightarrow \psi}$$

$$(\vee I)\frac{\Gamma \Rightarrow \phi}{\Gamma \Rightarrow \varphi\vee\psi}, \quad \frac{\Gamma \Rightarrow \psi}{\Gamma \Rightarrow \varphi\vee\psi} \qquad (\vee E)\frac{\Gamma \Rightarrow \varphi\vee\psi \quad \Delta,\varphi \Rightarrow \chi \quad \Theta,\psi \Rightarrow \chi}{\Gamma,\Delta,\Theta \Rightarrow \chi}$$

$$(\rightarrow I)\frac{\Gamma,\varphi \Rightarrow \psi}{\Gamma \Rightarrow \varphi\rightarrow\psi} \qquad (\rightarrow E)\frac{\Gamma \Rightarrow \varphi \quad \Delta \Rightarrow \varphi\rightarrow\psi}{\Gamma,\Delta \Rightarrow \psi}$$

[2] Observe that the versions of ($\vee$E) and ($\exists$E) given here are more complex than those cited previously. The added complexity gives no further power (Exercise 7.2.1), but is adopted here because it better matches the way that ($\vee$E) and ($\exists$E) are actually used in natural deductions.

$$(TND)\frac{\Gamma,\varphi \Rightarrow \psi \quad \Delta,\neg\varphi \Rightarrow \psi}{\Gamma,\Delta \Rightarrow \psi} \qquad (EFQ)\frac{\Gamma \Rightarrow \varphi \quad \Delta \Rightarrow \neg\varphi}{\Gamma,\Delta \Rightarrow \psi}$$

$$(\forall I)\frac{\Gamma \Rightarrow \varphi}{\Gamma \Rightarrow \forall\xi\varphi(\xi/\alpha)} \qquad (\forall E)\frac{\Gamma \Rightarrow \forall\xi\varphi}{\Gamma \Rightarrow \varphi(\alpha/\xi)}$$
provided α is not in Γ

$$(\exists I)\frac{\Gamma \Rightarrow \varphi(\alpha/\xi)}{\Gamma \Rightarrow \exists\xi\varphi} \qquad (\exists E)\frac{\Gamma \Rightarrow \exists\xi\varphi(\xi/\alpha) \quad \Delta,\varphi \Rightarrow \psi}{\Gamma,\Delta \Rightarrow \psi}$$
provided α is not in Δ or ψ

Given the familiar rules formulated in this new way, and given also the basic idea that a proof in a sequent calculus records, at each stage, the whole sequent that has been proved at that stage, it is really very easy to see how a proof, originally written as a proof in natural deduction, may now be rewritten as a proof in this sequent calculus. I give just one example for a detailed analysis. Turn back to the proof given on p. 258 of the sequent

$$\forall x \exists y(Fx \wedge Gy) \vdash \exists y \forall x(Fx \wedge Gy).$$

This proof is rewritten as a sequent calculus proof below. You will observe that, to save clutter, I have omitted the small signs to the left of each horizontal line saying which rule of inference is being applied at that line. As an exercise, restore those signs. It will be seen that the structure of this proof is exactly the same as the structure of the proof given on p. 258, on which it is modelled. Indeed the two proofs correspond perfectly, step by step,[3] and this is not just an accident which happens to hold for this particular example but not for others. It should be perfectly clear that the point holds quite generally. Since it really is very simple to rewrite a natural deduction proof as a proof in the corresponding sequent calculus, one could at this point pass on without more ado to the next topic. But perhaps it will be useful if I make two further observations at this point.

The first is that it is evidently very tedious to write out a proof in our sequent calculus, and especially if the proof is to be given in a tree structure. But we have already seen that tree proofs may be collapsed into linear proofs, and that much ink is saved thereby, so can we not apply the same idea to these new sequent calculus proofs too? The answer is that we certainly can, and that this does indeed economize on ink and paper. But this answer

---

[3] The correspondence would not be perfect if steps of interchange and contraction had been put in explicitly. As an exercise, put them in.

$$\dfrac{\forall x \exists y (Fx \wedge Gy) \Rightarrow (Gy \vee Gy) \vee (Fx \wedge Gy)}{\forall x \exists y (Fx \wedge Gy) \Rightarrow \exists y (Fc \wedge Gy)}$$

$$\exists y (Fx \wedge Gy) \Rightarrow \exists y A \wedge \forall x (Fx \vee Gy) \wedge \exists x A$$

$$\dfrac{Fa \vee Gb \Rightarrow Fa \vee Gb}{Fa \vee Gb \Rightarrow Fa} \qquad \dfrac{Fc \wedge Gb \Rightarrow Fc \vee Gb}{Fc \wedge Gb \Rightarrow Gb}$$

$$\dfrac{\forall x \exists y (Fx \wedge Gy), Fc \wedge Gb \Rightarrow Fa \wedge Gb}{\forall x \exists y (Fx \wedge Gy), Fc \wedge Gb \Rightarrow \forall x (Fx \wedge Gb)}$$

$$\forall x \exists y (Fx \wedge Gy), Fc \wedge Gb \Rightarrow \exists y \forall x (Fx \vee Gy)$$

$$\dfrac{\forall x \exists y (Fx \wedge Gy) \Rightarrow Fa}{(Fx \vee Gy) \vee \exists x A \Rightarrow (Gy \vee x A) \wedge \exists x A}$$

$$(Fx \vee Gy) \vee \exists x A \Rightarrow (Gy \vee x A) \wedge \exists x A$$

279

can be improved to one which is perhaps more interesting, namely that our existing method of writing natural deduction proofs in a linear form is *already* a way of writing the corresponding sequent calculus proofs in linear form. I illustrate the point with the same sequent as example. A linear proof, drawn up according to the method of Section 6.4, would look like this:

$\forall x \exists y(Fx \wedge Gy) \vdash \exists y \forall x(Fx \wedge Gy)$

1	(1)	$\forall x \exists y(Fx \wedge Gy)$	ASS
1	(2)	$\exists y(Fa \wedge Gy)$	1,$\forall$E
3	(3)	$Fa \wedge Gb$	ASS
3	(4)	Fa	3,$\wedge$E
1	(5)	Fa	2,3–4,$\exists$E
1	(6)	$\exists y(Fc \wedge Gy)$	1,$\forall$E
7	(7)	$Fc \wedge Gb$	ASS
7	(8)	Gb	7,$\wedge$E
1,7	(9)	$Fa \wedge Gb$	5,8,$\wedge$I
1,7	(10)	$\forall x(Fx \wedge Gb)$	9,$\forall$I
1,7	(11)	$\exists y \forall x(Fx \wedge Gy)$	10,$\exists$I
1	(12)	$\exists y \forall x(Fx \wedge Gy)$	6,7–11,$\exists$E

Because each line in this proof contains, on the left, an explicit mention of the assumptions that the formula in that line rests on, we can easily see each line as being itself a sequent, namely the sequent which has the listed assumptions to its left and the formula displayed to its right. When we look at the proof in this way, we see that it is already a proof in a sequent calculus, and the justification for each line is unaffected. In fact it is just short for this explicit sequent calculus version:

(1)	$\forall x \exists y(Fx \wedge Gy) \Rightarrow \forall x \exists y(Fx \wedge Gy)$	ASS
(2)	$\forall x \exists y(Fx \wedge Gy) \Rightarrow \exists y(Fa \wedge Gy)$	1,$\forall$E
(3)	$Fa \wedge Gb \Rightarrow Fa \wedge Gb$	ASS
(4)	$Fa \wedge Gb \Rightarrow Fa$	3,$\wedge$E
(5)	$\forall x \exists y(Fx \wedge Gy) \Rightarrow Fa$	2,3–4,$\exists$E
(6)	$\forall x \exists y(Fx \wedge Gy) \Rightarrow \exists y(Fc \wedge Gy)$	1,$\forall$E
(7)	$Fc \wedge Gb \Rightarrow Fc \wedge Gb$	ASS
(8)	$Fc \wedge Gb \Rightarrow Gb$	7,$\wedge$E
(9)	$\forall x \exists y(Fx \wedge Gy), Fc \wedge Gb \Rightarrow Fa \wedge Gb$	5,8,$\wedge$I
(10)	$\forall x \exists y(Fx \wedge Gy), Fc \wedge Gb \Rightarrow \forall x(Fx \wedge Gb)$	9,$\forall$I
(11)	$\forall x \exists y(Fx \wedge Gy), Fc \wedge Gb \Rightarrow \exists y \forall x(Fx \wedge Gy)$	10,$\exists$I
(12)	$\forall x \exists y(Fx \wedge Gy) \Rightarrow \exists y \forall x(Fx \wedge Gy)$	6,7–11,$\exists$E

Given a natural deduction proof in the linear form, then, it is even more simple to rewrite it as a linear proof in the corresponding sequent calculus. In fact it is so simple that we may perfectly well count the original proof *as a* proof in the sequent calculus, but one that uses a convenient technique of abbreviation. For practical purposes, this is by far the best approach. But for most of the present chapter we shall not be too much concerned over what is convenient in practice, for one does not usually introduce a sequent calculus for that purpose. Rather, the interest is theoretical. As we shall see, a sequent calculus is a useful tool for comparing two systems that at first look utterly different. And for this purpose it is probably more helpful to stick to the original way of writing a proof, namely as a tree structure.

A second point, worth adding here, concerns sequents with no formula on the right. If we start from the perspective of natural deduction, we might expect such sequents to be defined in terms of the more familiar sequents with just one formula on the right. The simplest method of doing this is to suppose that the language already contains the symbol $\perp$, with its own rule of inference

$$(\perp)\frac{\Gamma \Rightarrow \perp}{\Gamma \Rightarrow \varphi}.$$

Then clearly we can define

$$\Gamma \Rightarrow \quad \text{as short for} \quad \Gamma \Rightarrow \perp.$$

Alternatively, if $\perp$ is not available, but we do have (say) $\wedge$ and $\neg$, then we could instead define

$$\Gamma \Rightarrow \quad \text{as short for} \quad \Gamma \Rightarrow P \wedge \neg P.$$

It is artificial to pick on some particular contradictory formula to play this role, for no good ground could be given for choosing one rather than another, but in practice it works perfectly well. As a further alternative, we may, of course, accept sequents with no formula on the right as part of our primitive vocabulary, extending the usual structural rules to cover such sequents. Thus Thinning, Cutting, Interchange, and Contraction are to apply as before both when there is a formula on the right and when there is not, and there is also to be a new rule of Thinning *on the right*, which takes this form:

$$\frac{\Gamma \Rightarrow}{\Gamma \Rightarrow \varphi}.$$

EXERCISES

7.2.1.(*a*) Assuming the standard structural rules, show that the rules ($\vee$E) and ($\exists$E) given above are interdeducible with these more familiar versions, which are rules for introducing on the left:

$$(\vee E') \frac{\Gamma,\varphi \Rightarrow \chi \quad \Delta,\psi \Rightarrow \chi}{\Gamma,\Delta,\varphi\vee\psi \Rightarrow \chi} \qquad (\exists E') \frac{\Gamma,\varphi \Rightarrow \psi}{\Gamma,\exists\xi\varphi(\xi/\alpha) \Rightarrow \psi}$$
$$\text{provided } \alpha \text{ is not in } \Gamma \text{ or in } \psi$$

(*b*) Assuming the standard structural rules again, show that the rule ($\forall$E) given above is interdeducible with this rule for introducing on the left:

$$(\forall E') \frac{\Gamma,\varphi(\alpha/\xi) \Rightarrow \psi}{\Gamma,\forall\xi\varphi \Rightarrow \psi}.$$

(*c*) Consider once more the sequent

$$\forall x\exists y(Fx\wedge Gy) \Rightarrow \exists y\forall x(Fx\wedge Gy).$$

Construct a proof of this sequent using ($\exists$E') and ($\forall$E') in place of ($\exists$E) and ($\forall$E), and *not* using CUT.

7.2.2. Let us write a double horizontal line to signify that the sequent below the line follows from the ones above *and* conversely that the ones above each follow from the one below. Then what were called in Section 2.5 the 'basic principles' for $\wedge,\vee,\rightarrow,\neg$ may be formulated thus:

$$\frac{\Gamma \Rightarrow \varphi \quad \text{AND} \quad \Gamma \Rightarrow \psi}{\Gamma \Rightarrow \varphi\wedge\psi} \qquad \frac{\Gamma,\varphi \Rightarrow \chi \quad \text{AND} \quad \Gamma,\psi \Rightarrow \chi}{\Gamma,\varphi\vee\psi \Rightarrow \chi}$$

$$\frac{\Gamma,\varphi \Rightarrow \psi}{\Gamma \Rightarrow \varphi\rightarrow\psi} \qquad \frac{\Gamma \Rightarrow \varphi}{\Gamma,\neg\varphi \Rightarrow}$$

Assuming all the standard structural rules for a sequent calculus, show that these rules are interdeducible with the ones given in this section.

7.2.3. Consider a sequent calculus which has all the standard structural rules and in addition just this one pair of rules:

$$\frac{\Gamma \Rightarrow \varphi \quad \text{AND} \quad \Gamma \Rightarrow \psi}{\Gamma,\varphi\!\uparrow\!\psi \Rightarrow}.$$

(*a*) Give an interpretation of ↑ under which this rule is sound.

(*b*) Define ¬,∧,∨ in terms of ↑, and show how to prove, in this calculus, the rules for ¬,∧,∨ given in this section.

7.3. **Semantic Tableaux as a Sequent Calculus**

The sequent calculus of the last section was designed to fit proofs in a natural deduction system. In this section we shall find a sequent calculus to fit proofs by semantic tableaux. I begin by considering the tableau proofs that we actually use in practice, in which negation plays a special role. But in the next section I shall be concerned with the tableau rules as originally formulated in Section 4.2, using an explicitly semantical vocabulary. This will lead us to something very much more elegant. But it is more sensible to begin with the method used in practice, since that is likely to be more familiar.

At a first glance, the method of a sequent calculus seems not to apply to tableau proofs. For the method is that each step of the new proof records the sequent that is proved at the corresponding step of the original proof, but the individual steps of a tableau proof do not establish any sequent at all. Indeed, no sequent is established until the final step of the proof, when the last branch is closed, and until then we are simply exploring a hypothesis. Nevertheless, the hypothesis being explored can certainly be stated as a hypothesis about a sequent, and that is enough for us to be able to bring the method to bear. The sequents in question are sequents which have no formula on the right.

In more detail, a tableau proof begins with a (finite) list of formulae at its root, say Γ, and it puts forward the hypothesis that these formulae are consistent, i.e. not inconsistent. That is, the hypothesis, is

$$\Gamma \nvdash.$$

This is the negation of a sequent. When we then go on to develop the tableau, we argue that if these formulae which we have so far are consistent, then so too is the result of adding to them some further formulae, shorter than the ones we began with. But here we need to distinguish between branching and non-branching rules, for a branching rule will say that if these formulae that we have already are consistent, then *either* the result of adding this *or* the result of adding that must remain consistent. To illustrate, let us just look at the rules for $\wedge$. Using our present notation for when one sequent follows from another, but applying it now not only to sequents but also to their negations, we may say that the two rules for $\wedge$ are these:

$$\frac{\Gamma,\varphi\wedge\psi\nvDash}{\Gamma,\varphi\wedge\psi,\varphi,\psi\nvDash} \qquad \frac{\Gamma,\neg(\varphi\wedge\psi)\nvDash}{\Gamma,\neg(\varphi\wedge\psi),\neg\varphi\nvDash \ \ \text{OR} \ \ \Gamma,\neg(\varphi\wedge\psi),\neg\psi\vDash}.$$

Clearly, all the other tableau rules can be similarly formulated, but first let us introduce some simplifications.

The left-hand rule has the formula $\varphi\wedge\psi$ repeated in the bottom line, and similarly the right-hand rule repeats $\neg(\varphi\wedge\psi)$ in each bottom line. But this is superfluous. (*a*) It is superfluous from a semantic point of view, for the rules would be equally correct if these repetitions were dropped; and (*b*) is superfluous from the point of view of reflecting what actually happens in a tableau proof. For once a formula $\varphi\wedge\psi$ has been developed (in every branch on which it lies), and replaced by the simpler formulae φ and ψ, we never do go back to the original conjunction $\varphi\wedge\psi$. It plays no further role in the growth of the tableau and the closing of branches. Exactly the same applies to a formula $\neg(\varphi\wedge\psi)$; once it has been replaced by $\neg\varphi$ in one branch, and $\neg\psi$ in another, it is never referred to again. So we may simplify the rules just stated in this way:

$$\frac{\Gamma,\varphi\wedge\psi\nvDash}{\Gamma,\varphi,\psi\nvDash} \qquad \frac{\Gamma,\neg(\varphi\wedge\psi)\nvDash}{\Gamma,\neg\varphi\nvDash \ \ \text{OR} \ \ \Gamma,\neg\psi\nvDash}.$$

A further simplification turns these rules upside-down, by contraposition, and thus presents them as rules concerning sequents, and not the negations of sequents. For it is clear that B follows from A iff the negation of A follows from the negation of B. So we obtain

$$\frac{\Gamma,\varphi,\psi\vDash}{\Gamma,\varphi\wedge\psi\vDash} \qquad \frac{\Gamma,\neg\varphi\vDash \quad \Gamma,\neg\psi\vDash}{\Gamma,\neg(\varphi\wedge\psi)\vDash}.$$

Notice that at the same time the anomalous 'OR' which had appeared on the bottom of the rule for $(\neg\wedge)$ has now become an ordinary 'AND' on the top line, and so may be omitted in the usual way.

For convenience I gather together here all the tableau rules for truth-functors, treated in the same way, i.e. by first omitting repetitions as superfluous and then turning them upside-down. At the same time, since it is now a genuine sequent calculus that is being put forward, I write $\Rightarrow$ in place of $\models$. The rules become:

$$(BS)\ \frac{}{\Gamma,\varphi,\neg\varphi \Rightarrow}$$

$$(\wedge)\ \frac{\Gamma,\varphi,\psi \Rightarrow}{\Gamma,\varphi\wedge\psi \Rightarrow} \qquad\qquad (\neg\wedge)\ \frac{\Gamma,\neg\varphi \Rightarrow\quad \Gamma,\neg\psi \Rightarrow}{\Gamma,\neg(\varphi\wedge\psi) \Rightarrow}$$

$$(\vee)\ \frac{\Gamma,\varphi \Rightarrow\quad \Gamma,\psi \Rightarrow}{\Gamma,\varphi\vee\psi \Rightarrow} \qquad\qquad (\neg\vee)\ \frac{\Gamma,\neg\varphi,\neg\psi \Rightarrow}{\Gamma,\neg(\varphi\vee\psi) \Rightarrow}$$

$$(\rightarrow)\ \frac{\Gamma,\neg\varphi \Rightarrow\quad \Gamma,\psi \Rightarrow}{\Gamma,\varphi\rightarrow\psi \Rightarrow} \qquad\qquad (\neg\rightarrow)\ \frac{\Gamma,\varphi,\neg\psi \Rightarrow}{\Gamma,\neg(\varphi\rightarrow\psi) \Rightarrow}$$

$$(\neg\neg)\ \frac{\Gamma,\varphi \Rightarrow}{\Gamma,\neg\neg\phi \Rightarrow}$$

The rule that I have put at the top, called 'BS' for 'basic sequent', is, of course, the rule for closing branches. All the other rules are introduction rules, and there are no elimination rules. This, of course, corresponds to the fact that, in their original setting, all the tableau rules are elimination rules, allowing us to replace a longer formula by its shorter components. So, when one turns them upside-down, they naturally become introduction rules. And since at the moment our sequents have no formulae on the right, they must be rules for introducing on the left.

Now the point is that any tableau proof can be rewritten as a proof in this sequent calculus, simply by turning the whole thing upside-down. Let us begin with a very simple example. Here is a tableau proof of Peirce's law:

$\models((P{\rightarrow}Q){\rightarrow}P){\rightarrow}P$

$$\neg((P{\rightarrow}Q){\rightarrow}P){\rightarrow}P$$
$$|$$
$$(P{\rightarrow}Q){\rightarrow}P$$
$$\neg P$$
$$|$$

$$\neg(P{\rightarrow}Q) \qquad\qquad P$$
$$| \qquad\qquad\qquad =$$
$$P$$
$$\neg Q$$
$$=$$

When we analyse this proof we see that what it is saying, step by step, is this:

$$
\begin{array}{ll}
\text{Assume} & \neg(((P{\to}Q){\to}P){\to}P) \not\vDash \\
\text{Then} & (P{\to}Q){\to}P, \neg P \not\vDash \\
\text{So either} \quad \neg(P{\to}Q), \neg P \not\vDash & \text{or} \quad P, \neg P \not\vDash \\
\text{hence} \quad P, \neg Q, \neg P \not\vDash & \text{but this is not so} \\
\text{but this is not so.} &
\end{array}
$$

Turning the reasoning upside-down, we find that it is a piece of reasoning in our sequent calculus, going like this:

$$
(\neg{\to})\cfrac{(\mathrm{BS})\cfrac{}{P,\neg Q,\neg P \Rightarrow}}{(\to)\cfrac{\neg(P{\to}Q),\neg P \Rightarrow \qquad (\mathrm{BS})\cfrac{}{P,\neg P \Rightarrow}}{(\neg{\to})\cfrac{(P{\to}Q){\to}P,\neg P \Rightarrow}{\neg(((P{\to}Q){\to}P){\to}P) \Rightarrow}}}
$$

Each branch begins with what we are now calling a basic sequent, and each transition is made in accordance with one of the rules $(\to)$ or $(\neg{\to})$ as now formulated. (Again, I am omitting occurrences of interchange.) I shall give a rather longer example in a moment, but first I pause to consider the quantifier rules.

If we formulate the tableau rules for $\forall$ as we first formulated the rules for $\wedge$, we obtain these:

$$
(\forall)\cfrac{\Gamma,\forall\xi\varphi \not\vDash}{\Gamma,\forall\xi\varphi,\varphi(\alpha/\xi) \not\vDash} \qquad (\neg\forall)\cfrac{\Gamma,\neg\forall\xi\varphi \not\vDash}{\Gamma,\neg\forall\xi\varphi,\neg\varphi(\alpha/\xi) \not\vDash}
$$
$$
\text{provided } \alpha \text{ is not in } \Gamma \text{ or in } \varphi
$$

Now the repetitions of $\forall\xi\varphi$ and $\neg\forall\xi\varphi$ on the bottom lines are again superfluous from the semantic point of view; each rule would remain a correct rule if these repetitions were simply omitted. With the rule for $\neg\forall$ on the right we can add, as before, that such an omission would in addition reflect the structure of a tableau proof. For it is again true that once a formula $\neg\forall\xi\varphi$ has been developed, by dropping the quantifier $\forall\xi$ and putting a new name α in place of the variable ξ, then we never need to go back to that formula $\neg\forall\xi\varphi$ again, and it plays no further role in growing the tableau. So in this case there is no problem over dropping the repetition. But with the $\forall$

rule on the left there is a problem, since we have seen that in a tableau proof the same formulae $\forall \xi \varphi$ may have to be used several times over, first with one name and then with another. So in this case we have a choice: we can drop the repetition to obtain a simpler rule, but remembering that it does not fit so closely the structure of a tableau proof, or we can keep the repetition because sometimes it will be useful. The choice is merely a matter of taste, for the two rules to which we would be led as rules of a sequent calculus are

$$(\forall_1) \frac{\Gamma, \varphi(\alpha/\xi) \Rightarrow}{\Gamma, \forall \xi \varphi \Rightarrow} \qquad (\forall_2) \frac{\Gamma, \forall \xi \varphi, \varphi(\alpha/\xi) \Rightarrow}{\Gamma, \forall \xi \varphi \Rightarrow}$$

It is easily seen that these two rules are interdeducible. I show on the left how $\forall_2$ can be obtained, given $\forall_1$, and on the right how $\forall_1$ can be obtained, given $\forall_2$.

$$\text{(CONTR)} \frac{(\forall_1) \dfrac{\Gamma, \forall \xi \varphi, \varphi(\alpha/\xi) \Rightarrow}{\Gamma, \forall \xi \varphi, \forall \xi \varphi \Rightarrow}}{\Gamma, \forall \xi \varphi \Rightarrow} \qquad \text{(THIN)} \frac{\Gamma, \varphi(\alpha/\xi) \Rightarrow}{(\forall_2) \dfrac{\Gamma, \forall \xi \varphi, \varphi(\alpha/\xi) \Rightarrow}{\Gamma, \forall \xi \varphi \Rightarrow}}$$

I choose, then, to adopt the simpler rule $(\forall_1)$ as the official rule in the sequent calculus, though remembering that the analysis of a tableau proof may be more complex than this simple form suggests. (There is a similar choice over the rule for $\neg \exists$, where I choose in the same way.)

The four quantifier rules for our sequent calculus are therefore these.

$$(\forall) \frac{\Gamma, \varphi(\alpha/\xi) \Rightarrow}{\Gamma, \forall \xi \varphi \Rightarrow} \qquad (\neg \forall) \frac{\Gamma, \neg \varphi \Rightarrow}{\Gamma, \neg \forall \xi \varphi(\xi/\alpha) \Rightarrow}$$
$$\text{provided } \alpha \text{ is not in } \Gamma$$

$$(\exists) \frac{\Gamma, \varphi \Rightarrow}{\Gamma, \exists \xi \varphi(\xi/\alpha) \Rightarrow} \qquad (\neg \exists) \frac{\Gamma, \neg \varphi(\alpha/\xi) \Rightarrow}{\Gamma, \neg \exists \xi \varphi \Rightarrow}$$
$$\text{provided } \alpha \text{ is not in } \Gamma$$

I have made a small change in the formulations of the rules $(\exists)$ and $(\neg \forall)$, in order to simplify the statement of the provisos attached to those rules, but otherwise these rules are obtained in the same way as those for the truth-functors, i.e. just by deleting repetitions and then turning them upside-down.

When we transform a whole tableau proof, by turning it upside-down, and writing each step as an application of these sequent rules, we need to be wary of the discrepancy just noted between the form of the rules ($\forall$) and ($\neg\exists$) and the actual procedure of the proof. Where the original tableau proof was a simple one, with the $\forall$-rule and the $\neg\exists$-rule never applied more than once to the same formula, there is no problem; we just follow the simple recipe already illustrated, and everything comes out right. But where one of these rules is applied more than once, in our analysis of the proof we carry down the formula it is applied to until we reach the last application of the rule. The result is that when this analysis is turned upside-down to become a sequent proof, an extra step of contraction will be needed at the end. I illustrate the position by returning once more to the sequent

$$\forall x\exists y(Fx\wedge Gy) \models \exists y\forall x(Fx\wedge Gy).$$

A tableau proof of this is given in (P15). Notice that in this proof the $\forall$-rule

Tableau (P15)

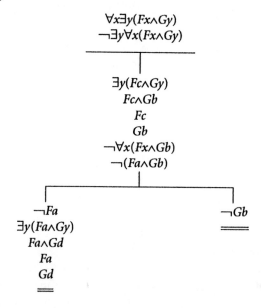

is applied twice to the first formula in the root, once as the very first step in the development, and then again just after the branch. Bearing this in mind, the analysis is:

Assume $\forall x \exists y (Fx \wedge Gy), \neg \exists y \forall x (Fx \wedge Gy) \not\models$

$\therefore \forall x \exists y (Fx \wedge Gy), \exists y (Fc \wedge Gy), \neg \exists y \forall x (Fx \wedge Gy) \not\models$

$\therefore \forall x \exists y (Fx \wedge Gy), Fc \wedge Gb, \neg \exists y \forall x (Fx \wedge Gy) \not\models$

$\therefore \forall x \exists y (Fx \wedge Gy), Fc, Gb, \neg \exists y \forall x (Fx \wedge Gy) \not\models$

$\therefore \forall x \exists y (Fx \wedge Gy), Fc, Gb, \neg \forall x (Fx \wedge Gb) \not\models$

$\therefore \forall x \exists y (Fx \wedge Gy), Fc, Gb, \neg (Fa \wedge Gb) \not\models$

$\therefore$ either $\forall x \exists y (Fx \wedge Gy), Fc, Gb, \neg Fa \not\models$

$\therefore \exists y (Fa \wedge Gy), Fc, Gb, \neg Fa \not\models$

$\therefore Fa \wedge Gd, Fc, Gb, \neg Fa \not\models$

$\therefore Fa, Gd, Fc, Gb, \neg Fa \not\models$

but this is not so

or $\forall x \exists y (Fx \wedge Gy), Fc, Gb, \neg Gb \not\models$

but this is not so.

We now turn the analysis upside-down to obtain our proof in the sequent calculus, at the same time writing $\Rightarrow$ for $\models$. This yields:

$$\cfrac{\cfrac{\cfrac{\cfrac{Fa, Gd, Fc, Gb, \neg Fa \Rightarrow}{Fa \wedge Gd, Fc, Gb, \neg Fa \Rightarrow}}{\exists y (Fa \wedge Gy), Fc, Gb, \neg Fa \Rightarrow}}{\forall x \exists y (Fx \wedge Gy), Fc, Gb, \neg Fa \Rightarrow \qquad \forall x \exists y (Fx \wedge Gy), Fc, Gb, \neg Gb \Rightarrow}}{\cfrac{\cfrac{\cfrac{\cfrac{\cfrac{\cfrac{\forall x \exists y (Fx \wedge Gy), Fc, Gb, \neg (Fa \wedge Gb) \Rightarrow}{\forall x \exists y (Fx \wedge Gy), Fc, Gb, \neg \forall x (Fx \wedge Gb) \Rightarrow}}{\forall x \exists y (Fx \wedge Gy), Fc, Gb, \neg \exists y \forall x (Fx \wedge Gy) \Rightarrow}}{\forall x \exists y (Fx \wedge Gy), Fc \wedge Gb, \neg \exists y \forall x (Fx \wedge Gy) \Rightarrow}}{\forall x \exists y (Fx \wedge Gy), \exists y (Fc \wedge Gy), \neg \exists y \forall x (Fx \wedge Gb) \Rightarrow}}{\forall x \exists y (Fx \wedge Gy), \forall x \exists y (Fx \wedge Gy), \neg \exists y \forall x (Fx \wedge Gy) \Rightarrow}}{\forall x \exists y (Fx \wedge Gy), \neg \exists y \forall x (Fx \wedge Gy) \Rightarrow}}$$

As you may check, each branch begins with a basic sequent, and each subsequent line follows from the line above it by the rules stated (except that steps of interchange have again been passed over in silence, and there is a final step of contraction).

EXERCISES

7.3.1. Rewrite six of your answers to Exercise 4.4.1 as proofs in the sequent calculus of this section.

7.3.2. Let S be the sequent calculus which contains just the rule for basic sequents and for the truth-functors as formulated in this section, the rules ($\exists$) and ($\neg\forall$) as in this section, the rules ($\forall$) and ($\neg\exists$) formulated *without* deleting the repetition, and interchange. Note that S does *not* contain ASS, THIN, CUT, or CONTR.
(*a*) Say how the changes to ($\forall$) and ($\neg\exists$) affect the recipe for rewriting tableau proofs as proofs in S.
(*b*) Show that every proof in S can be rewritten as a tableau proof of the same sequent. [Method: use induction on the length of the proof in S, working upwards from the bottom of the proof.]

7.3.3. Let S′ be like S of the previous exercise, except that it does not contain the rule BS for basic sequents but instead the rules ASS and THIN, with ASS in the form

$$(ASS) \; \frac{}{\varphi, \neg\varphi \Rightarrow}$$

Show that all the same sequents are provable in S and in S′. [Method: it is easy to prove BS as a derived rule of S′; for the converse, show that any use of THIN in S′ can be driven up the proof until it is applied to an instance of ASS.]

7.3.4. Let S″ be the system S of Exercise 7.3.2, except that in place of ($\wedge$) it has these two rules:

$$\frac{\Gamma, \varphi \Rightarrow}{\Gamma, \varphi \wedge \psi \Rightarrow}, \quad \frac{\Gamma, \psi \Rightarrow}{\Gamma, \varphi \wedge \psi \Rightarrow}$$

and in place of ($\neg\vee$) it has these two rules:

$$\frac{\Gamma, \neg\varphi \Rightarrow}{\Gamma, \neg(\varphi \vee \psi) \Rightarrow}, \quad \frac{\Gamma, \neg\psi \Rightarrow}{\Gamma, \neg(\varphi \vee \psi) \Rightarrow}$$

and in place of ($\neg\rightarrow$) it has these two rules:

$$\frac{\Gamma, \varphi \Rightarrow}{\Gamma, \neg(\varphi \rightarrow \psi) \Rightarrow}, \quad \frac{\Gamma, \neg\psi \Rightarrow}{\Gamma, \neg(\varphi \rightarrow \psi) \Rightarrow}$$

(*a*) Show that any sequent that can be proved in S″ can also be proved in S. [Hint: use the result of the previous exercise on thinning in S.]
(*b*) Show that, if we add to S″ the rule of contraction, then every sequent provable in S is also provable in the expanded S″.

(*c*) Show that, if we do not expand S″ by adding contraction, then it is not true that every sequent provable in S is provable in S″. [Hint: consider the sequent

$P \wedge \neg P \Rightarrow$.

This is not a basic sequent. So if it is provable in S″ there is a previous line in the proof. What could it be? (Note that only correct sequents are provable in S″.)]

(*d*) Show that, if we expand S by adding the rule of contraction, then no new sequents become provable. [For the simplest argument, use Exercise 7.3.2 and the reasoning which is applied to CUT on p. 182.]

7.4. Gentzen Sequents; Semantic Tableaux Again

We could pursue straightaway the comparison already hinted at between the sequent calculus corresponding to natural deduction and that corresponding to the tableau system. But at the moment negation is still playing a very special role in the tableau rules, and this is distracting. So I first adopt a new sequent calculus for the tableau system, which involves the use of a new kind of sequent altogether.

It is not an unreasonable suggestion that the unwanted occurrences of negation in many of the tableau rules can be removed if we recall that in the tableau system we abbreviate

$$\Gamma \Rightarrow \varphi \quad \text{for} \quad \Gamma, \neg \varphi \Rightarrow.$$

Applying this transformation to the rule for basic sequents, and to all the ¬-rules, they become

$$(\text{BS}) \ \frac{}{\Gamma, \varphi \Rightarrow \varphi}$$

$$(\neg \wedge) \ \frac{\Gamma \Rightarrow \varphi \quad \Gamma \Rightarrow \psi}{\Gamma \Rightarrow \varphi \wedge \psi}$$

$$(\neg \vee) \ ?$$

$$(\neg \rightarrow) \ \frac{\Gamma, \varphi \Rightarrow \psi}{\Gamma \Rightarrow \varphi \rightarrow \psi}$$

$$(\neg \neg) \ \frac{\Gamma, \varphi \Rightarrow}{\Gamma \Rightarrow \neg \varphi}$$

$$(\neg\forall) \; \frac{\Gamma \Rightarrow \varphi}{\Gamma \Rightarrow \forall\xi\varphi(\xi/\alpha)}$$

provided α is not in Γ

$$(\neg\exists) \; \frac{\Gamma \Rightarrow \varphi(\alpha/\xi)}{\Gamma \Rightarrow \exists\xi\varphi}$$

In every case, this turns a complex and unfamiliar negation rule into a simpler and more familiar rule, for introducing on the right, with no superfluous intrusion of negations. But there is one case, namely $(\neg\vee)$, to which the transformation cannot be applied, since it would lead to a sequent with *two* formulae to the right of $\Rightarrow$. It is true that one might try to avoid this by reformulating $(\neg\vee)$ as in Exercise 7.3.4, but we noted then that that introduced further complications of its own. So what we shall do now is to enlarge the notion of a sequent, so that it may have any (finite) number of formulae on the left *and* any (finite) number on the right. Such sequents are called Gentzen sequents, for they were introduced by Gerhard Gentzen (1934).

The idea, then, is that $\Gamma \Rightarrow \Delta$ will be a sequent, where both Γ and Δ may be lists of several formulae (or of none). The intended interpretation is that such a sequent will count as correct iff there is no interpretation which makes all the formulae in Γ true and all the formulae in Δ false. Since Γ and Δ are both constrained to be finite, this comes to the same thing as saying that the conjunction of all the formulae in Γ entails the disjunction of all the formulae in Δ. (For this purpose we may, if we wish, take the 'empty conjunction' as the formula $\top$ and the 'empty disjunction' as the formula $\bot$.) So such a sequent is always equivalent to one with just one formula on either side. That, of course, always was the case with the sequents we have considered previously. But just as previously we could set out our rules with several formulae on the left, without needing occurrences of $\wedge$ to bind them together into one, so now we can do the same on the right as well, without binding the several formulae together by occurrences of $\vee$. This restores the symmetry between $\wedge$ and $\vee$ that was so clearly missing in the natural deduction approach, and it gives us a great freedom to formulate elegant rules for the truth-functors and quantifiers, as we shall see. But as a preliminary let us first notice the structural rules for a sequent calculus employing these new Gentzen sequents.

So far as the standard rules are concerned, Assumptions will remain as before, Thinning and Interchange and Contraction will be extended so that they apply to both sides of a sequent, and Cut will be reformulated in a more powerful way, suited to the more complex sequents now available. That is to say, the standard structural rules are now these:

$$(ASS)\,\frac{}{\varphi \Rightarrow \varphi}$$

$$(THIN)\,\frac{\Gamma \Rightarrow \Delta}{\Gamma,\varphi \Rightarrow \Delta} \qquad\qquad (THIN)\,\frac{\Gamma \Rightarrow \Delta}{\Gamma \Rightarrow \varphi,\Delta}$$

$$(CUT)\,\frac{\Gamma_1 \Rightarrow \varphi,\Delta_1 \quad \Gamma_2,\varphi \Rightarrow \Delta_2}{\Gamma_1,\Gamma_2 \Rightarrow \Delta_1,\Delta_2}$$

$$(INT)\,\frac{\Gamma,\varphi,\psi,\Delta \Rightarrow \Theta}{\Gamma,\psi,\varphi,\Delta \Rightarrow \Theta} \qquad\qquad (INT)\,\frac{\Gamma \Rightarrow \Delta,\varphi,\psi,\Theta}{\Gamma \Rightarrow \Delta,\psi,\varphi,\Theta}$$

$$(CONTR)\,\frac{\Gamma,\varphi,\varphi \Rightarrow \Delta}{\Gamma,\varphi \Rightarrow \Delta} \qquad\qquad (CONTR)\,\frac{\Gamma \Rightarrow \varphi,\varphi,\Delta}{\Gamma \Rightarrow \varphi,\Delta}$$

If we wish to adopt a rule for basic sequents, in place of Assumptions and Thinning, then that rule must also be extended as Thinning has been extended, i.e. to

$$(BS)\,\frac{}{\Gamma,\varphi \Rightarrow \varphi,\Delta}\,.$$

These are the structural rules that one *expects* to find holding in a Gentzen sequent calculus, either adopted as primitive rules of the system or derived from other rules. (For example, thinning on the left is derivable from the natural deduction rules for $\wedge$, as we noted long ago; thinning on the right will now be derivable from the symmetrical rules for $\vee$; cutting may well be derivable from the rules for $\rightarrow$, depending on just what rules are adopted here.) But in particular cases a calculus may be specified which lacks one or more of these rules. However, all the calculi that will be considered here will contain Interchange as a primitive rule, and to avoid clutter I shall continue to leave the applications of this rule tacit.

I briefly illustrate the new freedoms with a few examples. The standard natural deduction rules for $\wedge$ are formulated as rules for introducing and eliminating on the right, and we could already have formulated a similar pair of rules for $\vee$, for introducing and eliminating on the left. But the duality of these rules can now be brought out much more clearly. To obtain a succinct formulation, let us again use a double horizontal line to signify that the inference holds both from top to bottom and from bottom to top. Then these rules are

$$\frac{\Gamma \Rightarrow \varphi,\Delta \quad \text{AND} \quad \Gamma \Rightarrow \psi,\Delta}{\Gamma \Rightarrow \varphi \wedge \psi,\Delta} \qquad \frac{\Gamma,\varphi \Rightarrow \Delta \quad \text{AND} \quad \Gamma,\psi \Rightarrow \Delta}{\Gamma,\varphi \vee \psi \Rightarrow \Delta}$$

(Previously we had to require Δ to be null in the rule for $\wedge$, and to be a single formula in the rule for $\vee$, and this destroyed the symmetry.) A more significant improvement, however, is that we can now give a much simpler pair of rules for $\wedge$, which introduce it and eliminate it on the left, and can match these with an equally simple pair of rules for $\vee$, which introduce it and eliminate it on the right:

$$\frac{\Gamma,\varphi,\psi \Rightarrow \Delta}{\Gamma,\varphi \wedge \psi \Rightarrow \Delta} \qquad \frac{\Gamma \Rightarrow \varphi,\psi,\Delta}{\Gamma \Rightarrow \varphi \vee \psi,\Delta}$$

As is familiar, the rules for $\wedge$ may be reformulated once more in this even simpler way:

$$\varphi,\psi \Rightarrow \varphi \wedge \psi \qquad \varphi \wedge \psi \Rightarrow \varphi, \quad \varphi \wedge \psi \Rightarrow \psi.$$

And these rules too can now be matched by dual rules for $\vee$:

$$\varphi \vee \psi \Rightarrow \varphi,\psi \qquad \varphi \Rightarrow \varphi \vee \psi, \quad \psi \Rightarrow \varphi \vee \psi.$$

As you are invited to discover, all these various ways of framing rules for $\wedge$ and for $\vee$ are equivalent to one another, given the standard structural rules in the background.

The situation with $\to$ is similarly improved, as Exercises 7.4.3 and 7.4.5 will show. But perhaps the most welcome liberation comes with the rules for $\neg$, for the pair TND and EFQ can now be put in this simple way:

$$\Rightarrow \varphi,\neg\varphi \qquad \varphi,\neg\varphi \Rightarrow.$$

These rules are adequate by themselves. So also would be either of these pairs of rules, the first for introducing and eliminating on the left, and the second for introducing and eliminating on the right

$$\frac{\Gamma \Rightarrow \varphi,\Delta}{\Gamma,\neg\varphi \Rightarrow \Delta} \qquad \frac{\Gamma,\varphi \Rightarrow \Delta}{\Gamma \Rightarrow \neg\varphi,\Delta}$$

While we had to require Δ to be empty, we had the oddity that the pair on the left was *not* adequate, though the pair on the right was adequate. (See Exercises 7.2.2(*b*) and 7.4.3.) This, I hope, is sufficient illustration of how the new style of sequent allows us much more freedom in the formulation of rules for truth-functors, and a considerable increase in elegance. But let us now come back to the question with which this section began, of how to improve our formulation of the tableau rules as a sequent calculus.

Our first formulation of the method of semantic tableaux in Sections 4.1–2 made overt use of semantical vocabulary, with formulae being explicitly assigned a truth-value, T or F. This was clumsy in practice, so in Section 4.3 we introduced an equivalent but abbreviated version, which eliminated the semantical vocabulary, but at the cost of giving a special role to negation. Let us now return to the original version, which may be somewhat long-winded but is also very much more elegant, as we noted at the time. In the original version truth and falsehood are symmetrically treated, and there is no special role for negation. How, then, should we formulate suitable sequent calculus rules to fit the original version of the semantic tableaux?

At the root of the tableau we have a set of formulae, some assigned the value T and some assigned the value F. This represents the hypothesis that truth-values can indeed be assigned as indicated. But if the proof is successful, it shows that this hypothesis runs into a contradiction, and hence that truth-values cannot be assigned as indicated. Now suppose we write 'on the left' all those formulae assigned the value T in the root, and 'on the right' all those assigned the value F. Then what is proved is that there is no interpretation which gives T to all those on the left and F to all those on the right. In other words, what is proved is the Gentzen sequent which has on its left all the formulae assigned T in the root and on the right all the formulae assigned F in the root. And it is not just the result of the whole proof that can be seen in this way, for indeed each step of the proof can be seen as reasoning about Gentzen sequents. We begin with the hypothesis that a certain Gentzen sequent is not correct, and the steps of developing this hypothesis are inferences that in that case certain further sequents are not correct either. The case of negation provides a convenient example. Suppose that our hypothesis so far is that a formula ¬φ is true, that certain other formulae Γ are all true, and that other formulae Δ are all false. Applying the rule for negation then represents this inference:

Suppose $\Gamma, \neg\varphi \not\Rightarrow \Delta$
Then $\Gamma \not\Rightarrow \varphi, \Delta.$

Similarly, if our hypothesis had been that ¬φ is false, then applying the negation rule would be inferring thus:

Suppose $\Gamma \not\Rightarrow \neg\varphi,\Delta$
Then $\Gamma,\varphi \not\Rightarrow \Delta.$

(Notice that, as in Section 7.3, we have deleted from these inferences the superfluous repetition of $\neg\varphi$.) It is clear that all the original tableau rules can be rephrased in this way.

When we do reformulate all the rules thus, and then turn them upside-down so that they become rules of a standard sequent calculus, the result is this:

$$(\text{BS}) \ \frac{}{\Gamma,\varphi \Rightarrow \varphi,\Delta}$$

$$(\wedge\Rightarrow) \ \frac{\Gamma,\varphi,\psi \Rightarrow \Delta}{\Gamma,\varphi\wedge\psi \Rightarrow \Delta} \qquad\qquad (\Rightarrow\wedge) \ \frac{\Gamma \Rightarrow \varphi,\Delta \quad \Gamma \Rightarrow \psi,\Delta}{\Gamma \Rightarrow \varphi\wedge\psi,\Delta}$$

$$(\vee\Rightarrow) \ \frac{\Gamma,\varphi \Rightarrow \Delta \quad \Gamma,\psi \Rightarrow \Delta}{\Gamma,\varphi\vee\psi \Rightarrow \Delta} \qquad\qquad (\Rightarrow\vee) \ \frac{\Gamma \Rightarrow \varphi,\psi,\Delta}{\Gamma \Rightarrow \varphi\vee\psi,\Delta}$$

$$(\rightarrow\Rightarrow) \ \frac{\Gamma \Rightarrow \varphi,\Delta \quad \Gamma,\psi \Rightarrow \Delta}{\Gamma,\varphi\rightarrow\psi \Rightarrow \Delta} \qquad\qquad (\Rightarrow\rightarrow) \ \frac{\Gamma,\varphi \Rightarrow \psi,\Delta}{\Gamma \Rightarrow \varphi\rightarrow\psi,\Delta}$$

$$(\neg\Rightarrow) \ \frac{\Gamma \Rightarrow \varphi,\Delta}{\Gamma,\neg\varphi \Rightarrow \Delta} \qquad\qquad (\Rightarrow\neg) \ \frac{\Gamma,\varphi \Rightarrow \Delta}{\Gamma \Rightarrow \neg\varphi,\Delta}$$

$$(\forall\Rightarrow) \ \frac{\Gamma,\varphi(\alpha/\xi) \Rightarrow \Delta}{\Gamma,\forall\xi\varphi \Rightarrow \Delta} \qquad\qquad (\Rightarrow\forall) \ \frac{\Gamma \Rightarrow \varphi,\Delta}{\Gamma \Rightarrow \forall\xi\varphi(\xi/\alpha),\Delta}$$
$$\text{provided } \alpha \text{ is not in } \Gamma \text{ or } \Delta$$

$$(\exists\Rightarrow) \ \frac{\Gamma,\varphi \Rightarrow \Delta}{\Gamma,\exists\xi\varphi(\xi/\alpha) \Rightarrow \Delta} \qquad\qquad (\Rightarrow\exists) \ \frac{\Gamma \Rightarrow \varphi(\alpha/\xi),\Delta}{\Gamma \Rightarrow \exists\xi\varphi,\Delta}$$
$$\text{provided } \alpha \text{ is not in } \Gamma \text{ or } \Delta$$

As before, all our rules are introduction rules, but they now pair nicely into rules for introducing on the left, labelled $(*\Rightarrow)$, and on the right, labelled $(\Rightarrow*)$, for each truth-functor or quantifier $*$. Also, the negation sign is no longer playing any special role, but occurs only in the pair of rules that deal with it. This calculus, then, represents in a much nicer way the principles that are at work in a tableau proof. As before we do not have the structural rules ASS and THIN, but instead the rule BS, which does the same work. Also, as before we do not have the rule CUT, since tableau proofs do not use any such rule. For this reason, the calculus is known as Gentzen's cut-free sequent calculus. Finally, the rules do include INT, if we need to state that rule separately, and as formulated here they need to include CONTR. But, as in Exercise 7.3.2, we could avoid this by reformulating ($\forall\Rightarrow$) and ($\Rightarrow\exists$) in this way:

$$(\forall\Rightarrow')\ \frac{\Gamma,\forall\xi\varphi,\varphi(\alpha/\xi)\Rightarrow\Delta}{\Gamma,\forall\xi\varphi\Rightarrow\Delta} \qquad (\exists\Rightarrow')\ \frac{\Gamma\Rightarrow\varphi(\alpha/\xi),\exists\xi\varphi,\Delta}{\Gamma\Rightarrow\exists\xi\varphi,\Delta}$$

Given this reformulation, and for completeness adding INT explicitly, the rules stated here exactly match the rules of the original tableau system, so it is easy to argue that whatever sequents can be proved in the one system can also be proved in the other.

EXERCISES

7.4.1. Rewrite the proof, given on p. 162, of the sequent

$$\forall x\exists y(Fx\wedge Gy)\Rightarrow\exists y\forall x(Fx\wedge Gy)$$

as a proof in Gentzen's cut-free sequent calculus.

7.4.2. Assuming all the standard rules for a calculus of Gentzen sequents, verify the assertion made in the text, that the various sets of rules cited for $\wedge$ and for $\vee$ on p. 294 are interdeducible.

7.4.3. Assuming all the standard structural rules, show that the Gentzen rules ($\rightarrow\Rightarrow$) and ($\Rightarrow\rightarrow$) are interdeducible with each of the following sets:

$$(a)\ \frac{\Gamma\Rightarrow\varphi,\Delta \quad \text{AND} \quad \Gamma,\psi\Rightarrow\Delta}{\Gamma,\varphi\rightarrow\psi\Rightarrow\Delta}$$

$$(b)\ \frac{\Gamma,\varphi\Rightarrow\psi,\Delta}{\Gamma\Rightarrow\varphi\rightarrow\psi,\Delta}$$

$(c)\ \psi\Rightarrow\varphi\rightarrow\psi \qquad \Rightarrow\varphi,\varphi\rightarrow\psi \qquad \varphi,\varphi\rightarrow\psi\Rightarrow\psi$

7.4.4. Assuming all the standard structural rules, consider this pair of rules for negation:

$$\frac{\Gamma, \varphi \Rightarrow \Delta}{\Gamma \Rightarrow \neg\varphi, \Delta}.$$

(*a*) Suppose first that in these rules Δ is required to be empty. Show that in that case the sequent $\neg\neg P \Rightarrow P$ is not provable. [Method: consider this three-valued table for negation:

φ	$\neg\varphi$
1	0
$\frac{1}{2}$	0
0	1

(Compare table VI on p. 198.) Count a sequent $\Gamma \Rightarrow \psi$ as correct iff the minimum of the values of the formulae in Γ is less than or equal to the value of ψ. Verify that on this interpretation the structural rules remain sound, and the two rules for $\neg$ are both sound, but the proposed sequent is not correct.]

(*b*) Allowing Δ to be non-empty, prove the sequent $\neg\neg P \Rightarrow P$. [Hint: you will find it useful to use CUT on $\Rightarrow P, \neg\neg P$ and $\neg P \Rightarrow \neg\neg\neg P$.]

(*c*) Show that the pair of rules in question is equivalent to the Gentzen pair $(\neg\Rightarrow)$ and $(\Rightarrow\neg)$. [For the argument in one direction you will need part (*b*); for the other direction you will need $P \Rightarrow \neg\neg P$.]

7.4.5. (This exercise continues Exercise 5.7.2.) Let GC be a sequent calculus for Gentzen sequents whose only truth-functor is $\rightarrow$. It has the standard structural rules and in addition just $(\rightarrow\Rightarrow)$ and $(\Rightarrow\rightarrow)$.

(*a*) Show that $(\Rightarrow\rightarrow)$ can equivalently be replaced by the pair of rules

$$\frac{\Gamma, \varphi \Rightarrow \Delta}{\Gamma \Rightarrow \varphi{\rightarrow}\psi, \Delta} \qquad \frac{\Gamma \Rightarrow \psi, \Delta}{\Gamma \Rightarrow \varphi{\rightarrow}\psi, \Delta}$$

(*b*) Let φ be a formula with $\rightarrow$ as its only truth-functor, and consider any assignment of truth-values to the letters in φ. Let Γ be the set of letters assigned T, and Δ be the set of letters assigned F. Prove:

> If φ is true on this assignment, then $\Gamma \Rightarrow \varphi, \Delta$ is provable in GC.
> If φ is false on this assignment, then $\Gamma, \varphi \Rightarrow \Delta$ is provable in GC.

[Method: use induction on the length of φ.]

(*c*) Deduce from (*b*) that if φ is a tautology, with $\rightarrow$ as its only truth-functor, then $\Rightarrow \varphi$ is provable in GC.

(*d*) Deduce from (*c*) that if $\Gamma \vDash \Delta$, and if $\rightarrow$ is the only truth-functor in Γ and in Δ, then $\Gamma \Rightarrow \Delta$ is provable in GC. [Hints: (1) you can define $\vee$ in terms of $\rightarrow$; (2) you will need to derive the following two further rules of GC:

$$\frac{\Gamma \Rightarrow \varphi \rightarrow \psi, \Delta}{\Gamma, \varphi \Rightarrow \psi, \Delta} \qquad \frac{\Gamma \Rightarrow (\varphi \rightarrow \psi) \rightarrow \psi, \Delta}{\Gamma \Rightarrow \varphi, \psi, \Delta}$$

Note, incidentally, that a rather quicker proof of this same result is contained in the reasoning that immediately follows.]

7.5. Comparison of Systems

As we showed in Chapter 4, the tableau system provides a complete proof procedure: every correct sequent can be proved in it. Our argument in Chapter 4 was directed to the second version of the tableau system, more convenient in practice, but giving a special role to negation. But it is easily shown that whatever can be proved in the second version of the tableau system can also be proved in the first (Exercises 4.3.1 and 4.3.2), so it follows that the first version of the tableau system is complete too. It is also clear that whatever can be proved in the first version of the tableau system can also be proved in Gentzen's cut-free sequent calculus, since we have just seen how the two correspond, rule for rule. It follows that this sequent calculus is also complete. Admittedly there is a difference between the two systems over what is to count as a sequent. Gentzen's system has sequents $\Gamma \Rightarrow \Delta$, where there may be many formulae on the right, whereas the second tableau system (to which our completeness proof applied) is primarily concerned with sequents $\Gamma \Rightarrow$ which have no formulae on the right. But, provided that standard rules for negation are available, this difference is of no importance. For if we let $\neg\Delta$ stand for the set of formulae which are the negations of the formulae in Δ we have

$$\Gamma, \neg\Delta \vDash \quad \text{iff} \quad \Gamma \vDash \Delta.$$

Any system, then, which can prove all correct sequents of the one sort can automatically prove all correct sequents of the other sort too.

Not only are the first tableau system, and Gentzen's cut-free sequent calculus, complete as wholes; they are also complete part by part, in the way we desired, but did not achieve, for our system of natural deduction. That is: the rules for each logical sign are by themselves complete for all sequents containing that sign and no other, and the various combinations of these rules are complete for all sequents containing the corresponding combinations of logical signs. This point is especially clear for the tableau rules, for when we are drawing up a tableau for a given set of formulae there simply is no opportunity to use any rules other than the rules for the logical signs in those

299

formulae. Other rules just cannot be brought to bear. The same applies too to Gentzen's corresponding sequent calculus, because every rule in that calculus is an introduction rule, and so a sign that is introduced into the proof at any point cannot later be got rid of. It must therefore appear in the final sequent proved. (Note here that we rely not just on the point that no sign is furnished with an elimination rule of its own, but also on the fact that CUT is absent;[4] for CUT is a kind of general elimination rule.)

Now we have not yet proved that the rules for natural deduction in Chapter 6 are complete—complete, that is, for the sequents standardly considered in natural deduction, namely those with just one formula on the right. (I shall call these 'natural deduction sequents'.) If our concern were simply with the completeness of that system as a whole, then we could abbreviate labour by observing that we do already have an independent proof that its rules for truth-functors are complete. This is because other truth-functors can be defined in terms of $\to$ and $\neg$, the natural deduction rules for $\to$ and $\neg$ are easily shown to imply the three axioms and the one rule of inference of our axiomatic system of Section 5.2, and that axiomatic system was proved to be complete in Section 5.5. (We also showed in Exercise 6.2.4 that the natural deduction rules for $\wedge$ and $\neg$ form a complete system, and again other truth-functors can be defined in terms of $\wedge$ and $\neg$.) Since, then, the natural deduction rules for the truth-functors are both sound and complete, and since the tableau rules for the truth-functors are likewise both sound and complete, it follows that whatever can be proved with the one set of rules can also be proved with the other. So the only task remaining would be to compare the quantifier rules of the two systems, and in particular to show that the natural deduction rules for the quantifiers imply those of Gentzen's cut-free system. Now, if we may assume the rules for negation as background rules, this is very simple. For in that case any Gentzen sequent (save for the empty sequent) may be reformulated as a natural deduction sequent, by the method just indicated. And if we do confine attention just to these sequents, then the rules ($\forall$I) and ($\exists$I) for natural deduction are just the same as the rules ($\Rightarrow\forall$) are ($\Rightarrow\exists$) of Gentzen's system, while the rules ($\forall$E) and ($\exists$E) are easily shown to be interdeducible with ($\forall\Rightarrow$) and ($\exists\Rightarrow$), as we observed in Exercise 7.2.1. So it follows that our natural deduction rules are also a complete set, and whatever can be proved in either system can also be proved in the other.

---

[4] Gentzen proved that adding CUT to his cut-free system would not increase the provable sequents (his 'cut-elimination' theorem). A version of that proof, but applied directly to tableaux, is given in the appendix to Chapter 4.

These last remarks compare the two systems as wholes, but it is instructive also to compare them part by part, and for this purpose I begin by noting an interesting feature of the Gentzen system. If we restrict attention to
sequents in which every formula is in prenex normal form (PNF), then any
sequent provable in Gentzen's system also has a proof in which all applications of quantifier rules come after all applications of rules for truth-
functors. In addition, all applications of the rule for basic sequents can be
confined to atomic formulae, so that no quantifiers get introduced in this
way. Such a proof therefore contains a sequent called the *midsequent* which
is quantifier-free, and such that all sequents following it are obtained just by
applying the rules for ∀ and ∃, and perhaps contraction. I outline the proof
of this point, leaving many of the details as an exercise.

First we show that the rule for basic sequents can be confined to atomic
formulae. The argument is by induction on the length of the formulae introduced by a use of that rule. We have two kinds of case to consider, (*a*) when
the formula is the main formula of that rule, i.e. the one which appears on
both sides of ⟹, (*b*) when the formula is an extra formula, appearing on one
side of the sequent only. For illustration, I give two clauses of the induction,
for ∧ and for ∀, first for case (*a*) and second for case (*b*) with the extra formula on the right.[5] (It will be seen that the argument for case (*b*) is merely
half of that for (*a*).)

Replace   by

$(a)(i)$ (BS) $\dfrac{}{\Gamma,\psi\wedge\chi \Rightarrow \psi\wedge\chi,\Delta}$ $(BS)\ \overline{}\quad (BS)\ \overline{}$

$$(BS)\ \dfrac{}{(\Rightarrow\wedge)\ \dfrac{\Gamma,\psi \Rightarrow \psi,\Delta \qquad \Gamma,\chi \Rightarrow \chi,\Delta}{(\wedge\Rightarrow)\ \dfrac{\Gamma,\psi,\chi \Rightarrow \psi\wedge\chi,\Delta}{\Gamma,\psi\wedge\chi \Rightarrow \psi\wedge\chi,\Delta}}}$$

$(a)(ii)$ (BS) $\dfrac{}{\Gamma,\forall\xi\psi \Rightarrow \forall\xi\psi,\Delta}$

$$(BS)\ \dfrac{}{(\forall\Rightarrow)\ \dfrac{\Gamma,\psi(\alpha/\xi) \Rightarrow \psi(\alpha/\xi),\Delta}{(\Rightarrow\forall)\ \dfrac{\Gamma,\forall\xi\psi \Rightarrow \psi(\alpha/\xi),\Delta}{\Gamma,\forall\xi\psi \Rightarrow \forall\xi\psi,\Delta}}}$$

Choose α so that it is not in Γ or Δ or ψ

---

[5] It may be noted that case (*a*) merely repeats what has already been proved as Exercise 4.2.2.

$(b)(i)$ $(BS) \dfrac{}{\Gamma \Rightarrow \Delta, \psi \wedge \chi}$ $(BS) \dfrac{}{\Gamma \Rightarrow \Delta, \psi}$ $(BS) \dfrac{}{\Gamma \Rightarrow \Delta, \chi}$

$(\Rightarrow \wedge) \dfrac{}{\Gamma \Rightarrow \Delta, \psi \wedge \chi}$

$(b)(ii)$ $(BS) \dfrac{}{\Gamma \Rightarrow \Delta, \forall \xi \psi}$ $(BS) \dfrac{\Gamma \Rightarrow \Delta, \psi(\alpha/\xi)}{}$

$(\Rightarrow \forall) \dfrac{\Gamma \Rightarrow \Delta, \psi(\alpha/\xi)}{\Gamma \Rightarrow \Delta, \forall \xi \psi}$

Choose α so that it is not in Γ or Δ or ψ

(It should be noted that steps of interchange have been left tacit throughout.) The other cases are all equally simple, as you are invited to discover.

With this point established, we now need to show that the proof can be rearranged further, so that all rules for truth-functors precede all rules for quantifiers. But this point is very obvious once we note that, by hypothesis, the formulae are all in PNF. So once a quantifier is prefixed to a formula, no truth-functor is ever applied to *that* formula. (Only further quantifiers can be prefixed to it.) Consequently, that formula must be what is called a *side* formula in any subsequent application of a rule for truth-functors, i.e. one that is not itself altered by the inference. This makes it obvious that the rules could have been applied in the reverse order. For example, our proof may have an application of $(\forall \Rightarrow)$ followed by one of $(\wedge \Rightarrow)$ in this way:

$$(\forall \Rightarrow) \dfrac{\Gamma, \varphi(\alpha/\xi), \psi, \chi \Rightarrow \Delta}{\Gamma, \forall \xi \varphi, \psi, \chi \Rightarrow \Delta}$$
$$(\wedge \Rightarrow) \dfrac{\Gamma, \forall \xi \varphi, \psi, \chi \Rightarrow \Delta}{\Gamma, \forall \xi \varphi, \psi \wedge \chi \Rightarrow \Delta}$$

It is evident at once that this can be replaced by

$$(\wedge \Rightarrow) \dfrac{\Gamma, \varphi(\alpha/\xi), \psi, \chi \Rightarrow \Delta}{\Gamma, \varphi(\alpha/\xi), \psi \wedge \chi \Rightarrow \Delta}$$
$$(\forall \Rightarrow) \dfrac{\Gamma, \varphi(\alpha/\xi), \psi \wedge \chi \Rightarrow \Delta}{\Gamma, \forall \xi \varphi, \psi \wedge \chi \Rightarrow \Delta}$$

(Again, steps of interchange are left tacit.) The position is entirely similar with the other cases, and it is clear that by successive transformations of this kind the desired position must eventually be reached.

Now let us come to our comparison between the rules of natural deduction and the rules of Gentzen's sequent calculus. The argument at the beginning of this section, showing that the natural deduction system is complete, can easily be extended to yield this result: for any combination of truth-functors and quantifiers, the natural deduction rules for these signs, *plus* the natural deduction rules for negation, form a complete set of rules for natural deduction sequents containing just those signs. But here it is essential to include a separate mention of the negation rules. In fact we have already seen, in Chapter 5 (p. 199), that the standard rules for $\rightarrow$ are not by themselves complete for $\rightarrow$, but need supplementing by the negation rules. We also saw in Exercise 6.3.4 that the same holds for the combination of logical signs, $\vee$ and $\forall$. Besides, the method of argument that we are here employing depends upon using negation to transform Gentzen sequents into natural deduction sequents, and so would not be available without the rules for negation. So from here onwards I set negation to one side, and consider both systems without their negation rules.[6]

It turns out that the two limitations already mentioned are the only limitations of the natural deduction rules. Combinations including $\rightarrow$ but not $\neg$ will not be complete, and need no further exploration. Considering, then, just $\wedge, \vee, \forall, \exists$, we already know that the combination of $\vee$ with $\forall$ is not complete, but we shall find that all other combinations are. That is, the natural deduction rules for $\wedge, \vee, \exists$ are complete, both severally and jointly, for natural deduction sequents containing any combination of these logical signs, and the same is true of the rules for $\wedge, \exists, \forall$. I prove these points in order. In each case my argument will assume that we are dealing with sequents in PNF, so that the Gentzen proof may be assumed to contain a quantifier-free midsequent. But this is no real restriction, for it is easily checked that the natural deduction rules for $\wedge, \vee, \exists$ suffice to show that every formula containing only those logical signs has an equivalent in PNF, and similarly with the rules for $\wedge, \exists, \forall$.

$\wedge, \vee, \exists$. We have already noted that the rules for $\wedge$ and $\vee$ are complete for those signs, both severally and jointly (Exercise 6.2.2; another proof is outlined in Exercise 7.5.2). Consider, then, any correct natural deduction sequent $\Gamma \vDash \varphi$, containing only $\wedge, \vee, \exists$ as logical signs. Since the sequent is correct, there is a proof of $\Gamma \Rightarrow \varphi$ in Gentzen's sequent calculus, and we may assume that this proof has a quantifier-free midsequent, say $\Gamma' \Rightarrow \Delta$. It is easily seen that Δ cannot be empty, so let us write δ for the single formula which is the disjunction of all formulae in Δ. Then $\Gamma' \Rightarrow \delta$ is a correct natural deduction sequent, containing only $\wedge$ and $\vee$ as logical signs, and hence is provable by the natural deduction rules for $\wedge$ and $\vee$. So what we have to

---

[6] The standard natural deduction rules without negation are all correct for intuitionist logic (see Ch. 5 n. 8 and Exercises 5.4.3, 5.4.4, and 6.3.4). Consequently what follows is, in a way, a comparison between intuitionist logic and classical logic, excluding negation.

show is that the Gentzen proof from the midsequent $\Gamma' \Rightarrow \Delta$ to the final sequent $\Gamma \Rightarrow \varphi$ can be matched by a corresponding proof in natural deduction from $\Gamma' \Rightarrow \delta$ to $\Gamma \Rightarrow \varphi$. The Gentzen proof will contain just applications of ($\exists\Rightarrow$), which alter the formulae in Γ', applications of ($\Rightarrow\exists$), which alter the formulae in Δ, and otherwise only interchanges and contractions.

From the natural deduction rules for $\vee$ we easily deduce that $\vee$ is associative, commutative, and idempotent. This ensures that interchanges and contractions within Δ can be matched by corresponding changes within the disjunction δ. From the rules ($\vee$E), ($\exists$I), ($\vee$I) we easily deduce this rule in natural deduction:

$$\frac{\Gamma \Rightarrow \varphi(\alpha/\xi) \vee \delta}{\Gamma \Rightarrow \exists\xi\varphi \vee \delta}$$

This ensures that changes to formulae in Δ brought about by applying ($\Rightarrow\exists$) can be matched in natural deduction by corresponding changes to the disjunction δ. And, of course, changes to formulae in Γ' brought about by applying ($\exists\Rightarrow$) can equally be brought about by applying ($\exists$E), since these are the same rule. It follows that each step of the Gentzen proof, from the midsequent on, can be matched in natural deduction, and this is the desired result.

I observe that this argument establishes that the rules for $\wedge,\vee,\exists$ are together complete for sequents containing all three of these signs, and that the rules for $\vee,\exists$ are complete for sequents containing these two signs. It does not, in fact, establish the completeness of the rules for $\wedge,\exists$, since the argument relies upon the rules for $\vee$ for its method of transforming Gentzen sequents to natural deduction sequents. But the case for $\wedge,\exists$ will be a consequence of the next argument, which uses a different method.

$\wedge, \forall, \exists$. Assume that $\Gamma \vDash \varphi$ is a correct sequent, containing only $\wedge,\forall,\exists$ as logical signs. Then as before there is a proof of it in the Gentzen sequent calculus, with a quantifier-free midsequent, say $\Gamma' \Rightarrow \Delta$. But in this case we show that we can confine attention to just one formula in Δ. For first, if there are several formulae in Δ, then it is clear from the form of the rules ($\Rightarrow\forall$) and ($\Rightarrow\exists$) that as the proof proceeds *each* of these formulae must be transformed eventually into the conclusion φ of the final sequent, and then they are amalgamated by contraction. And second, since the midsequent $\Gamma' \Rightarrow \Delta$ contains only $\wedge$, it is quite easy to show (Exercise 7.5.3) that there must be at least one formula in Δ, say φ', such that $\Gamma' \Rightarrow \varphi'$ is also provable. We can therefore take this as our midsequent, and discard any other formulae in Δ, so that the proof from the midsequent on uses natural deduction sequents throughout. But we have already observed that in this context the quantifier rules of natural deduction, and of Gentzen's calculus, are interdeducible with one another. This completes the argument.

We may conclude that the two failures of completeness already noted—namely in the rules for →, and in the rules for ∨ and ∀ together—are the only two weaknesses of this kind in the standard natural deduction system. I accordingly end this section with a brief reflection upon them.

It may be said that the position with the rules for → is not particularly disturbing. From a philosophical point of view one can argue that → is a poor reflection of the 'if' that occurs in natural languages, and that it is hardly surprising if the natural deduction rules (attempting to be 'natural') fit 'if' better than →. The sequents which are correct for →, but not provable from these rules, do indeed strike one as somewhat 'unnatural' (i.e. unnatural for 'if'). Besides, from the logician's point of view it may be said that the defect in the standard rules is quite easily remedied, simply by adopting other and stronger rules instead (e.g. Exercise 7.5.4). These other rules do not strike us as being particularly natural, but why should that matter? By contrast, the position with ∨ and ∀ is altogether more unsettling. There is no good philosophical reason for supposing that the meaning which the logician attaches to these symbols is in some way suspect, and in this case the defect appears not to be remediable. In the setting provided by natural deduction, there is no way (so far as I am aware) of formulating separate rules for ∨ and for ∀, which are both sound and complete for those two symbols when taken together.

The blame for this must fall on the general setting provided by natural deduction, i.e. on the fact that it restricts attention to sequents with just one formula on the right. It must be admitted that this is a very natural way to think of an argument, a proof, an inference, and so on. Such a thing, we say, may have many premises, but it can only have one conclusion. However, we have now seen that this very natural way of thinking introduces an asymmetry which is seldom pleasing (e.g. with the rule (∨E)) and in this particular case distinctly unwanted. If things are to be presented both neatly and effectively, then we need the extra expressive power that Gentzen sequents give us. I do not mean that we also need the particular way of reasoning with such sequents that is given by Gentzen's cut-free calculus. That calculus can be useful for particular purposes, as we have seen, mainly because its use of structural rules can be so tightly restricted. But there are also other and more liberal ways of reasoning with Gentzen sequents, as illustrated at the beginning of Section 7.4. My claim is just that the sequents themselves, with several formulae on the right, need to be available to us if we are to be able to say what we wish to.

It is true that these sequents are not very familiar to most people, but that, of course, is remediable. It is also true that we do think of an argument as having just one conclusion, and if we sometimes speak of there being several conclusions, we mean that the premisses imply *each* of these conclusions. This is not what a Gentzen sequent says. Rather, it represents an argument that distinguishes cases in this way: given these premisses, it may be that P, or it may be that Q; we cannot say which, but it must be one or the other. Finally, it is true that logicians have not, on the whole,[7] paid much attention to *practical* ways of reasoning with Gentzen sequents; they tend— as I have done so far—to consider them only in the context of a sequent calculus, and, of course, a sequent calculus is in practice a *very* cumbersome method of writing proofs. But this too is something that can be remedied, as my next section will show.

EXERCISES

7.5.1. Prove the assertion in the text that, for any combination of truth-functors and quantifiers, the natural deduction rules for those signs, *plus* the natural deduction rules for negation, form a complete set of rules for natural deduction sequents containing only the logical signs in question. [Method: the argument on p. 300 shows that, given negation, the natural deduction rules for the quantifiers imply the corresponding Gentzen rules; you need to apply the same line of thought to the truth-functors.]

7.5.2. Assume that the natural deduction rules for $\wedge$ are complete for all natural deduction sequents with $\wedge$ as their only logical symbol, and similarly for $\vee$ (Exercise 6.2.2). Show that the two sets of rules together are complete for all natural deduction sequents containing both $\wedge$ and $\vee$, but no other logical symbols. [Method: transform every correct Gentzen sequent into a natural deduction sequent by replacing the several formulae on the right by the single formula that is their disjunction. Then show that the natural deduction rules imply the corresponding Gentzen rules under this transformation, and infer that any Gentzen proof involving just these logical symbols can be matched by a natural deduction proof.]

7.5.3. Show that, if $\Gamma \vDash \Delta$, and the only logical symbol in this sequent is $\wedge$, then there is some formula φ in Δ such that $\Gamma \vDash \varphi$. [Method: use induction on the num-

---

[7] An exception is Shoesmith and Smiley (1978). My discussion in the next section is indebted to their much more thorough treatment.

ber of occurrences of $\wedge$ in Δ. For the case where there are none, the argument is straightforward; for the case where there is one or more, note that

$$\Gamma \models \varphi \wedge \psi, \Delta \quad \text{iff} \quad \Gamma \models \varphi, \Delta \quad \text{and} \quad \Gamma \models \psi, \Delta.]$$

7.5.4. Consider a sequent calculus for natural deduction which in place of the rule ($\rightarrow$E) has this rule:

$$(*) \frac{\Gamma, \varphi \rightarrow \psi \Rightarrow \varphi \quad \Delta \Rightarrow \varphi \rightarrow \chi}{\Gamma, \Delta \Rightarrow \chi}$$

(*a*) Deduce from (*) alone the sequent

$$\varphi, \varphi \rightarrow \chi \Rightarrow \chi.$$

(*b*) Using both this and ($\rightarrow$I), deduce further from (*) the sequent

$$(\varphi \rightarrow \psi) \rightarrow \varphi \Rightarrow \varphi.$$

(*c*) Argue from (*a*) and (*b*) that the two rules ($\rightarrow$I) and (*) are by themselves complete for $\rightarrow$. [Method: use Exercises 5.7.2 and 7.4.5.]

7.6. Reasoning with Gentzen Sequents

In natural deduction, as first presented in Chapter 6, proofs have a tree structure with the branches growing upwards. By contrast, the tableau proofs of Chapter 4 have a tree structure with branches growing downwards. When reasoning in practice with Gentzen sequents, and avoiding the labour of a full sequent calculus, one needs proofs which branch both upwards and downwards. The structure as a whole is a proof of the sequent which has on its left all the highest formulae of the structure, with nothing above them, and which has on its right all the lowest formulae of the structure, with nothing below them. So far as I am aware, the first person to propose proofs of this kind was W. C. Kneale (1956). Before we consider details of just what structure such a proof should have, let us look at a simple example to get the general idea.

As in natural deduction, Kneale's rules are presented as rules for the introduction and the elimination of whatever logical sign is involved. Let us begin just with his rules for $\wedge$ and $\vee$, which correspond to the Gentzen sequents

$$\varphi, \psi \Rightarrow \varphi \wedge \psi \qquad\qquad \varphi \wedge \psi \Rightarrow \varphi, \quad \varphi \wedge \psi \Rightarrow \psi$$
$$\varphi \Rightarrow \varphi \vee \psi, \quad \psi \Rightarrow \varphi \vee \psi \qquad \varphi \vee \psi \Rightarrow \varphi, \psi.$$

If we rephrase these in the form in which they will actually be used in proofs, and take over the familiar titles from natural deduction, they are

$$(\wedge I)\frac{\varphi \quad \psi}{\varphi \wedge \psi} \qquad\qquad (\wedge E)\frac{\varphi \wedge \psi}{\varphi}, \ \frac{\varphi \wedge \psi}{\psi}$$

$$(\vee I)\frac{\varphi}{\varphi \vee \psi}, \ \frac{\psi}{\varphi \vee \psi} \qquad (\vee E)\frac{\varphi \vee \psi}{\varphi \quad \psi}$$

Evidently $(\wedge I)$, $(\wedge E)$, and $(\vee I)$ are entirely familiar, but this version of $(\vee E)$ is new, and exploits the new idea that proofs may branch downwards as well as upwards. To see the rules in action, let us begin by considering a proof of the distribution law:

$$(\varphi \vee \psi) \wedge (\varphi \vee \chi) \Rightarrow \varphi \vee (\psi \wedge \chi).$$

Since we are now dealing in Gentzen sequents, the gist of this law may be simplified to

$$\varphi \vee \psi, \varphi \vee \chi \Rightarrow \varphi, \psi \wedge \chi.$$

A proof of the simplified version is this:

We can reconstruct from this a proof of the original version, which has just one sequent on either side, by adding extra steps on the top and on the bottom, thus:

You should compare this proof with the proof in natural deduction given on p. 247. It ought to be clear that while the basic idea of the proof is the same in each case, the present version has a structure which is easier to take in.

After this one example, let us come back to the general question of what structure a proof in this system must have. Something must be said on this point in order to rule out such obviously fallacious 'proofs' as the simple structure

$$\frac{\varphi \vee \psi}{\varphi \qquad \qquad \psi}$$
$$\overline{\varphi \wedge \psi}$$

or the slightly more complex but equally fallacious structure

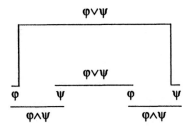

To deal with this kind of fallacy, Kneale stipulates that 'in the working out of [proofs] it is essential that token formulae which are already connected, either directly by one single horizontal line or indirectly through several horizontal lines, should not be connected again in any way.' (Kneale and Kneale 1962: 543). This is a simple ruling, and it does ensure that only correct sequents can be proved.

Since these structures are unfamiliar, I shall now describe them in more detail. Let us say that a position in a proof at which a formula may be written is a 'node' in the proof. Then a proof-structure is a finite array of nodes and horizontal lines obeying these conditions:

(1)   The structure may consist of just one single node and nothing more. But if there is more than one node, then every node is immediately above a line, or immediately below a line, or both. Moreover, every line is immediately below one or two nodes, or immediately above one or two nodes, or both. A node that is not immediately below any line is called a highest node; a node that is not immediately above any line is called a lowest node.

(2)   A path in the proof-structure is an alternating series of nodes and lines, beginning with a node, and such that: (a) no node or line

occurs more than once in the series; (*b*) every node, except the last, is followed by a line that is immediately above or below it, and every line is followed by a node that is immediately above or below it. It is said to be a path between its first member and its last. Then Kneale's ruling on the structure of proofs can be put in this way: between any two nodes in the proof-structure, there is one and only one path.

Finally, a proof is a proof-structure in which every node is occupied by a formula, in such a way that the several formulae immediately above and below the same horizontal line are related to one another in one of the ways specified by the various rules of inference. It is a proof of the sequent which has on its left all the formulae at its highest nodes, and on its right all the formulae at its lowest nodes.

It can be shown that, given rules of inference that are correct, any sequent proved by such a proof must also be correct (Exercise 7.6.2). But unfortunately it is not true that all correct sequents can be proved by such a proof. To see the difficulty let us consider another of the laws of distribution:

$$(\varphi \wedge \psi) \vee (\varphi \wedge \chi) \Rightarrow \varphi \wedge (\psi \vee \chi).$$

We expect the proof to split into two parts, one showing that

$$(\varphi \wedge \psi) \vee (\varphi \wedge \chi) \Rightarrow \varphi$$

and the other showing that

$$(\varphi \wedge \psi) \vee (\varphi \wedge \chi) \Rightarrow \psi \vee \chi.$$

There is no problem about the proof of these two parts individually. Here they are:

$$(\varphi \wedge \psi) \vee (\varphi \wedge \chi)$$

$\varphi \wedge \psi$	$\varphi \wedge \chi$
φ	φ

$$(\varphi \wedge \psi) \vee (\varphi \wedge \chi)$$

$\varphi \wedge \psi$	$\varphi \wedge \chi$
ψ	χ
$\psi \vee \chi$	$\psi \vee \chi$

But when we seek to put the two together, to form a proof of the sequent we desire, there is no evident way of doing so. The only suggestion that comes to hand is this:

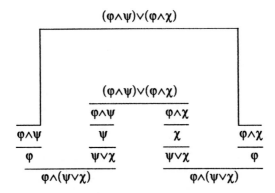

But, as we have observed, this is not a permitted proof structure.

The cause of the difficulty is quite straightforward: the rules do not allow us to perform a contraction within a proof. We apply contraction when we *report* one of these diagrammatic proofs as establishing this or that sequent; for example, the proof

$$\frac{(\varphi\wedge\psi)\vee(\varphi\wedge\chi)}{\underset{\varphi}{\overline{\varphi\wedge\psi}}\qquad \underset{\varphi}{\overline{\varphi\wedge\chi}}}$$

is taken as establishing the sequent

$$(\varphi\wedge\psi)\vee(\varphi\wedge\chi)\Rightarrow\varphi,$$

even though the proof-structure has two lowest nodes, while the sequent has only one formula on the right. So at this point we are in effect employing a contraction (on the right). But at the moment we have no way of doing this *within* a proof.

The remedy is therefore equally straightforward: we must liberalize the rules so that contractions are allowed. As a 'structural' rule for all proofs in the new notation, I therefore set down

$$\text{(CL)}\ \frac{\varphi}{\varphi\quad\varphi}\qquad\text{(CR)}\ \frac{\varphi\quad\varphi}{\varphi}$$

311

(Here 'CL' is short for 'contraction on the left', and 'CR' for 'contraction on the right'.) To illustrate how the new rules work, we may now finish our proof of the sequent

$$(\varphi\wedge\psi)\vee(\varphi\wedge\chi) \Rightarrow \varphi\wedge(\psi\vee\chi).$$

Here is the result:

$$
\begin{array}{c}
\text{(CL)} \dfrac{(\varphi\wedge\psi)\vee(\varphi\wedge\chi)}{(\varphi\wedge\psi)\vee(\varphi\wedge\chi)} \qquad\qquad (\varphi\wedge\psi)\vee(\varphi\wedge\chi)
\end{array}
$$

In this proof the individual proofs of the two sequents

$$(\varphi\wedge\psi)\vee(\varphi\wedge\chi) \Rightarrow \varphi$$
$$(\varphi\wedge\psi)\vee(\varphi\wedge\chi) \Rightarrow \psi\vee\chi$$

are reproduced once each, and each of them is taken to end with a step of (CR). They are then tied together with a single step of (∧I) at the bottom of the proof, and to bring out the fact that each has the same premiss they are also tied together with a step of (CL) at the top.

The intended use of these new rules (CL) and (CR) does, of course, conflict with the account given earlier of what a proof-structure is, so we must revise it in this way. Retaining the same definition of a path between two nodes, clause (2) must now be modified to this:

(2′) Between any two nodes in the proof-structure there is at least one path; and there is more than one path only if at least one of the lines in each path is a step of contraction.

An alternative way of saying the same thing would be this: the result of deleting from a proof all horizontal lines marking steps of contraction will fragment the whole structure into a number of substructures, and these substructures must then be proof structures as originally defined.

With contraction now catered for in the definition of a proof-structure, let us turn briefly to the other structural rules. Interchange is automatically covered by the fact that, when we have a rule of inference which has two separate formulae above the line, or two separate formulae below, we allow those formulae to occur in either order. That is, we make no distinction here between the left and the right positions. Assumption is also a consequence of the definition of a proof, since a formula φ standing on its own is a proof, namely a proof of the sequent φ ⟹ φ. Cutting too is built into the account, in the same way as with natural deduction, since one can always put one proof on top of another. But we are missing any automatic provision for Thinning. I therefore adopt two rules which explicitly provide it, the first for thinning on the left and the second for thinning on the right.

$$(\text{TL}) \frac{\varphi \quad \psi}{\varphi} \qquad (\text{TR}) \frac{\varphi}{\varphi \quad \psi}$$

Of course, the first is provable from the rules for ∧, and the second is provable from the rules for ∨, but we may wish to consider systems which lack either ∧ or ∨.

Let us now return to the rules for the truth-functors. For ease of reference I repeat here the rules for ∧ and ∨ that we have seen already, and I add rules for → and ¬ that are again taken from Kneale (with a trivial modification).

$$(\wedge\text{I}) \frac{\varphi \quad \psi}{\varphi\wedge\psi} \qquad\qquad (\wedge\text{E}) \frac{\varphi\wedge\psi}{\varphi}, \quad \frac{\varphi\wedge\psi}{\psi}$$

$$(\vee\text{I}) \frac{\varphi}{\varphi\vee\psi}, \quad \frac{\varphi}{\varphi\vee\psi} \qquad\qquad (\vee\text{E}) \frac{\varphi\vee\psi}{\varphi \quad \psi}$$

$$(\rightarrow\text{I}) \frac{}{\varphi \quad \varphi\rightarrow\psi}, \quad \frac{\psi}{\varphi\rightarrow\psi} \qquad\qquad (\rightarrow\text{E}) \frac{\varphi \quad \varphi\rightarrow\psi}{\psi}$$

$$(\neg\text{I}) \frac{}{\varphi \quad \neg\varphi} \qquad\qquad (\neg\text{E}) \frac{\varphi \quad \neg\varphi}{}$$

The rules for → are worth a brief comment. The first introduction rule takes an unexpected form; that is because it is aiming to have the same effect as the more natural rule

$$\frac{\neg\varphi}{\varphi\to\psi}$$

but to do so without explicitly using a negation sign. Given the rule $(\neg E)$ we can easily deduce the more natural version thus:

$$(\neg E)\ \frac{\neg\varphi \qquad (\to I)\ \dfrac{\varphi \qquad \varphi\to\psi}{\ }}{\ }$$

And the converse deduction is just as easily done using $(\neg I)$. I observe incidentally that we could apply the same transformation to the familiar rule $(\to E)$, and our rules for $\to$ would then be

$$\frac{\neg\varphi}{\varphi\to\psi}, \quad \frac{\psi}{\varphi\to\psi} \qquad \frac{\varphi\to\psi}{\neg\varphi \quad \psi}$$

Comparing these rules with those for $\vee$ we see at once how $\to$ might be defined in terms of $\vee$ and $\neg$, or how $\vee$ may be defined in terms of $\to$ and $\neg$.

I give just one example of a proof using the rules for $\to$, namely a proof to establish Peirce's law, in the form

$$\Rightarrow ((\varphi\to\psi)\to\varphi)\to\varphi.$$

Since this sequent has no formula on the left, it is clear that we must use the first rule $(\to I)$ to obtain it;[8] in fact we use this rule twice, and the other two rules for $\to$ once each.

$$(\to I)\ \frac{}{((\varphi\to\psi)\to\varphi)\to\varphi} \qquad (\to E)\ \frac{(\varphi\to\psi)\to\varphi \qquad (\to I)\ \dfrac{\varphi\to\psi \quad \varphi}{\ }}{(CR)\ \dfrac{\varphi}{\ }} \\ (\to I)\ \frac{\varphi}{((\varphi\to\psi)\to\varphi)\to\varphi}$$

(To save clutter, I have omitted a final step of contraction). You are encouraged to try some further proofs in this system in the exercises.

Let us now turn to the quantifiers, and first $\forall$. Supposing that we are still

---

[8] Observe that none of these rules allow for the discharge of an assumption. That technique was forced on us in natural deduction by the limitation to sequents with only one formula on the right; but it is now no longer needed.

aiming to copy the idea behind the rules for natural deduction, so that what is wanted is an introduction rule and an elimination rule, then clearly we can take over the familiar elimination rule, and our problem will be to find a suitable proviso for the introduction rule[9]

$$(\forall I)\ \frac{\varphi}{\forall \xi \varphi(\xi/\alpha)} \qquad (\forall E)\ \frac{\forall \xi \varphi}{\varphi(\alpha/\xi)}$$
provided ... ?

Now the ordinary rule $(\forall I)$ of natural deduction corresponds to the rule $(\Rightarrow \forall)$ formulated for Gentzen sequents, which is this:

$$\frac{\Gamma \Rightarrow \varphi, \Delta}{\Gamma \Rightarrow \forall \xi \varphi(\xi/\alpha), \Delta}$$
provided α is not in Γ or Δ

This naturally leads to the following proviso: when seeking to apply $(\forall I)$ we must ensure that the name α to be generalized upon does not occur in the formulae that are then *either* at the highest nodes of the proof, *or* at the lowest nodes, except, of course, for the displayed formula φ that is to be generalized.[10] But this is still not sufficiently clear. For to judge whether the rule, as now formulated, has been correctly applied, we need to know at what stage in the construction of the whole proof it was applied, and we cannot tell this just by looking at the finished proof.

To see the problem, consider the following suggested proof:

$$(\neg I)\ \frac{}{\quad} $$
$$(\exists I)\ \frac{Fa}{\exists x Fx} \qquad (\forall I)\ \frac{\neg Fa}{\forall x \neg Fx}$$

If the order of the three steps in this proof is taken to be first $(\neg I)$, then $(\forall I)$, then finally $(\exists I)$, then the step of $(\forall I)$ must be condemned as incorrect. For when it is applied the name a still occurs in a formula at a lowest node, namely in Fa. But if instead the order is taken to be first $(\neg I)$, then $(\exists I)$, then finally $(\forall I)$, there is nothing to object to. But we cannot tell, just by looking at the finished proof, what the order was supposed to be. Nor can we say that

---

[9] Kneale's own rules for the quantifiers are quite unclear, so I pay them no attention here.

[10] If the same formula φ that we wish to generalize is at several lowest nodes, then *either* we must bring all these together by contraction before applying $(\forall I)$, *or*—to save the need for this—we may allow ourselves to generalize several occurrences of the same formula simultaneously. In that case it is all formulae at highest nodes and all *other* formulae at lowest nodes that must lack the relevant name.

so long as there is *some* way of looking at the proof which would validate a given step of ($\forall$I), then that step is correct. For consider now the alleged proof

$$(\neg\text{I})\frac{}{Fa} \qquad \frac{}{\neg Fa}$$
$$(\forall\text{I})\frac{Fa}{\forall xFx} \qquad (\forall\text{I})\frac{\neg Fa}{\forall x\neg Fx}$$

For each of these two applications of ($\forall$I), taken singly, there is some way of validating it, namely by taking it as the last of the three steps of the proof. But the proof as a whole is not correct, for they cannot both be the last step, and whichever we choose to be the last step then the other was not a correct application of ($\forall$I).

If we look for a feasible way of writing proofs, which will ensure that these complexities are brought into the open, then I think the best plan is to say that when a step of ($\forall$I) is to be applied, the whole of what is taken to be the proof at that stage is encircled, say with a dotted line, which coincides with the solid line marking that step of ($\forall$I). We then check to see that the highest nodes in that circle do not contain the name to be generalized upon, nor do any of the lowest nodes except the one[11] to which ($\forall$I) is to be applied. Thus our correct proof above should be marked as on the left and not as on the right

$$\boxed{\begin{array}{cc} Fa & \neg Fa \\ \hline \exists xFx & \forall x\neg Fx \end{array}} \qquad \boxed{\begin{array}{cc} Fa & \neg Fa \\ \hline \exists xFx & \forall x\neg Fx \end{array}}$$

Our final and incorrect proof could only be marked in this way with circles that intersect, as in

$$\begin{array}{cc} Fa & \neg Fa \\ \hline \forall xFx & \forall x\neg Fx \end{array}$$

We shall avoid fallacies of this sort simply by stipulating that our dotted circles must never intersect.

To give just one simple illustration, here is a proof of the sequent

$$\forall x(Fx \lor P) \Rightarrow \forall xFx \lor P,$$

---

[11] Or perhaps more than one, so long as all the nodes to which ($\forall$I) is simultaneously applied contain the same formula. See previous note.

which proved so awkward in a natural deduction setting. Now the proof is perfectly straightforward:

$$
\begin{array}{c}
\text{(VI)} \dfrac{(\forall E) \dfrac{\forall x(Fx \vee P)}{Fa \vee P}}{\begin{array}{c} \text{(}\lor\text{E)} \dfrac{}{Fa} \qquad \text{(}\lor\text{I)} \dfrac{P}{\forall xFx \vee P} \\ \forall xFx \end{array}} \\
\text{(}\lor\text{I)} \; \overline{\forall xFx \vee P}
\end{array}
$$

Finally, let us turn briefly to $\exists$. Here, of course, the introduction rule is perfectly straightforward, and it is the elimination rule that needs a proviso. When we consider what this proviso ought to be, in the light of our reflections on ($\forall$I), and taking into account the relevant rule in the Gentzen sequent calculus, we see that it calls for a revision in the way we have been thinking of an elimination rule. We have been thinking of it, as we did in natural deduction, as a rule for eliminating a sign, considering the proof as something that starts from the top and proceeds downwards. But now our proofs are in principle symmetrical upwards and downwards, and they can equally well be thought of as starting from the bottom and proceeding upwards. Seen in this way, what we have been calling an 'elimination' rule is simply a rule for introducing in the upwards direction. Given this perspective, the correct formulation for ($\exists$E) presents no problem: it must refer to a completed proof *below* it, just as ($\forall$I) refers to a completed proof *above* it.

So the position that we reach is this. The four quantifier rules, diagrammatically presented, are

$$
\text{(}\forall\text{I)} \; \dfrac{\varphi}{\forall \xi \varphi(\xi/\alpha)} \qquad\qquad \text{(}\forall\text{E)} \; \dfrac{\forall \xi \varphi}{\varphi(\alpha/\xi)}
$$

$$
\text{(}\exists\text{I)} \; \dfrac{\varphi(\alpha/\xi)}{\exists \xi \varphi} \qquad\qquad \text{(}\exists\text{E)} \; \dfrac{\exists \xi \varphi(\xi/\alpha)}{\varphi}
$$

Let us say that an 'end formula' of a proof is a formula that is either a highest or a lowest formula of it. Then the provisos on ($\forall$I) and ($\exists$E) are

> Provided that the dotted line encircles a proof in which α does not occur in any end formula, except the displayed end formula φ.

And there is a general proviso on the dotted circles, namely

Dotted circles cannot intersect one another.

The system of rules thus provided is, as you are invited to argue, both sound and complete.

To give a simple example of a proof using the $\exists$ rules, I consider the sequent

$$\exists x Fx \wedge P \Rightarrow \exists x(Fx \wedge P).$$

This sequent is dual to the sequent in $\forall$ and $\vee$ just considered, and you will see that the proofs of the two are also now dual to one another:

$$
\begin{array}{c}
(\wedge E)\dfrac{\exists x Fx \wedge P}{\exists x Fx} \\
(\exists E)\dfrac{}{Fa} \quad ----\quad (\wedge E)\dfrac{\exists x Fx \wedge P}{P} \\
(\wedge I)\dfrac{}{Fa \wedge P} \\
(\exists I)\dfrac{Fa \wedge P}{\exists x(Fx \wedge P)}
\end{array}
$$

To give a more complex example, using rules for both $\exists$ and $\forall$, I return to our old friend, the sequent

$$\forall x \exists y(Fx \wedge Gy) \Rightarrow \exists y \forall x(Fx \wedge Gy).$$

A tableau proof of this sequent was given on p. 162, and then rewritten as a proof in Gentzen's cut-free sequent calculus as Exercise 7.4.1. There was also a natural deduction proof on p. 258. Here is another proof, in the system of this section

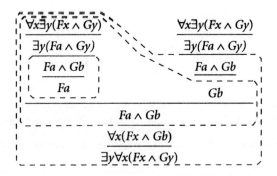

The proof should not be read from top to bottom, nor from bottom to top, but outwards from the middle. Its innermost stage is the encircled part proving the sequent $Fa \land Gb \Rightarrow Fa$. We apply ($\exists E$) to this, thus proving the sequent $\exists y(Fa \land Gy) \Rightarrow Fa$. After a couple more steps we come to the next encircled part, proving the sequent $\forall x \exists y(Fx \land Gy), Gb \Rightarrow Fa \land Gb$. We apply ($\forall I$) to this, to obtain $\forall x \exists y(Fx \land Gy), Gb \Rightarrow \forall x(Fx \land Gb)$. A couple more steps added to this proof yields the last part of the whole proof to be encircled, which has established the sequent $\forall x \exists y(Fx \land Gy), Fa \land Gb \Rightarrow \exists y \forall x(Fx \land Gy)$. One application of ($\exists E$) to this, and a final step of ($\forall E$), then yields the sequent we want. (If desired, we could have finished off with a step of contraction on the left, at the top of the whole proof.)

EXERCISES

7.6.1. Find proofs of the following sequents (*a*) in the tableau system of Section 4.3, (*b*) in the natural deduction system of Sections 6.2 and 6.3, (*c*) in the system of the present section:

    (1) $(P \rightarrow Q) \rightarrow Q \Rightarrow (Q \rightarrow P) \rightarrow P$.
    (2) $P \rightarrow (Q \lor R) \Rightarrow (P \rightarrow Q) \lor R$.
    (3) $\forall x Fx \rightarrow \exists x Gx \Rightarrow \exists x(Fx \rightarrow Gx)$.
    (4) $\forall x \exists y(Fx \lor Gy) \Rightarrow \exists y \forall x(Fx \lor Gy)$.

In which system is it easiest to find proofs? Which system yields the tidiest proofs? [Warning: In each case the natural deduction proofs will have to use some negation rules; use any that seem convenient.]

7.6.2. Show that the proof system of this section is sound. [Method: Argue the case first for quantifier-free 'Kneale proofs', in which contraction is not allowed. (Use induction on the number of horizontal lines in the proof; note where you need to use the hypothesis that no two nodes are connected by more than one path.) Then expand the argument to allow for contraction as well, and finally add the quantifier rules.]

7.6.3. Show that the proof system of this section is complete. [Method: show that whatever can be proved in Gentzen's cut-free sequent calculus can also be proved in this system.]

Part III

FURTHER TOPICS

8

Existence and Identity

8.1. Identity

We shall use '$a=b$' as short for 'a is the same thing as b'. The sign '$=$' thus expresses a particular two-place predicate, and since we generally write a predicate-symbol in front of the name-letters that fill its gaps, you might have expected the same here. Very occasionally this can be convenient (Exercise 8.1.2), but it is confusing to have the same sign '$=$' appearing in these two roles. So let us say that officially the letter 'I' is the identity predicate, and it is to have just the same grammar as the familiar two-place predicate-letters. For example, 'Iab' is a formula. But almost always we shall 'abbreviate' this formula to '$a=b$'. Similarly, we shall abbreviate the formula '$\neg Iab$' to '$a \neq b$'.

It is easy to see how to incorporate the new symbol into our formal languages. First, the formation rules are extended, so that they include a clause stating that, if τ_1 and τ_2 are any terms (i.e. names or variables) then $I\tau_1\tau_2$ (or $\tau_1 = \tau_2$) is a formula. Second, the intended meaning of this symbol is reflected in a suitable rule for interpretations of the language. An interpretation I is said to be a *normal* interpretation iff it satisfies the condition that, for any name-letters α and β,

$$|\alpha = \beta|_I = T \quad \text{iff} \quad |\alpha|_I = |\beta|_I.$$

Alternatively, if our interpretations are specified by a recursion on satisfaction rather than truth, then the relevant condition is

$$\sigma \text{ sats } \tau_1 = \tau_2 \quad \text{iff} \quad \sigma(\tau_1) = \sigma(\tau_2).$$

Given this intended interpretation, it is clear that we have as correct theses for identity

$$\models \alpha=\alpha$$
$$\alpha=\beta \models \varphi(\alpha/\xi) \leftrightarrow \varphi(\beta/\xi).$$

(Recall that the consequent of the second thesis means: if you start with a formula containing occurrences of α, and substitute β for some, but not necessarily all, of those occurrences, then the two formulae have the same truth-value.) These two together are usually taken as the basic principles for identity. With scant regard for history, the second of them is often called Leibniz's law, but the first has no special name (except that once upon a time it was called 'the' law of identity).

It is easy to see how these two theses may be used to furnish rules of proof for identity. For example, in an axiomatic system we could adopt the two axiom-schemas

$$\vdash \alpha=\alpha$$
$$\vdash \alpha=\beta \rightarrow (\varphi(\alpha/\xi) \leftrightarrow \varphi(\beta/\xi)).$$

In a tableau system we could adopt the rules

$$
\begin{array}{ccc}
\Big| &
\begin{array}{c} \alpha=\beta \\ \varphi(\alpha/\xi) \\ \big| \\ \varphi(\beta/\xi) \end{array} &
\begin{array}{c} \alpha=\beta \\ \varphi(\beta/\xi) \\ \big| \\ \varphi(\alpha/\xi) \end{array} \\
\alpha=\alpha & &
\end{array}
$$

(Here the left rule means that, for any name α, you may introduce the formula $\alpha=\alpha$ at any point on any branch.) Similarly, in a natural deduction system we could adopt the rules

$$(=\!I) \dfrac{}{\alpha=\alpha} \qquad (=\!E) \dfrac{\alpha=\beta \quad \varphi(\alpha/\xi)}{\varphi(\beta/\xi)}, \quad \dfrac{\alpha=\beta \quad \varphi(\beta/\xi)}{\varphi(\alpha/\xi)}$$

There are alternative rules that one may adopt instead (Exercise 8.1.1), but these just suggested are probably the most convenient and the most usual.

It is quite straightforward to show that these rules are complete for identity. That is, every correct sequent with identity as its only logical symbol can be proved from these rules alone, and every correct sequent containing identity and other logical symbols can be proved from these rules for identity and the rules for the other symbols, provided that those other rules are complete for the other symbols. The simplest tactic is to modify the argument given in Chapter 4 to show the completeness of the tableau rules. That argument involved a particular recipe to be followed in the construction of tableaux, a recipe which involved a cycle of three stages, namely (1) apply the rules for truth-functors in all possible ways, but without repetitions, (2) apply the rules for ∃ and for ¬∀, but only once to each formula, (3) apply the rules for ∀ and ¬∃ in all possible ways, but without introducing any new name-letters. (There is an exception to (3): if the first time that we come to (3) there are no name-letters already on the branch, then just one name may be introduced arbitrarily, in order to get started.) Now that we have rules for identity present as well, we add a fourth stage to this cycle, namely: (4) apply the identity rules in all possible ways to all name-letters already on the branch. This means (*a*) introduce $\alpha=\alpha$ for any name-letter α on this branch, (*b*) if $\alpha=\beta$ is on the branch, then substitute β for α in all possible ways in all formulae on the branch containing α, and (*c*) also substitute α for β in all possible ways in all formulae on the branch containing β. Since we have a general restriction that no formula is ever to be written more than once on the same branch, this stage (4) applying the identity rules must terminate. When it does, we start the whole fourfold cycle again, and go on repeating it *ad infinitum* unless either the tableau closes or no further moves are possible.

I briefly recapitulate the proof already given in more detail in Chapter 4. Either the procedure finds a closed tableau at some stage, or it does not. If it does, then in view of the soundness of the rules of proof we know that the set of formulae Γ at the root of the tableau is inconsistent, i.e. $\Gamma \vDash$. If it does not, then we are left with an open branch, either a finite open branch, if the procedure has halted, or otherwise an infinite open branch. (Strictly speaking, this should be an infinite series of finite open branches, each extending the last. But it is easier to think in terms of a single infinite branch.) Whichever of these is the case, I argued that there is an interpretation showing that $\Gamma \nvDash$, i.e. an interpretation which has a domain with one item for each name on the branch, and which assigns truth to each atomic formula on the branch. For it follows from this that it also assigns truth to *all* formulae on the branch, and hence to all formulae in Γ. Now we again need a small modification: wherever α=β is on the branch, the interpretation is to assign to α and to β the same member of the domain as their denotation. So it is a *normal* interpretation, treating identity as it should be treated. And there cannot be any obstacle to this stipulation, since we have ensured that, wherever α=β is on the branch, the result of interchanging α and β in any formula on the branch is again a formula on the branch, and therefore the two are alike in truth-values (for both are true).

The notion of identity has many uses. One, of course, is in the analysis of arguments expressed in ordinary language, but I set that aside, since the subject is not treated in this book. Another is in the classification of relations, and another in the definition of what may be called 'numerical quantifiers'. I shall now say a little about each of these. But there are also others, and the whole of this chapter is concerned with identity in one way or another.

A relation such as 'x is taller than y' is called a *quasi-ordering* relation. This means that it is transitive, asymmetrical, and in addition satisfies this further thesis: if x is taller than y, but not taller than z, then z is taller than y. That is, for 'R' as 'taller than' we have

(1) $\forall xyz(Rxy \wedge Ryz \rightarrow Rxz)$
(2) $\forall xy \neg (Rxy \wedge Ryx)$
(3) $\forall xyz(Rxy \wedge \neg Rxz \rightarrow Rzy)$.

It may be noted, incidentally, that an equivalent version of the third condition is

$$\forall xyz(\neg Rxz \wedge \neg Rzy \rightarrow \neg Rxy).$$

That is, this third condition states that the *negation* of R is transitive. In view of these three conditions, we may define 'x is the same height as y' for 'x is neither taller nor shorter than y', i.e.

(4) $\forall xy(x \approx y \leftrightarrow \neg Rxy \wedge \neg Ryx)$.

Then we can prove that being the same height as must be an equivalence relation, i.e. it must be transitive, symmetrical, and reflexive:

(5) $\forall xyz(x \approx y \wedge y \approx z \rightarrow x \approx z)$
(6) $\forall xy(x \approx y \rightarrow y \approx x)$
(7) $\forall x(x \approx x)$.

Many relations that naturally strike one as 'ordering' relations, in that they can be regarded as arranging things in an 'order' from less to more, are of this type. But a *fully* (or *totally*) ordering relation, arranging things in a *linear* order, is one in which the relation ≈ defined above is in fact identity.

To secure this result we replace clause (3) above by the stronger clause (3′) stating that R is connected, namely

(3′) $\forall xy(x{\neq}y \rightarrow Rxy \lor Ryx)$.

A relation R which satisfies (1)–(3′), must also satisfy the original (1)–(3), as I now show. I give what is called an 'informal' proof. This is not a proof in any particular proof system. The general idea is that one may use any rule of proof that is 'sufficiently obvious', and there is quite a lot of ordinary English in the proof, explaining what is going on at each step. Here it is:

If R satisfies (1) and (3′), then R satisfies (3).

Proof. Assume R satisfies (1) and (3′), and suppose for *reductio ad absurdum* that R does not satisfy (3). This means that there are objects a,b,c such that

(a) $Rab \land \neg Rac \land \neg Rcb$.

Considering the second clause, $\neg Rac$, and observing that by (3′) R is connected, we have

(b) $a{=}c \lor Rca$.

Bringing in the first clause of (a), and applying distribution, we then have

(c) $(a{=}c \land Rab) \lor (Rca \land Rab)$.

Applying Leibniz's law to the first disjunct, this yields

(d) $Rcb \lor (Rca \land Rab)$.

Observing that by (1) R is transitive, and applying this to the second disjunct, we infer

(e) $Rcb \lor Rcb$,

i.e.

(f) Rcb.

But this contradicts the third clause of our premiss (a). So we have our *reductio*, and the result is proved.

There is much more that could be said about ordering relations—a little of it will emerge from Exercise 8.1.2—but I do not pursue this topic further. Instead I mention another important way in which identity is used in the classification of relations, namely in the definition of what is called a *one–one* relation. This is the amalgamation of two simpler conditions. We say that a relation R is *one–many* iff

$$\forall xyz(Rxz \land Ryz \to x=y).$$

and it is *many–one* iff

$$\forall xyz(Rzx \land Rzy \to x=y).$$

(You will see that 'one–many' means, in effect 'for anything on the right there is at most one on the left', whereas 'many–one' means 'for anything on the left there is at most one on the right'.) A one–one relation is one that satisfies both of these conditions, i.e. it is both one–many and many–one. A neat way of amalgamating the two conditions is

$$\forall xyzw(Rxz \land Ryw \to (x=y \leftrightarrow z=w)).$$

These ideas will recur in what follows, so I do not develop them any further now. Let us turn instead to our other topic involving identity, namely the 'numerical quantifiers'.

To say that there is at least one thing x such that Fx we need only use an existential quantifier.

$$\exists xFx.$$

To say that there are least two such things we need identity as well, as in

$$\exists x(Fx \land \exists y(Fy \land y \neq x)).$$

Similarly, to say that there are at least three we need a formula such as

$$\exists x(Fx \land \exists y(Fy \land y \neq x \land \exists z(Fz \land z \neq y \land z \neq x))).$$

It is clear that there is a pattern in these formulae. Using '$\exists_n x$' to mean 'there are at least n things x such that', and using 'n'' for 'the number after n' we can sum up the pattern in this way:

$$\exists_1 x(Fx) \leftrightarrow \exists xFx$$
$$\exists_{n'} x(Fx) \leftrightarrow \exists x(Fx \land \exists_n y(Fy \land y \neq x)).$$

One can use this pattern to define any specific numeral in place of 'n'. Interestingly, we find the *same* pattern when we look into 'exactly n' rather than 'at least n'. If we represent 'there are exactly n things x such that' by the simple 'nx', we have

$$0x(Fx) \leftrightarrow \neg\exists xFx$$
$$n'x(Fx) \leftrightarrow \exists x(Fx \land ny(Fy \land y \neq x)).$$

Using these definitions, one can represent in 'purely logical' vocabulary such apparently 'arithmetical' theses as

$$2x(Fx \wedge Gx) \wedge 3x(Fx \wedge \neg Gx) \rightarrow 5x(Fx).$$

One can prove such theses too, by 'purely logical' means, assuming that our rules for identity are counted as a part of 'pure logic'. But we shall leave it to the philosophers to dispute about the relationship between this thesis and the genuinely arithmetical thesis

$$2 + 3 = 5.$$

As my final topic in this section I consider what is called the 'pure theory of identity'. In this theory the language is restricted to one that contains truth-functors and quantifiers as usual, the identity predicate, but no other specified predicates nor any schematic predicate-letters. Thus *every* atomic formula in the language is built from the identity predicate and two terms. This theory is decidable. That is, there is a decision procedure which we can apply to determine whether any given sequent in the language of the theory is or is not a correct sequent. The crucial point is that there is a procedure for driving the quantifiers in, until no quantifier is in the scope of any other, except that for this purpose we count a numerical quantifier as a *single* quantifier. (Of course, when the numerical quantifier is analysed in terms of the familiar quantifiers and identity, then it will turn out to contain one quantifier within the scope of another.)

Here is a recipe for driving the quantifiers in. In practice there will be many short cuts that one can exploit, as we observed when considering a similar recipe for a language containing only one-place predicate-letters (Section 3.7). But here I pay no attention to short cuts, and just give the basic recipe. We may assume for simplicity that we start with a formula in which all quantifiers are existential. We begin with an innermost quantifier, i.e. one which has no further quantifiers in its scope, and we express the quantifier-free formula that is the scope of that quantifier in DNF. Using the law

$$\exists x(\varphi(x) \vee \psi(x)) \; =\!\!\models \; \exists x \varphi(x) \vee \exists x \psi(x),$$

we distribute the existential quantifier through the disjunction. Then, using the law

$$\exists x(\varphi \wedge \psi(x)) \; =\!\!\models \; \varphi \wedge \exists x \psi(x)$$
provided x is not free in φ,

we confine each resulting quantifier to that part of the conjunction that contains the variable bound by it. The result is that each quantifier, say $\exists x$, comes to govern a conjunction of clauses $x=y_i$ and $x{\neq}y_i$. If one of these clauses is $x{\neq}x$, we replace the whole by $\bot$; if all the clauses are $x=x$, we replace the whole by $\top$; otherwise we delete any clauses $x=x$, so that the variables y_i in question are all other than x. We then consider two cases.

Case (1): Some positive identity occurs in the scope of $\exists x$, so by rearrangement we have,

$$\exists x(x=y_i \wedge \varphi(x)),$$

where $\varphi(x)$ is either lacking or contains a conjunction of identities and non-identities each containing the variable x.

Since we have

$$\models \exists x(x=y_i)$$
$$\exists x(x=y_i \wedge \varphi(x)) =\models \varphi(y_i)$$

in the first case we replace the whole just by $\top$, and in the second by $\varphi(y_i)$, i.e. by the result of substituting y_i for x throughout $\varphi(x)$. In either case the quantifier $\exists x$ has been eliminated.

Case (2): All the clauses in the scope of $\exists x$ are negative. Say, for the sake of illustration, that there are three of them, and we have

$$\exists x(x{\neq}y_1 \wedge x{\neq}y_2 \wedge x{\neq}y_3).$$

Then we replace the whole by the *disjunction* of the following five clauses:

$$y_1{=}y_2 \wedge y_2{=}y_3 \wedge \exists_2 x(x{=}x)$$
$$y_1{=}y_2 \wedge y_2{\neq}y_3 \wedge \exists_3 x(x{=}x)$$
$$y_1{\neq}y_2 \wedge y_2{=}y_3 \wedge \exists_3 x(x{=}x)$$
$$y_1{\neq}y_2 \wedge y_1{=}y_3 \wedge \exists_3 x(x{=}x)$$
$$y_1{\neq}y_2 \wedge y_1{\neq}y_3 \wedge y_2 \neq y_3 \wedge \exists_4 x(x{=}x).$$

The disjunction is found by considering what relations of identity and non-identity could hold between the variables y_1–y_3 and then saying in each case how many objects there must be if there is to be something x different from all of them. (As you may check, the number of disjuncts in the disjunction grows quickly as the number of distinct variables y_i increases.)

In this way the quantifier $\exists x$, which had several variables y_i other than x within its scope, is either eliminated altogether (in case (1)) or replaced by a number of numerical quantifiers which have no occurrences of y_i in their scopes. In subsequent operations, these new formulae with numerical quantifiers are treated as atomic formulae. Bearing this in mind, we can therefore drive in the next innermost quantifier, and then the next, treating each in turn in the same way. The result will be that either all the quantifiers have been eliminated altogether, so that the whole formula has become a truth-function just of the formula $\top$, or we are left with a truth-function of clauses of the form $\exists_n x(x{=}x)$. The final step, then, is to devise a way of testing sequents composed of formulae of this kind, but I leave this final step to you.

This method just described is very tedious in practice, but has some theoretical interest, (*a*) because it illustrates how the method of driving quantifiers in can sometimes be applied even where we have two-place predicates to consider, and (*b*) because the method can be extended to some more interesting cases, as you are invited to discover (Exercise 8.1.5).

EXERCISES

8.1.1. Consider the identity rules as given for natural deduction.

(*a*) Show that we do not need to assume *both* of the rules given as (=E), since either can be deduced from the other if (=I) is given. [Hint: A proof using just one step each of (=I) and (=E) will show that $\alpha{=}\beta \vdash \beta{=}\alpha$.]

(*b*) Show that, in the presence of (=E), ($\exists$I), and ($\exists$E), the rule (=I) may be replaced by

$$\vdash \exists\xi(\xi{=}\alpha).$$

(*c*) Show that, in the presence of ($\exists$I), ($\exists$E), and standard rules for the truth-functors, the stated rules for identity may be replaced by this pair:

$$\varphi(\alpha/\xi) \dashv\vdash \exists\xi(\xi{=}\alpha \wedge \varphi).$$

8.1.2. Let us write $\bar{R}$ for the negation of the relation R, $R{\cup}S$ for the disjunction of two relations R and S, and $R{\cap}S$ for their conjunction. In connection with this notation, let us also use I for the identity relation. Thus

$$\forall xy(\bar{R}xy \leftrightarrow \neg Rxy)$$
$$\forall xy(R{\cup}S)xy \leftrightarrow Rxy \vee Sxy)$$
$$\forall xy(R{\cap}S)xy \leftrightarrow Rxy \wedge Sxy)$$
$$\forall xy(Ixy \leftrightarrow x{=}y).$$

The conditions for R to be an ordering relation were given as

R is transitive	$\forall xyz(Rxy \wedge Ryz \rightarrow Rxz)$
R is asymmetrical	$\forall xy\neg(Rxy \wedge Ryx)$
R is connected	$\forall xy(x{\neq}y \rightarrow Rxy \vee Ryx).$

Let us say more precisely that these conditions define an ordering in the sense of $<$, or briefly a $<$-ordering, since they are evidently satisfied by $<$ among numbers. But the associated relation $\leqslant$ can also be said to be, in its different way, an ordering relation. It satisfies the analogous conditions

R is transitive	$\forall xyz(Rxy \wedge Ryz \rightarrow Rxz)$
R is antisymmetrical	$\forall xy(Rxy \wedge Ryx \rightarrow x{=}y)$
R is strongly connected	$\forall xy(Rxy \vee Ryx)$.

Let us say that these conditions define a $\leqslant$-ordering.

(*a*) Prove, informally if you wish,

(1) R is a $<$-ordering iff $\bar{R}$ is a $\leqslant$-ordering.

(2) $R \cap \bar{T}$ is a $<$-ordering iff $R \cup I$ is a $\leqslant$-ordering.

(*b*) Refute

(1) R is a $<$-ordering iff $R \cup I$ is a $\leqslant$-ordering.

(2) R is a $\leqslant$-ordering iff $R \cap \bar{T}$ is a $\leqslant$-ordering.

[Hint: for part (*a*) the example of an informal proof given in the text will be useful.]

8.1.3.(*a*) What would be wrong with the following scheme for defining the numerical quantifier 'there are at least n'?

$$\exists_1 x(Fx) \leftrightarrow \exists x Fx$$
$$\exists_{n'} x(Fx) \leftrightarrow \exists_n x(Fx \wedge \exists y(Fy \wedge y{\neq}x)).$$

(*b*) Suppose that new numerical quantifiers $\forall_n$ are defined by the scheme

$$\forall_0 x(Fx) \leftrightarrow \forall x \neg Fx$$
$$\forall_{n'} x(Fx) \leftrightarrow \forall x(\neg Fx \vee \forall_n y(Fy \wedge y{\neq}x)).$$

What is the right interpretation of these quantifiers?

8.1.4. Fill in two details omitted from the decision procedure outlined for the pure theory of identity, namely

(*a*) How should one replace the formula

$$\exists x(x{\neq}y)$$

by a formula in which y is not in the scope of any quantifier?

(*b*) Give a decision procedure for sequents in which every formula is a truth-function of numerically quantified formulae $\exists_n x(x{=}x)$. [Hint: If you use the argument on pp. 122–3 as a model, notice that if $n \geqslant m$ then

$$\exists_n x(x{=}x) \vDash \exists_m x(x{=}x)$$

If you prefer, you may use the argument on p. 185 as a model].

8.1.5.(*a*) Show how the decision procedure for the pure theory of identity can be extended so that it becomes a decision procedure for the theory of identity *and* one-place predicates together.

(*b*) The theory of dense order without first or last elements is given by the following axioms (cf. Exercise 3.10.2):

(1) $\exists xy(x{<}y)$.

(2) $\forall x \neg(x{<}x)$.

(3) $\forall xyz(x<y \wedge y<z \rightarrow x<z)$.
(4) $\forall xy(x\neq y \rightarrow x<y \vee y<x)$.
(5) $\forall xy(x<y \rightarrow \exists z(x<z \wedge z<y))$.
(6) $\forall x(\exists y(x<y) \wedge \exists y(y<x))$.

Show that this theory is decidable, by showing how the quantifiers in any formula of the theory may be driven in, and so eliminated. [Hints: according to the axioms of the theory

(1) We may replace clauses $\neg(x<y)$ by $(x=y \vee y<x)$.
(2) We may replace clauses $\neg(x=y)$ by $(x<y \vee y<x)$.
(3) We may replace a clause such as

$$\exists x(y_1<x \wedge y_2<x \wedge x<z_1 \wedge x<z_2)$$

by the disjunction of the three clauses

$$y_1<y_2 \wedge y_2<z_1 \wedge y_2<z_2$$
$$y_1=y_2 \wedge y_2<z_1 \wedge y_2<z_2$$
$$y_2<y_1 \wedge y_1<z_1 \wedge y_1<z_2.$$

Please note that these three hints do not cover all cases.]

8.2. Functions

Functions were briefly mentioned in Section 2.1. I now give a more formal treatment, but one that relies upon a convenient simplification.

We said originally that a function would be defined upon a certain domain of objects, so that if you take any object from that domain as the input to the function, then the function will yield just one object as its output for that input. In the received terminology, the inputs to a function are called its arguments, and the output for a given input is called the value of the function for that argument. So the chief characteristic of a function, then, is that it has one and only one value for each of its appropriate arguments. But usually we allow that not *everything* need be counted as an appropriate argument for the function, i.e. that the function need not be defined for all arguments whatever, but only for arguments of a suitable kind. The simplification to be imposed is that we shall *not* allow this; on the contrary, all functions are to be taken as 'defined everywhere', or in other words every function is to have one and only one value for any object whatever taken as argument, i.e. any object from the whole domain that our quantifiers range over. (Another way of saying the same thing is that all our functions are to be *total*, rather than *partial*, functions.) It must be admitted that this assumption is not very realistic, and it introduces a problem which will underlie most of the rest of this chapter. But the reason for imposing it is that it enables us to extend our formal languages to include functional expressions in a very simple way.

A function may take any number of arguments. The simplest kind of function is a one-place function, which takes just one object at a time as argument, and yields a value for that one argument. An example from arithmetic would be the function expressed by 'the square of . . .'; an example from every day would be the function expressed by 'the father of . . .'. But there are also two-place functions, such as that expressed by 'the sum of . . .' or 'the product of . . .' in arithmetic, and again there are three-place functions, and so on. (Functions of more than two places are usually complex, and put together from several simpler functions. For example, the arithmetical expression '$(x+y)\cdot z$' indicates a three-place function, which we could express in words as 'the result of multiplying the sum of x and y by z'. But there is nothing to stop one introducing simple three-place functions if there is a need for them.) In the other direction, we can, if we wish, speak of zero-place functions, but this is just a new-fangled name for a familiar item. For a zero-place function is something which cannot take any argument, but just has a single value, and that is to say that it has the same role as a name. Names, then, can be regarded as expressing zero-place functions if one wishes, but we already have a perfectly good notation for names, and do not need a new one. We do, however, need a new notation to represent other functions.

We shall use the letters

$$f, g, h, f_1, g_1, h_1, f_2, \dots$$

as schematic function-letters. They take the place of particular expressions for functions, just as our schematic name-letters and predicate-letters take the place of particular names and predicates. For official purposes we shall regard each function-letter as furnished with a superscripted numeral (greater than 0) to show how many places that function has. But, as with predicate-letters, we shall always omit these superscripts in practice, since the rest of the notation will convey this information. The arguments to the function will be written in a pair of round brackets to the right of the function-letter, separated by commas where there is more than one argument. So our function-letters will appear in contexts such as

$$f(a), \quad g(a,b), \quad g(f(a),b).$$

The last example should be noted. If we start with the name a, and supply it as argument to the one-place function f, then the resulting expression $f(a)$ is in effect another name, but a complex one. (We can read '$f(a)$' as 'the f of a'.) So *it* can then be supplied as argument to another function, or to the same function again, and so on indefinitely. In this way we can now form very complex names indeed. And by starting with a variable in place of a name-letter we can also form what might be called 'complex variables', though that is not the usual terminology.

For example, consider the arithmetical expression

$$3x^2 + 2x + 1.$$

Suppose that we use

$$f(x,y) \quad \text{for} \quad x+y$$
$$g(x,y) \quad \text{for} \quad x \cdot y.$$

Then this expression can be analysed as

$$f(f(g(3,g(x,x)),g(2,x)),1).$$

If you put in a particular numeral in place of the variable x, then the whole expression becomes a complex name of some number. But if you leave x as a variable, then you have an expression that behaves just like a complex name, except that it contains a free variable within it. So you obtain an open sentence by putting this expression into the gap of a one-place predicate, for example, the predicate '$\ldots = 0$'. Then you can form a closed sentence by adding a quantifier to bind the free variable, as in

$$\exists x[f(f(g(3,g(x,x)),g(2,x)),1) = 0].$$

Returning to the familiar notation, this just says

$$\exists x[3x^2 + 2x + 1 = 0].$$

Evidently much of school mathematics is concerned with procedures for discovering the truth-value of sentences such as these.

Of course, in the particular case nothing is gained by using the new letters $f,g,\ldots$ to re-express what is already expressed perfectly well by the familiar notation of mathematics. The example does illustrate how in mathematics one does use functional expressions in quite complex ways, but the main purpose of the letters $f,g,\ldots$ is not to 'abbreviate' particular functional expressions, but to act as schematic letters standing in for *any* such expressions. They allow us to frame general logical laws that apply to all functions without exception. To see how they do this we must see how such schematic letters can be added to the logical framework that we have already.

First we add function-letters to the vocabulary of our language. Using

these letters, we now add to the formation rules (p. 78) a recursive characterization of what is to count as a *term*, which goes like this:

(1) A name-letter is a term.
(2) A variable is a term.
(3) If θ^n is an n-place function-letter ($n>0$), and if $\tau_1,...,\tau_n$ is a series of n
terms (not necessarily distinct), then $\theta^n (\tau_1,...,\tau_n)$ is a term.
(4) There are no other terms.

The other formation rules remain as before, except that when complex
terms become available it increases clarity if the predicate-letters are supplied with brackets and commas, as the function-letters are. This means that
the clause for atomic formulae should now be rephrased in this way:

If Φ^n is an n-place predicate-letter (or is the two-place identity predicate I^2), and if $\tau_1,...,\tau_n$ is a series of n terms, not necessarily distinct, then
$\Phi^n (\tau_1,...,\tau_n)$ is a formula.

(Of course, we can for simplicity omit these extra brackets and commas
when there is no need for them.) It is to be observed that formulae given by
this rule are still called *atomic* formulae, since they do not have any proper
subformulae, but nevertheless they may now be very complicated, if the
terms that they contain are complicated.

The intended interpretation for a function-letter is, of course, that it be
interpreted as a function defined on the domain $\mathcal{D}$ of the interpretation, i.e.
a function yielding an object in that domain as value for each object, or
series of objects, from the domain as argument(s). Where θ^n is a function-
letter, we use $|\theta^n|_I$ for the value that the interpretation I assigns to θ^n. Then
what we have just said is that $|\theta^n|_I$ is to be a function from $\mathcal{D}_I^n$ into $\mathcal{D}_I$. The
relevant clause for evaluating expressions containing function-letters is
simply

$$|\theta^n(\tau_1,...,\tau_n)|_I = |\theta^n|_I(|\tau_1|_I,...,|\tau_n|_I).$$

This merely spells out the original intention in an obvious way.

Let us now turn to the rules of inference, and for definiteness let us
concentrate first on the natural deduction rules. Just as name-letters enter
into the rules of inference only as part of the quantifier rules, so too with
function-letters. But there is no need to make any alteration in the rules ($\forall$I)
and ($\exists$E), which are rules involving a name-letter stipulated to be *new*, i.e.
one that does not occur in the assumptions to the proof (nor—in the case of
($\exists$E)—in the conclusion). For the point of this stipulation is to ensure that
the name-letter may be interpreted as naming *anything* in the domain, and

that is why these rules are correct rules. So if we were to extend the rule, by allowing it to apply not only to name-letters but also to the complex terms built up from name-letters and function-letters, we should again have to ensure that these complex terms could be interpreted as naming *anything* in the domain. Now this could be done, by stipulating that *every* name-letter and *every* function-letter in the complex term had to be new. But there would be no point in doing so, since it merely complicates the statement of the rule without allowing us to prove any more with it. So in the case of ($\forall$I) and ($\exists$E) we shall make no change in the rules, and they remain as rules formulated just for names. The change comes in the simpler rules ($\forall$E) and ($\exists$I), which were initially formulated just for name-letters, but with no conditions on these name-letters. So there is nothing to prevent us from generalizing these rules so that they apply to all terms, however complex, and we shall do so. They are therefore restated in this way:

$$(\forall E)\ \frac{\forall\xi\phi}{\phi(\tau/\xi)} \qquad (\exists I)\ \frac{\phi(\tau/\xi)}{\exists\xi\phi}$$

where τ may now be any term at all.

But there is one qualification to be made here. I am assuming that only closed formulae may occur in a deduction, since the semantic turnstile $\models$ is defined only for closed formulae, and each step of a deduction should establish a semantically correct sequent. In that case, one must, of course, require that the term τ figuring in these rules be a *closed term*, i.e. a term such that no variable occurs free in it. (This means, in the present context, a term such that no variable at all occurs in it, for at present we have no way of binding a variable *within* a term.) But, as I have noted, in some books open formulae may figure in deductions, and in that case τ in these rules is permitted to contain free variables. On this approach we must further stipulate that the term τ be so chosen that all occurrences of variables that are free in τ remain free in $\varphi(\tau/\xi)$, or in other words that the variables in τ do not get captured by quantifiers already in φ. If this is not observed, then fallacies will result. For example, ($\forall$E) does not allow us to infer from the contingent premiss

$\forall x\exists y(x{\neq}y)$

to the impossible conclusion

$\exists y(y{\neq}y)$.

Similarly, then, it must not allow us to infer from the necessary premiss

$\forall x\exists y(x{=}y)$

to the contingent conclusion

$$\exists y (f(y) = y).$$

I add briefly that what has been said about the natural deduction rules (∀I) and (∃E), namely that they remain unchanged, applies also to the corresponding tableau rules (—∀) and (∃), and to the corresponding Gentzen rules (⇒∀) and (∃⇒). Similarly, what has been said about the natural deduction rules (∀E) and (∃I), namely that they are liberalized by writing τ in place of α, applies also to the corresponding tableau rules (∀) and (—∃), and to the corresponding Gentzen rules (∀⇒) and (⇒∃).

It turns out, then, that the result of admitting function letters is that the language becomes very much more complicated, but the rules of inference are scarcely affected. There is one small liberalization, but that is all. However, the reason why we have been able to keep these rules so simple is that we have been relying on the assumption noted at the beginning of this section, namely the assumption that every function is always defined for every argument. So far as concerns our ordinary and everyday use of functional expressions, this assumption is wholly unrealistic. For example, 'the father of . . .' is very naturally viewed as a functional expression, but we certainly do not suppose that absolutely everything has a father. Rather, we say that this function is defined only for certain kinds of argument (e.g. persons) but not for others (e.g. stones). The case is the same in mathematics too, where functions have a very important role to play, as we have seen. Naturally, in arithmetic we are only concerned with whether such functions as addition, subtraction, multiplication, and so on, are defined *for numbers*; we do not bother about whether they happen to be defined for other things too. This is compatible with the proposed logic, provided that our intended domain of quantification contains only the numbers, as in arithmetic it will do. However, not all arithmetical functions are defined even for all numbers as arguments. As every schoolboy knows, an exception is 'x divided by y', since division by zero is not defined, and all kinds of fallacies result from ignoring this point.

Where we have a function that is not defined for certain arguments, it is always possible to introduce a surrogate function that is defined for all arguments, by stipulating arbitrarily what value the function is to have in the cases hitherto undefined. For example, suppose that $f(x,y)$ abbreviates 'the number which results upon dividing x by y'. Then, as we have said, $f(x,y)$ is not defined for $y=0$, and it is equally not defined if x or y is not a number at all. But we could introduce the surrogate function f' by setting

$$f'(x,y) = \begin{cases} f(x,y), & \text{if } x \text{ and } y \text{ are both numbers, and } y \neq 0 \\ 0 & \text{otherwise.} \end{cases}$$

Then we have

$$f'(4,2) = f'(6,3) = 2.$$

And in addition

$$f'(4,0) = f'(\text{the moon},3) = f'(\text{the moon, the sun}) = 0.$$

But one has no sympathy with such surrogate functions. It is very much more natural to say that there is *no* number which can be obtained upon dividing 4 by 0, and *nothing* which counts as the result of dividing the moon by the sun. And it is surely perverse to suppose that the 'nothing' which comes from the latter division is 'the same thing' as the perfectly good number which results upon dividing 0 by 4.

The assumption that all functions are everywhere defined is, then, something that one would much rather do without. Yet we cannot easily abandon it, for if we do, then the simple rules of inference for function-letters must be abandoned too. This is because the rules of inference for name-letters are based upon the assumption that a name does always stand for something, as we noted way back in Section 3.1. And our present rules of inference treat functional expressions such as $f(a)$ as complex name-symbols, not differing in any important way from a simple name-letter. Consequently, these rules just assume that $f(a)$ does always stand for something, and without this assumption they would not be correct. Now you might say that the initial assumption about names is unrealistic, and we should seriously consider whether we can do without it. I shall take up this question from Section 4 onwards. But you might instead say that the present trouble arises only because functional expressions have been treated as if they were names, and that this is the point that needs revision. I take up this suggestion in the next section.

EXERCISES

(These exercises are exercises in applied logic, using function symbols.)

8.2.1. The theory of groups can be presented as having in its vocabulary just identity and a single two-place function $f(x,y)$ which we write as '$x \cdot y$'. The usual laws for identity apply, and in addition these three axioms:

(A1) $\forall xyz(x\cdot(y\cdot z) = (x\cdot y)\cdot z)$
(A2) $\forall xy\exists z(x = z\cdot y)$
(A3) $\forall xy\exists z(x = y\cdot z)$.

In this theory, prove

(1) $a = a\cdot c \vdash c = c\cdot c$. [Use $\exists z(c = z\cdot a)$.]
(2) $c = c\cdot c, d = d\cdot d \vdash c = d$. [Use $\exists z(c = d\cdot z), \exists w(d = w\cdot c)$.]
(3) $a = a\cdot c \vdash b = b\cdot c$. [Use (1), (2), and $\exists z(b = b\cdot z)$.]
(4) $\vdash 1x\forall y(y = y\cdot x)$. [Recall that '$1x$' means 'there is exactly one x such that'. It is easily shown from (3) that there is at least one, and from (2) that there is at most one.]

Given the result (4) we are evidently entitled to introduce a name for the unique entity x such that $\forall y(y = y\cdot x)$. We shall call it '1'. Thus we have

(4') $\vdash \forall y(y = y\cdot 1)$.

Continue to prove

(5) $a = c\cdot a \vdash c = c\cdot c$. [Similar to (1).]
(6) $\vdash a\cdot 1 = 1\cdot a$. [Use (2), (4), (5).]
(7) $a\cdot b = 1 \vdash b\cdot a = 1$. [The proof goes via $(b\cdot a)\cdot(b\cdot a) = b\cdot a$, and the result follows from this by (2) and (4').]
(8) $a\cdot b = 1, a\cdot c = 1 \vdash b = c$. [Use (6) and (7).]
(9) $\vdash \forall x 1y(x\cdot y = 1)$. [Use (8) and (A3).].

Given this result, we are evidently entitled to introduce a one-place function $f(x)$, to represent the fact that for each x there is one and only one item $f(x)$ such that $x\cdot f(x) = 1$. We shall write $f(x)$ as x^{-1}, so we have

(9') $\vdash \forall x(x\cdot x^{-1} = 1)$.

I remark incidentally that the constant 1 is called the identity of the group, and the function x^{-1} the inverse function of the group.

8.2.2. (continuing 8.2.1). Suppose that the axioms for a group are given as

$\forall xyz(x\cdot(y\cdot z) = (x\cdot y)\cdot z)$
$\forall x(x = x\cdot 1)$
$\forall x(x\cdot x^{-1} = 1)$.

(These axioms simply *assume* the existence of the constant 1 and the inverse function x^{-1} just proved.) Prove from these axioms the original axioms (A1)–(A3) of Exercise 8.2.1. [You will need to establish a couple of lemmas on the way, but I leave you to find them.]

8.2.3. Consider a theory which is supposed to axiomatize elementary arithmetic. It has in its vocabulary a constant 0, a one-place function $f(x)$ which we write as x', meaning the number after x, and two two-place predicates, namely = and <. We assume the usual laws for identity and in addition these eight axioms:

(A1) $\forall x(x'\neq 0)$.
(A2) $\forall xy(x'=y' \to x=y)$.
(A3) $\forall x(x\neq 0 \to \exists y(x=y'))$.
(A4) $\forall xyz(x<y \wedge y<z \to x<z)$.
(A5) $\forall xy\neg(x<y \wedge y<x)$.
(A6) $\forall x\neg(x<0)$.
(A7) $\forall xy(x<y \to x'<y')$.
(A8) $\forall xy(x<y' \leftrightarrow (x=y \vee x<y))$.

(*a*) Prove, informally if you wish, that the axioms imply

    (9) $\forall x\exists y(x<y \wedge \forall z(x<z \to y=z \vee y<z))$.

(*b*) Show by an interpretation that the axioms do *not* imply

    (10) $\forall xy\ (x\neq y \to x<y \vee y<x)$.

[Hint: an interpretation that verifies (A1)–(A8) must contain a set of elements corresponding to the natural numbers, i.e. with a first member (to interpret 0) and for each member a next (to interpret x'), and the relation < must be connected on this set. But consider how to add *further* elements to the interpretation, still satisfying axioms (A1)–(A8), but not connected with the elements that correspond to the natural numbers.[1]]

(*c*) Suppose that we add (10) to the axioms (A1)–(A8) as a further axiom. Show that in that case the axiom (A2) becomes superfluous.

(*d*) Show that, even if (10) is added to the axioms, still there is an interpretation in which all the axioms are true and yet this domain does not have the intended structure of the natural numbers. [Hint: your answer to part (*b*) will also answer this.]

I remark as an aside that *no* set of axioms which we can formulate in elementary logic will constrain an interpretation to have just the structure of the natural numbers. (That is a consequence of the compactness theorem; the discussion on pp. 183–4 may give a suggestion as to how it might be proved.)

8.3. Descriptions

A functional expression such as 'the father of *a*' is a special case of what is called a *definite description*. This is a singular noun-phrase, beginning with the definite article 'the', which one might naturally think of as purporting to refer to just one thing. (In a sentence such as 'The seventh child is most likely to have second sight', the phrase 'the seventh child' is a definite description

---

[1] Further hint, to be consulted if really needed:

Take the domain to consist of both the natural numbers and the signed integers, and assume that no natural number is itself a signed integer.

if, in the context, there is some particular child that is referred to, but not if the remark is intended as a generalization over all seventh children.) We can form a definite description out of any one-place predicate 'Fx' by adding a suitable prefix at the front, as in 'the thing x such that Fx'. Functional expressions are expressions of this kind, but in their case the object is always described by means of a one–many relation that it bears to some other object (or pair of objects, etc.) For example, 'the father of a' is easily seen as short for 'the thing x such that x fathered a', and similarly '$a + b$' is easily seen as short for 'the number x which results upon adding a and b'. Definite descriptions do quite often have this structure, but they do not have to. For example, 'the only man here with a blue beard' is a perfectly good definite description, but it is not naturally seen as involving any one–many relation.

It is quite natural to suppose that one uses a definite description only when one believes that, in the context, it describes one and only one thing. But (a) a little reflection shows that there are clear exceptions to this generalization. For example, one who says 'There is no such thing as the greatest prime number' is using the definite description 'the greatest prime number', but not because he believes that there is some one thing that it describes. Besides (b) even if the speaker does *believe* that his description singles out some one thing, still he may be mistaken. For example, I may say to someone, in all sincerity, 'I saw your dog in the park yesterday, chasing squirrels'. The expression 'your dog' is clearly a definite description (short for 'the dog that belongs to you'), and no doubt I would not have said what I did unless I believed that the person in question owned a dog. But I may have got it all wrong, and perhaps that person has never owned a dog. In that case I have made a definite claim, but a false claim, for I could not have seen your dog if in fact there is no such thing.

Even in ordinary speech, then, we do in fact use definite descriptions which fail to refer. And if we are going to admit descriptions into our logic, then we certainly cannot overlook this possibility. For you can form a definite description out of any one-place predicate whatever, by prefixing to it the words 'the x such that', but it would be idiotic to suppose that every one-place predicate is satisfied by exactly one object. So although a definite description looks like a name (a complex name), and in many ways behaves like a name, still it cannot *be* a name if names must always refer to objects. We therefore need some other way of handling these expressions, and it was Bertrand Russell (1905) who first provided one.

Russell introduces the notation

$$(\imath x{:}Fx)$$

to represent 'the x such that Fx'. (The symbol ⅎ is a Greek iota, upside-down.) In his symbolism this expression can take the place of a name, as in the formula

$G(\imath x{:}Fx)$.

But although the expression behaves like a name in this way, still Russell's theory is that it is not really a name. For the expression is introduced by a definition which stipulates that this whole formula is short for

$\exists y(\forall x(Fx \leftrightarrow x{=}y) \wedge Gy)$.

That is, the formula makes this complex claim: 'There is one and only one thing such that F (it), and in addition G (that thing)'. Consequently, when the definite description is not uniquely satisfied, the whole formula is false.

That is only a rough outline of Russell's theory, and we soon see that more is needed. For consider the formula

$\neg G(\imath x{:}Fx)$.

Here we must choose whether to apply the proposed analysis just to the part $G(\imath x{:}Fx)$, or to the whole formula. In the first case the $\neg$ remains at the front, undisturbed by the analysis, and we obtain

$\neg\exists y(\forall x(Fx \leftrightarrow x{=}y) \wedge Gy)$.

In the second case the $\neg$ is itself taken into the analysis, and we get

$\exists y(\forall x(Fx \leftrightarrow x{=}y) \wedge \neg Gy)$.

In the first case we say, for obvious reasons, that the $\neg$ has major scope (or wide scope), and the definite description has minor scope (or narrow scope); in the second case we say that the definite description has major scope, and the $\neg$ has minor scope. Evidently it can make a difference whether we assign the scope in one way or the other. So this at once reveals an important way in which definite descriptions differ from names on this theory, for in orthodox logic names are not regarded as having scope, whereas on Russell's theory definite descriptions certainly do. We need, then, some way of representing these scopes in our formal notation.

Russell had his own way (which I shall come to in a moment), but I think that nowadays the preferred method is to say that it was a mistake in the first place to allow definite descriptions to take the place of names. After all, if they have scopes while names do not, this must lead to trouble. So the suggestion is that the main idea behind Russell's analysis is much better presented if we 'parse' definite descriptions not as names but as quantifiers, for we all know that quantifiers must have scopes. On this proposal, the definite article 'the' is to be treated as belonging to the same category as the acknowledged quantifier-expressions 'all' and 'some'. In English all three of these expressions occur in prefixes to noun-clauses which can take the place of names, but which in standard logical notation are pulled to the front of the open sentences which represent their scopes, precisely in order to reveal what the scope is. We can think of the analysis in this way. If we start with

All men are mortal,

then the scope of the quantifying phrase 'all men' may be explicitly represented in this way:

($\forall$ men x)(x is mortal).

And then the structure of this quantifying phrase itself may be revealed by rewriting it in this form:

($\forall x$:x is a man)(x is mortal),

where the colon ':' abbreviates 'such that'. We can repeat the same suggestions both for '$\exists$', representing 'some', and for the new quantifier 'I' which I now introduce as representing 'the' when regarded as a quantifier. ('I' is, of course, a capital Greek iota, written both upside-down and back to front, as befits a quantifier.) So we now have sentences of the pattern

($\forall x$:Fx)(Gx).
($\exists x$:Fx)(Gx).
(Ix:Fx)(Gx).

The prefixes are to be read, respectively, as

For all x such that Fx
For some x such that Fx
For the x such that Fx.

These prefixes are restricted quantifiers, and as a final step they in turn may be analysed in terms of the unrestricted quantifiers used in elementary logic. Upon this analysis, the three sentence-patterns we began with are transformed into

$\forall x(Fx \rightarrow Gx)$.
$\exists x(Fx \wedge Gx)$.
$\exists x(\forall y(Fy \leftrightarrow y=z) \wedge Gx)$.

If 'the' is regarded in this way as a quantifier, then, of course, it will make a difference whether we write $\neg$ before or after (Ix:Fx), just as it makes a difference whether we write it before or after ($\forall x{:}Fx$) and ($\exists x{:}Fx$). But I remark here that in the case of I it makes a difference only when the definite description is not uniquely satisfied. Let us borrow Russell's notation once more, and abbreviate

$$\exists x\forall y(Fy \leftrightarrow y{=}z)$$

to

$$E!(\imath x{:}Fx)$$

('$E!$' is for 'exists'). Then it is perfectly simple to prove that

$E!(\imath x{:}Fx) \models (Ix{:}Fx)(\neg Gx) \leftrightarrow \neg(Ix{:}Fx)(Gx).$
$E!(\imath x{:}Fx) \models (Ix{:}Fx)(P \wedge Gx) \leftrightarrow P \wedge (Ix{:}Fx)(Gx).$
$E!(\imath x{:}Fx) \models (Ix{:}Fx)(Gx \wedge Hx) \leftrightarrow (Ix{:}Gx)(Gx) \wedge (Ix{:}Fx)(Hx).$
$E!(\imath x{:}Fx) \models (Ix{:}Fx)\forall y(Rxy) \leftrightarrow \forall y(IxFx)(Rxy).$

In fact the last three of these sequents hold without the premiss $E!(\imath x{:}Fx)$, but in place of the first we then have

$$\neg E!(\imath x{:}Fx) \models \neg(Ix{:}Fx)(Gx)$$

and hence also

$$\neg E!(\imath x{:}Fx) \models \neg(Ix{:}Fx)(\neg Gx).$$

From a technical point of view, there is nothing wrong with the definition of I just introduced, but it is extremely tedious in practice. I illustrate with a couple of examples from arithmetic. Suppose that we have a couple of three-place predicates representing addition and multiplication thus:

$Sxyz$: adding x and y yields z.
$Pxyz$: multiplying x and y yields z.

From these we can, of course, form the definite description quantifiers

$(Iz{:}Sxyz)$
$(Iz{:}Pxyz)$.

And we can use these to analyse arithmetical sentences containing '+' and '·'. For example, the simple statement

$$a + b = b + a$$

can be analysed in this way:

$(Ix{:}Sabx)(Iy{:}Sbay)(x{=}y)$.

This is already a little unexpected, but—one might say—perhaps we could get used to it. Consider, then, something just a bit more complicated, such as

$$a \cdot (b+c) = a \cdot b + a \cdot c.$$

After some thought, one sees that the analysis must be this:

$$(\mathrm{I}x{:}Sbcx)(\mathrm{I}y{:}Paby)(\mathrm{I}z{:}Pacz)(\mathrm{I}u{:}Paxu)(\mathrm{I}v{:}Syzv)(u{=}v).$$

And with the present notation there appears to be no way of introducing any simplifications.

Contrast with this what the position would have been if we had retained the original symbol ı, conceived as an operator which produces from an open sentence, not a quantifier, but a (complex) name. We could then have written

$$a + b = b + a$$

in the simpler form

$$(\mathrm{ı}x{:}Sabx) = (\mathrm{ı}x{:}Sbax).$$

And we could indeed have returned to the original notation, which is simpler still, by saying: let us *abbreviate*

$$a + b \quad \text{for} \quad (\mathrm{ı}x{:}Sabx).$$

This abbreviation is available with $(\mathrm{ı}x{:}Sabx)$, since in this expression the variable x is bound by the prefix $\mathrm{ı}x$, and no occurrences of x outside the expression are relevant to its interpretation. Hence an abbreviation may omit the variable x altogether. But we cannot do the same with the quantifier $(\mathrm{I}x{:}Sabx)$, since this quantifier is used to bind *further* occurrences of x. Consequently, if an abbreviation omits x from $(\mathrm{I}x{:}Sabx)$, then the rest of the formula must fall into confusion. Thus the quantifying notation, apparently needed in order to represent scopes explicitly, also prevents one from using the simple and traditional notation of ordinary mathematics.

Russell himself proposed an ingenious way out of the difficulty. Suppose that we begin with definite descriptions construed as variable-binding quantifiers. Thus, to continue with the same example, the description 'the x such that $Sabx$' occurs in contexts of the kind

$$(\mathrm{I}x{:}Sabx)(\text{---}x\text{---}x\text{---}).$$

Then, to obtain Russell's own notation, for each subsequent occurrence of x, bound by $(\mathrm{I}x{:}Sabx)$, we write instead the namelike expression $(\mathrm{ı}x{:}Sabx)$. At the same time we write ι in place of I in the original quantifier, but change its surrounding brackets to square brackets, in order to show which occurrences of this expression are quantifiers and which are not. Thus we reach

$$[\iota x{:}Sabx](\text{---}(\iota x{:}Sabx)\text{---}(\iota x{:}Sabx)\text{---}).$$

This is the notation Russell uses himself, and, as I have indicated, it is easily seen as just a variation on the natural way of representing descriptions as quantifiers. But in practice it has two great advantages. First, there is now no obstacle to abbreviating a definite description in a way that omits its variable *x*. Thus, in place of the formula above we may write simply

$$[a{+}b](\text{---}(a{+}b)\text{---}(a{+}b)\text{---}).$$

Second, we may introduce a convention by which the initial quantifying expression $[\iota x{:}Sabx]$ or $[a{+}b]$ may be omitted altogether. Russell's basic idea here is that such a quantifier may be omitted when its scope is the smallest possible, i.e. when its scope is an atomic formula, but it must be shown explicitly when it includes in its scope either truth-functors or other quantifiers. In practice, however, he *also* allows the omission of a description-quantifier when its scope contains other *description*-quantifiers. Thus he would omit *both* description-quantifiers from

$$[a{+}b][b{+}a]((a{+}b) = (b{+}a))$$

and he would omit *all five* from

$$[b{+}c][a{\cdot}b][a{\cdot}c][a{\cdot}(b{+}c)][(a{\cdot}b) + (a{\cdot}c)]((a{\cdot}(b{+}c)) = ((a{\cdot}b) + (a{\cdot}c))).$$

To avoid ambiguity, then, we need further conventions to tell us in what order the description-quantifiers are to be restored when more than one has been omitted, and this order must take account of the fact that a complex description may contain another description inside itself, as the second example illustrates. But I shall not delay to formulate such conventions. The basic idea is, I hope, clear enough.

Russell's own procedure, then, is a very ingenious way of getting the best of both worlds. In practice, definite descriptions are for the most part treated as names, since this is by far the most convenient notation, but in theory they are treated as quantifiers, since in theory they are assigned scopes, and quantifiers have scopes whereas names do not. Moreover, theory and practice fit quite nicely with one another, because in contexts where we need to make *serious* use of descriptions we always assure ourselves first that the descriptions are uniquely satisfied. And when a description is uniquely satisfied then it does behave like a name, since all ways of assigning its scope are equivalent to one another.[2] But the theory will still accommodate descriptions that are not uniquely satisfied, just because in theory they are quantifiers and not names.

Despite Russell's ingenious compromise, I think one still feels that there is a tension in this theory, just because descriptions are officially introduced in one way but then treated as much as possible in a different way. The need for this tension arises because, although descriptions do behave very much as names do, still we began by saying that they could not actually *be* names, since a description can fail to refer but a name cannot. But it is now time to look once more at that very basic assumption: why must we say that a name cannot lack a reference?

EXERCISES

8.3.1. Prove by an informal argument, with just enough detail to be convincing, that the following formulae are all equivalent. (Hence any of them might have been used to provide a Russellian analysis of 'the *F* is *G*'.)

   (1) $\exists x(\forall y(Fy \leftrightarrow y{=}x) \wedge Gx)$
   (2) $\exists x \forall y(Fy \leftrightarrow y{=}x) \wedge \forall x(Fx \rightarrow Gx)$
   (3) $\forall x \forall y(Fx \wedge Fy \rightarrow x{=}y) \wedge \exists x(Fx \wedge Gx)$.

8.3.2.(*a*) Prove, by any means you like, the sequents cited on p. 345.
(*b*) Show in detail how these justify the claim that, where a definite description is uniquely satisfied, all ways of assigning its scope are equivalent.

8.3.3. Taking the domain to be the real numbers, use the definite description quantifier I, and the predicates *Sxyz* and *Pxyz* of p. 345, to give an analysis of

   (1) $a+(b+c) = (a+b)+c$.
   (2) $(a+b)^2 = a^2 + 2ab + b^2$.
   (3) $\dfrac{a}{b} + \dfrac{c}{d} = \dfrac{a{\cdot}d + b{\cdot}c}{b{\cdot}d}$.

Is (3), in your analysis, a true statement?

8.4. Empty Names and Empty Domains

A name is said to be empty if it denotes nothing, and we assumed at the beginning of Chapter 3 that names could not be empty. That is, we did not

---

[2] For some qualifications that seem to be needed here, see the appendix to this chapter.

allow name-letters to be interpreted as empty. Equally, we did not allow the domain of an interpretation to be empty. These decisions are connected, for if domains are allowed to be empty, then one must also allow names to be empty, as I now show.

Assume, for *reductio*, that a domain may be empty but that names must not be. Now in an empty domain it is clear that any formula beginning with an existential quantifier must be interpreted as false. Retaining the usual relation between $\exists$ and $\forall$, it then follows that any formula beginning with a universal quantifier must be interpreted as true. It is, as one says, 'vacuously' true. It should be observed that this ruling does fit with the semantics originally given for the quantifiers on p. 85. For if I is an interpretation with an empty domain, then there is no variant interpretation I_α for any name α. This is because a variant interpretation I_α must retain the same domain as I, but must also interpret α, and it cannot do both if the domain of I is empty but α cannot be interpreted as empty. But the semantics for $\exists$ says that $\exists\xi\varphi$ is to be interpreted as true in I iff there is a variant interpretation I_α which ..., and we have just said that in an empty domain there is no such variant. Similarly, the semantics for $\forall$ says that $\forall\xi\varphi$ is to be interpreted as true in I iff for all variant interpretations I_α..., and this is vacuously the case if I has an empty domain. In an empty domain, then, $\forall\xi\varphi$ is always true and $\exists\xi\varphi$ is always false.

With this understanding it is clear that the sequent

$$\forall xFx \vDash Fa$$

remains correct, even if we include interpretations with an empty domain. For still there is no interpretation which makes $\forall xFx$ true and Fa false. To be sure, an interpretation with an empty domain will always make $\forall xFx$ true, but it cannot make Fa false, for since a has no interpretation on an empty domain, neither does Fa. In an entirely similar way the sequent

$$Fa \vDash \exists xFx$$

remains correct, for again there is no interpretation which makes Fa true and $\exists xFx$ false. By the Cut principle, you expect it to follow that the sequent

$$\forall xFx \vDash \exists xFx$$

must also be correct, and yet clearly this cannot be so, since the empty domain provides a counter-example. So one has to conclude that, in the situation envisaged, the Cut principle must fail. And in fact if you look back to the proof of that principle given on pp. 31–2 and p. 97, you will see that it requires an assumption which cannot be satisfied if we have empty domains but no empty names.

Not only does the Cut principle fail in this situation, but so also does what one might well call 'the oldest rule in the book', namely Modus Ponens. We need only a small modification of the example to make this point. By the same reasoning as before, the two sequents

$$\models Fa \vee \neg Fa$$
$$\models (Fa \vee \neg Fa) \to \exists x(Fx \vee \neg Fx)$$

remain correct, even if empty domains are permitted, as you may easily check. But their consequence by Modus Ponens, namely

$$\models \exists x(Fx \vee \neg Fx),$$

is no longer correct in this situation. These results seem to me to be wholly intolerable,[3] and I infer that any proposal that leads to them must therefore be rejected. In particular, then, we must reject the proposal that domains can be empty whereas names cannot.

The reason why this proposal led to an intolerable result was because it implies that there are formulae—i.e. those containing name-letters—which can only be interpreted on some of the permitted domains, but not on all. This situation is avoided if both names and domains may be interpreted as empty. For in that case a name *can* be interpreted on the empty domain, namely by interpreting it as denoting nothing. On this proposal the sequent

$$\models (Fa \vee \neg Fa) \to \exists x(Fx \vee \neg Fx)$$

is no longer correct. To see this clearly, take '*Fa*' as abbreviating '*a* exists'. Then on any domain $Fa \vee \neg Fa$ will be true, for if *a* is interpreted as denoting something in that domain, then *Fa* will be true, and if *a* is interpreted as not denoting—which it must be, if the domain is empty—then $\neg Fa$ will be true. But yet there is an interpretation in which $\exists x(Fx \vee \neg Fx)$ is false, namely one with an empty domain. In a similar way, both of the sequents

$$\forall x Fx \models Fa$$
$$Fa \models \exists x Fx$$

must be rejected as incorrect, if names may be empty as well as domains, as you are invited to work out for yourself. The two 'intolerable' results just mentioned are thus prevented on the new proposal. More generally you will find that the proof of the Cut principle originally given on p. 97 is now rescued.

[3] One has to admit that the results are *accepted* in Hodges (1977).

I conclude that if empty domains are permitted, then empty names must be permitted too. There is no equally strong argument for the converse conditional, that if empty names are permitted, then empty domains must be permitted too, but only a challenge: what motive might there be for allowing the one but not the other? This, however, brings us to what is obviously the main question: what positive motives are there for allowing either? Well, in each case the chief motive is that this represents a genuine possibility that should not be ignored. I offer three lines of argument for this conclusion. The first is a tricky line of argument, running into several problems and open to some quite plausible objections, which I shall not explore in any detail. So here I merely sketch the argument, since I think that it does have *some* force, but I do not pretend that what I say here adds up to a conclusive case. The second and third lines of argument are altogether more straightforward, and I think it is clear that they make a very strong case.

1. The first argument begins from the premisses (*a*) that logic is by tradition supposed to be an a priori science, i.e. one that needs no assistance from empirical enquiry, but also (*b*) that logic is used in the practical assessment of real arguments. Now, when we are aiming to test a real argument, the first thing that we need to do is to determine the domain of discourse of the argument, i.e. the domain over which the quantifiers employed are intended to range, and in practice one chooses different domains for different arguments. For example, one can often say that, for the purposes of this argument, only people need be included in the domain, or only items of furniture, or only cities, or whatever it may be. One can tell what the domain is supposed to be just by understanding what is being said at each point in the argument. But then, if the evaluation of the argument is to proceed a priori, we should not be relying upon our empirical knowledge when selecting a domain. Yet if domains have to be non-empty, then this cannot be avoided, for we cannot know a priori that there are people, or bits of furniture, or cities, and so on. A similar argument evidently applies to names. One cannot tell a priori whether a name that is being used as the name of a person really does denote a person, since one cannot tell a priori whether that alleged person does exist. Hence if our logic requires that an expression can be counted as a name only when it does denote something, then the logical testing of an argument cannot after all be an a priori process, as it was supposed to be.

This line of argument is open to various objections. One might try to avoid the point about domains by saying that logic never *requires* us to confine attention to this or that special domain, and we can always take the domain to be 'everything whatever' if we wish to. Then it can be added that, for logical purity, the domain should always be taken in this way, just because we *can* know a priori that there is at least *something*. But this reply raises many problems. For example, it could be argued (i) that logic does require one to confine attention to a special domain if the predicates (and functions) being considered are only defined on that special domain; (ii) that we cannot in fact make sense of the alleged domain of 'everything whatever'; (iii) that even if we can make sense of this domain, still our knowledge that it is non-empty cannot be a priori. I shall not pursue these problems any further.

Turning to the point about names, one might say that philosophers are now familiar with several theories of names, and some of them do seem to have the consequence that one cannot understand a name unless it does denote something. From this it may be inferred that one cannot understand a name without *knowing* that it denotes something, and hence that this knowledge must count as a priori. Again there are many problems. For example, (i) the inference from 'understanding requires that the name denotes' to 'understanding requires *knowing* that the name denotes' is surely questionable; (ii) whether it follows that this knowledge is a priori is also questionable, and must depend upon a detailed account of what a priori knowledge is; anyway (iii) the position invites this general response: if one cannot understand a genuine name without understanding that it is non-empty, then there can be only very few expressions that qualify as genuine names—perhaps only demonstratives such as 'this'. Once more, I shall not pursue these problems any further.

I remark finally about this line of argument that in any case one might wish to question the premiss upon which it is based. It certainly is part of the tradition that the study of logic contrasts with, say, the study of physics, on the ground that logic is a priori and physics is not. But there are plenty of philosophers nowadays who would call this tradition into question. I pass on, then, to my two other lines of argument, which do not invoke the notion of a priori knowledge.

2. The second argument retains the premiss that we are supposed to be able to apply our logic to test ordinary arguments for validity. Now, as I said in Section 1.2, an argument is a valid argument iff it is not possible for all its premisses to be true and its conclusion false. But in logic we do not study particular propositions, and particular arguments built from them, but proceed schematically, by working with formulae and sequents. A sequent is not itself a particular argument, but is rather a general pattern of argument, which actual arguments may exemplify. The idea is that if in our logic we can

show that a certain pattern of argument is a correct pattern, then it should follow that all arguments exemplifying that pattern are correct, i.e. valid, arguments. But how is this supposed to follow? Well, we count a pattern of argument as a correct pattern if there is no interpretation which makes all the premisses true and the conclusion false, and this is supposed to imply that in any argument of that pattern there is no possible situation in which all its premisses are true and its conclusion is false. The implication evidently depends upon the point that the interpretations considered in logic do exhaust all the possible situations for an actual argument. But this will not be so if interpretations are not permitted to have empty domains or empty names. For it *is* possible that there should have been nothing in the domain specified, whatever the specification, and it *is* possible that a named object should not have existed. These are genuine possibilities, even if we know (perhaps, in some cases, a priori) that they do not obtain in fact.

Someone may say: but why should we bother to take into account these possibilities which we know are not realized? I take this to be a proposal to amend the definition of validity for arguments, by building in a clause saying that a possibility can be ignored if it is known (or anyway, if it is *well known*?) that it is not realized. But this is quite contrary to the spirit of logic. We can see this clearly if we look back to an interesting episode in the development of the subject. It is well known that Aristotle's system of syllogistic logic accepted as correct some laws which nowadays we reject, for example

$$\models (\text{Some } Fs \text{ are } G) \text{ or } (\text{Some } Fs \text{ are not } G).$$

The explanation is that Aristotle was failing to take into account the possibility of there being no *Fs* at all. So we say today that several of the argument-patterns which he accepted as correct are not actually correct, for they need the extra premiss

There are some *Fs*.

We may concede to him that very often this extra premiss would state only what was well known both to the arguer and to his audience, and so it would be unsurprising if in practice it was often omitted. After all, in practice we often do omit all kinds of premiss as too obvious to need an explicit statement. But still we should insist that logic alone cannot certify the argument to be correct until the extra premiss is explicitly put in. So too, it seems to me, with the possibility of a whole domain of quantification being empty, and of a named object failing to exist. What is still today the standard logic ignores these possibilities, but that means that it is sometimes *mistaken* in which arguments it counts as valid. For some of these arguments require extra premisses, stating that a named object does exist, or that at least something exists, if they are to be valid in the proper sense. Again we may concede that in practice these extra premisses very often go without saying, since they are well known to all participants. But that should not prevent us from insisting that pure logic can certify such an argument to be valid only if the missing premisses are explicitly put in.

3. My third argument no longer concerns the practical application of logic in testing ordinary arguments, but the role that elementary logic has as forming the basis on which to build more advanced logics. Here I briefly consider just one such more advanced logic, namely modal logic, which studies the two sentence-functors 'it is possible that' and 'it is necessary that'. These are abbreviated to '$\Diamond$' and '$\Box$' respectively. One sets out such a logic by first assuming the appropriate elementary logic, and then adding more rules or axioms to deal with the modal sentence-functors. A standard rule for this purpose, adopted in many systems, is the so-called rule of necessitation, stating that what can be proved is necessary:

If $\vdash \varphi$ then $\vdash \Box\varphi$.

But this rule is clearly incorrect if as our underlying elementary logic we take the logic studied up to this point, which does not permit empty names. For in this logic we have, for any name a,

$\vdash \exists x(x=a)$.

But we do *not* want

$\vdash \Box\exists x(x=a)$.

For even though Margaret Thatcher does exist—and even if the name 'Margaret Thatcher', used as we use it, would not have existed unless Margaret Thatcher had existed—still it is not a necessary truth that Margaret Thatcher exists. On the contrary, it is evidently possible that she should not have done. (For she would not have existed if her mother had died at the age of 10, and that is something that might have happened). An entirely similar point holds about empty domains. In the logic studied up to now we have, e.g.

$\vdash \exists x(x=x)$.

But we do *not* want

$\vdash \Box\exists x(x=x)$.

For it is a possibility that nothing should have existed at all.

It may be replied to this argument that the rule of necessitation is not sacrosanct, and there is in principle no reason why we should not retain our existing elementary logic and modify or abandon this rule. That is, no doubt, an avenue that one might explore. But it is surely a more straightforward course to modify the elementary logic so that only necessary truths can be proved in it. The rest of this chapter presents such a modification.

EXERCISES

8.4.1. Look back to the proof in section 3.7 that for every formula there is an equivalent formula in PNF.
(*a*) Explain where that proof breaks down if empty domains are permitted.
(*b*) Show that this breakdown cannot be repaired, i.e. that there is a formula which has no equivalent in PNF, if empty domains are permitted.
(*c*) Do you think this provides a good argument for saying that empty domains should not be permitted?

8.4.2. If you know of any philosophical arguments in favour of the dictum 'existence is not a predicate', consider whether those arguments show that the traditional logic is right to discount the possibility of a named object not existing.

8.5. Extensionality Reconsidered

In Section 3.1 I introduced two principles about names which underlie the whole treatment of names in the traditional logic. One was that a name always has a denotation, and I have just been arguing that this principle should be rejected. The other was the principle of extensionality, that if two different names denote the same object, then they behave as if they were the same name, i.e. either may be substituted for the other in any context. This is reflected, of course, in the adoption of Leibniz's law,

$$a = b \models (Fa \leftrightarrow Fb),$$

as a principle governing identity. I noted at the time that in a natural language there would be many occurrences of names that seemed to conflict with this principle, but said that for the purposes of elementary logic these must just be set aside. For we cannot recognize anything as an occurrence of a name unless the principle of extensionality applies to it. But if we decide to jettison the first principle, that names must always have denotations, then what becomes of the second?

Well, since there do seem to be many exceptions to this second principle, one might wish to jettison it as well. And there would be good reason to do so if we were trying to develop a more advanced logic concerning what is necessary or possible, or what is knowable a priori, or simply what is known or believed or held probable or something of the sort. For in such contexts as these the principle of extensionality very frequently seems to fail. But that is not our present task. At the moment we are simply considering the ordinary and straightforward areas of language which one usually regards as subject only to elementary logic, and not needing an advanced treatment. Is there any need to say that in these simple contexts extensionality must be abandoned once empty names are permitted?

There is not. On the contrary, there is a great need to retain the principle so far as possible, for, as I pointed out (p. 74), it is built into the ordinary semantics for elementary logic. For example, when a name-letter is interpreted as denoting something, then all that we provide by way of an interpretation is the object denoted. Similarly, all that we provide by way of interpretation for a one-place predicate-letter is the set of objects that it is true of. There is nothing in this simple apparatus that could explain how a predicate might be 'true of' an object under one name but not under another, and it would clearly be going beyond the confines of elementary logic if we tried to introduce a more complex apparatus. I conclude that extensionality must be retained when we are dealing with names that do denote, so the problem is: how are we to explain extensionality for names that do not denote? I think the answer is quite straightforward. If the truth-value of a predication depends only on *what* the name denotes, so that it must remain the same for any other name denoting the same thing, then when it turns out that the name denotes nothing, that fact *itself* must determine the truth-value. So the truth-value will remain the same for any other name that also denotes nothing.

To illustrate, consider the simple predicate 'x is a horse'. It is undeniable that if in place of 'x' we have a name that denotes something, then whether the whole is true or not depends only on whether the thing denoted is a horse. And it cannot possibly happen that two names denote the same thing, but one of them denotes a horse and the other does not. So the principle of extensionality is certainly satisfied in this case. It is also satisfied with names that denote nothing, if we say—as seems to me very reasonable—that only what exists can be a horse. Thus it is not true that Jupiter is a horse, principally because Jupiter does not exist, though in this case one may wish to add that even if he did exist, he still would not be a horse. (Here is an interesting question for philosophers: how do you know that?) Equally, it is not true that Pegasus is a horse, and again this is because Pegasus does not exist (and never did). Here one is tempted to say that if Pegasus had existed he would have been a horse. By the same token, he would have been winged. So there would have been a winged horse. But as things are, there are no winged horses, since Pegasus is not a horse. And this is simply because Pegasus does not exist (now, or at any other time).

Two comments may be made at once. First, there are people who will protest that 'Pegasus is a horse' should be accepted as true, and one must admit that we do often talk in this way. When our discourse is about fictional characters, it appears that we take a domain of quantification that includes these characters, and we count it as true that P if the relevant story says (or implies) that P, and as false that P if the relevant story says (or implies) that $\neg P$. From a logical point of view, however, one cannot take this proposal seriously, since it must lead to a breakdown in elementary logical laws. Thus $P \vee \neg P$ will not be true when the relevant story says nothing either way, and, worse, $P \wedge \neg P$ *will* be true when the relevant story is inconsistent. So we would do better to say that this way of talking is really a shorthand. We talk as if we took it to be true that P when all that we really mean—or should mean—is that it is true that *it is said in the story that P*. To apply this to the example in hand, we should continue to insist that

Pegasus is a horse

is *not* true, but we add that there is a related statement which *is* true, namely

It is said in Greek mythology that Pegasus is a horse.

The two statements are, of course, different statements, and the first would follow from the second only if whatever is said in Greek mythology is true. But the fact is that most of what is said in Greek mythology is not true, and this includes the claim 'Pegasus is a horse'.

Second, there are people who, when persuaded that 'Pegasus is a horse' is not true, think that the same should therefore apply to 'Pegasus is not a horse'. Their thought is that *neither* of these can be true if Pegasus does not exist. But I see no reason to agree. For negation is so defined that '$\neg P$' counts as true in any situation in which 'P' is not true, and so in the present situation '$\neg$(Pegasus is a horse)' *is* true. If this is rejected, then certainly the familiar logic can no longer be upheld, and we would apparently need a 'third truth-value', i.e. 'neither true nor false'. But such a reaction is surely too extreme. Observe, first, that we must certainly reject the perfectly general principle that *nothing* can be true of *a* unless *a* exists, for when *a* does not exist it is quite clear that '$\neg$(*a* exists)' *is* true of *a*. It follows that when '*Fa*' implies '*a* exists', and the truth is that $\neg$(*a* exists), then also the truth is that $\neg Fa$. People who are still uneasy about this may perhaps be placated by this suggestion: perhaps they are understanding 'Pegasus is not a horse' not as the negation of 'Pegasus is a horse', but as equivalent to

(Pegasus exists) $\land \neg$(Pegasus is a horse).

Certainly, *this* is no more true than 'Pegasus is a horse'.[4]

To return to the original question concerning extensionality, I propose that this principle be preserved in an elementary logic which admits empty names by the ruling that all empty names are to behave alike, i.e. that substituting any one for any other will always leave truth-values unchanged. The suggested elucidation of this is that where '*F*' represent an *atomic* predicate, such as '. . . is a horse', then '*Fa*' will be false whenever '*a*' denotes nothing. The truth-values of more complex sentences containing '*a*' will then be determined in the usual way by the truth-values of their atomic components; in particular, if '*Fa*' is false when '*a*' denotes nothing, then '$\neg Fa$' will be true when '*a*' denotes nothing. I observe here that this gives the right result when '*Fa*' is '*a* exists'. This is an atomic statement, so by the suggested ruling, when '*a*' denotes nothing we shall have '*a* exists' as false and '$\neg$(*a* exists)' as true. This is evidently as it should be.

This ruling has an effect upon what sentences of ordinary language we can accept, for logical purposes, as made up from a predicate and a name. For example, consider a sentence

John is painting a picture of *a*.

It is quite easy to see this sentence as satisfying the principle of extensionality when the name '*a*' does denote something, but we still have a problem when it does not. Previously we had to say that we cannot count this as a sentence of the form '*Fa*' when '*a*' fails to refer, since our stipulation was that all names must refer. Now we do not rule it out on this ground, but we must still rule it out nevertheless. For 'Pegasus' refers to nothing, and so does 'Jupiter', so if we accept

---

4 Philosophers will note at this point that I am making no distinction between on the one hand saying or implying that Pegasus exists, and on the other hand *presupposing* this point. That is a fair comment, but one which I do not propose to discuss. Presupposition can have no place in elementary logic.

John is painting a picture of Pegasus

as containing the name 'Pegasus', then we must also accept

John is painting a picture of Jupiter

as obtained from it by substituting one empty name for another. But then our extensionality principle would require us to say that the two sentences must have the same truth-values, which is wholly paradoxical, since it is clear that a picture of Pegasus is not at all the same thing as a picture of Jupiter. The result then is that for the purposes of elementary logic we still cannot accept 'John is painting a picture of Pegasus' as made up from a name 'Pegasus' and a predicate 'John is painting a picture of . . .'.

This situation is common. Where previously we had to say that an apparent example of name-plus-predicate structure could not be accepted at face value, just because the name was empty, so now we quite often have to reach the same conclusion, but on the different ground that empty names do not all behave alike in that context. But this does not happen always, and there are some sentences which we can now recognize as having the form '*Fa*' but could not have done before. The simplest and most prominent examples are the sentences

$\neg(a$ exists$)$.

Previously we had to say that no such sentence was of the form '*Fa*', because we required that, for any admissible sentence '*Fa*',

$Fa \vDash \exists xFx.$

Naturally, this does not hold for '$\neg(a$ exists$)$' in place of '*Fa*'. But with our revised conception it no longer has to.

Let us move on, then, to consider just what rules of inference do hold on the revised conception.

EXERCISE

8.5.1. Consider the sentence

John is writing a story about King Arthur.

Do we have to say that this sentence means one thing if King Arthur did exist, but a different thing if there was no such person?

8.6. Towards a Universally Free Logic

A 'free' logic is one in which names are permitted to be empty. A 'universally free' logic is one in which the domain of an interpretation may also be empty, and our object now is to formulate such a system. In this section I approach the topic by asking how the familiar rules of inference need to be modified for this purpose. For definiteness, I shall concentrate attention upon the rules required for a tableau system of proof.

As I argued on pp. 357–8, the rules for the truth-functors are not affected by the new view of names and domains, so we may turn at once to the quantifier rules. The familiar tableau rules are

$$
\begin{array}{cccc}
\forall\xi\varphi & \neg\forall\xi\varphi & \exists\xi\varphi & \neg\exists\xi\varphi \\
| & | & | & | \\
\varphi(\tau/\xi) & \neg\varphi(\alpha/\xi) & \varphi(\alpha/\xi) & \neg\varphi(\tau/\xi)
\end{array}
$$

provided α is new

But the intended interpretation is now that the quantifiers range only over existing things (as before), whereas the terms are not so restricted, and this means that each rule requires a modification. First, the two outer rules need to be weakened. For, if τ is a term that fails to denote, then from the premiss that all *existing* things satisfy φ it will not follow that τ satisfies φ. (For a clear counter-example take $\varphi(\tau/\xi)$ as 'τ exists'.) So here we need to add the extra premiss that τ exists, if the inference is to remain sound. The same evidently applies to the rule for $\neg\exists$. By contrast, the two inner rules can be strengthened. For example, the premiss to the $\exists$ rule tells us that there *exists* something satisfying φ, and we argue as before that we can therefore introduce a name α for that thing, provided that the name is a new name, i.e. one that has not already been used for anything else. It then follows as before that α satisfies φ, but now we can *also* add something further, namely that α exists. Abbreviating 'α exists' to '$E!\alpha$', our four rules therefore need modifying in this way:

$$
\begin{array}{cccc}
\forall\xi\varphi & \neg\forall\xi\varphi & \exists\xi\varphi & \neg\exists\xi\varphi \\
E!\tau & | & | & E!\tau \\
| & E!\alpha & E!\alpha & | \\
\varphi(\tau/\xi) & \neg\varphi(\alpha/\xi) & \varphi(\alpha/\xi) & \neg\varphi(\tau/\xi)
\end{array}
$$

provided α is new

So far this is all very straightforward, and all free logics are in agreement. It is easy to see that the quantifier rules do need modifying in these ways, and

360

that the modified rules are sound under the revised conception. Hence we cannot prove from them any sequents which must now be counted as incorrect, such as

$$\forall x Fx \models \exists x Fx$$

or

$$\models \exists x (Fx \vee \neg Fx)$$

or indeed

$$\models \exists x E!x.$$

But we can prove some new sequents which are correct on the new conception, such as

$$\models \forall x E!x.$$

The next thing to ask, therefore, is whether we can prove *all* such sequents, i.e. whether the new quantifier rules are complete for the new conception.

The answer to this depends upon what exactly the new conception is. In particular, I have argued in the last section that the principle of extensionality should be extended to empty names by requiring that all empty names behave alike, and this is a thesis that can certainly be formulated in the vocabulary now being used, thus

$$\text{EXT:} \quad \neg E!\tau_1, \neg E!\tau_2 \models \varphi(\tau_1/\xi) \leftrightarrow \varphi(\tau_2/\xi)$$

('EXT' is for 'extensionality'.) But we certainly cannot prove this principle from the quantifier rules already stated. Now some free logics do not adopt this principle EXT, and they may count the four quantifier rules already given as complete. But I have argued that EXT should be adopted, and since we cannot prove it from what we have already, on my conception these four rules are not complete. Suppose, then, that EXT is added as a new rule of inference. Will that give us a complete system? Well, in a sense, yes.[5] But our present rules use $E!$ as a primitive and undefined predicate, because they do not yet say anything about identity. Once we add identity, however, $E!$ will surely be definable, for we expect it to be true that

$$E!\tau =\models \exists \xi (\xi = \tau).$$

So before I come back to the question of completeness, I now proceed to consider what rules we ought to have for identity in a free logic. (On this question there is no general agreement amongst logicians.)

---

[5] But also, in a sense, no. The position will be clarified in the following section.

The principle of extensionality for names that do denote objects holds under the new conception just as much as it did under the old. So we may lay it down that

LL: $\tau_1 = \tau_2 \models \varphi(\tau_1/\xi) \leftrightarrow \varphi(\tau_2/\xi)$

('LL' is for 'Leibniz's law'). On this there is universal agreement, so far as I know. But it is not so clear whether we should retain the other principle for identity,

$\models \tau = \tau$

for *all* terms τ whatever, or whether we should say that only existent things can be identical with anything, and hence that only they can be self-identical.

We should observe first that EXT has this implication: if even non-existent things are still counted as self-identical, then all non-existent things must be counted as identical with one another. For, as an instance of EXT, we have

$\neg E!a, \neg E!b \models (a=a \leftrightarrow a=b).$

If, then, $a=a$ holds for all names a whatever, whether or not a exists, we can infer

$\neg E!a, \neg E!b \models a=b.$

This apparently says that there is at most one non-existent thing. As such, it is a principle well suited to the approach whereby a name that appears to denote nothing is always treated, despite appearances, as denoting something —either some arbitrarily chosen and familiar object, such as the number 0, or perhaps a specially invented object called 'the null object'. (This 'null object' must then be a member of *all* domains, even those that we think of as empty, since it must be possible to interpret a name-letter on any domain.) But such an approach is hardly attractive. I have already noted (pp. 338–9) that we obtain unwanted truths if we suppose that what appears to name nothing does actually name an arbitrarily chosen but familiar object. We do not get this consequence with 'the null object', since it is not a familiar object already figuring in familiar truths. On the contrary, it is a wholly unfamiliar object, invented just to be the thing that all otherwise empty names denote. As such, one must admit that it is technically convenient, and a neat way of upholding the principle that all empty names behave alike. But, at the same time, it is sheer fantasy, and we do not actually *need* any such fantasy. We can perfectly well say that a name may be interpreted as denoting nothing, without having to suppose that this 'nothing' is really something, but a strange thing.

If we do dispense with the fantasy, then the suggestion that all non-existent things are identical with one another will get no support in this way, and I think that it gets no support in any other way either. But there is an argument against it. For I have said that a good general principle is that when F represents an atomic predicate, and a a name that denotes nothing, then Fa is to be false. This principle seems to me to work very well for a wide range of simple atomic predicates. But then we have only to add that identity is to be regarded as a simple atomic predicate, and we have a definite ruling on the present issue: if a does not exist, then $a=b$ is always to be false, whatever b may be; hence as a special case $a=a$ is false too.[6]

Now the sequent

$$b=a \models a=a$$

is provable just from LL by itself. Hence by the quantifier rules we already have a proof of

$$\exists x(x=a) \models a=a.$$

The decision that $a=a$ is to be true only when a exists now allows us to affirm the converse

$$(*) \quad a=a \models \exists x(x=a).$$

It follows that either $a=a$ or $\exists x(x=a)$ would do equally well as our analysis of $E!a$. It turns out, however, that there is an advantage in choosing the first. For if we write $\tau=\tau$ in place of $E!\tau$ (and $\alpha=\alpha$ in place of $E!\alpha$) in the quantifier rules as formulated on p. 360, then it turns out that $(*)$ is deducible, whereas if we write $\exists\xi(\xi=\tau)$ instead, then $(*)$ will be needed as a separate postulate. I therefore adopt this decision. We shall have as a definition

$$E!\tau \quad \text{for} \quad \tau=\tau.$$

Our basic rules will then be the four quantifier rules of p. 360, but with $E!$ eliminated in favour of its definition, and in addition just EXT and LL as further rules. In the context of a tableau system of proof, these are formulated as

---

[6] One *might* claim that identity should *not* be regarded as a simple atomic predicate. In a *second*-order logic it may be defined thus:

$$a=b \quad \text{for} \quad \forall F(Fa \leftrightarrow Fb).$$

On this definition it is not atomic, and $a=a$ is always true, whether or not a exists. (Similarly, $a=b$ is true if neither a nor b exists.)

$$\begin{array}{cccc}
\tau_1 \neq \tau_1 & \tau_1 \neq \tau_1 & \tau_1 = \tau_2 & \tau_1 = \tau_2 \\
\tau_2 \neq \tau_2 & \tau_2 \neq \tau_2 & \varphi(\tau_1/\xi) & \varphi(\tau_2/\xi) \\
\varphi(\tau_1/\xi) & \varphi(\tau_2/\xi) & | & | \\
| & | & \varphi(\tau_2/\xi) & \varphi(\tau_1/\xi) \\
\varphi(\tau_2/\xi) & \varphi(\tau_1/\xi) & &
\end{array}$$

This completes our combined theory for quantifiers and identity together.

I remark here that some free logics adopt the principle that, if Φ^n is any *atomic* predicate-letter, then for $1 \leq i \leq n$

$$\Phi^n(\tau_1,...,\tau_n) \models E!\tau_i.$$

I think, however, that this is due to a confusion. I have already said that I think this is a very reasonable thesis where Φ^n is an atomic *predicate*, but predicates are not the same as *predicate-letters*. On the contrary, the role of the predicate-letter is to take the place of *all* kinds of predicates, and not only atomic ones. That is why the principle of uniform substitution for predicate-letters is a correct principle.

A similar principle that is sometimes proposed applies this idea to function-letters. The suggestion is that if θ^n is any n-place function-letter, then we should have, for $1 \leq i \leq n$,

$$E!\theta^n(\tau_1,...,\tau_n) \models E!\tau_i.$$

But I think that this suggestion too should be rejected. No doubt many familiar functions do obey the proposed condition that they are defined— i.e. have a value which exists—only for arguments which themselves exist. But there seems to be no reason to insist that all functions whatever must be like this. For example, it is often useful to introduce, for any predicate, its corresponding 'characteristic function'. The definition takes this form: given a predicate F—a one-place predicate, for simplicity—we introduce the corresponding function f defined so that

$$f(\tau) = 1 \text{ if } F(\tau)$$
$$f(\tau) = 0 \text{ if } \neg F(\tau).$$

Such a function must provide a counter-example to the proposed principle. For, as we have said, even where τ does not exist, still either $F(\tau)$ or $\neg F(\tau)$ will be true, so in any case $f(\tau)$ will be defined. I shall not, then, add any further principles of this sort.

In fact I prefer not to add function-letters at all, since there is nothing that can be laid down as a general principle to say when a function is or is not defined for a given argument. So the system that I have been considering so far is one in which the only closed terms are simple name-letters, and there is therefore no practical distinction between the letters τ and α. But I shall now proceed to add definite descriptions as further terms. As I have noted, functions are a special case of descriptions, so if descriptions are available, then we do not need to make any further provision for functions. And because a definite description necessarily has an internal structure, it is easy to say when there is such a thing as it describes, namely when the description is uniquely satisfied.

Since our system allows names to be empty, the chief objection to treating definite descriptions as (complex) names has now disappeared, and I shall therefore treat them in this way. Accordingly, given any formula φ containing a free occurrence of the variable ξ, the expression $(\imath\xi{:}\varphi)$ will be a term. Since all occurrences of ξ in this term are bound (by the initial prefix $\imath\xi$, if they are not already bound in φ), the term will be a closed term provided that there are no other variables free in φ. In that case, the rules that have been stated as applying to all terms τ will apply to it. If we wish to allow our rules to apply also to open formulae, which may contain open terms, then as before (p. 337) we need to make sure that the substitution-notation is so explained that all occurrences of variables that are free in τ remain free in $\varphi(\tau/\xi)$. Once this is done, the extension presents no further problem. If we wish to allow for vacuous occurrences of the prefix $\imath\xi$, i.e. occurrences in which it is attached to a formula φ containing no free occurrences of ξ, then this is harmless. In nearly all cases it will lead to a term $(\imath\xi{:}\varphi)$ that does not denote, though there is one exception (Exercise 8.6.4). Finally, the obvious principle for when a definite description has a denotation, is this:

$$E!(\imath\xi{:}\varphi) \ \leftrightarrow \ \exists\zeta\forall\xi(\varphi \leftrightarrow \zeta{=}\xi).$$

A stronger principle from which this follows, and which I adopt as an axiom-schema governing descriptions, is this:

$$\text{(PD)} \ \ \forall\zeta(\zeta{=}(\imath\xi{:}\varphi) \leftrightarrow \forall\xi(\varphi \leftrightarrow \zeta{=}\xi)).$$

('PD' is for 'principle of descriptions'.) Considered as a rule of inference for the tableau system, the rule is that any instance of this principle may be added to the root of any tableau.

In the following section I set out the system that we have just reached in a more formal manner, give an explicit account of the intended semantics, and outline a completeness proof with respect to that semantics. It will be convenient to have a name for the system; I shall call it the system B ('B' for 'Bostock').

EXERCISES

8.6.1.(*a*) Using the tableau rules for quantifiers and for identity as formulated for the system B on pp. 360 and 364, prove

(1) $\vdash \forall x(x=x)$.
(2) $a=a \dashv\vdash \exists x(x=a)$.
(3) $\exists x(x \neq x) \vdash$.
(4) $\forall x(x \neq x) \vdash \forall x F x$.

(*b*) Show that the following are not provable from these rules:

(5) $\forall x(x \neq x) \vdash$
(6) $a \neq a \vdash$.

8.6.2. Rewrite the tableau rules given in this section as rules for use in natural deduction. [Method: first express the tableau rules as rules for a Gentzen sequent calculus, as in Sections 7.3 and 7.4, and then consider how they may be restricted to sequents with just one formula on the right.]

8.6.3.(*a*) Explain why vacuous quantifiers in the system B can make a difference, and we no longer have

If ξ is not free in φ then $\forall \xi \varphi \dashv\vdash \varphi$.

[Hint: Consider the implications of part (4) of Exercise 8.6.1(*a*).]
(*b*) In the light of this explanation, say where exactly the proof on p. 98 would break down for the system B.
(*c*) State a new rule for vacuous quantifiers, suited to the system B.

8.6.4. Let φ be a closed formula, so that in the term $(\imath\xi:\varphi)$ the prefix $\imath\xi$ binds no variable. Show that, according to the principle PD, the formula $E!(\imath\xi:\varphi)$ is true in an interpretation I iff (1) the domain of I contains one and only one object, and (2) φ is interpreted as true in I.

8.7. A Formal Presentation

To give a formal presentation of the system B, we must begin by specifying its language. The vocabulary is

name-letters:	$a,b,c,d,e,a_1,...$
variables:	$x,y,z,w,u,v,x_1,...$
predicate-letters:	$P^n,Q^n,R^n,S^n,T^n,F^n,G^n,H^n,P^n_1,... \ (n \geqslant 0)$
predicate:	I for identity, usually written $=$

truth-functors: $\neg, \wedge, \vee, \ldots$
quantifiers: $\forall, \exists$
term-forming operator: $\imath$

(Brackets are also used as punctuation, to show grouping.) The formation rules, which simultaneously define both what a term is and what a formula is, are:

(1)(*a*) A name-letter is a term.
   (*b*) A variable is a term.
(2)(*a*) If Φ^n is an *n*-place predicate-letter, and if $\tau_1,\ldots,\tau_n$ is a series of *n* terms (not necessarily distinct), then $\Phi^n(\tau_1,\ldots,\tau_n)$ is a formula.
   (*b*) If τ_1 and τ_2 are terms, then $I(\tau_1, \tau_2)$ is a formula (but we usually write $\tau_1 = \tau_2$).
(3)   If φ and ψ are formulae, so are $\neg\varphi$, $(\varphi\wedge\psi)$, $(\varphi\vee\psi)$,...
(4)   If φ is a formula and ξ a variable, then $\forall\xi\varphi$ and $\exists\xi\varphi$ are formulae.
(5)   If φ is a formula and ξ a variable, then $(\imath\xi{:}\varphi)$ is a term.
(6)   There are no other terms or formulae.

On this account open formulae, and open terms, are accepted as being formulae and terms, and they are also permitted to contain vacuous occurrences of $\forall$, $\exists$, and $\imath$. But I shall confine attention to closed formulae and closed terms in what follows, since open formulae will receive no interpretation, and will not figure in the rules of inference. We could if we wished confine attention further to formulae and terms lacking vacuous occurrences of $\forall$, $\exists$, and $\imath$, for nothing of importance would be lost thereby.

The next task is to explain what counts as an interpretation of these terms and formulae. We define what it is for I to be an interpretation of a language L containing some, but not necessarily all, of the vocabulary just listed. This will be the case iff:

(1) There is a domain $\mathcal{D}_I$ of the interpretation I. This may be any set you like, including the empty set.
(2) Each name-letter α in L is interpreted by I either as denoting some element $|\alpha|_I$ of $\mathcal{D}_I$, or as denoting nothing. In the latter case we say that $|\alpha|_I$ is a *gap*.
(3) Each *n*-place predicate-letter Φ^n of L is a assigned by I a set $|\Phi^n|_I$ of *n*-tuples as its extension.[7] The members of these *n*-tuples must be *either* members of $\mathcal{D}_I$, *or* gaps.

---

[7] For the application of this clause to zero-place predicate-letters, see Sect. 3.4 nn. 11 and 12.

This interprets the non-logical vocabulary of L. Turning to the logical vocabulary, to deal with atomic formulae we have:

(4) For any predicate-letter Φ^n and any series of a n closed terms $\tau_1,...,\tau_n$,

$$|\Phi^n(\tau_1,...,\tau_n)|_I = T \quad \text{iff} \quad \langle |\tau_1|_I,...,|\tau_n|_I \rangle \in |\Phi^n|_I.$$

To deal with the truth-functors we have

(5) For any closed formulae φ and ψ,

$$|\neg\varphi|_I = T \quad \text{iff} \quad |\varphi|_I \neq T$$
$$|\varphi \wedge \psi|_I = T \quad \text{iff} \quad |\varphi|_I = T \text{ and } |\psi|_I = T$$
$$|\varphi \vee \psi|_I = T \quad \text{iff} \quad |\varphi|_I = T \text{ or } |\psi|_I = T$$

etc.

To deal with the quantifiers we again need the notion of an interpretation I_α which is an α-variant interpretation of the interpretation I. An α-variant interpretation is exactly like I except perhaps in the interpretation that it assigns to α, and in addition it must interpret α as denoting some member of the domain $\mathcal{D}_I$, i.e. it cannot interpret α as denoting nothing. (Hence, if I has an empty domain, there are no α-variant interpretations of I.) Then we have

(6) For any formula φ with at most one free variable ξ,

$$|\forall\xi\varphi|_I = T \quad \text{iff} \quad \text{for any name } \alpha \text{ not in } \varphi, \text{ and for any } \alpha\text{-variant interpretation } I_\alpha \text{ of } I,$$
$$|\varphi(\alpha/\xi)|_{I_\alpha} = T.$$

$$|\exists\xi\varphi|_I = T \quad \text{iff} \quad \text{for some name } \alpha \text{ not in } \varphi, \text{ and for some } \alpha\text{-variant interpretation } I_\alpha \text{ of } I,$$
$$|\varphi(\alpha/\xi)|_{I_\alpha} = T.$$

The clause for identity is the obvious one:

(7) For any terms τ_1 and τ_2,

$$|\tau_1 = \tau_2|_I = T \quad \text{iff} \quad \text{both } \tau_1 \text{ and } \tau_2 \text{ are interpreted in } I \text{ as denoting something, and}$$
$$|\tau_1|_I = |\tau_2|_I.$$

And finally the clause for the description-operator is this:

(8) For any formula φ with at most one free variable ξ: if there is some name α not in φ, and some α-variant interpretation I_α of I, such that $|\forall\xi(\varphi \leftrightarrow \xi = \alpha)|_{I_\alpha} = T$ then

$$|(\imath\xi{:}\varphi)|_I = |\alpha|_{I_\alpha}.$$

If there is not, then $|(\imath\xi{:}\varphi)|_I$ is a gap.

(This means that if there is just one object in the domain that satisfies φ, then (ıξ:φ) denotes that object; if there is not, then it denotes nothing.)

This completes the definition of an interpretation, so we can now say what it is for a sequent in this language to be a correct sequent. For simplicity, I confine attention to those sequents that are basic from the tableau point of view, namely with no formulae on the right. The definition is, as expected,

> Γ ⊨   iff   every formula in Γ is closed, and there is no interpretation
> in which every formula in Γ is true.

We can now turn from questions of semantics to questions of proof, first defining Γ ⊢, and then considering the relation between ⊨ and ⊢. But I take this in two stages, beginning with the subsystem which does not yet include the description operator.

As in the previous section, I shall concentrate just on the tableau rules of proof. The standard rules for the truth-functors, and the rule for closing branches, are taken over unchanged from p. 156: I do not repeat them here. The rules for the quantifiers are as given on p. 360, but with *E!* eliminated according to its proposed definition. For ease of reference, I repeat them here:

$$
\begin{array}{cccc}
\forall\xi\varphi & \neg\forall\xi\varphi & \exists\xi\varphi & \neg\exists\xi\varphi \\
\tau=\tau & | & | & \tau=\tau \\
| & \alpha=\alpha & \alpha=\alpha & | \\
\varphi(\tau/\xi) & \neg\varphi(\alpha/\xi) & \varphi(\alpha/\xi) & \neg\varphi(\tau/\xi)
\end{array}
$$

provided α is new

The rules for identity (and for non-existence) are as on p. 364. Again, I repeat them for ease of reference:

$$
\begin{array}{cccc}
\tau_1\neq\tau_1 & \tau_1\neq\tau_1 & \tau_1=\tau_2 & \tau_1=\tau_2 \\
\tau_2\neq\tau_2 & \tau_2\neq\tau_2 & \varphi(\tau_1/\xi) & \varphi(\tau_2/\xi) \\
\varphi(\tau_1/\xi) & \varphi(\tau_2/\xi) & | & | \\
| & | & \varphi(\tau_2/\xi) & \varphi(\tau_1/\xi) \\
\varphi(\tau_2/\xi) & \varphi(\tau_1/\xi)
\end{array}
$$

All of these rules are to be taken as applying to closed formulae only; open formulae do not occur in proofs, since they equally do not appear in the sequents that those proofs establish. It is easily seen that each rule is sound, with respect to the semantics specified, so I spend no more time upon that point.

One might have expected that together they would form a complete set of rules for the system with quantifiers and identity, but without the description-operator, because of the way that the semantics has been set up to mirror them closely. But in fact they do not. The cause of the trouble is not that the rules do not contain enough information, but that tableau proofs are limited to a very strict form which does *not* include any analogue to the Cut rule for natural deduction. Here is an example of a simple sequent which is a correct sequent according to the semantics specified, but which is not provable from the rules just given:

$$a{\neq}a, Fa, \neg Fb, \forall xFx \models.$$

It is easily checked that the sequent is not provable, for when one sets out to draw up a tableau with these four formulae at its root one finds that there is no tableau rule at all which can be applied. But it is also easy to see that the sequent is correct, for it must be the case either that $b{=}b$ or that $b{\neq}b$. If $b{=}b$, then by the $\forall$ rule we cannot have both $\neg Fb$ and $\forall xFx$; but if $b{\neq}b$ then by EXT we cannot have all of $a{\neq}a$, Fa, $\neg Fb$. The remedy is clear: we must allow ourselves to introduce the alternative hypotheses $b{=}b$ and $b{\neq}b$ within the course of a tableau proof.

This is done by introducing a further rule:

$$\tau{=}\tau \qquad\qquad \tau{\neq}\tau$$

which has exactly this effect. (As we shall see, the rule may be confined, if we wish, to terms τ that already occur on the branch in question.) I observe that the rule is an analogue, in the tableau system, to a special case of the Cut rule. For, seen in terms of a sequent calculus, the rule says

$$\frac{\Gamma \not\Rightarrow}{\Gamma,\tau{=}\tau \not\Rightarrow \quad \text{OR} \quad \Gamma,\tau{\neq}\tau \not\Rightarrow}$$

Turning this upside-down, and removing negation signs to obtain a rule for a Gentzen sequent calculus, it becomes

$$\frac{\Gamma,\tau{=}\tau \Rightarrow \Delta \quad \Gamma \Rightarrow \tau{=}\tau, \Delta}{\Gamma \Rightarrow \Delta}$$

I shall therefore call this rule CUT=, i.e. a Cut rule for =.

With the addition of the new rule CUT= we do now have a complete basis for the system B with quantifiers and identity, but without the description-operator. I give a brief outline of the completeness proof, leaving the details to you (Exercise 8.7.1), since the general strategy is by now familiar. The proof will follow the lines of the completeness proof of Chapter 4, as extended in Section 8.2, by providing a recipe for constructing tableau proofs which must yield either a closed tableau or an open branch leading to an interpretation verifying all the formulae on that branch. So in particular the interpretation verifies all the formulae at the root of the tableau, showing them to be consistent. The recipe is this:

Initial step: Apply the rule CUT= to all name-letters occurring in the formulae at the root of the tableau. After this initial step the rule CUT= need never be applied again. (This is because the recipe will not allow the introduction of any further name-letters except by application of the rules ($\exists$) and ($\neg\forall$), and for a letter α introduced in this way it is already specified that $\alpha=\alpha$.)

Subsequent cycle of rules: With the restriction that no formula is ever to be written more than once on the same branch, continue to apply the remaining rules in this fourfold cycle:

(1) Apply the rules for truth-functors in all possible ways.
(2) Apply the rules ($\exists$) and ($\neg\forall$) in all possible ways, with the restriction that they are not to be applied more than once on the same branch to any formula.
(3) Apply the rules ($\forall$) and ($\neg\exists$) in all possible ways. (Note that the new form of these rules ensures that they can only be applied to names already on the branch.)
(4) Apply the rules EXT and LL in all possible ways.

This procedure must lead either to a closed tableau or to a tableau with an open branch—either a finite branch, if at some stage no more rules can be applied, or to an infinite branch (if we may speak in this way). If the result is an open branch, then we use it to construct an interpretation in this way. For each name α on the branch, either $\alpha=\alpha$ or $\alpha\neq\alpha$ is on the branch. If $\alpha\neq\alpha$ is on the branch, then α is interpreted as denoting nothing, and on this interpretation the semantics ensures that $\alpha=\alpha$ is interpreted as false, and hence $\alpha\neq\alpha$ is interpreted as true. If $\alpha=\alpha$ is on the branch, then α is interpreted as denoting something, and if $\alpha=\beta$ is also on the branch, then α and β are interpreted as denoting the same thing. (Note here that if $\alpha=\beta$ is on the branch, then so are $\alpha=\alpha$ and $\beta=\beta$, since these each result by applying LL to $\alpha=\beta$.) Thus if $\alpha=\beta$ is on the branch, then by the semantics it is interpreted as true. The domain of the interpretation is then to consist just of one object for each name α such that $\alpha=\alpha$ is on the branch, with the rider that the same object is used both for α and for β iff $\alpha=\beta$ is on the branch. Extensions for the predicate-letters that occur in some formula on the branch are then constructed so as to ensure that an atomic formula is interpreted as true iff that formula is on the branch, i.e. by including $\langle|\alpha_1|,...,|\alpha_n|\rangle$ in the extension of Φ^n iff $\Phi^n(\alpha_1,...,\alpha_n)$ is on the branch. This cannot lead to any contradiction, for we have ensured that (a) if α is interpreted as denoting something, then $|\alpha|=|\beta|$ only if $\alpha=\beta$ is on the branch, and so by LL $\Phi^n(...,\alpha,...)$ is on the branch iff $\Phi^n(...,\beta,...)$ is also on the branch; and (b) if α is interpreted as denoting nothing, so that $|\alpha|$ is a gap, then for any other name β such that $|\beta|$ is also a gap we have both $\alpha\neq\alpha$ and $\beta\neq\beta$ on the branch, and so again by EXT $\Phi^n(...,\alpha,...)$ is on the branch iff $\Phi^n(...,\beta,...)$ is on the branch.

I make one further remark at this point. It may happen that there are no names α on the branch at all. In that case, by our stipulation, the domain of the interpretation is to be taken as empty. The only atomic formulae that can occur on the branch are then zero-place predicate-letters, i.e. sentence-letters, and any such sentence-letter is to be interpreted as true. All other atomic formulae are interpreted as false. Moreover, the only quantified formulae to occur on the branch must be ones that begin either with $\forall$ or with $\neg\exists$, and we have already noted that all such formulae are interpreted as true in an empty domain.

The rest of the argument is a straightforward induction on the length of the formula φ to show that every formula φ on the branch is interpreted as true in this interpretation. I leave this to you.

I now come to consider the full system B, which contains in addition the description-operator ı. But I shall proceed somewhat obliquely, first introducing a new constant name, say *, with the fixed interpretation that * denotes nothing. (Thus * corresponds in a way to ⊥. It is stipulated that ⊥ does not, in any situation, state a truth; and similarly it is stipulated that * does not, in any situation, denote an object.) You may think of *, if you wish, as short for a definite description such as ($ıx:x\neq x$), but at present I am pursuing an approach in which * is introduced as a constant *before* descriptions are generally available. It is clear that we need one new rule of inference to govern the constant *, namely that $*\neq*$ may be introduced into a proof at any stage. It is also clear that the completeness proof just outlined may be extended to show that, if we add the new constant * to the system just considered, and the new rule for it, then the extended system is also complete.

The point of this is that, with the new constant * available, we may introduce the description-operator by an explicit definition. The basic thought here is that for any formula ψ with a free occurrence of ζ the formula

$$\psi((\imath\xi{:}\varphi)/\zeta)$$

must be equivalent to

$$\exists\zeta(\zeta{=}(\imath\xi{:}\varphi) \wedge \psi) \vee (\neg\exists\zeta(\zeta{=}(\imath\xi{:}\varphi)) \wedge \psi(*/\zeta)).$$

This is provable just from the rules already introduced for quantifiers and identity, provided that those rules are taken to apply not just to name-letters but also to terms such as $(\imath\xi{:}\varphi)$. But we can go on to eliminate $(\imath\xi{:}\varphi)$ from this formula by applying our principle PD for descriptions, since this allows us to substitute for one another

$$\zeta{=}(\imath\xi{:}\varphi) \quad \text{and} \quad \forall\xi(\varphi \leftrightarrow \xi{=}\zeta).$$

So we obtain, as equivalent to the original

$$\exists\zeta(\forall\xi(\varphi \leftrightarrow \xi{=}\zeta) \wedge \psi) \vee (\neg\exists\zeta\forall\xi(\varphi \leftrightarrow \xi{=}\zeta) \wedge \psi(*/\zeta)).$$

The suggestion is that $\psi((\imath\xi{:}\varphi)/\zeta)$ be defined as an abbreviation for this.

As it stands, such a proposed definition is ambiguous, for the same reason as before (p. 343), e.g. because it does not tell us whether, in a formula such as $\neg\psi((\imath\xi{:}\varphi)/\zeta)$, the $\neg$ is to be taken into the definition or left outside it. In the system B this ambiguity is of no importance, for whichever choice we make the results are equivalent, but a proper definition should be unambiguous. To remove the ambiguity we may stipulate first that the definition is to apply only where the initial formula ψ is an *atomic* formula. But another ambiguity is that even an atomic formula may contain several descriptions, as in

$$(\imath x{:}Fx) = (\imath x{:}Gx)$$

or it may contain the same description several times, as in

$$(\imath x{:}Fx) = (\imath x{:}Fx)$$

or it may indeed contain one description inside another, as in

$$(\imath x{:}x = (\imath y{:}Gy)) = a.$$

Again, all ways of applying the definition would actually yield equivalent results in the system B, but still we should stipulate some definite way of applying it. Let us say, then, that in any atomic formula containing descriptions the leftmost occurrence of $\imath$ is to be eliminated first, in accordance with the definition proposed. If, when this is done, there are still further occurrences of $\imath$, then again we look for the atomic formulae that contain them, and once more we eliminate the leftmost occurrence in each atomic formula in accordance with the definition proposed. Proceeding in this way, we must in the end eliminate all occurrences of ι, and in such a way that we end with a formula equivalent to the original.

It follows that *one* way of introducing descriptions into the system B is by adding the new constant ∗ and the suggested definition. This is easily shown to be a *complete* basis for descriptions, since we can argue thus. Take any correct sequent containing some descriptions. By the definition suggested the descriptions can be eliminated from this sequent, leaving us with another correct sequent containing only the vocabulary of B, without descriptions but with ∗ added. But we have already observed that B, with ∗ but without descriptions, is complete. So the correct sequent with descriptions eliminated is provable in it. And hence the correct sequent that we began with, including descriptions, is also provable when the definition of descriptions is added.

It follows further that if, instead of adding the new constant ∗ and the definition, we add the principle PD as an axiom, then again we have a system that is complete for B with descriptions. For (1) in this setting the rules of B are taken as applying to terms (ιξ:φ) as well as to simple name-letters; (2) we may define ∗ as, say, (ιx:x≠x), and the rule ⊢ ∗≠∗ is then provable from PD; and (3) it follows that from PD we can prove an equivalence corresponding to the definition of the last paragraph. Hence whatever can be proved from the constant ∗ and the definition can also be proved from PD. Since the former system is complete, it therefore follows that the latter is too.

The full system B, then, contains the eight rules initially specified for quantifiers and identity, the extra rule CUT= needed to loosen a little the very strict strait-jacket of a tableau proof, and the axiom PD for descriptions. These rules define Γ⊢ᵦ. As I remarked earlier, it is clear the rules are individually sound with respect to the semantics given, and we have now shown that they are together a complete set of rules. Thus

$$\Gamma \vdash_B \text{ iff } \Gamma \vDash.$$

This completes my exposition of the system B.

EXERCISES

8.7.1. Fill in the details of the completeness proof outlined for B with quantifiers and identity but without descriptions.

8.7.2. With descriptions counted as terms, and with PD added as an axiom, prove

(1) $\vdash_B (\iota x{:}x{\neq}x) \neq (\iota x{:}x{\neq}x)$.

(2) $\psi(\tau/\zeta) \;_B{\dashv}{\vdash}_B \; \exists\zeta(\zeta{=}\tau \land \psi) \lor (\neg\exists\zeta(\zeta{=}\tau) \land \psi((\iota x{:}x{\neq}x)/\zeta)))$.

8.8. Appendix: A Note on Names, Descriptions, and Scopes

A standard assumption in logic is that names do not have effective scopes. For example, it does not make any difference whether we see the formula $\neg Fa$ as obtained by first supplying the name a as subject to the predicate F, and then negating the result, or as obtained by first negating the predicate F and then supplying the name a as subject to this complex predicate. We may look at it either way. On Russell's analysis of definite descriptions, this gives us a clear contrast between names and descriptions, for it is a feature of his analysis that descriptions must have scopes. To use the same example, if we see the formula $\neg F(\imath x{:}Gx)$ as got by first supplying $(\imath x{:}Gx)$ as subject to the predicate F, and then negating the result, the whole will be true if $(\imath x{:}Gx)$ fails to exist and F represents an atomic predicate. But if we see it as got by first negating the predicate F, and then supplying $(\imath x{:}Gx)$ as subject to this complex predicate, we get the opposite result. This is the difference between

$$(\mathrm{I}x{:}Fx)(\neg Gx) \quad \text{and} \quad \neg(\mathrm{I}x{:}Fx)(Gx).$$

This point suggests the following thought. If it is really true that definite descriptions have scopes whereas names do not, then Russell must be right to claim that definite descriptions are not names. If, however, this is not really true, then it does no harm to treat descriptions as complex names, which is what the system B does.

Now, provided that names are allowed to be empty, as descriptions evidently can be, this question cannot be decided at the level of elementary logic. For, as I have pointed out (Exercise 8.3.2), in elementary logic when we assign the scope of a description in one way rather than another, this can make a difference only if the description is empty, and the difference that it then makes is just that some versions imply that the description is not empty whereas others do not. (Thus, concerning the examples of the last paragraph, the first implies that $(\imath x{:}Gx)$ is not empty, and the second does not; on the contrary it is true if F is atomic and $(\imath x{:}Gx)$ is empty.) But we can get exactly the same effect with names, not by assigning them scopes, but by including or excluding explicitly existential clauses. For example, the distinction just noted for a description $(\imath x{:}Gx)$ can be reproduced for a name a as the distinction between

$$E!a \wedge \neg Fa \quad \text{and} \quad \neg(E!a \wedge Fa).$$

Thus all the work that could be done, in elementary logic, by making scope-distinctions either for names or for descriptions, can equally well be done instead by adding explicitly existential clauses at appropriate points in the formula. I conclude that, at the level of elementary logic, there is no call to assign scopes either to names or to descriptions.

It may be replied that, when we move to a more complex level of discourse, where we cannot make do just with the resources of elementary logic, the advantage of

Russell's analysis of descriptions becomes clear. For example, Kripke (1980: 48–9) has argued that, where a is a name, the sentence

It might not have been that $a=a$

is unambiguous, and always false. But if in place of the name a we take a description $(\imath x{:}Fx)$, then—he says—we must make a distinction. The proposition

It might have been that $(\imath x{:}Fx)\neg(x=x)$

is always false: there is no possibility of there being one and only thing which is F but not self-identical. But, in contrast, it is very often true to say

$(\imath x{:}Fx)(\text{It might have been that } \neg(\imath y{:}Fy)(x=y))$.

This is true because it means that, concerning the one and only thing that is F, it might not have been the one and only thing that is F—either because it might not have been F or because something else as well might have been F. But—he claims—there is no similar point to be made about a name a: we cannot say that, concerning the thing that is a, it might not have been a.

For the sake of argument, let us grant that Kripke is essentially right on this point. Nevertheless, one might still find the point unimpressive, since there are many other non-extensional contexts where—at least at first sight—scope-distinctions seem to be needed just as much for names as for descriptions. To adapt an example of Quine's (1960: 141–56), consider the sentence

Ralph believes that the man in the brown hat is a spy.

This may be taken in two ways. It can be understood as saying that Ralph believes to be true what is said by the whole sentence 'the man in the brown hat is a spy', or as saying that Ralph believes to be *true of* a certain person what is expressed by the predicate 'that he is a spy', where the person in question is in fact the one man here in a brown hat, though Ralph may be unaware of this fact. The distinction is that in the first case the words 'the man in the brown hat' are taken as part of the report of what Ralph believes, whereas in the second case they are the speaker's way of referring to a particular person, which need not also be Ralph's way of referring to him. In the jargon, the sentence is said to be understood *de dicto* in the first case and *de re* in the second. Now at first sight it is tempting to say that the distinction is one of scope. In the first case we have

Ralph believes that $(\imath x{:}x$ is wearing a brown hat$)$ $(x$ is a spy$)$

and in the second case we have

$(\imath x{:}x$ is wearing a brown hat$)$ Ralph believes that $(x$ is a spy$)$.

But here one must notice that exactly the same ambiguity occurs when we have a name in place of the description, as in

Ralph believes that Bernard J. Ortcutt is a spy.

Again, the name 'Bernard J. Ortcutt' may be taken as reporting part of the content of Ralph's belief, or it may be taken as the speaker's way of telling us who is the object of Ralph's belief. Should we conclude, then, that in contexts such as these both names and descriptions should be assigned scopes?

Quine, for one, would not wish to look at it in this way. On his suggestion the ambiguity is better viewed, not as a question of the scope of the name or description, but as an ambiguity in the prefix 'Ralph believes that'. We can construe this prefix as an operator that forms a sentence from a sentence, or we can construe it as an operator that forms a sentence from a name and a predicate taken separately, where only the predicate represents what is believed, and the name is used to say what it is believed of. In the second case, then, the more perspicuous rendering is

Ralph believes, of Bernard J. Ortcutt, that he is a spy.

As Quine insists, we must be able to understand belief-sentences *both* in the one way *and* in the other. Belief is what he calls a 'multigrade relation', relating a believer either to a sentence, or to an object and a one-place predicate, or perhaps to two objects and a two-place predicate, and so on.

It is a question for philosophical disputation whether Quine's way of looking at these sentences is better or worse than the way which assigns scope to referring expressions, or whether the apparent disagreement between these two approaches is one that disappears on a closer analysis. I shall not here take this dispute any further. But in any case we can say that contexts of this kind provide no motive for *distinguishing* names from descriptions. Bearing this in mind, let us look back once more to Kripke's case for saying that descriptions do have scopes whereas names do not. Clearly Quine would wish to distinguish between

(1) It might have been that a was not a.
(2) It might have been, concerning a, that it was not a.

The first takes 'it might have been that' to be operating on a whole sentence, whereas the second takes it to be operating on a name and a predicate taken separately. Now for the sake of argument we may agree with Kripke that (1) is always false, whereas (2) may be true where 'a' is a description, but not where 'a' is a name.[8] But this, we may suggest, is a peculiar feature of the way that names interact with modal operators such as 'it might have been that', and is to be explained by the fact that names are what Kripke calls 'rigid designators'. This means (roughly) that names continue to designate the same thing as we shift our attention from one possible situation to another, whereas most descriptions do not. But this point by itself would not prevent us from saying that descriptions may be treated as complex names, for it does not in any way imply that descriptions have scopes whereas names do not. On the contrary, the only 'scope-distinction' that is here envisaged is a distinction in how the prefix 'it might have been that' is to be understood, and this has no tendency to show that definite descriptions are not complex names.

---

[8] Actually, one could perfectly well claim that (2) will be true wherever 'a' is a name that might have been empty. To avoid this objection, change the example to

It might have been, concerning a, that it existed but was not a.

References

This list includes a few books which I have used but not referred to elsewhere.

BERNAYS, P. (1926), 'Axiomatische Untersuchungen des Aussagenkalküls der *Principia Mathematica*', *Mathematische Zeitschrift*, 25: 305–20.
—— See Hilbert.

BETH, E. W. (1955), 'Semantic Entailment and Formal Derivability', Mededelingen van de Koninklijke Nederlandse Academie van Wetenschappen, Afdeling Letterkunde, NS 18: 309–42. Repr. in Hintikka (1969).

CARROLL, LEWIS (C. L. Dodgson) (1896), *Symbolic Logic* (Clarendon Press: Oxford).

CHURCH, A. (1936), 'A Note on the *Entscheidungsproblem*', *Journal of Symbolic Logic*, 1: 40–1, 101–2.
—— (1956), *Introduction to Mathematical Logic*, i (Princeton University Press: Princeton).

FREGE, G. (1879/1967), *Begriffsschrift—eine der arithmetischen nachgebildete Formelsprache des reinen Denkens* (Nebert: Halle). Eng. trans. in van Heijenoort (1967).
—— (1892/1960), 'Über Sinn und Bedeutung'. Trans. as 'On Sense and Reference', in his *Philosophical Writings*, ed. P. T. Geach and M. Black (Blackwell: Oxford).

GENTZEN, G. (1934/1969), 'Untersuchungen über das logische Schliessen', *Mathematische Zeitschrift*, 39: 176–210, 405–31. Eng. trans. in his *Collected Papers*, ed. M. E. Szabo (North-Holland: Amsterdam, 1969).

GÖDEL, K. (1930/1967), 'Die Vollständigkeit der Axiome des logischen Funktionenkalküls', *Monatshefte für Mathematik und Physik*, 37: 349–60. Eng. trans. in van Heijenoort (1967).

HENKIN, L. (1949), 'The Completeness of the First-Order Functional Calculus', *Journal of Symbolic Logic*, 14: 159–66. Repr. in Hintikka (1969).

HERBRAND, J. (1930/1967), 'Recherches sur la théorie de la démonstration', *Travaux de la Société des Sciences et des Lettres de Varsovie*, 3/33. Eng. trans. in van Heijenoort (1967).

HILBERT, D., and BERNAYS, P. (1934), *Grundlagen der Mathematik*, i (Springer: Berlin).

HINTIKKA, J. (ed.) (1969), *The Philosophy of Mathematics* (Oxford University Press: Oxford).

HODGES, W. (1977), *Logic* (Penguin: Harmondsworth).

JEFFREY, R. C. (1967, 1981), *Formal Logic: Its Scope and Limits* (McGraw-Hill: New York).

KALMÁR, L. (1934–5), 'Über die Axiomatisierbarkeit des Aussagenkalküls', *Acta litterarum ac scientiarum Regiae Universitatis Hungaricae Francisco-Josephinae, sectio scientiarum mathematicarum*, 4: 248–52.

KLEENE, S. C. (1952), *Introduction to Metamathematics* (Van Nostrand: New York).

—— (1967), *Mathematical Logic* (Wiley: New York).

KNEALE, W. C. (1956), 'The Province of Logic', in H. D. Lewis (ed.), *Contemporary British Philosophy*, 3rd ser. (George Allen & Unwin: London).

—— and KNEALE, M. (1962), *The Development of Logic* (Clarendon Press: Oxford).

KRIPKE, S. A. (1965), 'Semantical Analysis of Intuitionistic Logic I', in J. N. Crossley and M. A. E. Dummett (eds.), *Formal Systems and Recursive Functions* (North-Holland: Amsterdam).

—— (1980), *Naming and Necessity* (Blackwell: Oxford).

LEMMON, E. J. (1965), *Beginning Logic* (Nelson: London).

ŁUKASIEWICZ, J. (1936), 'Zur Geschichte der Aussagenlogik', *Erkenntnis*, 5: 111–31.

—— (1948), 'The Shortest Axiom of the Implicational Calculus of Propositions', *Proceedings of the Royal Irish Academy*, 52A3.

—— and TARSKI, A. (1930/1956), 'Untersuchungen über den Aussagenkalkül', *Comptes rendue des séances de la Société des Sciences et des Lettres de Varsovie*, 3: 30–50. Eng. trans. in Tarski (1956).

MATES, B. (1972), *Elementary Logic*, 2nd edn. (Oxford University Press: Oxford).

MENDELSON, E. (1964), *Introduction to Mathematical Logic* (Van Nostrand: London).

MEREDITH, C. A. (1953), 'Single Axioms for the Systems (C,N), (C,O) and (A,N) of the Two-Valued Propositional Calculus', *Journal of Computing Systems*, 1: 155–64.

NEWTON-SMITH, W. H. (1985), *Logic* (Routledge & Kegan Paul: London).

NICOD, J. (1917), 'A Reduction in the Number of the Primitive Propositions of Logic', *Proceedings of the Cambridge Philosophical Society*, 19: 32–41.

POST, E. L. (1921), 'Introduction to a General Theory of Elementary Propositions', *American Journal of Mathematics*, 43: 163–85. Repr. in van Heijenoort (1967).

PRIOR, A. N. (1955), *Formal Logic* (Clarendon Press: Oxford).

QUINE, W. V. (1951), *Mathematical Logic*, 2nd edn. (Harvard University Press: Cambridge, Mass.).

—— (1952), *Methods of Logic* (Routledge & Kegan Paul: London).

—— (1960), *Word and Object* (MIT Press: Cambridge, Mass.).

ROSSER, J. B. (1953), *Logic for Mathematicians* (McGraw Hill: New York).

RUSSELL, B. (1905), 'On Denoting', *Mind*, 14: 479–93. Repr. in *Bertrand Russell: Logic and Knowledge*, ed. R. C. Marsh (George Allen & Unwin: London, 1956); and in *Bertrand Russell: Essays in Analysis*, ed. D. Lackey (George Allen & Unwin: London, 1973).

—— and WHITEHEAD, A. N. (1910–13), *Principia Mathematica*, i–iii (Cambridge University Press: Cambridge).

SCOTT, D., *et al.* (1981), *Notes on the Formalization of Logic* (Sub-faculty of Philosophy: Oxford).

SHOESMITH, D. J., and SMILEY, T. J. (1978), *Multiple-Conclusion Logic* (Cambridge University Press: Cambridge).

SMILEY, T. J. See Shoesmith.

TARSKI, A. (1956), *Logic, Semantics, Metamathematics*, trans. J. H. Woodger (Clarendon Press: Oxford).

—— See Łukasiewicz.

TENNANT, N. W. (1978), *Natural Logic* (Edinburgh University Press: Edinburgh).

VAN HEIJENOORT, J. (1967), *From Frege to Gödel: A Source Book in Mathematical Logic 1879–1931* (Harvard University Press: Cambridge, Mass.).

VON NEUMANN, J. (1927/1961), 'Zur Hilbertschen Beweistheorie', *Mathematische Zeitschrift*, 26: 1–46. Repr. in his *Collected Works* (Pergamon Press: New York).

WHITEHEAD, A. N. See Russell.

List of Symbols

(The page-reference is to the first introduction of the symbol)

List of Axioms and Rules of Inference

1. Structural Rules

I give the rules here in their most general form (cf. p. 293).

> Assumptions (ASS) $\varphi \vDash \varphi$

> Thinning (THIN)
> on the left   If $\Gamma \vDash \Delta$ then $\Gamma,\varphi \vDash \Delta$
> on the right   If $\Gamma \vDash \Delta$ then $\Gamma \vDash \varphi,\Delta$

> Cutting (CUT)   If $\Gamma_1 \vDash \varphi,\Delta_1$ and $\Gamma_2,\varphi \vDash \Delta_2$ then $\Gamma_1,\Gamma_2, \vDash \Delta_1,\Delta_2$

> Interchange (INT)
> on the left   If $\Gamma,\varphi,\psi,\Delta \vDash \Theta$ then $\Gamma,\psi,\varphi,\Delta \vDash \Theta$
> on the right   If $\Gamma \vDash \Delta,\varphi,\psi,\Theta$ then $\Gamma \vDash \Delta,\psi,\varphi,\Theta$

> Contraction (CONTR)
> on the left   If $\Gamma,\varphi,\varphi \vDash \Delta$ then $\Gamma,\varphi \vDash \Delta$
> on the right   If $\Gamma \vDash \varphi,\varphi,\Delta$ then $\Gamma \vDash \varphi,\Delta$

Until Gentzen sequents become available (in Sect. 7.4) the rules are restricted to cases where no more than one formula appears on the right. For purposes of a sequent calculus (Ch. 7) we interpret 'Γ', 'Δ', . . . as schematic letters for finite sequences of formulae, and it becomes necessary to state INT and CONTR explicitly. For other purposes these letters may be taken as representing sets of formulae, in which case INT and CONTR go without saying. If desired, one may replace ASS and THIN by

> Basic Sequents (BS) $\Gamma,\varphi \vDash \varphi,\Delta$

2. Basic Principles for Truth-Functors (p. 33) and Quantifiers (pp. 97–8)

Negation	$\Gamma,\neg\varphi \vDash$	iff $\Gamma \vDash \varphi$
Conjunction	$\Gamma \vDash \varphi\wedge\psi$	iff $\Gamma \vDash \varphi$ and $\Gamma \vDash \psi$
Disjunction	$\Gamma,\varphi\vee\psi \vDash$	iff $\Gamma,\varphi \vDash$ and $\Gamma,\psi \vDash$

Conditional	$\Gamma \vDash \varphi \rightarrow \psi$ iff $\Gamma, \varphi \vDash \psi$
$\forall$-introduction ($\forall$I)	If $\Gamma \vDash \varphi$ then $\Gamma \vDash \forall \xi \varphi(\xi / \alpha)$
	provided α does not occur in Γ
$\forall$-elimination ($\forall$E)	$\forall \xi \varphi \vDash \varphi(\alpha / \xi)$
$\exists$-introduction ($\exists$I)	$\varphi(\alpha / \xi) \vDash \exists \xi \varphi$
$\exists$-elimination ($\exists$E)	If $\Gamma, \varphi \vDash$ then $\Gamma, \exists \xi \varphi(\xi / \alpha) \vDash$
	provided α does not occur in Γ

Once Gentzen sequents become available, 'Δ' may be added on the right in all cases. This makes a real difference in the case of the conditional, and of ($\forall$I); cf. pp. 305–6. Until then, it is useful to give two versions of the principles for disjunction and for $\exists$-elimination, one as stated here and the other with a single formula on the right. If there is something further on the right, then the restrictions on ($\forall$I) and ($\exists$E) must add that α should not occur in it. When complex terms become available (as in Sect. 8.2), we may generalize ($\forall$E) and ($\exists$I) by writing 'τ' in place of 'α', and adding 'provided τ is closed'.

3. Tableau System

I give the rules here in the simplified form which is most convenient in practice (p. 156), and in practice one omits the labels shown here.

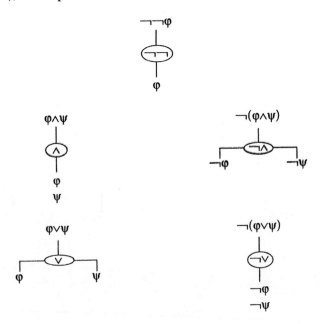

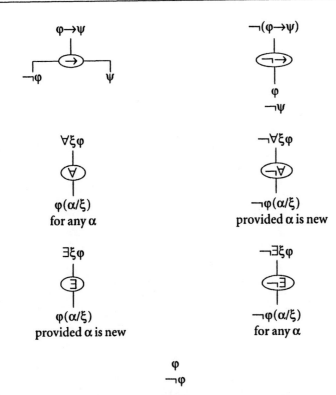

4. Axiomatic System (pp. 194, 221)

Axioms: (A1) ⊢ φ→(ψ→φ)
         (A2) ⊢ (φ→(ψ→χ))→((φ→ψ)→(φ→χ))
         (A3) ⊢ (¬φ→¬ψ)→(ψ→φ)
         (A4) ⊢ ∀ξφ → φ(α/ξ)
         (A5) ⊢ ∀ξ(ψ→φ)→(ψ→∀ξφ)
               provided ξ is not free in ψ

Rules: DET If ⊢ φ and ⊢ φ→ψ then ⊢ ψ
         GEN If ⊢ φ then ⊢ ∀ξφ(ξ/α)

For use in proofs by assumptions, the rule DET is generalized to

Modus Ponens (MP) If Γ ⊢ φ and Γ ⊢ φ→ψ then Γ ⊢ ψ

And the rule GEN is generalized to (∀I), as in (2) above, but with '⊢' for '⊨'.

5. Natural Deduction System

I formulate the rules here in a way that is neutral between tree proofs and linear proofs (see pp. 277–8).

($\wedge$I)   If $\Gamma \vdash \varphi$ and $\Delta \vdash \psi$ then $\Gamma, \Delta \vdash \varphi \wedge \psi$

($\wedge$E)   If $\Gamma \vdash \varphi \wedge \psi$ then $\Gamma \vdash \varphi$ and $\Gamma \vdash \psi$

($\vee$I) $\Gamma \vdash \varphi$ or $\Gamma \vdash \psi$ then $\Gamma \vdash \varphi \vee \psi$

($\vee$E)   If $\Gamma \vdash \varphi \vee \psi$ and $\Delta, \varphi \vdash \chi$ and $\Theta, \psi \vdash \chi$ then $\Gamma, \Delta, \Theta \vdash \chi$

($\rightarrow$I)   If $\Gamma, \varphi \vdash \psi$ then $\Gamma \vdash \varphi \rightarrow \psi$

($\rightarrow$E)   If $\Gamma \vdash \varphi$ and $\Delta \vdash \varphi \rightarrow \psi$ then $\Gamma, \Delta \vdash \psi$

The rules for quantifiers are ($\forall$I), ($\forall$E), ($\exists$I), ($\exists$E) as given in (2) above, but with '$\vdash$' in place of '$\models$', and with one formula supplied on the right for ($\exists$E).

6. Gentzen's Cut-Free Sequent Calculus

This is a reformulation of the original rules for a tableau system (pp. 147, 150) but turned upside down and presented as rules for a sequent calculus (p. 296).

$$(BS) \frac{}{\Gamma, \varphi \Rightarrow \varphi, \Delta}$$

$$(\wedge \Rightarrow) \frac{\Gamma, \varphi, \psi \Rightarrow \Delta}{\Gamma, \varphi \wedge \psi \Rightarrow \Delta} \qquad (\Rightarrow \wedge) \frac{\Gamma \Rightarrow \varphi, \Delta \quad \Gamma \Rightarrow \psi, \Delta}{\Gamma \Rightarrow \varphi \wedge \psi, \Delta}$$

$$(\vee \Rightarrow) \frac{\Gamma, \varphi \Rightarrow \Delta \quad \Gamma, \psi \Rightarrow \Delta}{\Gamma, \varphi \vee \psi \Rightarrow \Delta} \qquad (\Rightarrow \vee) \frac{\Gamma \Rightarrow \varphi, \psi, \Delta}{\Gamma \Rightarrow \varphi \vee \psi, \Delta}$$

$$(\rightarrow \Rightarrow) \frac{\Gamma \Rightarrow \varphi, \Delta \quad \Gamma, \psi \Rightarrow \Delta}{\Gamma, \varphi \rightarrow \psi \Rightarrow \Delta} \qquad (\Rightarrow \rightarrow) \frac{\Gamma, \varphi \Rightarrow \psi, \Delta}{\Gamma \Rightarrow \varphi \rightarrow \psi, \Delta}$$

$$(\neg \Rightarrow) \frac{\Gamma \Rightarrow \varphi, \Delta}{\Gamma, \neg \varphi \Rightarrow \Delta} \qquad (\Rightarrow \neg) \frac{\Gamma, \varphi \Rightarrow \Delta}{\Gamma \Rightarrow \neg \varphi, \Delta}$$

$$(\forall \Rightarrow) \frac{\Gamma, \varphi(\alpha/\xi) \Rightarrow \Delta}{\Gamma, \forall \xi \varphi \Rightarrow \Delta} \qquad (\Rightarrow \forall) \frac{\Gamma \Rightarrow \varphi, \Delta}{\Gamma \Rightarrow \forall \xi \varphi(\xi/\alpha), \Delta}$$
provided α is not in Γ or Δ

$$(\exists \Rightarrow) \frac{\Gamma, \varphi \Rightarrow \Delta}{\Gamma, \exists \xi \varphi(\xi/\alpha) \Rightarrow \Delta} \qquad (\Rightarrow E) \frac{\Gamma \Rightarrow \varphi(\alpha/\xi), \Delta}{\Gamma \Rightarrow \exists \xi \varphi, \Delta}$$
provided α is not in Γ or Δ

The structural rules INT and CONTR, as given in (1) above, should be added. But note that the system does not contain ASS, except as a special case of BS, or THIN or CUT. The last is important.

7. Identity

There are many ways of formulating rules or axioms (pp. 324, 331). For definiteness I give here a pair of axioms, more economical than those cited

$\vdash \alpha = \alpha$

$\vdash \alpha = \beta \rightarrow (\varphi(\alpha/\xi) \rightarrow \varphi(\beta/\xi))$

8. Free Logic (System B)

I give a formulation suited for tableau proofs (in the simplified notation). The rules for the truth-functors are as usual. The rules for the quantifiers are (p. 360)

$$
\begin{array}{cccc}
\forall\xi\varphi & \neg\forall\xi\varphi & \exists\xi\varphi & \neg\exists\xi\varphi \\
E!\tau & \mid & \mid & E!\tau \\
\mid & E!\alpha & E!\alpha & \mid \\
\varphi(\tau/\xi) & \neg\varphi(\alpha/\xi) & \varphi(\alpha/\xi) & \neg\varphi(\tau/\xi)
\end{array}
$$

The proposed definition of $E!$ is (p. 363)

$E!\tau$ for $\tau = \tau$

So, under this definition, these rules involve identity. The remaining rules for identity, using the same definition, are LL and EXT, which may be formulated (more economically than on p. 364) as

$$
\begin{array}{cc}
\tau_1 = \tau_2 & \neg E!\tau_1 \\
\varphi(\tau_1/\xi) & \neg E!\tau_2 \\
\mid & \varphi(\tau_1/\xi) \\
\varphi(\tau_2/\xi) & \mid \\
& \varphi(\tau_2/\xi)
\end{array}
$$

To complete the system, for tableau purposes, it is important also to add the rule CUT =

$$
\begin{array}{cc}
\mid & \\
E!\tau & \neg E!\tau
\end{array}
$$

The system may be complicated by adding a constant, $*$, for 'the constant empty name'. The rule governing it is simply

$$\begin{array}{c} | \\ \neg E!* \end{array}$$

Or, better, it may be complicated by adding a description operator, $\imath$, and this principle for descriptions (PD)

$$\forall \zeta (\zeta = (\imath \xi{:}\varphi) \overset{|}{\leftrightarrow} \forall \xi (\varphi \leftrightarrow \zeta = \xi))$$

Index

Printed in the United Kingdom
by Lightning Source UK Ltd.
108343UKS00001B/64-66